PUBLIC RELATIONS WRITING:
STRATEGIES AND SKILLS

PUBLIC RELATIONS WRITING: STRATEGIES AND SKILLS

Robert E. Rayfield
California State University, Fullerton

Lalit Acharya
University of Southern California

J. David Pincus
California State University, Fullerton

Donn E. Silvis
California State University, Dominguez Hills

 Wm. C. Brown Publishers

Book Team

Editor *Stan Stoga*
Developmental Editor *Jane F. Lambert*
Production Coordinator *Carla D. Arnold*

Wm. C. Brown Publishers

President *G. Franklin Lewis*
Vice President, Publisher *Thomas E. Doran*
Vice President, Operations and Production *Beverly Kolz*
National Sales Manager *Virginia S. Moffat*
Group Sales Manager *John Finn*
Associate Executive Editor *Edgar J. Laube*
Senior Marketing Manager *Kathy Law Laube*
Marketing Manager *Kathleen Nietzke*
Managing Editor, Production *Colleen A. Yonda*
Manager of Visuals and Design *Faye M. Schilling*
Production Editorial Manager *Julie A. Kennedy*
Production Editorial Manager *Ann Fuerste*
Publishing Services Manager *Karen J. Slaght*

WCB Group

President and Chief Executive Officer *Mark C. Falb*
Chairman of the Board *Wm. C. Brown*

Cover design by Kay Dolby Fulton

Cover image by Ted Lacey

Library of Congress Catalog Card Number: 90–82183

ISBN 0–697–03174–8

Printed in the United States of America by Wm. C. Brown Publishers,
2460 Kerper Boulevard, Dubuque, IA 52001

10 9 8 7 6 5 4 3 2 1

CONTENTS

PART 3 · WRITING: CRAFTING PRECISE MESSAGES 117

PREFACE

Public relations writing is much more than putting words on paper. It is a complete process, demanding considerable thought and analysis. Unfortunately, the thinking and analysis aspects of the writing process are all too often ignored or taken for granted. This text is driven by the strong belief that writing designed to achieve public relations objectives extends beyond mere style and format. Writing is first and foremost a strategic thinking process. Our purpose is to help future public relations practitioners learn how to research and analyze issues, integrate this information into a plan, write and communicate the message, and evaluate its impact on target audiences.

Public relations writing is frequently thought to be much like journalistic writing. While this is sometimes the case in style, often both rationale and content are quite different. Public relations writers are advocates both for their clients and the publics those clients seek to influence. Balancing these sometimes conflicting interests adequately requires systematic consideration of the interests of each group in each message, as well as the accuracy and comprehensiveness which journalism demands. Consequently, strategies and tactics in public relations writing are mutually interdependent.

We see the outstanding features of this text as these:

1. It treats writing for public relations as an integrated process involving decision making and technical actions. In addition to consideration of the factors noted above, our approach includes practical application of communication and other social science theory. This text presses students to systematically apply predictive theory in solving public relations writing problems.

2. It is the first such text we know which helps students manage writing actions in a strategic and comprehensive manner. Most modern public relations practitioners spend more time managing writing actions than they do actually writing. At the corporate and agency levels, much of the writing, graphics and message production chores are "farmed out" to specialists and free-lancers. The comprehensive writing course needs to prepare the student to manage these problems, since innumerable writing, layout and editing decisions are required.

3. "Writing Exercise Assignments" and "Food for Thought" segments at the end of each chapter help the instructor and student immediately incorporate new knowledge into realistic writing scenarios. Numerous other exercises, as well as comprehensive sets of questions and answers, are provided in the separately packaged instructor's manual. In addition, the references noted at the end of each chapter are designed to help the interested student learn more about an area.

4. Leading professionals and academics in the field offer helpful comments on various aspects of public relations writing in the "Professional Tip" features found in each chapter.

5. The text can be useful to those in widely different writing programs. Public relations education programs come in all shapes and sizes. Some are large, with many different, narrowly-focused courses; others are small with but a handful of broadly-focused courses. Some are independent entities, others are sequences or tracks within umbrella communications or journalism departments, and still others are one or two courses in a communication, journalism or speech communication curriculum.

Whatever the shape or size, writing is an essential component of public relations education. But the approaches to teaching public relations writing—naturally and necessarily—differ with the size and breadth of a program. This comprehensive text, while focused on the writing process, touches many issues on the cutting edge of professional public relations today. We believe this contextual perspective is vital to students' understanding of how writing fits into the practice of public relations.

However, the text has the flexibility to adapt to various course concepts. The full text fits the complete semester course program, or one encompassing two quarters. It can also serve as the single text for a course which combines writing with other public relations education—with proper instructor input. With desired emphasis, it works well in a one-quarter course. Suggested alignments for these and several course situations are included in the instructor's manual.

We believe this text represents the increasing focus on strategy and analysis engulfing professional public relations today. Public relations practitioners must think, plan and act in processes similar to those used in business if they are to merit top management positions. We hope this book can help enable tomorrow's public relations practitioner to think and write from a professional public relations management perspective.

ACKNOWLEDGMENTS

There is no way we can thank all those who helped shape this book. Mentors such as Alan Scott, Glen Broom and Jim Grunig inspired us in the beginning with a true appreciation of the field. Colleagues praised and shamed us into doing our best. Hundreds of students in dozens of writing classes let us know when we were right or wrong and, by their writing, taught us what to teach. Our editor at Wm. C. Brown, Stan Stoga, prodded until it was done. To all of these, and many more, we express appreciation.

A number of people also participated directly in production of the book by providing comments for quotation, reading and correction, and discussion. To them we express special thanks:

Surekha Acharya, Orange Coast Community College
Paul H. Alvarez, Ketchum Public Relations
Edward Bernays, public relations counsel, Boston
Marv Braman, Sanders Associates, Inc.
William Corbett, American Institute of Certified Public Accountants
Wendell Crow, California State University, Fullerton
H. J. Dalton, LTV Corporation
R. F. Dalton, corporate advertising, Dow Chemical USA
Roger D'Aprix, Towers, Perrin, Forster and Crosby, Inc.
David Ferguson, Hill and Knowlton, Inc.
Nancy Friedman, U.S. Justice Department
Mary Lou Galician, Arizona State University
Walter Gerson, University of Redlands
James E. Grunig, University of Maryland
Barbara W. Hunter, Hunter Mackenzie Cooper, Inc.
Norm Leaper, International Association of Business Communicators
Otto Lerbinger, Boston University
Julian Levine, TRW Space & Defense Sector
Wilma Mathews, AT&T
Wayne Overbeck, California State University, Fullerton
Karen Pincus, University of Southern California
Betsy Ann Plank, Illinois Bell

Tony Rimmer, California State University, Fullerton
Students in public relations writing, California State University, Fullerton, and California
State University, Los Angeles
Frank Winston Wylie, California State University, Long Beach.

In addition, we thank the following persons who provided careful review and thoughtful comments on our manuscript in its prepublication form:

William Baxter, Marquette University
William Brody, Memphis State University
Richard Dubiel, University of Wisconsin, Stevens Point
James Measell, Wayne State University
Guy Meiss, Central Michigan University
Michael Parkinson, Southern Illinois University
Maureen Rubin, California State University, Northridge
Karyn Rydacki, Northern Michigan University

Robert E. Rayfield
Lalit Acharya
J. David Pincus
Donn E. Silvis

THINKING: WHERE WRITING BEGINS

PUBLIC RELATIONS WRITING: A DIFFERENT BREED OF CAT • • •

Introduction

The Essence of Good Writing

"Pity the readers," writes *Slaughterhouse Five* author Kurt Vonnegut. "They have to identify and make sense of thousands of little marks on paper. They have to **read,** an art so difficult that most people don't really master it even after having studied it all through grade school and high school—12 long years."

In this chapter, we begin our look at the special art of writing for public relations, keeping in mind those who receive our words.

In many ways, writing for public relations is like other writing. It conveys thoughts from one person to another. Its aim is to make readers understand, accept and comply with some message. The writer wishes to amuse, inform, educate, provoke or persuade the reader—or perhaps all of these. The writer may be conveying original thoughts, or those of others. It is a concept connoting great power.

But, make no mistake. It is the readers who are in charge. They enter the writer's arena ready to receive, ignore or reject messages.

We, the writers, come to our readers on their terms. They cannot be forced to consider our message if they don't want to. If they open the sports pages and find opera news, they may ignore it. So we place messages in proper settings. If readers find our communication hurried or harried, they may be confused. So we make our messages direct and clear. If our purpose is to convince, we ask readers to accept our messages for reasons that will appeal to them. Good writing demands that we use the correct set of language symbols necessary to achieve our objectives, and not one symbol more or less. "Jesus wept." "Time and tide wait for no man." "This nation, of the people, by the people, for the people. . . ." "Great Britain declared war against Germany today." "Ask not what your country can do for you. . . ." The world's memorable messages have generally been brief and compelling. Whether emotional or rational, they have been direct, simple and clear.

That is the kind of writing we would like to help you learn. We will endeavor to teach the basic rules, concepts and techniques you must master to write effectively for public relations. We will use examples that demonstrate this mastery. Repeatedly, we will ask you to review and apply the marks of a successful writer—thinking, planning, writing, delivering and evaluating—to your writing tasks. We will provide you with exercises on which you can practice this approach.

Strategies and Skills

By now, it is clear that effective public relations messages cannot be produced by simply putting words down on paper. There should be a five-part strategy behind almost every successful public relations writing effort.

1. First, the writer **thinks** about the problem the writing will address, defines it precisely, researches its background and circumstances, and considers all feasible writing approaches. One way to stop people from smoking would be to ban it. Another would be to show them the horrors of death from lung cancer. A third might be to show them how their health and self esteem could improve if they didn't smoke. Which is the best? There are no easy answers. The choice of strategy would depend upon the writer's objectives, and the audience's expectations and attitudes.

2. Second, the writer **plans** a writing strategy that best fits the nature and needs of the client organization, its environment and its targeted publics. Writers must consider the legality and ethics of the communication as well as the channels available for distributing the message. A strategy for raising money for a performing arts center might be a gala premiere, with $1,000-per-seat tickets. How can writers reach people who might attend? How can they help to publicize future productions?

3. Next the writer **prepares** the copy. The message is tailored to each public and medium. Then it is edited and rewritten to the writer's satisfaction and reviewed by pertinent members of the client organization. For example, a financial message not reviewed by legal and financial staffs may be a bomb ready to explode.

4. The writer then makes sure the right messages are **delivered** to the right places at the right time **through the proper channels.** Publicity releases on a charity relay race must be delivered to newspaper, radio and TV sports editors well before their respective deadlines.

5. Finally the writer **evaluates** the impact of the message. Was the message published or broadcast? Was it heard or read? Was it understood and acted upon favorably? Was it cost effective? The writer analyzes and records this information so it may be applied to future writing challenges.

Unfortunately, public relations writers do not always thoroughly follow each of these steps. They may be hampered by a lack of time and money. But most know the importance of the strategic approach. A skilled publicist may be able to teach a talented student the mechanics of writing an acceptable press release in a few hours. But learning to think strategically takes time. The necessity for thought and planning comes into sharper focus when one considers that a sloppy writer can trigger a lawsuit which could far exceed that writer's total income for a decade.

Recapping the writing process, it is clear that only through proper thought and planning can we produce the most effective messages. To do less is to waste time, effort and money. Today's professional atmosphere does not easily tolerate ineffectiveness.

Agreeing on the Jargon: Some Key Terms

Communication theory holds that communication is more efficient when there is a common language. Like everyone else, public relations writers need to agree upon the terms germane to their profession.

The following paragraphs list a number of such terms and their working definitions. The definitions are not intended to be comprehensive since these can get very lengthy. We offer a brief and easily understandable definition of each of them for your quick reference and use. It is important for you to learn, understand and apply these meanings to your work. On our part, these definitions provide a common ground on which to base instruction.

Journalism

Journalism is a report of events as they appear at the moment of writing. Its objective is to provide news or opinion through print, broadcast or electronic channels. "A journalist may write an account that is entertaining as well as newsworthy; but a person who writes for sheer entertainment only . . . is not a journalist" (Agee, Ault and Emery 1976, 11). Because journalists often become public relations writers, journalistic and public relations writing are sometimes confused with each other. Public relations writers practice journalism and many other kinds of writing.

Advertising

Advertising is controlled persuasion through mass and specialized media on behalf of clients (Wright, Winter and Zeigler 1982, 10). Advertisers normally control the message by paying for it and are thus able to dictate when and where it will appear. When one reads, hears or sees an ad, there is little doubt about whose goods, services or ideas are being offered for sale. Public relations writers often support advertising by writing corporate or image ads. While advertising and public relations functions sometimes overlap, they are conceptually quite different. Advertising creates sales, whereas public relations creates understandings. And, unlike ads, public relations messages are not paid for. They depend on their newsworthiness for getting published or broadcast.

Marketing

In its broadest sense, marketing is a management function that identifies customers, determines their wants, develops appropriate products and gets them to the customers (Bovee and Arens 1982, 166–68). Thus, advertising is a function of marketing, although marketing can be accomplished without advertising. Public relations is sometimes confused with marketing. Some public relations writing, such as institutional advertising copy or product publicity, certainly supports the marketing function.

Promotion

Promotion is the creation of "interest in a person, product, institution or cause through special activities" (Newsom and Scott 1985, 503). It is generally thought of as publicity or media exposure without direct cost. Public relations writers often help promote clients through stories and interviews. New products can be promoted without paying advertising costs when the products themselves are newsworthy. When Proctor and Gamble first introduced Crest toothpaste, it received considerable free promotion in the media because it was the first to be acknowledged by a respected dental group to stop or slow down tooth decay.

Publicity

Publicity is unpaid and uncontrolled mass communication (Nolte and Wilcox 1984, 4). A newspaper article or radio announcement about a 10K run for charity would probably be publicity. The media carry the information without cost because it is socially responsible and newsworthy. But media may use publicity when, where and how they choose. The "uncontrolled" notation really means that the placement and distribution are controlled by the media, not the public relations writer or the client.

Public Affairs

Public affairs has three usages in communication. In journalism, the term refers to reporting of public events, especially those involving government agencies. In the military services and other branches of government, it is often used as an umbrella title for all functions of public communication. In business, it is used to refer to those public relations functions relating to politics and government.

Communication

Communication is the process by which information is passed from one person or organization to another. Public relations writers begin each communication with print symbols. But their information may be transmitted through many channels. The communication which began as a page of copy may reach its audience through an item in the calendar section of a newspaper, a television interview by the client, or in private conversation between a lobbyist and a politician. Communication is successful if the public receiving it understands the message as the writer meant to be understood. No human communication is perfect, but knowing how it works can improve its effectiveness (Newsom and Wollert 1985, 18–27).

Channels

Channels are the vehicles used to transmit public relations messages to target audiences. Public relations writers move their messages through many channels. Among these are mass channels such as newspapers, magazines, radio, television, film and billboards, as well as interpersonal channels, such as speeches and private conversations. Public relations writers attempt to get the best possible effect from their messages by selecting the best channel for each message to each target public.

Message

The message is the specific set of symbols used to convey a specific thought. It may be written or spoken, verbal or nonverbal, and auditory or pictorial. For example, a writer wishing to convince people to contribute to the United Negro College Fund might do so today with a ten-second radio public service announcement, repeating the well-known slogan, "A mind is a terrible thing to waste."

Client

For our purposes, a client is a person or organization for whom public relations tasks are undertaken. The client might be the marketing division of a corporation making a request through a public relations firm. But the client might also be the president of a public relations agency for whom the writer works, or the director of public relations in a nonprofit agency or corporation.

Opinion

An opinion is a person's expressed belief about a subject. An opinion is open to considerable change over time. Public relations writers often incorporate individual and public opinion into their messages. Expert opinions may provide new perspectives or add credibility. The opinions of groups of people help determine what public relations actions need to be taken.

Public

A public is any group of people with something in common. Some believe that members of a public must share this "sense of commonness" (Cutlip, Center and Broom 1985, 157).

A public may be defined with increasing precision. This can help the public relations writer fashion a message with the most effective appeal. "Women who swim" is a public. "Women under 30 who swim" is a more easily addressed public. And, "California women under 30 who swim" is an even more targetable public, having gender, age and geographical boundaries. A public may change, of course. And, one may belong to many publics at once. Public relations usually classifies publics into two major categories: (1) **Internal:** those publics within the client organization. These might include top and middle management, supervisors and workers. (2) **External:** those outside publics which may affect or be affected by the client organization. These include suppliers, wholesalers, customers, special interest groups and other organizations.

Sometimes the terms "audience" and "public" are used interchangeably. However, an audience is those people who receive a given message. Our desired public may be all employees of a company, but our audience will be only those employees who read our message in the newsletter.

Public Opinion

This is the prevailing view of some public on a given subject. Public relations writers often determine and incorporate public opinion into their writings. But public opinion does not necessarily represent the truth. Determining public opinion is costly and is usually applied to important issues. "Most scholars agree that public opinion represents a **consensus,** which emerges over time, from all expressed views that cluster around an issue in debate, and that this consensus exercises power" (Cutlip, Center and Broom 1985, 157).

Public Relations

"Public relations helps an organization and its publics adapt mutually to each other" (definition adopted by the Public Relations Society of America, Spring 1988, Wilcox, Ault and Agee 1989, 5). According to the 1978 Public Relations World Congress (Black 1979, xi) and the Public Relations Society of America (*Public Relations Journal* 1987, 6), public relations specifically involves:

1. Researching societal trends, analyzing them and predicting their consequences; anticipating, analyzing and interpreting public opinion, attitudes and issues.

2. Counseling clients on policy, action and communication; recommending actions to change organizations or their publics.

3. Researching and planning programs of action and communication to achieve the informed public understanding necessary to meet the organization's objectives.

4. Conducting dynamic and continuing programs of action and communication necessary to meet the organization's objectives.

5. Determining the effects of these actions on the intended publics, comparing actual effects with those planned, and revising actions and communications to better support organizational goals and objectives; analyzing lessons learned from these evaluations, and applying them to future programs.

Writing for Public Relations

Though public relations writing shares much in common with other forms of writing, its purposes and content are often quite different from other writing forms. It conforms to the general writing concepts noted at the beginning of this chapter. It often adopts the writing style of journalism. However, it is, as the saying goes, "a different breed of cat." Noted below are some types of public relations writing, with a brief explanation for each. These will be explored in detail in later chapters.

Personal Communications

Personal communications range from informal conversations to major speeches. Organizational leaders often get help from public relations writers for such communication. Examples of personal communications support which public relations writers provide include cards, one-liners, "elevator speeches," memoranda and letters:

Cards, One-liners and "Elevator Speeches"

Public relations writers often research, outline and type on cards pertinent points for chief executive officers to make in conversation with other important executives. The key is to get the essence of the message into a few memorable words and phrases. The "elevator speech" is a brief message designed for use in a personal conversation with an executive, presumably while the elevator is between floors. A one-liner is a short, pithy and forceful sentence. An example of an anti-capital punishment one-liner might be: "How many rich people ever went to the electric chair?"

Memoranda

Memos are informal internal notes used to pass organizational information, reminders or even persuasive messages. They are helpful in communicating with fellow workers, bosses and subordinates. Public relations writers often write memos as brief records of meetings, to gain support for ideas or to explain plans or reports. Sometimes they draft personal notes for CEOs using this format.

Letters

Although they are not always personal, letters are designed to be person-to-person communications. They are used to communicate directly with outside publics, and to accompany reports, proposals, position papers, plans and other impersonal communications. These tell readers what is in the packages and what action is requested. One of the most difficult letters to write is the "pitch letter," so called because it makes a "pitch," or appeal, to readers, trying to persuade them to accept program concepts, use promotions or participate in campaigns.

Specialized Communications

These communications for limited audiences include formal proposals, position papers, annual and quarterly reports, and organizational communications.

Formal proposals are made to client organizations' top management, requesting and specifying communications programs to fill perceived needs. You might, for example, write a formal proposal for an aircraft manufacturer's national headquarters, which would include your plan for the roll-out ceremony of the company's 10,000th airplane.

Position papers are documents detailing official organizational views on important issues. If you worked for an electric utility, you might be asked to write a paper which articulated the company's official position on nuclear power.

Annual and quarterly reports are comprehensive accountings to stockholders and financial analysts on the status and future of a public organization. Public relations writers usually coordinate the preparation of these, as well as write portions of them.

Organizational communications, also called "internal public relations" and other different names in public relations, generally refers to planned communication within an organization. Depending on the size and orientation of the organization, it may publish fliers, newsletters and magazines, and produce motion picture films, radio and television broadcasts, and video and audio tapes to communicate with employee publics. Many public relations writers are exclusively involved in writing and editing for these communications.

Public Communications

Usually designed for a specific public, these include writing brochures, speeches, news releases, feature stories, corporate advertising, and radio and television comments.

Brochures are informational or persuasive pamphlets covering single or multiple topics. They are usually double or triple folded with single-column printing. They may be used for general distribution but usually focus on a single public. An example would be a Red Cross brochure telling prospective donors how to go about giving blood.

Speeches are among the most demanding forms of public communications. Top managers often do not have time to research or draft their own speeches. Also, many

TABLE 1.1.   Types of Public Relations Writing

Personal Communications

Cards, One-Liners and Elevator Speeches
Memoranda
Letters

Communications for Limited Audiences

Formal Proposals
Position Papers
Annual and Quarterly Reports
Organizational Communications

Public Communications

Brochures
Speeches
News Releases
Feature Stories
Corporate Advertising
Radio and Television

---

times organizational messages demand more careful thought and preparation than top management can give them. So public relations writers provide ideas, background research, speech drafts and other support.

News releases are stories about client activities that are prepared in formats acceptable to specific media, such as newspapers or television stations. News releases are the mainstay of public relations. Most media coverage for clients is initiated by newsworthy releases written by public relations writers.

Feature stories are articles public relations writers often prepare about interesting people, places and things within their organizations. These may appear in the clients' own internal publications or in commercial newspapers or magazines.

Corporate advertising takes place frequently when companies decide that stories they most want certain people to receive are not being used by the media. So they have advertising and public relations people work together to write advertising messages and pay to have them published. These range from communications to improve the image of the company among certain publics to ads discussing prominent issues not directly related to the company or its products.

Radio and television materials which public relations writers prepare include public service announcements, new product stories, video news releases, interviews and a host of other communications for broadcast on behalf of clients. A company executive's participation in a television talk show is usually based upon a public relations writer's research and drafts. Though the words spoken may not be those of the writer, the drafts help the executives with key aspects of the subjects they will be discussing.

Table 1.1 reviews some types of public relations writing.

What Are We Trying to Achieve?

The writing tasks noted above are diverse, each requiring different experience and knowledge. But all have a common core which differentiates them from other forms of writing. Primary among these is **advocacy.** The public relations message, regardless of form, takes a stand. It speaks "for" and champions the client. Writers who don't subscribe to this tenet may not belong in public relations. Of course, advocacy ceases to be an issue when writers have ethical reservations about the messages under consideration.

Secondly, all public relations copy is to some extent **persuasive.** We don't want people to just hear what we say. We want them to do something about it. Our persuasive intent ranges from desiring readers to be properly informed to asking for their intellectual, physical and economic support for a cause. But public relations persuasion falls short of selling products.

Thirdly, public relations copy must be **authoritative** and **accurate.** The public relations writer speaks for the president, the board of directors, the stockholders and employees of the organization. Any error or erroneous supposition on the part of the writer reflects on the entire group, to say nothing of the legal problems it might cause. Therefore, a message should not be released to the media or public until all concerned are agreed that it is accurate.

Lastly, each public relations message is **designed for a specific time, place, public and communication channel.** And it is intended to elicit a specific response from that public. This precise message design and its handling are important to success.

How Is It Different from Journalism?

Because many journalists switch to jobs in public relations, public relations writing is often perceived to be journalistic writing. This is essentially true for news releases and most publicity. The publicity release must be composed in journalistic style, and is accurate, brief, clear and newsworthy. Otherwise, it will never meet the standards of the newspaper editor and broadcast news director or be used.

But for other forms of public relations writing, the similarities with journalistic writing recede or vanish. Table 1.2 provides an outline for comparison.

Some of the differences are significant and worthy of comment:

1. The traditional journalist tries to present all available information on a story—positive and negative—and let the reader decide who is right or wrong. The public relations writer also provides pertinent information on the story. The truth is not hidden. But information is presented in a manner that persuades the reader of the correctness of the client's cause. It is not ethical for the public relations writer to support an illegal or immoral cause. However, given the correctness of the client's cause, the writer then becomes an advocate for that cause.

TABLE 1.2. Some Comparisons of Journalism and Public Relations Writing

Factor	Journalism	Public Relations
Accuracy	Best possible to meet deadline	Always, regardless of time
Brevity	Always, with pyramid	Usually with pyramid
Clarity	Always	Always
Honesty	Always	Always
Completeness	All pertinent facts, regardless of effect	Normally, except for unverified facts, others' releases and trade secrets
Attribution	Generally	Always
Optimism	Bad news is good news.	Be optimistic on client's behalf.
Criticism	Let the chips falls where they may.	Show the client in the best possible light.

2. Traditional journalists present facts and reasoned arguments. They rarely inject emotion into news stories, relegating it to the feature story or column. When public relations writers prepare news releases, they generally follow journalistic writing guidelines. But for other types of writing, public relations writers may use emotional appeals to persuade their audiences. Sentiment is critical to the success of some writing tasks.

3. Finally, public relations writers compose for several media. While journalists normally write solely for one medium, print or broadcast, public relations writers are expected to master the writing styles and formats for all media. Thus, the public relations writer may follow up a release on a new plant opening with a radio public service announcement for the client organization's favorite charity. This, in turn, may be followed by a storyboard on a new product for a television station's business news segment.

How Important Is It?

A Critical Function

Public relations writing performs a critical function in our complex society. No reporter can assemble a comprehensive story about an organization without reviewing a series of releases, fact sheets, biographies, speeches and backgrounders produced by a public relations office. While reporters add their own research to verify and complete the story, public relations writings can save them considerable research time and effort. And public relations specialists provide information which accurately represents the organization's outlook on issues related to the story.

A PROFESSIONAL TIP:
Public Relations Writing and Journalism

Public relations writing, unlike journalism news, takes a point of view or position, normally that of the organization or client. Hence the public relations practitioner who wishes to advocate a position needs to learn the art of persuasive writing. But the essential journalism skills of truthfulness, accuracy, completeness, brevity and clarity are equally needed for public relations writing.

Public relations writing offers some latitude on what is said and how, but there can never be any compromise on accuracy and truthfulness. Since the first "gatekeeper" or decision-maker through whom public relations writing must flow is usually a journalism-schooled editor, writing in acceptable journalistic style is a must.

The public relations person must always keep in mind, though, the ultimate audience to whom the message is directed. Messages must be relevant, interesting and believable to this ultimate audience for communication to occur. Without communication, the public relations goal usually cannot be achieved.

H. J. (Jerry) Dalton Jr., APR, is manager, corporate communications, for the LTV Corp. He has been practicing public relations for almost 40 years. As a brigadier general, he headed the U.S. Air Force's worldwide public affairs activity. He has worked for two large corporations and was the 1990 president of the Public Relations Society of America.

Presidents of major charities and corporations who do a great deal of public speaking do not always have time to research and draft fresh and inspiring speeches. They depend on speech writers for ideas and at least the first draft of every important public message.

Organizational Communication

No organization is successful for long without a competent organizational communication program. Employees must be surveyed to determine their attitudes. News about the organization has to be gathered and prepared. It may appear in broadcast scripts, audio-visual recordings, newspaper or magazine photographs and articles, provided to all employees. Continuing employee feedback must be synthesized and analyzed for organizational decision makers. Motivational messages and key information must be passed from management to workers. Quarterly, semi-annual and annual reports must be prepared and presented to corporate stockholders. The outside environment must be examined for its impact on the organization. Plans and programs must be prepared to meet the challenges of tomorrow.

The Information Society

Additionally, there are definite societal, economic and legal trends that demand effective public relations writing and make it indispensable to modern business and society. One of these is the coming of what social forecaster John Naisbitt calls the "Information Society" (Naisbitt 1982, 11–38). Due to satellites, computers and international economies, information moves around the world faster and in more sophisticated ways than ever before. All of us are exposed daily to many times more information than our parents were. Sometimes we miss messages that are important to our well-being. Often we are bombarded by so many that we don't know which to attend to. In such a media-rich society, information specialists are needed to help get messages quickly and in easily understandable forms to people who need them. Public relations writers assist in such processes by translating complex business, economic, political and social information into easily-understood messages that are channeled through the mass media to the people who need them.

Social Investment

A second trend which underscores the need for intelligent public relations writing is the economic trend called "social investment." During the 1980s, some people determined to invest only in companies whose social outlooks and actions reflected their own. Thus, pacifists refused to invest in arms manufacturers, and those opposed to apartheid refused to invest in companies with interests in South Africa. One social investment fund specialist has claimed that "today, socially conscious investing is becoming 'mainstream across the country' " (Council of Economic Priorities 1986, 1).

In light of this trend, many U.S. businesses are taking unprecedented socially responsive steps. They have divested themselves of socially questionable holdings, hired more minority employees and provided more direct support for the arts and education. While public relations counselors assist in this process, public relations writers play a central role in telling pertinent publics what actions their client organizations have taken to demonstrate social consciousness.

Legal Communication Requirements

Finally, public relations writing helps client organizations fulfill their legal requirements for communications. Since 1933, the U.S. Congress and government agencies have been mandating that public companies must take specific actions so that current and potential stockholders may make informed and intelligent investment decisions. These range from the specifications for a minimum size of type in annual reports (for easier reading) to the need for prompt and widespread disclosure of major corporate actions. These requirements must be met accurately and promptly for the sake of the investor and the survival of the organization. Public relations writers help fill this need by writing financial releases, preparing stock information for customers and analysts, and producing quarterly and annual corporate reports.

Thus, writing for public relations is a varied, endless cycle, without which the organization cannot effectively run. Without successful writing support, the organization cannot hope to achieve and maintain an understanding with the outside publics it serves or the democratic electorate which allows it to exist.

Not surprisingly, the writing task is the single most important thing a person must master in order to be a successful public relations practitioner. Countless professionals repeat the dictum: "You can't be a successful public relations practitioner until you are a successful public relations writer." It is easier to be a competent writer if one enjoys writing. But it is not essential. What is essential is reasonable intelligence, the ability to analyze and solve problems, patience and endless attention to detail.

What Makes It Complicated?

Little Tolerance for Error

Public relations writing is complicated precisely because of its importance. First, it tolerates little error. If one writes copy for a CEO which says that the company owns 29 ocean-going tankers instead of the 35 it actually owns, someone will catch the error. If it is the CEO, the writer may be lucky. If it is an investigative reporter looking for hidden tankers, the company's credibility may be tarnished.

If copy is prepared with spelling, grammar or other technical errors, it probably will not be used. Reporters rely on editors to correct and edit their copy. Many public relations writers do not have such support, however, and their flawed copy goes directly to the media. Media editors generally believe that if writers don't care enough to be technically correct, then what they have written can't be very important. Worse, writers who are careless with words may also be careless with facts. Thus, the effectiveness of writers and their organizations is weakened by errors.

Complications of Circumstance

Public relations writing is also complicated by circumstance. Reporters want all the known information. If something goes wrong, they want to know how bad it is, who is responsible for the error and what is going to be done about it. These are reasonable enough requests, except that the organization's media relations people don't always have all the answers. Even when they do, the client may not want all the facts made public. The reason may be personal (bosses quite understandably don't like to appear stupid), financial (a negative message might make a company's stock drop five points overnight), legal (top managers may be reluctant to publicly admit guilt for fear of a civil suit), or strategic (company trade secrets are as carefully protected as national defense secrets).

Directors or writers attempt to persuade the client that early self-disclosure is best for the long-range health of the organization, as well as the soul. But they may be directed not to provide the media complete information, even when the information is available. It is difficult to prepare such releases in a professional manner. Balancing the media's right to know with the client's right to privacy complicates the public relations writing process considerably, making it all the more important.

Protecting Clients and Other Parties

Finally, public relations writing is complicated because, whatever the situation, the message must be designed to advance or protect the client without unnecessarily offending or compromising other parties. On first thought, it would be easy to say: "Our company is blameless. Mayor Jones ordered the sewage dumped into the river." But we would not make such a charge without careful consideration. If it is true, then city officials should make the statement. But perhaps the information we have is wrong. Perhaps there were extenuating circumstances. Public relations writers tend to give other parties the benefit of the doubt. Sometimes that makes their writing less complete than it might be. They avoid speculations on the actions and motivations of others. They need to consider all aspects of a story before writing about it. A reporter filing a story close to deadline can be forgiven an error. A public relations writer, whose copy is always final, will not be so easily forgiven. That is what makes writing for public relations so different, interesting and important.

Chapter Summary

This chapter helped begin the thinking process for the public relations writer. It discussed some of the elements of what is professionally considered "good" writing. These include directness, simplicity, reading ease and relevance of material. Strategies behind successful writing were emphasized: **thinking, planning, writing, delivering** and **evaluating.**

We discussed key terms for the text. Special attention was given to publics, public opinion and public relations. You were advised on the precise use in public relations of terms such as advertising, marketing, publicity and public relations, and how these terms differ and are related.

You learned that public relations writing has several unique characteristics and forms. It was categorized into personal communications, specialized communications and public communications.

We showed public relations writing to be a discipline requiring advance thought, careful research and complete accuracy. Unlike journalism, persuasion and advocacy are central to it. It can make important contributions to complex societies, since news media need its information, and organizations need its internal and external support.

You found that public relations writing is complicated. It tolerates little error, must balance between the media's right to know and the client's right to privacy, and must advocate the client's case without unnecessarily offending others.

In this chapter you were introduced to the public relations writing structure. You were challenged to think about the nature of public relations writing, how it is like other writing and how it differs. Professional writers **think, plan** and then **write.** Having first considered what the public relations writing process is about, they then write to achieve the best result. We believe you will also find this approach best for you.

A Writing Exercise

Situation. A business major from a local college begins sounding off about "parasites" in business. She claims these are functions which reduce profits, but offer no contribution to the "bottom line." She sees public relations as the worst of these parasites. While noting that advertising has been shown to increase sales, she says nobody seems to be able to measure the effects of public relations. She calls it "a fraud perpetrated by five wasted writers who send out thousands of claptrap releases that few publish and nobody reads."

Assignment. Write a 200–500 word letter to the editor of the business school newsletter. Use it to explain to business majors just what public relations is. Include a brief justification for public relations writing, discussing its necessity, objectives and value. Build your argument around points made in this chapter. Take great care that your letter is technically perfect. Make certain your word usage, sentence structure, spelling, abbreviation and capitalization are correct. Make your copy "camera ready," i.e., absolutely clean and neat, with no pencil corrections or strikeovers. If you do not have an automatic correcting capability in your computer, word processor or typewriter, whiteovers (but not pen or pencil marking) are acceptable. The letter should be so clean that if someone made a photocopy of your letter, no error would be visible in it.

This first assignment should begin your search for writing excellence. Nothing less is acceptable. Get used to it.

An Editing Exercise

Situation. You are a new intern with Perkins Public Relations, a central U.S. firm which employs 15 people and specializes in agricultural public relations. As a first assignment, your boss asks you to review, edit and rewrite a proposed news release which has been drafted for a chemical client by your predecessor.

Assignment. Read the draft below carefully, keeping in mind the major points covered in this chapter. Edit and rewrite it to the best of your ability, keeping in mind those points and employing your best writing skills. Your copy should be typed neatly, double-spaced, error-free and photo-ready.

New Insectorcide for Corn

Qwik-Kill, Inc., one of the nation's best known insectorcide companies, put a new anti-rat chemical on the market this week. Called Corn Care Rat Kill, it attacks rats' nervous systems, giving them intense pain and bleeding upon contact and death within 15 minutes. One application to a corn stowage bin is guaranteed by Kwik-Kill Inc. to kill all rats in the bin in less than an hour. It is harmless to humans but will cause pain, vomiting and agonizing death to cats eating more than a quart of it. Corn Care Rat Kill can be dropped right into a corn stowage bin on top of the corn. It evaporates after three hours and leaves no residue. It does not dissolve dead rats, however. They will remain in the corn, rotting, until cleared out. According to the Department of Agriculture, no other product on the market is as effective as Corn Care Rat Kill in killing rats without damage to the product. AgChem, a competitor, makes Ratgo, a similar product. Ratgo is only 75 percent as effective as Corn Care Rat Kill, but it costs 15 percent less.

Food for Thought

1. Scientists often express great thoughts in complex words. Einstein's "Theory of Relativity" is incomprehensible to many. How can the communications writer explain complex issues such as communications theory in simple language?
2. One of the problems with the term "public relations" is that its meaning to the layperson has little to do with its professional use. What name would you give the function if everyone involved agreed to use it, and why?
3. Public relations writing is at times critical to the survival of a corporation. Why then is the function one of the first to be cut during economic hard times?

4. Many journalists appear to believe public relations writing to be of inferior quality. How are some ways that this perception might have come about and what can public relations writers do to change it?
5. What do you see as the most critical responsibility for today's public relations writer, and why?

References for Further Study

Agee, Warren K., Phillip H. Ault and Edwin Emery. *Introduction to Mass Communications,* 5th ed. New York: Harper & Row, 1976.

Black, Sam, ed. *Public Relations in the 1980s: Proceedings of the Eighth Public Relations World Congress.* New York: Pergamon Press, 1980.

Bovee, Courtland L., and William F. Arens. *Contemporary Advertising.* Homewood, Ill.: Richard D. Irwin, 1982.

Center, Allen H. *New Technology and Public Relations.* New York: Foundation for Public Relations Research and Education, 1988.

Council of Economic Priorities. *Newsletter* N86–6, June 1986.

Cutlip, Scott M., Allen H. Center and Glen M. Broom. *Effective Public Relations,* 6th ed. Englewood Cliffs, N.J.: Prentice-Hall, 1985.

Naisbitt, John. *Megatrends: Ten New Directions Transforming Our Lives.* New York: Warner Books, 1982.

Newson, Doug, and Alan Scott. *This is PR: The Realities of Public Relations,* 3d ed. Belmont, Calif.: Wadsworth, 1985.

Newson, Doug, and James A. Wollert. *Media Writing: News for the Mass Media.* Belmont, Calif.: Wadsworth, 1985.

Nolte, Lawrence N., and Dennis L. Wilcox. *Effective Publicity: How to Reach the Public.* New York: Wiley, 1984.

Public Relations Journal, Register Issue, 1987–1988 (June 1987):6.

Wilcox, Dennis L., Phillip H. Ault and Warren Agee. *Public Relations: Strategies and Tactics,* 2nd ed. New York: Harper & Row, 1989.

Wright, John S., Willis L. Winter, Jr. and Sherilyn K. Zeigle. *Advertising,* 5th ed. New York: McGraw-Hill, 1982.

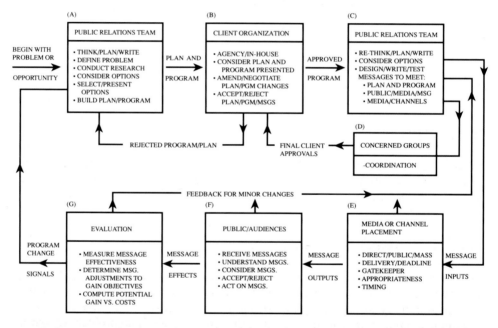

(A)

PUBLIC RELATIONS TEAM

BEGIN WITH
PROBLEM OR

OPPORTUNITY

- THINK/PLAN/WRITE
- DEFINE PROBLEM
- CONDUCT RESEARCH
- CONSIDER OPTIONS
- SELECT/PRESENT
  OPTIONS
- BUILD PLAN/PROGRAM

PLAN AND

PROGRAM

(B)

CLIENT ORGANIZATION

- AGENCY/IN-HOUSE
- CONSIDER PLAN AND
  PROGRAM PRESENTED
- AMEND/NEGOTIATE
  PLAN/PGM CHANGES
- ACCEPT/REJECT
  PLAN/PGM/MSGS

APPROVED

PROGRAM

(C)

PUBLIC RELATIONS TEAM

- RE-THINK/PLAN/WRITE
- CONSIDER OPTIONS
- DESIGN/WRITE/TEST
  MESSAGES TO MEET:
  - PLAN AND PROGRAM
  - PUBLIC/MEDIA/MSG
  - MEDIA/CHANNELS

REJECTED PROGRAM/PLAN

FINAL CLIENT
APPROVALS

(D)

CONCERNED GROUPS

-COORDINATION

FEEDBACK FOR MINOR CHANGES

(G)

EVALUATION

PROGRAM
CHANGE

SIGNALS

- MEASURE MESSAGE
  EFFECTIVENESS
- DETERMINE MSG.
  ADJUSTMENTS TO
  GAIN OBJECTIVES
- COMPUTE POTENTIAL
  GAIN VS. COSTS

MESSAGE

EFFECTS

(F)

PUBLIC/AUDIENCES

- RECEIVE MESSAGES
- UNDERSTAND MSGS.
- CONSIDER MSGS.
- ACCEPT/REJECT
- ACT ON MSGS.

MESSAGE

OUTPUTS

(E)

MEDIA OR CHANNEL
PLACEMENT

- DIRECT/PUBLIC/MASS
- DELIVERY/DEADLINE
- GATEKEEPER
- APPROPRIATENESS
- TIMING

MESSAGE

INPUTS

▶ **Figure 2.1.** The public relations writing process model. The public relations writing process is generally a continuous loop of thinking, planning, writing, delivery and evaluation. Every public relations writing project begins with a problem or opportunity presented to the public relations management team (A). From there, a plan and program are sent back to the client for approval (B). Once the plan is approved, it is passed to the public relations writing team (C) for messages. After messages are coordinated among all concerned parties (D) and given final client approval, they are sent to media contacts (E), who may send them to publics (F) through broadcast or print media, and are evaluated (G) for their effectiveness by the public relations team. Evaluation may call for minor changes, which are made directly by writers. If major changes are needed, the problem goes back to the public relations management team for reconsideration (A).

THINKING ABOUT THE WRITING PROBLEM • • •

Introduction

In this chapter, we consider the thought processes required to be effective public relations writers. We do this by tying these processes to the actions required to produce effective messages for public relations. A useful way to do this is through a model.

The Public Relations Writing Process Model

The importance of thinking, planning, writing, delivering and evaluating public relations messages was emphasized in chapter 1. Now we will examine these processes as a continual activity we call the **public relations writing process.** The model allows us to examine a public relations message at each step in its life, from problem to concept to planning to execution and to evaluation. This model, as displayed in figure 2.1, will be referred to periodically as we proceed through the study of how to write for public relations. Follow the explanations of segments of the model and see how they relate to one another. Keeping an image of the model in mind will help you understand each step in the process.

Problem Identification

The writing process begins when a problem or opportunity comes to the attention of the public relations team. The term "opportunity" is noted because some public relations programs are designed more to take advantage of promising situations than to solve problems. However, since public relations programs may also be responses to client problems, and "problem" is the term generally used, both "problems" and "opportunities" are called "problems." We will use the practice here, except in special cases.

The Public Relations Team (A)

The public relations team consists of management and all those involved in problem solving (see box A of figure 2.1). Public relations writers are usually members of such teams. Having received the problem, the public relations team defines it and conducts appropriate research. Thus begins the **think** portion of the writer's endless **think-plan-write** process. After considering all feasible outcomes and costs, the team selects the optimal solution.

Based on that projected solution, its members devise and write a program plan. Planning is one of the public relations writer's most important assignments. The public relations plan is a documentation of the goals, objectives, strategies and tasks required to solve a problem. It describes steps needed to achieve each objective, the people and tasks involved, the order of each activity, the time schedule required to complete it and a budget for costs (Baskin and Aronoff 1988, 123–146).

Plans should be written to achieve the solution most efficiently. But they should also appeal to key members of the client organization. One might expect that achieving either one of these objectives would ensure the other, but this is not always the case. An endorsement by a certain film star might be the most effective way of spreading news about a new product. But if the client organization's CEO dislikes the star, even the most efficient plan may be doomed.

The Client Organization (B)

Once the public relations team completes the plan, it goes to the client organization for consideration and approval. Copies are typically sent to key client managers (for example, the CEO, and marketing, advertising and public relations directors), along with representative copies of copy and art work. Although formal proposals are usually submitted, the client is persuaded of the program's value through a specially-prepared briefing. Briefings are usually scripted and coordinated by public relations writers. At this point the client either accepts the plan, rejects it or accepts it with changes. Since clients usually have strong notions of what they want a program to be, and are very sensitive to cost-benefit ratios, the last course of action is normal. Thus, writers may have to rewrite segments of the plan to gain the client's acceptance.

The Public Relations Team (C)

When the program plan is finally approved, it goes back to the public relations team for implementation. At this point, the writers rethink the entire program. Having satisfied themselves that the process has been thoroughly thought out, they compose the messages and coordinate the art required.

Concerned Groups (D)

After the messages have been written, edited, rewritten, checked and rechecked by the public relations team, they go through a coordination process. Involved in this process are client groups having a primary interest in the project, legal representatives and some level of client management. For example, a new product publicity campaign is usually reviewed by marketing, engineering and production personnel. After the review, everything which had to be changed goes back through the public relations team and client organization for final approval.

Media or Channel Placement (E)

Next, messages are sent to designated channels or media in order to reach specific publics. Media selection is based on the nature and urgency of the message, as well as the size, location and composition of the publics it is meant to reach. A campaign for property rezoning might require that one message be personally presented by the CEO of the client organization to the city council. A public campaign against drunk driving, on the other hand, might require that multiple messages be relayed to mass audiences via radio, television and newspapers. Letters accompany such messages, briefly explaining their intent and importance to editors or program directors.

Publics (F)

Messages reach the targeted publics through the media or other channels. As you will see, the messages published or broadcast by the media are not always the same as those sent to them. The writers' messages eventually reach some publics, though not always the desired ones. Audiences must not only receive the messages, but also understand, be convinced and act on them in the desired manner in order to achieve the desired public relations objectives. It is a long and tenuous chain of action from problem to plan to public to action.

Evaluation (G)

Throughout the process, program success is measured and fed back to decision makers. Minor changes are accomplished directly by the public relations writing team (C). Major errors, detected by more formal evaluation procedures, are returned as program change signals to the starting point of the process (A). Based on this feedback, public relations writers rethink, replan and rewrite to correct the flaws in the program. This cycle continues throughout the life of the public relations program.

Theory in Public Relations Writing

A theory is a set of related statements about a subject, based on research and contemplation, that can be tested and used to predict results of planned actions (Schramm 1963, 10). Theory, as it applies to public relations writing, can be usefully studied within the framework of the public relations writing model. Several theories will be discussed for each component of the model. We address here, however, only those concepts which have direct application to writing, especially public relations writing.

The Client Organization (B)

A message is generally more effective when it is presented by a credible, liked or respected client representative (Hovland, Janis and Kelly 1953; Whitehead 1968; Berlo, Lemert and Mertz 1969–70; McGinnies and Ward 1974; Horai, Naccari and Fatoullah 1974; McGuire 1985). Source credibility generally depends on several factors, including the source's perceived:

1. knowledge of or expertise in the subject addressed,
2. trustworthiness,
3. attractiveness,
4. objectivity,
5. self-confidence,
6. familiarity to the audience,
7. concern for the audience, and
8. control of the situation.

Knowing the importance of the source to the message's success, the public relations writer attributes the message to the highest possible authority in the client organization, unless the credibility of this source is known to be weak. Thus, for an important message from a corporation, the best source would normally be its president or CEO. Table 2.1 compares a routine release with one using a highly credible source.

Clients and Business Theories

Client organizations are also affected by business and economics theories that are applied by organizations routinely, sometimes unconsciously, to writing-related decisions (Hall and Goodale 1986, 94–104). Table 2.2 describes a few of these theories, noting how they may apply to public relations writing.

TABLE 2.1. Neutral versus Highly Credible Source

As the comparison demonstrates, a news source which is credible due to recognized expertise can increase media use and reader acceptance of a message.

Release from Neutral Source

Valerie Unlimited today announced production of a new lightweight jet aircraft engine for small and private aircraft—called the Jetlite.

The engine is designed to give light aircraft the same efficiency and low-maintenance values jet engines gave to airline fleets two decades ago. Breakthroughs in lightweight alloys and fuel economy caused Valerie to go ahead now.

The engine is rated at 500 horsepower—about the same as most gasoline-driven light aircraft engines today. It is meant to be tail-mounted.

Production begins this month at Valerie's sole Dania, Fla., factory. The company has been in business two years. This is its first product.

Release from a Highly Credible Expert Source

A. V. Jones, president of Valerie Unlimited, today announced production of a new lightweight engine for small and private aircraft—called the Jetlite. Jones, an aeronautical engineer, has worked on jet engine design for 22 years. He retired two years ago as head of engine design for Cal Tech's Jet Propulsion Laboratory.

"The engine is designed to give light aircraft the same efficiency and low-maintenance values jet engines gave to airline fleets two decades ago," Jones said. "Breakthroughs in lightweight alloys and fuel economy caused us to go ahead now."

Jones described the engine as rated at 500 horsepower, about the same as gasoline-driven light aircraft engines today. He said it's meant to be tail-mounted.

Production begins this month at Valerie's sole Dania, Fla., factory. Jones started the company two years ago, after retiring. This is its first product.

TABLE 2.2. Some Management Theory Useful in PR Writing

Theoretical School	*Principle*	*Value to Writing*
Classical	Division of Labor	Full-time writers are more efficient.
	Worker Incentive	Rewarding publics who support messages increases support.
Behavioral	Individual goals over organizational goals	Placing publics' goals first is to the organization's long range benefit.
	Full individual development needs group development.	Publics which share a common purpose respond fully.
	Hawthorne Effect	Individual attention causes positive public response, regardless of its purpose.

A PROFESSIONAL TIP:
Information Theory

To write clearly, one must "research" the task. Use information theory to reduce uncertainty. Experiments in the field tell us that a "bit"—a measure of amount of information—can reduce uncertainty by one-half. Use the "bit" concept as illustrated in this example: if someone chooses a number between 1 and 32, you can, by asking the right questions and getting only a yes or no response, determine the number by asking no more than five questions. Fine-tune from the general to the specific. Never say "dog" when you can say "pit bull." The reader wants the essence—the orange juice concentrate—without the water.

Otto Lerbinger, APR, is a professor and the public relations program coordinator for the department of mass communication and public relations at Boston University. He is also publisher of *pr reporter*, and editor of its supplement, *purview*. He is author or co-author of five books on public relations.

The Public Relations Team (A & C)

The public relations team's job is to think about the problem or opportunity assigned and to consider all possible avenues of action in an objective, comprehensive fashion. It is useful to look at some theories that influence public relations specialists in these considerations. These range from straightforward application of **information theory** to interesting but less supportable contentions that "the medium is the message."

Information theory applies mathematics to communications systems concepts and applications. One of its best known applications shows that, in a binary logic system, each "bit" of information can reduce uncertainty by half (see Professional Tip: Information Theory).

TABLE 2.3.   Grunig and Hunt's Problem-Solving Behavioral Molecule

1. **Detect:** Begin to think about behavior when a problem is detected in the environment.
2. **Construct:** Define the problem. Consider all solutions. Choose feasible solutions.
3. **Define:** Detail each feasible solution, step by step.
4. **Select:** Choose the best solution, all things considered.
5. **Confirm:** Consider every aspect; confirm the selection.
6. **Behave:** Carry out the solution.
7. **Detect:** Based on feedback from results, continue or resume the process.

Source: James E. Grunig and Todd Hunt, *Managing Public Relations* (New York: Holt, Rinehart & Winston, 1984), 104–111. Used with permission.

Systems theory presents an organization as a set of interacting subsystems. All these subsystems are interrelated so that any change in one affects all the others and the organization itself. Within the system there is a constant pressure to maintain it on a steady course. A corporation is a system whose subsystems may include production, marketing, finance, personnel, advertising and public relations departments. If a corporation is programmed to produce 7 percent net profit annually and one of its products becomes outmoded, it will compensate for that loss by updating the product or increasing sales in other areas.

The systems process works like this:
1. The organizational system steadily performs its functions.
2. Some internal or external force disturbs its equilibrium.
3. The system feedback detects unwanted changes.
4. The system locates the probable cause or causes of the problem.
5. The most efficient correction possible is made.
6. The system returns to its steady state.

Many current management concepts spring from systems theory. Grunig and Hunt (1984, 105–110) show how problem-solving fits the systems model in describing the steps in their **Behavioral Molecule** (see table 2.3).

It also subsumes the Public Relations Writing Process Model:

1. Detect. We begin to think about a response when we detect a problem in the environment. We may do this through research or have a reaction thrust upon us, as when we experience a fire.

2. Construct. Here we begin to formulate solutions. We define the problem, brainstorm, consider every possible alternative, and choose primary and alternative solutions.

3. Define. In this step we carefully detail how each possible alternative can be pursued. If the problem is that people in a town strongly object to noise from a factory operated by a client, there might be two alternatives:

A. Try to convince the people that the noise is necessary and not harmful, or,

B. Try to reduce the noise levels as much as possible, using public relations to convince the people that the client is doing its best to resolve the problem.

A third possibility of moving the factory to another location might be discarded as impractical.

4. Select. Here, options are progressively eliminated, leaving the best possible strategy. Some options might be eliminated because they would violate professional ethics, others because they could be too costly, still others due to possible legal problems. Eventually, the best alternative is selected. In the example described in the previous step, (B) appears to be the most feasible option. But what if plant engineers found that further noise reduction was technologically impossible? Alternative (B) would then no longer be viable, so option (A) would win out.

5. Confirm. Having made a decision, the managers step back and reconsider it from every possible angle. What is the probability of failure? What are the human, material and monetary costs of such a failure? Step (A) above could be rendered useless if someone could prove that the factory noise was physically harmful to people. If the alternative becomes risky upon such consideration, we go back to the previous step and begin again. If it holds up, we move on.

6. Behave. Now, the action takes place. Releases are sent. Stories are written. Speeches are given. The writers are now primary action agents.

7. Detect. The process begins again. Feedback during the "behave" phase reveals how well the actions are succeeding. This feedback is applied to alter actions in the "behave" phase and to generate new ones. The process, a never ending one, continues (see table 2.3).

A long-used explanation of effects is the **hierarchy-of-effects theory.** This traditional theory of communication posits four steps in the persuasion process, with each step a prerequisite for the next (Ray 1973, 147–176). These steps are:

1. **Awareness:** People become aware of a message.
2. **Understanding:** They understand it.
3. **Conviction:** They become convinced of its correctness.
4. **Action:** They act in suggested ways.

Although this approach to communication effects still has considerable following, there is evidence that these steps may not always work, be sequential or even be connected. A person may act on a message without ever understanding it. And he or she may act in a particular way for personal reasons; then seek reinforcement for that action in a message. However, the hierarchy-of-effects theory is a useful framework for understanding communication which has proven to be routinely effective.

TABLE 2.4. Typology of Media Effects

There are five two-way distinctions of effects. Under this typology, there are thirty-two possible communications effects.

1. Individual versus social effects
2. Direct versus indirect effects, depending on the presence of other effects
3. Content specific effects versus diffuse effect of the media content in general
4. Attitudinal or behavioral effects versus cognitive effects
5. Effects altering attitudes, knowledge or behavior versus effects which stabilize them

Source: Jack M. McLeod and Byron Reeves, "On the Nature of Mass Media Effects," G. Cleveland Wilhoit and Harold deBock (eds.), *Mass Communication Review Yearbook,* (Vol. 2) pp. 245–282, copyright 1981. Reprinted by permission of Sage Publications, Inc.

The **multiple effects theory** implies that mass media can have many kinds of effects, caused either by media content or the time people spend with media (Chaffee 1980, 78–108; McLeod and Reeves 1981, 245–282). Its effects can be individual or social, direct or indirect, or dependent upon content or simply media absorption. It might change only knowledge, attitudes or behavior, or all three. As many as 32 communications effects are possible when we apply all these considerations, the least possible of which might be convincing people to act directly in ways the client desires (see table 2.4); the most probable being indirect knowledge. Public relations writers need to understand how multiple effects theory may be applied when considering delivering messages through the mass media.

Here is how you might apply the multiple effects theory (following table 2.4) in considering a campaign to convince pregnant women not to drink alcoholic beverages:

1. You are after individual effects right now in order to protect unborn babies. Social effects are important, but you'll consider them later.
2. You want a direct message to these women: "Don't drink because it can harm your baby."
3. You want content specific effects now, but would like general mass media support for the message in the long run.
4. You are trying to change a specific behavior.
5. You want to change knowledge, attitudes and behavior of women who drink while pregnant. There is little likelihood that pregnant women who don't drink now will begin doing so.

Some **advertising theories** which have been specifically tested and developed in advertising and marketing can be useful for public relations writers (Weilbacher 1984, 460–470):

Pressure-Response. These theories postulate that the more messages about a product or service that consumers receive and are aware of, the more likely they are to buy the product or service. Implications for public relations writing are that, all other things being equal, the more a message is repeated, the more effective it becomes. Beyond a certain point, however, this repetition loses its value. For example, one study found that more than four ads on a subject to an audience led to negative reaction, despite the fact that the subject was a worthy charity (McGuire 1985, 18).

Active Learning. Advertising informs people in ways that may get them to change their attitudes toward a product or service. When this occurs, learning theory implies that, the more the increase in favorable attitude, the greater the probability of purchase. This type of response is more likely when there is some risk in the selection of alternatives and the customer is actively seeking information. A public relations AIDS prevention campaign designed to get certain publics to use condoms might take the active learning approach.

Low Involvement. These theories hold that a great deal of advertising information is absorbed by the consumer without conscious effort. Accordingly, over time similar messages may cause a subconscious change in the consumer's awareness and evaluation of the product, and lead to a purchase. Low-key cigarette ads may best be understood through these theories. Most public relations campaigns are designed to stimulate conscious thought, but this approach can help enhance positive attitudes over time. Annual community fund drives might be regularly reinforced in this way by low involvement "It works for all of us" messages.

Balance and Dissonance Reduction. These theories hold that people strive for harmony among their attitudes, values, beliefs and opinions. Accordingly, when this harmony is disrupted, they change one or more of these variables to reduce the inner conflict (see, for example, Festinger 1957). By way of example, let's say that you bought an unknown stereo on a whim. That causes you, a knowledgeable stereophile, some dissonance but you convince yourself that the system is really superior (maybe your gut feeling was really scientifically sound). Then you begin watching ads on that system and reading brochures and analyses about it. You let your new knowledge persuade you that you really got a good buy and the dissonance vanishes. But this is a backwards communication process, because you acted first, then had an attitude change and finally began learning. As a public relations writer, you could not use this system to convince people, since you wouldn't know about the dissonance until they had already taken some action. But you can disseminate favorable information on an issue of interest to help people who might be experiencing dissonance over it.

Market Segmentation. Consumers daily receive increasingly more media messages, each with a potentially diminished impact. But they appear to cope with this information overload by classifying brands into easily remembered categories (Ray 1982, 225–246). Marketing research identifies categories with common characteristics, then combines product usage, attitude, demographics and psychographics to find market segments. Organizations then position products and services to fit these segments. Public relations may use segmentation through a comprehensive analysis of donors to charity. Having learned that a segment of donors gave freely to feed hungry children, we could emphasize that aspect of our charity in addressing this group.

Media and other Channels of Communication (E)

Here we consider concepts which may help us use the channels of communication most effectively (see box E, figure 2.1).

1. The channel which most facilitates persuasion is interpersonal communication (McGuire 1968, 225–229). This follows the notion that the more senses one appeals to (sight, hearing, touch, smell), the more effective the communication. So, if your public is small, nearby and available readily, you would want the most credible speaker to present it in person. The message should be reinforced through mass media and other channels in some cases. But the primary effort should be interpersonal.

2. If the personal approach is not possible, you will want to consider which medium is most appropriate, given the message and the public. Marshall McLuhan made "the medium is the message" a common phrase (1965). Most would not go so far, but certain media are more effective in certain circumstances. **Radios** are so portable one can reach a public almost anywhere—at home, while driving or at the beach. Radio is also the least distracting medium and is at least partially heard while the listener does other things.

Television is more effective than radio in certain ways since it can be both seen and heard. But it is much more difficult to carry around and requires considerably more attention. **Print media** communicate using symbols and pictures. Most, like newspapers, are easy to carry and can be read almost anywhere. But they must be read. If you are trying to convince high school dropouts to stay off drugs, print would probably be your last choice because dropouts watch and listen, but seldom read.

Certain media are more useful for certain messages. If you wanted to reach Michigan residents in February with a tourism promotion for the Virgin Islands, television would be your clear choice because of the visual contrast it would offer to reality. Passing informational or educational messages might require a different approach, however. Since most Americans get most of their news from television, you might think that would always be your first choice. But if your message is long or complex, you might wish to shift to newspapers since gaining news and understanding are why most people read them (Witt 1983, 45–58).

3. The agenda setting theory states that public beliefs about the relative importance of issues are significantly shaped by the amount of attention the media devote to them (McCombs and Shaw 1972, 176–87). It also argues that media shape beliefs by making people aware of positions or options. Clearly, the absence of media coverage or positions on an issue could have equal impact. This impact is greater on issues we might know only through the media, such as problems in Afghanistan, and less on issues which directly affect us, such as inflation.

Public relations writers apply this theory in two ways. By calling media attention to an important issue of interest to our clients, we may get the issue much broader coverage. Many successful charities exist because public relations specialists ignited media and public interest.

Secondly, public relations writers can bring media attention to messages which are related to issues on the current media agenda. The tragic death of a young girl in New York from alleged parental abuse gave new life to efforts to get people to attend free seminars on how to combat this problem.

4. The spiral of silence theory maintains that most people tend to be silent if their views contradict the majority view because they fear losing group membership. Thus, the majority view appears much stronger than it really is. This causes a spiraling process that increasingly establishes that view as the prevailing one (Noelle-Neumann 1974, 43–51). Thus, the theory holds, when media take a consistent position over time, public opinion will tend to move in that direction. Public relations messages can be used to reinforce media support for a client's position. If media oppose the client's cause, public relations must make extraordinary efforts to make the client's position publicly known.

5. The transactional theory of news maintains that there are two main values in news: value to the public and value to the media organization (McManus 1987). Figure 2.2 shows these plotted on a two-dimensional graph.

Orientational or civic value news is of value to publics because it informs them about the world and helps them to cope with it. Media organizations, on the other hand, primarily value news which is exciting, perhaps because it entertains, frightens or amuses, thus gaining more readers or viewers and greater profits. Graphically, the four quadrants of these dimensions are:

A. News of *high social-civic/orientation value* **and** *high organizational/entertainment value.* Such news is both interesting and important. When U.S. Senator Gary Hart removed himself from contention for the Democratic Party's presidential nomination in 1987, it was important because it affected the party's chances of winning the next presidential race. It was also interesting because the decision involved alleged infidelity.

B. News of a *low social-civic/orientation* **and** *high organizational/entertainment value.* This is interesting, but unimportant news. Opening of the first Kentucky Fried Chicken franchise in the People's Republic of China would likely fit that quadrant.

C. News of a *low social-civic/orientation* **and** *low organizational/entertainment value.* This is dull and unimportant news. It would likely be cut by the editor or used to fill a space requiring a few column inches of print or a few seconds of air time. Public relations releases about new products of minor significance often fit into this category.

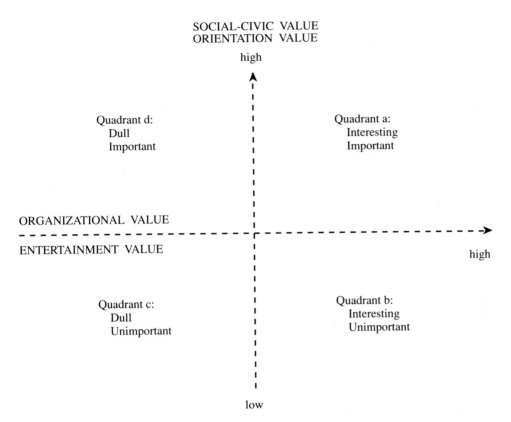

SOCIAL-CIVIC VALUE
ORIENTATION VALUE

high

Quadrant d:
Dull
Important

Quadrant a:
Interesting
Important

ORGANIZATIONAL VALUE

ENTERTAINMENT VALUE

high

Quadrant c:
Dull
Unimportant

Quadrant b:
Interesting
Unimportant

low

▶ **Figure 2.2.** Dimensions in the transactional theory of news. The theory posits two fundamental news values: organizational value, which allows the medium to sell its product for profit, and social-civic value, which provides the media user with information of value in coping with society. The public relations writer attempts to maximize both these values in each story. Source: John McManus, "A Transactional Theory of News." Paper presented to the Western Communication Educators Conference, Fresno, California, 14 November 1987. Used with permission.

D. News of a *high social-civic/orientation* and *low organizational/entertainment value.* This news would be important to the society, but dull to most readers. An in-depth review of the national budget might fit this quadrant.

This two-dimensional depiction encompasses most of the factors that go into story selection by media gatekeepers, including applicability, profitability, readership and service to society. Public relations writers would wish all their work to fall into Quadrant A. Unfortunately, the story assigned cannot always be both interesting and important. But both values can be emphasized where possible.

Publics/Audiences (F)

1. Receiving the Message: Theory may also be used to predict how publics will receive and use messages. Each message competes with several others at any given time to capture a reader, listener or viewer's attention. Proven attention-getting techniques generally involve pleasantness, interest and change. A television public service announcement may begin with a striking sunset to set the scene for aid to the elderly. A radio PSA may use a seductive feminine voice (the pleasure of sexual stimulation) to convince men that regular exercise is good for their hearts. A radical new layout may catch a reader's interest.

Visual Cues. Color affects readers' and viewers' interest. Bold colors normally indicate strength. Red connotes excitement and sensuality, blue implies coldness and green recalls nature. Pastels seem friendly, warm and nonthreatening. Earthtones or neutrals have been found to be conducive to business (Wilcox, Ault and Agee 1986, 180; 1989, 197). Meanings associated with color vary with culture. For example, white connotes purity in our culture, but signifies death in some others. Research tells us that the following sight, sound and print cues are usually attention getters:

Sight:
Pleasing or startling color contrasts
New or unusual sights
Familiar scenes or people
Appeal to sexual tastes
Visual humor

Sound:
Pleasant sounds (music, poetry, nature sounds)
Contrasting sounds (loud/quiet, harsh/soft)
Familiar sounds (recognizable voices, city noises)
Sexual appeal (words used, tone of voice)
Audible humor (jokes, situations)

Print:
Size of type, photo/art or white space
Pleasant or startling color use
Appealing or distracting graphics
Commanding lead sentences
Humorous words, photos or art

2. Selective Exposure: The differing natures, needs and desires of people also influence what messages they will receive, as well as how these messages will be understood (Berelson, Lazarsfeld and McPhee 1954, 220). Many people choose to read, watch or listen only to messages that are reinforcing or comforting. Truck drivers who work long hours on the road and whose only recreation is sports are unlikely to read the local newspaper's calendar section. Thus, they may never be exposed to your organization's 25th anniversary announcement in that section.

3. Selective Perception: Many simply block out information contrary to their personal attitudes and beliefs. How many times have you heard two people argue over the same news article, one claiming it is biased toward the liberals, the other insisting its bias is conservative (the opposites of their own political persuasions)? Given this reality, how can you, as a public relations writer, avoid having a message not reach its mark? The best way is to know your publics so well that you can predict which types of messages its members will likely avoid or misconstrue.

4. The Situation: Situational theory holds that publics differ in how much they are aware of an issue and how much they think they can influence it (Grunig and Hunt 1984, 147–160). Communication behaviors, it implies, can best be understood by measuring how members of publics perceive situations affecting them. Situational theory projects eight kinds of publics, with these four major types:

A. Publics Active on All Issues. These publics consist of people who have a high sense of involvement, readily recognize problems and see little to constrain their actions. They are activist publics who will do something, once they are convinced of the right course.

B. Publics Apathetic on All Issues. Such publics have low sense of involvement, do not recognize problems readily and feel constrained from action on all issues. They are difficult to target and are out of the mainstream of society. They often include the poor, the unwanted and those who prefer isolation.

C. Publics Active on Pervasive Issues. These people do not recognize problems readily and are afraid to get involved on most issues. But they become active on issues that affect nearly everyone in the population. If a client is concerned with a "gut issue"—inflation, wages, taxes, the price of gasoline—public relations writers may be able to get members of this public to pay attention.

D. Single-Issue Publics. These are also generally people with a low sense of involvement, low problem recognition and high constraint recognition. They will not usually get involved. But every once in a while an issue comes along which they will pursue doggedly, ignoring other issues. Such publics might support "Save the Whales" to the exclusion of other issues, including other animal protection efforts. One must hit the "right" issue to attract them and that's very difficult to do.

5. Arousal: This theory maintains that people change psychologically when they are emotionally aroused. Such an effect could be achieved by an absorbing or exciting message. People so aroused seem to have extra adrenaline and act more quickly and with greater than normal intensity (Becker 1987, 460). Most research in this area has investigated the negative aspects of this arousal, primarily child violence stemming from watching violent television programs. On the positive side, people are more likely to remember the content of a message if they are somewhat aroused by it. This aspect of the theory makes it useful for public relations writers. Emotional messages designed to prompt contributions often use arousal in a positive way.

Understanding the Message

Having received the message, the audience must be able to understand it in order to be persuaded. In general, that calls for messages which are simple, clear and straight-forward. For purely visual messages, that is difficult to predict. For print and audio, however, research has shown that "readability," the average person's ease in compre-hending a message, can be predicted with reasonable success (Rayfield, 1977). This area is further discussed in chapter 7. In general, the shorter the average word and sentence length of a passage, the easier it will be to comprehend.

Considering the Message

Although mass media reach more people with messages than do other channels, re-search indicates that mass media alone seldom convince (McGuire 1968, 228–229). They convey information, but getting consideration requires more than that. Most people make considerations and decisions only after they discussed a message with a trusted expert (Berelson, Lazarsfeld and McPhee 1954, 220; Baskin and Aronoff 1988, 149–157). That means that if you have a message which requires careful consideration, you need to reach not only the pertinent publics, but also those they might discuss it with.

Public relations experts often take steps to benefit from this "two-step flow." When corporations offer messages to potential stockholders on new offerings, they also make sure that stock analysts and columnists are fully informed. New product promotions target innovators and early adapters, as well as the desired buying publics (Rogers and Shoemaker 1971, 183–84). Innovators are the first people to try new themes, ideas and things. Early adopters are less pioneering than innovators, but are also leaders in public activities.

Accepting the Message

The effectiveness of the type of message used depends in part on the characteristics of the audience addressed (Hovland, Lumsdaine and Sheffield 1949, 201–227). If you know that your audience is poorly educated or is sympathetic to your message, you can be more effective with it by presenting only arguments that are favorable to your client. Since public relations writers can never be sure of these factors, however, they do best always to present both supporting and contrary arguments. This procedure also works best for groups with higher education or those who are initially opposed to the writer's position.

Acting on the Message

How successful we are in getting audiences to comply with our recommendations de-pends to some extent on our objectives. We communicate in order to entertain, inform or instruct, or persuade. All public relations messages contain an element of persuasion. But it is easier to get people to believe that a client organization is doing good things in Guam than to get them to contribute funds for education in Guam. The greater the personal involvement we desire, the more difficult the challenge.

Elaboration Likelihood: The Elaboration Likelihood Model of Persuasion shows two routes by which people may be persuaded: central and peripheral (Petty and Cacioppo 1987). The *central route* depends on quality of arguments, as well as reaching people who have the desire and ability to examine the issue. The *peripheral route* depends on cues and source credibility to get response. Using it, the announcer's voice or video picture may be more effective than words. It is less resistant to counterarguments than the central route. Persuasion via the peripheral route works best on issues which don't directly impact on those being persuaded. An emotional television appeal for donations to charity with "volunteer operators standing by to take your pledge right now" uses the peripheral route.

Cultivation: This theory reveals that people develop common images of the external world after repeated exposure to particular kinds of messages or images in the mass media (Gerbner and Gross 1976, 173–199). Implications of this theory for public relations writers are worth noting. For example, constant television watchers in an inner city are probably more likely to think they will become victims of street crime than others. Consequently, getting them to support gun control legislation may not be possible.

Fear: One reason people act on messages is out of fear. After a 1989 earthquake in Southern California, people who had previously ignored messages on earthquake preparation began to seek out this information. Mild-to-moderate fear appeals help in the persuasion process. But messages arousing high levels of fear can be counterproductive, making audiences so anxious that they tune out the threatening message (Hovland, Janis and Kelley 1953, 56–98). For example, in a television PSA asking people to seek out AIDS information, an AIDS patient weakened by the disease might be helpful. But one showing victims in pain might destroy the effectiveness of your message.

Evaluation, Feedback and Change (G)

As boxes E, F and G in figure 2.1 show, evaluation and feedback are critical to effective public relations writing. Theory is valuable for explaining and applying these processes as well. To ensure effectiveness, public relations writers need to monitor their programs at each step in the planning, writing and production process. This evaluation is also necessary to convince clients that the results are worthwhile. Corporate managers are usually most interested in results which support objectives such as: (a) survival of the organization, (b) growth, (c) improvement of products or services, (d) profit, (e) maintenance and improvement of the organization's facilities, and (f) quality, satisfaction and productivity of the employees. Public relations actions which do not measurably support these objectives are generally considered unnecessary frosting on the cake.

Management by Objectives: One way to provide measurable support for management objectives is through the systems theory-related management process called Management by Objectives (Nager and Allen 1984, 55–86, 167–227). Public relations-MBO creates general statements of goals and precise objectives as a framework for solving problems in support of the organization's overall goals and objectives.

"To improve the Image of the Torin Company in Sebor City" might be a PR-MBO goal for that company. Objectives derived from that goal should be precise, quantitative, timebound and measurable. A PR-MBO objective in support of the Torin Company's goal could be: "Complete by January 1, a random survey of at least 1,000 citizens of Sebor City, using the Standard Objective Attitude Survey, to determine the present image of the Torin Company in Sebor City."

Having determined goals and objectives, public relations writers then convince management that these goals and objectives support organizational aims and will adequately address the problem.

Evaluation might call for determination of what level of achievement of the objectives can be rated "average," "superior" or "excellent." This type of evaluation system supports the systems approach and focuses evaluators on the original objectives and goals desired. Systems theory views a problem as an intrusion into the smooth progress of the organization in pursuit of its goals. Public relations writing, like all other subsystems, must work to eliminate or control problems in its area so that the organization can maintain its steady state.

The Writing Problem

Having considered the developmental process of writing and how theory may be applied to it, we examine writing itself. Consider writing as a problem-solving process.

Problem solving in public relations writing is similar to all problem solving in a system. The public relations writing subsystem is a part of the public relations system, which is in turn part of the organizational suprasystem. For the organization, a problem is any set of circumstances which disturbs or may disturb its smooth and progressive operation.

Let us say that a corporation operates at a steady state, manufacturing high technology products for the U.S. Department of Defense. Specifications for the products call for extreme precision and low volume. Therefore, the unit price is high compared to less precise commercial equivalents. Then an investigative reporter includes the costs in a series on government waste. Other mass media pick up the story.

Corporate managers realize that a problem is at hand. For them, the transaction is being misrepresented. The $500 hammer being complained about is made of a special lightweight metal required for products used in space. It must be able to operate at minus 55 degrees Celsius without crystallization. It must be able to withstand 5,000 pounds of torque under these conditions. They believe that the unit price is fair, but realize that continued negative publicity will cause the product to be canceled.

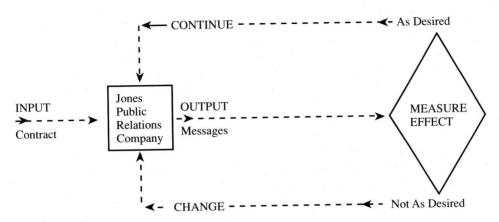

▶ **Figure 2.3.** An open system

   Management turns to its public relations department to help restore equilibrium. Its media relations staff writes news and broadcast releases explaining the reasons for the high costs and distributes them to all media. The staff produces and distributes a video news release in which the engineer who designed the hammer explains why it is so costly. If these explanations are compelling, interested publics will adopt them and the negative pressure will ease. The corporation can continue the contract.

   All problems disturb the equilibrium of the organizational system, calling for problem-solving actions to maintain normal operations. The closed system ignores such disturbances and will ultimately fail. The open system is designed to detect problems and correct them. Figure 2.3 portrays an open public relations system.

Nonworkable Problems

Public relations writers should be aggressive in writing to solve problems. However, they must also recognize their limitations. Some suggestions follow.

   No Writing Solution: Writers must be able to affect the problem with messages, otherwise they cannot control it. If messages can't be written and executed in pursuit of a solution, then it is not a writing problem.

   Noncomprehension: If the targeted public cannot understand the writer's language, then a writing solution is not possible. That failure to understand may be because the sender and receiver speak different languages, because the public cannot read the message or because the two worlds are so different that sender and receiver don't relate to one another.

   Media/Channel Availability: If the medium necessary to deliver the message to the intended publics is not available, writing and distributing the message will do no good. During the 1970s and 1980s some businesses found that no matter how many messages they delivered in any number of ways to the media, their messages were not broadcast

TABLE 2.5. Steps in the Analysis of a Writing Problem

---

 1. Think about the problem which has been assigned.
 2. Discuss it thoroughly with the public relations team.
 3. Articulate the writing problem. Write it out.
 4. Conduct and evaluate research to reduce uncertainty.
 5. Consider solutions which support organizational goals.
 6. Review all possible objectives and select the best.
 7. Decide on an action strategy.
 8. Conduct and record planning.
 9. Determine the writing actions needed.
10. Determine the writing evaluations needed.

---

or published. They perceived that American media wanted only to inform the public about negative business news. Some took the extraordinary step of buying advertisements in order to get their corporate stories to those publics.

Writing Constraints: The public relations writer must work within a complex set of constraints on what may be said, based on regulations covering commercial speech, corporate political expression, lobbying, foreign agent activities, labor-management communications, securities trading, Federal Communications Commission rulings, and libel, privacy and copyright laws. The nature of these constraints will be discussed in chapter 14.

Thinking about the Problem

Having considered theory and problem solving in general, we can go through the problem-solving process step-by-step. In the chapter on planning (see chapter 3), we'll cover problem solving as a part of the planning process in detail. But the problem-solving process is essential to high quality public relations writing and it can be approached systematically. Table 2.5 lists a logical series of "Steps in the Analysis of a Writing Problem" for your consideration.

These steps are simply an organized way for you to analyze public relations problems. In essence, they force you to articulate the problem, consider what information is already available and what actions have already been taken to resolve the problem. Then you can decide what you don't know and how much more information you need to reduce uncertainty to an acceptable level. Restating the problem based on your understanding of it, you can then determine goals, objectives and actions needed to resolve the problem. Finally, you can decide how to construct, deliver and evaluate the messages needed for each public and for each channel.

In essence, that's how public relations writing should be done. We think and plan before we write. During the entire process, we apply theory in order to make our writing as effective as possible. Communication is too important to be undertaken lightly. Adequate preparation is necessary.

Chapter Summary

This chapter helped us learn to think about the writing problem. In it we looked at the public relations writing problem through a writing process model. As the model shows, once the public relations team is presented with a problem or opportunity, the team researches it, plans a program and passes it to the client organization. After amendment, the client organization passes back an approved program to the public relations team for rethinking, replanning and rewriting. From there, message inputs go to appropriate media or other output channels. Message outputs from these channels reach the desired publics in some altered form. Having received, understood and considered the message, the publics exhibit some kinds of effects. These are evaluated against message objectives by the public relations team, which alters the message to better achieve desired effects. The public relations writing process is a continuous one.

Several communications-related theories were examined within each component of the writing process model. Discussion showed how each might be used in public relations writing. See table 2.6 for brief theoretical applications.

Next, the writing problem was examined in the context of traditional problem-solving processes under systems theory. A system operates to maintain itself in a steady goal state. When conditions within or outside the system cause it to fail to meet its desired objectives, the system changes to regain its equilibrium. Public relations writers were asked to think about solving problems in a comprehensive way, beginning with an outlined systematic analysis.

Writing Exercise One

Situation. You are an administrative aide (public relations) for a U.S. senator from a Bible Belt state. The senator has declared himself a candidate for nomination by the Democratic Party for president of the United States. He is running a solid second in the national public opinion polls. No major primaries or state caucuses have yet taken place, but his home state caucus is tomorrow.

It is noon and the senator has just come from a press meeting. Because of alleged drug abuse by a U.S. Supreme Court nominee, a question came up in the meeting about drugs. Your senator admitted that he had smoked marijuana "on several occasions" while in college in his home state. This is a criminal offense in the state, and was at

TABLE 2.6. Theory in Brief: Applications That Can Improve Results

---

Agenda Setting.   Getting the media to discuss your client's issue can increase the issue's importance in the minds of members of your public.

Arousal.   Messages which emotionally arouse may get quicker, more intense results.

Canalization.   Behavior is initially instigated to reduce a drive. Therefore, if the product, idea or service supported in your message can be seen by your public as gratifying that drive, then your message has a better chance of being effective.

Consistency.   Messages which show a public how its stand on one issue is at odds with beliefs which it espouses can cause the public to reconsider its stand on that issue.

Credibility.   Your message has a better chance of being effective if the person seen as its source is highly credible. Components of credibility are perceived: expertise on the subject, trustworthiness, attractiveness, objectivity, dynamism, similarity to the audience, concern and power. (See table 2.1.)

Cultivation.   People who are exposed to a great deal of mass communication develop common images of the external world. If your message fits those common images, it will have a better chance of being accepted.

Elaboration Likelihood.   People are usually persuaded to act via one of two routes. The central route depends on rationality and the quality of arguments. The peripheral route depends more on cues and source credibility. It works quickly and on those who aren't directly impacted by the issue. The public relations writer could have a need for each approach.

Ethnocentrism.   Each public tends to view its own norms and values as absolute and use them as a standard against which to judge information received. If the central idea of your message fits the ethnocentric norms and values of its intended publics, then it has a better chance of being accepted.

Fear Appeal.   Mild fear appeal helps to persuade publics. Too much fear appeal is counterproductive. Generally, emphasizing positive results is more effective than emphasizing negative results.

Hierarchy of Effects.   Four basic sequential steps in traditional persuasion are: awareness of the message, understanding the message, being convinced by the message and acting in the desired manner. Though the hierarchy is not always correct and is refuted by some, it remains a logical way to consider persuasion.

Identification.   If members of your public identify with the person who presents your message, they are more likely to be influenced by the message.

Learning.   Behavior followed by reward will tend to be repeated and behavior that is not rewarded will fade away. Your message should in some way reward your public for complying with it.

Marginal Man.   In a society certain traits are normally associated with one another. Those who don't fit are "marginal." If your spokesperson fits the generally-accepted trait grouping, he or she will be more acceptable. A corporate spokesperson who wears robes and is a communist does not seem to be appropriate for a stockholder public.

Medium Is the Message.   A communications medium shapes society without regard to its message or intended purpose. Television is a "cool" medium, requiring that the audience supply more information and giving it a sense of deep involvement. Movies are "hot" and audience involvement is less.

TABLE 2.6.   Theory in Brief: Applications That Can Improve Results (*continued*)

Modeling.   If media examples support your position, publics who are exposed to a great deal of mass media will be more likely to support it also.

Opinion Leaders.   On most issues, there are people who hold strong opinions, are articulate and are prone to action. Public relations writers do well to determine leaders of publics on issues and make special efforts to address them first.

Pleasantness of the Message.   All other things being equal, messages which are pleasing to the senses are better received. Good use of color and graphics makes it more likely that your message will be read.

Political Economy.   Forces created by the economic interests of the media have an impact on the media and their publics. If your message supports the interests of those who have significant economic or political control over the media, it has a better chance of being selected.

Pressure-Response Theories.   The more times the message is delivered, the more likely it is to be effective. Research reveals that there is a limit to the effectiveness of repetition, however.

Principle of Least Effort.   People act so as to put out the least possible effort overall. If your message shows your public that following its cause is the easiest route, that increases your chance of success.

Sapir-Whorf Hypothesis.   Language is more than a means of communicating. It is a framework for interpreting reality in the world around us. For your message to be effective, it must conform to the reality language of the public to whom it is addressed.

Segmentation.   Publics classify and remember products, services and ideas associated with categories for which they have interest. A family which gets clothes very dirty would be interested in a soap especially designed for dirty clothes.

Selective Exposure.   People read, view or listen most closely to those messages with which they think they will agree. Your message to a public which is expected to be supportive should make an effort to attract that public, such as a visual appeal.

The Significant Other.   A person often acts as the person he or she most admires would approve. If you know your public's "significant others," you can call for action which can be approved.

Situation.   Publics differ on issues to the extent that they are aware of the issues and respond to issues. The public relations writer should be especially aware of single-issue publics and publics active on pervasive issues only.

Stratification.   People seek fulfillment of their own desires, rather than the desires and ambitions of others. Your message should make clear how the reader or listener can meet his or her own objectives by complying with it.

Third-Person Effect.   Individuals exposed to a communication will expect it to have a greater effect on others than on themselves. This notion is to the advantage of the writer preparing counter messages, such as those against cigarette advertising.

Transactional Theory of News.   Two main values in news are public value (the good of society) and organizational value (this sells more papers). Public relations releases which have both will have a better chance of acceptance.

the time (although the law against smoking marijuana was seldom enforced). You and the senator both know that such an admission can be the kiss of death back home, but he wishes to remain in the race. He told the press that he considered the act a mistake and was sorry he had done it. But something more is in order.

Assignment. Analyze the situation, applying steps 1–4 of the "Steps in the Analysis of a Writing Problem" (see table 2.5). Then, identify one theoretical precept that you can apply which may help. Explain why. Finally, write a one-page press release for the senator to read to the press and to members of the state caucus tonight. The senator says: "We only have one chance, and that's tonight. If my home state doesn't endorse me, how can I expect anyone else to?"

Rules. Use any heading specified by your instructor. Double space your copy. Use no more than 27 lines of copy. Make sure all copy is technically perfect and that the release is camera-ready.

Writing Exercise Two

Situation. You are a student at a major university. The president of your student environmental group, "Save the World," has asked you to prepare a letter to the editor of the university newspaper. In it, you are to convince student readers not to buy products that come in aerosol spray cans because of the detrimental effect aerosol spray has on the ozone layer. You want to do an especially good job, so you decide to approach it in two ways and see which is the best.

Assignment. Prepare two drafts of the letter, based on considerations in this chapter. Apply the theoretical considerations of **fear appeal** in the first draft and **balance and dissonance reduction** in the second. Then decide which you will send, and why.

Rules. Each letter should be at least 150 words in length, typed, double-spaced, error-free and camera-ready.

Food for Thought

1. Many say the Japanese people during World War II were victims of the spiral of silence theory. What are some steps a homogeneous people like the Japanese can take during peacetime to keep their government and mass media from making them victims?

2. Do you think it is ever appropriate for public relations writers to attempt to use the arousal theory to get results? If so, give an example. If not, why not?
3. Following the Vietnam War, the Khmer Rouge caused perhaps two million Cambodians to die in the new Communist Kampuchea. Could the agenda setting theory be used to hold American media responsible for our not knowing of this tragedy until years later? Why or why not?
4. If "the medium is the message," what medium should be used to tell a corporation's publics about its loss of $20 million due to a computer error? Why?
5. What theory would you use to convince pertinent publics that "Pet Parfum" should be used to keep house dogs smelling nice? How would you phrase the message?

References for Further Study

Baskin, Otis, and Craig Aronoff. *Public Relations: The Profession and the Practice.* Dubuque, Iowa: Wm. C. Brown, 1988.

Becker, Samuel L. *Discovering Mass Communication,* 2nd ed. Glenview, Ill.: Scott, Foresman, 1987, 452–471.

Berelson, Bernard R., Paul F. Lazarsfeld and William N. McPhee. *Voting: A Study of Opinion Formation in a Presidential Campaign.* Chicago: University of Chicago Press, 1954.

Berlo, David K., James B. Lemert and Robert J. Mertz. "Dimensions for Evaluating the Acceptability of Message Sources." *Public Opinion Quarterly* 33:4(Winter 1969–1970):563–576.

Broom, Glen M. "Co-orientational Measurement of Public Issues." *Public Relations Review* 3(Winter 1977):110–119.

Chaffee, Steven H. "Mass Media Effects: New Research Perspectives." G. Cleveland Wilhoit and Harold deBock, eds., *Mass Communication Review Yearbook,* 1. Beverly Hills, Calif.: Sage, 1980, 77–108.

Cutlip, Scott M., Allen H. Center and Glen M. Broom. *Effective Public Relations,* 6th ed. Englewood Cliffs, N.J.: Prentice-Hall, 1985.

DeFleur, Melvin L., and Sandra Ball-Rokeach. *Theories of Mass Communication,* 4th ed. New York: Longman, 1982.

Festinger, Leon. *A Theory of Cognitive Dissonance.* Stanford, Calif.: Stanford University Press, 1957.

Gerbner, George, and Larry Gross. "Living with Television: The Violence Profile." *Journal of Communication* 26:2(1976):173–199.

Grunig, James E., and Todd Hunt. *Managing Public Relations.* New York: Holt, Rinehart & Winston, 1984.

Guilford, J. P., and Benjamin Fruchter. *Fundamental Statistics in Psychology and Education,* 5th ed. New York: McGraw-Hill, 1973.

Hall, Douglas T., and James G. Goodale. *Human Resource Management: Strategy, Design and Implementation.* Glenview, Ill.: Scott, Foresman, 1986.

Horai, J., N. Naccari and E. Fatoullah. "The Effects of Expertise and Physical Attractiveness upon Opinion Agreements and Liking." *Sociometry* 37(1974):601–606.

Hovland, Carl I., Arthur A. Lumsdaine and Fred D. Sheffield. *Experiments in Mass Communication.* New York: Wiley, 1949.

Hovland, Carl I., Irving L. Janis and Harold H. Kelley. *Communication and Persuasion: Psychological Studies of Opinion Change.* New Haven, Conn.: Yale University Press, 1953.

Insko, Chester A. *Theories of Attitude Change.* New York: Appleton-Century-Crofts, 1967.

Lerbinger, Otto. *Designs for Persuasive Communication.* Englewood Cliffs, N.J.: Prentice-Hall, 1972.

McCombs, Maxwell E., and Donald L. Shaw. "The Agenda Setting Function of the Press." *Public Opinion Quarterly* 36(1972):176–187.

McGinnies, Elliott, and Charles D. Ward. "Persuasibility as a Function of Source Credibility and Locus of Control: Five Cross Cultural Experiments." *Journal of Personality* 42(1974): 360–371.

McGuire, William J. "Nature of Attitudes and Attitude Change." Gardener Lindzey and Elliot Aronson, eds., *Handbook of Social Psychology,* 2nd ed., 3. Reading, Mass.: Addison-Wesley, 1968, 136–314.

McGuire, William J. "Recent Advances in Persuasion Research." Paper presented to the 38th National Conference of the Public Relations Society of America. Detroit, November 12, 1985.

McLeod, Jack M., and Steven H. Chaffee. "Interpersonal Approaches to Communication Research." *American Behavioral Scientist* 16(1973):469–500.

McLeod, Jack M., and Byron Reeves. "On the Nature of Mass Media Effects." G. Cleveland Wilhoit and Harold deBock, eds., *Mass Communication Review Yearbook,* 2. Beverly Hills, Calif.: Sage, 1981, 245–282.

McLuhan, Marshall. *Understanding Media: The Extension of Man.* New York: McGraw-Hill, 1965.

McManus, John. "A Transactional Theory of News." Paper presented to the Sixth Annual Western Communication Educators Conference, California State University at Fresno, Fresno, Calif., November 14, 1987.

McQuail, Denis. *Mass Communication Theory: An Introduction.* London: Sage, 1984.

Nager, Norman R., and T. Harrell Allen. *Public Relations Management by Objectives.* New York: Longman, 1984.

Noelle-Neumann, Elizabeth. "The Spiral of Silence: A Theory of Public Opinion." *Journal of Communication* 24(Spring 1974):43–51.

Pavlik, John V. *Public Relations: What Research Tells Us.* Beverly Hills, Calif.: Sage, 1987.

Petty, Richard, and John Cacioppo. *Communication and Persuasion.* New York: Spring-Verlag, 1987.

Ray, Michael L. "Marketing Communication and the Hierarchy-of-Effects." Peter Clarke, ed., *New Models for Communication Research. Annual Reviews of Communication Research* 2(1973):147–176. Beverly Hills, Calif.: Sage.

Ray, Michael L. *Advertising and Communication Management.* Englewood Cliffs, N.J.: Prentice-Hall, 1982, 225–246.

Rayfield, Robert E. "Two Experiments in Computer Analysis of Newspaper Prose." Unpublished doctoral dissertation, The University of Texas at Austin, Austin, Texas, 1977, 102–210.

Rogers, Everett M., and F. Floyd Shoemaker. *Communication of Innovations: A Cross-Cultural Approach,* 2nd ed. New York: The Free Press, 1971.

Schramm, Wilbur. "The Challenge to Communication Research." Ralph O. Nafziger and David M. White, eds., *Introduction to Mass Communication Research.* Baton Rouge, La.: Louisiana State University Press, 1963, pp. 3–31.

Schramm, Wilbur. "The Challenge to Communication Research." Ralph O. Nafziger and David M. White, eds., *Introduction to Mass Communication Research.* Baton Rouge, La.: Louisiana State University Press, 1963, 3–31.

Severin, Werner J., and James W. Tankard, Jr. *Communication Theories: Origins, Methods, Uses,* 2nd ed. New York: Longman, 1987.

Weilbacher, William M. *Advertising,* 2nd ed. New York: Macmillan, 1984.

Whitehead, J. L. "Factors of Source Credibility." *Quarterly Journal of Speech* 54(1968): 59–63.

Wilcox, Dennis L., Phillip H. Ault and Warren K. Agee. *Public Relations: Strategies and Tactics.* New York: Harper & Row, 1986.

Wilcox, Dennis L., Phillip H. Ault and Warren K. Agee. *Public Relations: Strategies and Tactics,* 2nd ed. New York: Harper & Row, 1989.

Witt, Evans. "Here, There and Everywhere: Where Americans Get Their News." *Public Opinion* 6:4(1983):45–48.

P A R T

2

PLANNING AND RESEARCH: REDUCING UNCERTAINTY

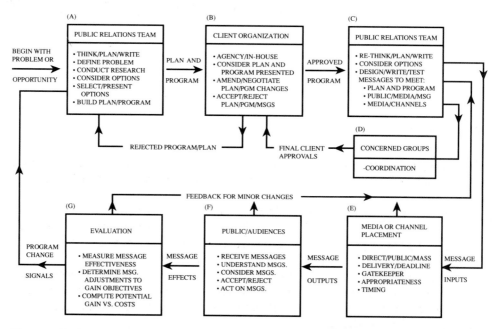

(A) PUBLIC RELATIONS TEAM	(B) CLIENT ORGANIZATION	(C) PUBLIC RELATIONS TEAM
• THINK/PLAN/WRITE • DEFINE PROBLEM • CONDUCT RESEARCH • CONSIDER OPTIONS • SELECT/PRESENT OPTIONS • BUILD PLAN/PROGRAM	• AGENCY/IN-HOUSE • CONSIDER PLAN AND PROGRAM PRESENTED • AMEND/NEGOTIATE PLAN/PGM CHANGES • ACCEPT/REJECT PLAN/PGM/MSGS	• RE-THINK/PLAN/WRITE • CONSIDER OPTIONS • DESIGN/WRITE/TEST MESSAGES TO MEET: • PLAN AND PROGRAM • PUBLIC/MEDIA/MSG • MEDIA/CHANNELS

BEGIN WITH PROBLEM OR

OPPORTUNITY

PLAN AND

PROGRAM

APPROVED

PROGRAM

REJECTED PROGRAM/PLAN

FINAL CLIENT APPROVALS

(D)
CONCERNED GROUPS

-COORDINATION

FEEDBACK FOR MINOR CHANGES

(G) EVALUATION	(F) PUBLIC/AUDIENCES	(E) MEDIA OR CHANNEL PLACEMENT
• MEASURE MESSAGE EFFECTIVENESS • DETERMINE MSG. ADJUSTMENTS TO GAIN OBJECTIVES • COMPUTE POTENTIAL GAIN VS. COSTS	• RECEIVE MESSAGES • UNDERSTAND MSGS. • CONSIDER MSGS. • ACCEPT/REJECT • ACT ON MSGS.	• DIRECT/PUBLIC/MASS • DELIVERY/DEADLINE • GATEKEEPER • APPROPRIATENESS • TIMING

PROGRAM CHANGE

SIGNALS

MESSAGE

EFFECTS

MESSAGE

OUTPUTS

MESSAGE

INPUTS

After considering all outcomes and costs, the team selects the optimal solution. Based on that projected solution, its members devise and write a program plan. The public relations plan is a documentation of the goals, objectives, strategies, and tasks required to solve a problem. The completed program and plan are reviewed, amended, and approved by the client.

THE PLAN IS NOTHING:
PLANNING IS EVERYTHING • • •

Introduction

The second key in the **think-plan-write** philosophy of this book is the planning process (block A, figure 2.1). Without a clear plan, writers can easily lose sight of where they want to go.

All successful writers plan before they write. Some experienced public relations writers do much of their planning in their heads, jotting down notes as guidelines. Others, like 40-year professional David Ferguson, use simple but effective planning concepts that apply universally (see Professional Tip: Planning).

Most writers tailor their planning efforts to the complexity of the project. In this chapter we will cover the public relations writer's planning process in detail. Writer's experience and expertise allow them to judge how much of the process to use. Beginners should use the entire process.

Planning Defined

A plan is a projection or blueprint of how a task can be accomplished. It can be long or short, simple or complex. What matters is that it works for its planners, managers, and followers. Plans for the construction of a modern airplane are hundreds of thousands of pages long, weigh hundreds of pounds and may be impossible for one person

A PROFESSIONAL TIP:
Planning

I approach every writing assignment as though I had been asked to create a cantaloupe. First, I consider the basic idea of the piece I'm writing (the seeds). Next, I add the supporting material (the meat), and finally, the beginning and end that hold it all together (the skin). I find that by thinking of writing in this way, I avoid overconcern about the "opening grabber" and "closing clincher," and build my pieces from the central idea out.

David Ferguson, APR, is a senior consultant for Hill and Knowlton Inc. Public Relations in Chicago. Prior to joining Hill and Knowlton, Ferguson served United States Steel in public relations and public affairs for 37 years, retiring in 1984 as general manager, public affairs, central. He is a former president of the Public Relations Society of America.

to read in a lifetime. On the other hand, President Franklin D. Roosevelt's plan for General Dwight D. Eisenhower for conducting European military operations during World War II was simple: "Find the German army and destroy it." Public relations plans cover all aspects of projects whether simple or complex. The writers' plans are guides to completing writing projects. A writing plan can be generally defined for our purpose as:

A written document detailing a logical sequence of ideas and actions to complete a writing assignment.

Why Plan?

The title of this chapter, "The Plan Is Nothing: Planning Is Everything," overstates its case. But it notes a key reason for planning in public relations writing. The experience of planning forces writers to articulate and document their thoughts. Great visions don't necessarily result in great writing. Writing out a plan makes the writer look at decisions to be made, such as the actions required, their potential costs and implications even before the messages are formed.

A second reason is the road map nature of the plan. Few people would drive through strange places without maps. The plan helps writers best decide what actions need to be taken and messages composed to achieve their objectives (Lavine and Wackman 1988, 90–127).

Third, the plan also helps public relations specialists coordinate their work. In a complex program, it is useful to know exactly which are your assignments and which are others' assignments, and how these fit together.

Next, because planning forces you to think through the project, it minimizes the need for *ad hoc* crisis decisions. As you know, such decisions can be influenced as much by adrenalin and emotion as by logic. By planning the project, you can see where crises might occur and consider your options should they occur. Suppose you were a corporate newsletter editor who planned to interview the new chief executive officer immediately after her arrival at company headquarters, just in time to make your copy deadline. Adequate planning would force you to consider that she might be late, and steps to take if she were. Good planning dictates that you are ready with an alternative course of action.

Last, all other things being equal, good planning can also give you an edge over your competitors. The well-planned program is invariably smoother and more efficient. While public relations specialists seldom compete directly, their organizations certainly do so.

In this chapter, we will speak alternatively about: (a) **planning,** which is the process by which we logically construct the plan, and (b) **plans,** which are the written documents in which the planning process is detailed. Both are important for the public relations writer.

Pre-planning Actions

Before you receive a project that merits writing assignments, several organizational planning actions should have been completed. Since that is sometimes not the case, we'll note those actions.

The Mission Statement

Writers need to be familiar with the mission statements of the client organizations they are writing for. If the organization does not have one, check the articles of incorporation for a corporation, or the constitution or charter of a noncorporate agency or association (Haberman and Dolphin 1988, 33). These tell you what the client organization was chartered to do.

The mission statement of a charity organization might read:

> **The mission of Food for Friends is to improve the human condition in Carter County by: arousing public interest in the plight of the unfortunate, recruiting members to assist in the cause, soliciting wholesome food (or gifts which will be bartered for food) from appropriate donors in the county, and distributing this food equitably among needy inhabitants of the county.**

Next, you should verify that the mission statement is appropriate. Sometimes, organizational purposes change drastically. At other times, the real mission is much more prosaic than the formal statement implies. Usually the statement can be evaluated by reading it to client representatives and asking for comments.

Organizational Goals

According to management by objectives parlance, goals are general directions that a management wants its organization to take. They are broad indicators from which precise objectives are derived (Nager and Allen 1984, 11, 56–60). They normally identify the overall responsibilities of a function. It is important that everything you write supports your client's goals. Here are some goals a progressive corporation might write:

1. **Make the corporation survive and prosper.**
2. **Protect the well-being of members of the corporation and all publics associated with it.**
3. **Protect property of the corporation, its members and all publics associated with it.**
4. **Protect and enhance the corporation's standing with all publics.**
5. **Ensure that all corporate endeavors are undertaken to provide high quality goods or services at fair profits.**
6. **Assure that the corporation acts as a good citizen in all its endeavors.**

Public Relations Goals

Normally there is at least one public relations goal supporting each organizational goal. A public relations goal supporting 2., above, might read:

> **Assist in protecting the well-being of members of the corporation and all publics associated with it by conceiving, writing and distributing proactive and reactive safety messages.**

TABLE 3.1. Public Relations Management by Objectives

Management by Objectives. One way to improve planning is through the systems theory-related management process called Management by Objectives (Nager and Allen 1984, 55–86, 167–227). PR-MBO creates goals which are general statements of directions which will help solve problems. "To improve the image of the Torin Company in Sebor City" might be such a goal. Then, objectives are formed in support of each goal. Insofar as possible, objectives are precise, quantitative, timebound and measurable. Some objectives in support of the goal above might be:

1. Complete by January 1, a random survey of at least 1,000 citizens of Sebor City, using the Standard Objective Attitude Survey, to determine the present image of the Torin Company in Sebor City.
2. Conduct an in-company campaign during February–March which will cause an increase of twenty percent or more in community service activity by Torin employees in Sebor City during April–June.
3. Repeat the survey during the month of July, with an objective of 10 percent average score increase in the SOAS.

Organizational and Public Relations Objectives

Objectives in PR-MBO are usually precise, timebound, measurable actions to be conducted according to a designated strategy in support of specific goals. Organizational and public relations group goals don't normally provide guidance for specific writing assignments, as objectives do. Having read through them once, you'll know if they are useful.

Project Goals and Objectives

Each project (and often each writing assignment) has its own goals and objectives. Writing goals and objectives are often subsumed under those of the entire project. Sometimes the writing project merits its own. For an example of goals and objectives for a public relations project which contains writing objectives, see table 3.1.

Planning for a Writing Assignment

Here we discuss the entire planning process and the formal or informal record you will retain of the process. It is important to keep the plan as brief as possible, recording all the information needed to follow the decisions it reflects and the directions it provides. This may include information which may be incidental to the planning process, but is necessary for the plan to be followed.

The planning guide indicates the steps necessary to plan a writing assignment. Writers omit steps which aren't needed for a particular plan, but most find it useful to have a complete guide for review. In discussing the process, we will review a sample case step-by-step. At its completion, we'll note steps usually followed for a minor assignment. Table 3.2 is a planning guide.

TABLE 3.2. Planning for a Writing Assignment

---

1. Write the problem statement.
2. Show research pertinent to planning and action decisions.
3. State the public relations writing goal or goals.
4. List public relations objectives supporting each goal.
5. Indicate the strategy to be used.
6. Select the appropriate plan.
7. Match publics, channels and messages.
8. Indicate the schedule of activities required.
9. Indicate the program budget.
10. Indicate how each objective will be measured.

The Writer's Planning Guide

There are 10 steps in this planning guide for writing, which is based in part on Nager and Allen's "PR-MBO Writing System" (1984, 101–165). These 10 steps can encompass the planning for even the most complex assignment. For each step listed below, two elements are provided: (A) the information to be recorded in the plan, and (B) the planning process which supports it, with notes accompanying an example.

1.A. Write the problem statement.
   B. Rephrase as necessary the problem presented to you. In chapter 2 we saw that a problem or opportunity is given to the public relations team (see figure 2.1) via one or more of several means. The team then goes through the thinking process to establish the precise problem and its possible solution. Here we are concerned with the public relations writing problem, either in isolation or as part of an overall public relations problem. The problem statement you end up with may not be the same that was initially given to you.

   > In this example, you are a public relations writer for Slick Oil Co. Your corporation, which grosses $20 million annually and employs 200 people, pumps and delivers crude oil. Its main activity is pumping oil from its ocean wells in the Santa Barbara Channel off the coast of California. The oil is pumped into company barges, which are then towed to refineries on the Southern California coast. Your company has just been awarded the 1,000-member Oil Producers Association's "Annual Oil Production Safety Award." George Slick, the company president and CEO, drops into the office with the news. He hands you the letter and certificate and says, "See if you can't get us some good PR on this."

There are a number of unanswered questions in our Slick Oil Company example. You must think about these and seek answers just to be able to pose the problem properly. How should the program be handled? Should the boss get all the credit? Or, should the pumping teams or the company be recognized as a whole? How much money can you spend? Should you buy an ad? Will the award be made formally? If so, when and where? Then you reconsider. It's up to the public relations team to propose solutions. That's what you'll do.

So you restate the problem in a way you hope will allow you to make the most of it:

> **To obtain maximum positive exposure and good will for Slick Oil Company's receipt of the Oil Producers Association's Annual Oil Production Safety Award.**

Now you go to work.

2.A. List all research information pertinent to your planning and action decisions.
   B. Like any other problem, a writing problem needs research. In thinking about the problem, one makes a number of considerations about what research needs to be done.

Preceding Facts: What are the facts preceding this problem or opportunity which are important to know and record? What are the background facts about this problem? Again, research is used to get the pertinent information. To the extent that it is unique, much of this information will be recorded in the plan.

> For our example, research tells us that oil, a vital natural resource for any industrialized society, is especially critical to the U.S. Our nation, which was an oil exporter a few decades ago, now imports as much as 60 percent of its oil. Imported oil is a strategic liability, since it can be shut off in times of crisis. So, American oil which can be pumped and refined at competitive costs, as that coming from offshore rigs, is valuable. But oil pumped from the ocean can be spilled. Such spills not only result in lost oil, but disturb the marine ecology and ruin beaches for surfing and swimming. In coastal areas such as Southern California, the danger of oil spills has had cause groups, fishermen, and tourist and recreation industries up in arms for some time.
>
> The Oil Producers Association, a national 1,000-member association of oil producers, seeing the potential problems of oil spills, established its Annual Oil Production Safety Award in 1980 to encourage safe production. The award is given annually to the U.S. oil producer having the best record in terms of human, animal, plant, equipment and facility safety. The awardee is selected from among association members by its executive committee. Winning the award for offshore operations is considered especially noteworthy in the industry.

Actions Taken and Results: Actions with public relations significance often take place before public relations experts know a problem exists. Sometimes these other actions are unintended, as when uninstructed telephone operators respond to calls immediately after a crisis. Sometimes they are deliberate actions by management. In the plan, you should record what prior actions were taken with what observable results.

> In our example, the Oil Producers Association's executive committee met and selected Slick Oil as its winner of the year. The Certificate of Award has been received at company headquarters. A 250-word news release has been sent by the association to the 10 largest oil trade publications. Most domestic oil producers are now aware that Slick won the award. There has been no mention in national, regional or Santa Barbara media of the award.

Research Already Completed and Findings: Often, others conduct and complete considerable research that bears directly on the problem. Your plan will include this research.

In the Slick Oil case, no research has been completed beyond that noted above.

Further Research: Here we note any additional research required and findings for whatever is completed. You would like to know everything. But since research is costly, you try for the minimum necessary to make useful decisions. The plan will outline important findings which influence action.

In the Slick Oil example, you asked for and got answers in these areas.

—Was Slick just lucky, or were there significant reasons why the company won the award? Oil producers are generally perceived as being interested only in the bottom line, the profit. But George Slick, who runs Slick Oil as a private company, doesn't fit the mold. He is a native of Santa Barbara, loves the beaches, and was an avid surfer in his younger days.

Ten years ago, he went to work for Slick Oil, owned and operated by his father, after completing a degree in petroleum engineering. Two years later, his father died of a massive heart attack and George inherited the company. Because of his personal interest in a clean water environment, he was disturbed by the potential for massive oil spills in the Santa Barbara Channel and their impact on the environment. So he designed and built special floating dams (called oil booms) costing $180,000 each around all Slick pumping operations to catch spills. Additionally, he instituted a safety training operation for all Slick employees involved in pumping operations.

—Is there a local angle on the award? This is a powerful news criterion. Yes. We know that George Slick is a native of the area. That will help. Further research tells us that the City of Santa Barbara's leaders are extremely sensitive to oil spills and their negative impact. Several city government officials have been active in a movement to end offshore oil exploration, drilling and production.

Other research provides some understanding of the national, regional and local significance of the award. The U.S. president and key members of his administration favor off-shore oil development. They might publicly praise anything positive about it. Since the association's award is the only one of its kind, we should be able to get some national attention. But that is not Slick's primary interest.

Restating the Problem: Sometimes research and analysis convince the public relations team that the original problem statement is inaccurate. It could be that the problem is one public relations activities cannot affect until some other action is taken by the client organization. More often, the problem statement needs refocusing, based on research.

In the Slick Oil case, the original problem statement can stand. It was carefully fashioned and nothing has been learned in research to change it.

3.A. State the public relations writing goal or goals.

  B. Fully understanding the problem or opportunity, the public relations team can now set public relations goals or specific writing goals. If current strategic (long range) or tactical (specific) goals are adequate, new ones are not needed.

One of Slick Oil's strategic public relations goals for the year is "to enhance the image of Slick Oil in Southern California as a safe and efficient handler of natural resources." This supports Slick Oil's primary strategic goal of "bringing oil and petroleum products from their sources to desired destinations at maximum profit, commensurate with the quality of effort that will reflect public responsibility and ensure company survival."

Therefore, Slick's supporting public relations goal for the above strategic goal might read: "Create, produce, deliver and evaluate messages to maximize recognition and image enhancement in Southern California for Slick Oil Company's receiving the Oil Producers Association's Annual Safety Award."

4.A. State the public relations objectives supporting the goal or goals.

B. Here the plan documents selected objectives. It might also list other objectives rejected and why, especially if they seem to be superior to the ones chosen. This is a complex stage where much thought and discussion are often called for and basic choices made. Even though the general direction may be clear, the best way to get there may not. For it is here that basic choices are made. All feasible alternatives are critically considered. Those accepted are prioritized by importance. Here the problem-solving process can come into heavy play. Each selected objective must meet the following criteria:

1. Does it support stated goals and objectives?
2. Can it be attained?
3. Is it affordable?
4. How would its attainment affect the problem?
5. How would its failure affect the problem?

In this case, the selective objectives would be those problem-solving actions which support the goal, and are feasible and supportable. Some selected objectives to support Slick Oil's goals could be:

A. Arrange for the mayor of Santa Barbara to formally present the award to company President George Slick this month. The city should welcome this opportunity to show that its leaders can be positive about actions related to offshore oil production. Slick Oil public relations writers will draft a proclamation for the mayor and a brief acceptance speech for Slick.

B. Inform all local media one week prior to the presentation. Slick Oil public relations will provide news releases and fact sheets on the company, the award and George Slick.

C. Research, plan, write, distribute and get printed in a statewide publication with circulation of 500,000 or more during the next quarter, a 2,000–4,000 word feature on George Slick, emphasizing his personal contributions to oil production safety.

D. Write, produce and offer to all Pacific Coast television stations a two-minute video news release on the award and its background.

E. Write, produce and offer to all Pacific Coast radio stations a five-minute feature on George Slick, his local origins, his surfing days, education, operation of the company, environmental concerns and the award.

5.A. Indicate the strategy to be used.

B. Here we use the term "strategy" to mean an overall concept that unifies, synergizes and propels the objectives toward their goals. Sometimes the strategy is fashioned around a single event. For example, if the goal is to increase current public recognition of a long-established company, the unifying strategy might be the celebration of a corporate anniversary. At other times, developmental strategies might be used, expanding from teaser releases on a new product to an all-out multi-media campaign just prior to the introduction of the product.

In the Slick Oil example, the strategy is clear. The company CEO is worth considerable attention because he is native to the area where we want to make the most impact. More importantly, he contradicts the stereotypical oil producer. Therefore, the public relations campaign can be built around the boss, George Slick.

6.A. Select the appropriate plan.

B. Managerial plans have several designations (Baskin and Aronoff 1988, 123–46). Here you indicate your choice and rationale, unless they are obvious.

Business plans are generally categorized as either "strategic" or "tactical." Strategic plans deal with long-range organizational development. Tactical plans focus on specific problems or events. The Slick Oil example clearly calls for the latter.

Plans can also be either "standing" or "single use." Standing plans are used for strategic planning and for recurring events such as a nonprofit organization's annual charity event. A single-use plan is prepared for a specific, unique event. Since Slick has not won this award before and may not again soon, our example requires a single-use plan.

Plans are also sometimes designated by type. A "budget plan" has an obvious purpose. An "operational plan" usually projects how a unit will operate during the year. A "campaign plan" specifies a sequence of concepts and actions necessary to achieve the goals and objectives of a specific public relations campaign. Our example case fits the campaign type.

7.A. Match publics, channels and messages.

B. A key function in the effectiveness of public relations writing is matching each selected public with the media or medium best capable of reaching it. As noted in chapter 1, the more precisely each public is defined, the easier the match. Messages can then be designed in the proper format, style, length, language and complexity for each public-channel match. How to prepare those messages and deliver them will be subjects of chapters 7, 8 and 9. The theory behind development was covered in chapter 2.

In our Slick Oil example, the first objective called for the mayor of Santa Barbara to present the Oil Producers Association's safety award to George Slick at a public ceremony and for George to make an acceptance speech. Writers drafting the mayor's and Slick's remarks are working on multiple publics. The immediate audience for both will be the city council and council visitors (most of whom will be Slick Oil employees). The channel of delivery will be the public speech. But the writers hope that larger audiences, consisting of area people favoring or opposing off-shore oil development, Santa Barbara residents and other recreation-minded Southern Californians, will receive the messages through the media. So, while the format, style and length would fit the immediate audience, the language and content would have to fit larger, more dispersed publics.

The second objective of the Slick Oil campaign was to inform the local media. This would be done initially by media alerts mailed out by media relations personnel. Public relations writers would concentrate on a general news release and fact sheets. The news release would be fashioned for the broadest possible publics, with newspaper, radio and television versions. These would key on the dichotomy that George Slick, an oil producer and transporter, is also a conservationist and former surfer. Succinct fact sheets on the company, the award and Slick would be written for editors and reporters. Note that no effort is being made to reach the national audience. That would be left to area news service offices, which would receive all media alerts and information.

The third objective called for a feature on George Slick for a statewide publication. This would be sent to Sunday magazines of the major newspapers whose readers are middle class and fairly well informed on issues. The feature would focus on Slick's unique personality and accomplishments, with the award representing a culmination of and recognition for his efforts.

The fourth objective was a two-minute video news release. This would be designed for viewers of local television as straight news and focus on those general viewers who are not well informed on off-shore oil concerns. It would show Slick supervising installation of an oil boom, talking to a safety class and receiving the award.

The final Slick Oil campaign objective was a five-minute radio feature, intended for "drive time" listeners. It would consist mostly of George Slick's voice discussing his youth and surfing, the company and his environmental concerns and activities.

8.A. Indicate the schedule of activities required.

B. This step calls for sequential listing of all activities required to accomplish the stated objectives through the chosen strategy: (1) the action, (2) its participant(s), (3) location(s), (4) time(s), (5) method(s) used and (6) supporting rationale. Obvious inputs are omitted. A partial activities list for the Slick Oil example is shown in table 3.3.

9.A. Indicate program budget.

B. The campaign, program or item budget should show the anticipated costs for human and material goods and services purchases, facilities and equipment rented or used in-house, work days spent by supervisors and workers, and for each activity. Public relations writers do not often prepare budgets, but should have some knowledge of costs to select and justify actions taken. For example, the five-minute radio feature on Slick might involve the following costs:

1. One work day by public relations writers researching and preparing background notes, and an outline and questions for the announcer ($96).
2. Three hours preparation and interview by a free-lance announcer, using his equipment ($150).
3. One hour of George Slick's time taping the interview ($80).
4. Audio tapes to send to 50 selected stations ($87.50).

TABLE 3.3.   Schedule of Activities, Oil Producers Safety Award to Slick Oil

Action Required	Person Responsible	Location	Date/Time	Method	Rationale
Get mayor to make award	PR director	City Hall	Friday 11 A.M.	Phone call	Schedule award
Draft mayor proclamation	PR writers	Office prior	1 week	Speech	
Draft Slick acceptance	PR writers	Office	1 week prior	Speech	
Inform media	Media relations manager	As needed	ASAP	Phone calls	
Inform media	PR writers	Office	ASAP	News release	
Inform media	PR writers	Office	ASAP	Fact sheets	
Prepare feature	PR writer J. Brown	Office as required	2 weeks from OK		
Prepare VNR	PR writers, audiovisual	Office studio	3 weeks from OK		
Prepare radio interview	PR writers, audio announcer	Studio as required	3 weeks from OK		

5. Duplication of 50 audio tapes from the master, in-house ($60).
6. 0.07 work day preparing cover letter ($2.50).
7. Duplication of 50 cover letters on bond ($12.50).
8. Packaging 50 audio tapes and cover letters ($10).
9. Mailing 50 audio tapes with cover letters ($25).

Total cost: ($523.50).

10.A. Indicate how each objective will be measured.

B. One of the most valuable and difficult aspects of PR-MBO is the way in which it measures the value of an action. PR-MBO says effort alone doesn't count. You may have prepared three days for the interview, but if you didn't get it done, your accomplishment is zero. But the easy thing about PR-MBO is that if you have properly designed your objectives, their accomplishment is your measure of effectiveness. In some cases it's as simple as saying accomplishing 90 percent or more of the objective is excellent, 70–89 percent is acceptable, and anything else is unacceptable. Of course, evaluation is normally more complex than that, as you will learn in chapter 12.

In essence, we evaluate a program by the quality and completeness of preparation, its conduct (Is it working?) and impact. Sometimes programs which seem to be going well backfire at the last minute and fail to achieve their objectives. Others don't appear to be doing well during the preparation phase, but finish well and meet all their objectives.

One complication of evaluating public relations writing is that its contributions often cannot be separated from those of the presenter. If the *Los Angeles Times* reports that the mayor of Santa Barbara made a great speech at the awards ceremony, how much of the credit goes to Slick's public relations writers, how much to the mayor's speaking ability and how much to a possible bias by the reporter?

Not all the Slick Oil campaign objectives lend themselves well to direct evaluation of public relations writing. For example, in scoring the "state publication" objective, one could measure whether or not it was written, if its length was between 2,000 and 4,000 words, and whether or not it was printed in a statewide publication with a circulation of 500,000 or more.

Planning Steps for a Minor Assignment

A simple writing assignment requires planning, but not to the extent needed in a complete campaign. In this section, we'll discuss the steps inherent in such abbreviated plans.

Here is the assignment. You are a senior student studying public relations at a major university. For the past two years you have also been a part-time writer for the university's public affairs office. On May 1, the director says, "I've got an assignment that's right up your alley." The president wants to start a new scholarship, "The Dollar Scholarship." She wants each graduating senior to donate $1 to the scholarship as he or she marches into the auditorium on graduation day. This will provide a useful scholarship if 4,000 or more of the 5,000 graduating seniors contribute. The director wants you to write an editorial for the op-ed section of the May 15 pre-graduation issue of the school newspaper. He has already spoken to the editor, who says the paper will publish the piece if it's well done. "Give me your writing plan next week," concludes the director.

Here is the writing plan you devise:

Writing Plan for The Dollar Scholarship

1. **The problem statement.** Write an op-ed piece for the May 15 issue of the *Daily Collegian* which will convince seniors of the need for "The Dollar Scholarship" and get them to support the university president's plan.

2. Pertinent research information.
   Preceding Facts.
   a. Supported by president. Apparently her idea.
   b. Fund-raising research previously completed.
      Actions Taken and Results. None.
      Research Already Completed and Findings. None.
   Research Required:
   a. Interview with president (one hour). She got the idea from a graduating senior. Believes it can provide a needed scholarship, unite seniors and help convince them to donate as alumni. Will be handled by development office. Committee of five seniors selected by her will select scholarship recipient based on overall grades and demonstrated need. She hopes this will become an annual event.
   b. Interview with senior class president (30 minutes). He is supportive, has been looking for a unifying action like this, will publicly endorse it.
   c. Random phone survey with 50 seniors. All were supportive. Most (40) felt all seniors could afford the $1. Some (15) thought the money ought to go to a minority student. Half said more communication was required, since not all seniors read the campus paper.
   d. No parallel cases, but several cases of student-initiative scholarship drives. Those that failed either lacked administration endorsement or received very little publicity.

   Restate the Problem. Same.

3. The public relations writing goal. Create, produce, deliver and evaluate messages which will convince university students of the need to support scholarships for the university.

4. Public relations objectives supporting the goal.
   a. (Assigned) Write a publishable quality op-ed article for the May 15 edition of the *Daily Collegian* that will persuade at least 4,000 of the 5,000 graduating seniors to contribute $1 to the president's "Dollar Scholarship" fund.
   b. At least five 30-second PSAs on the campus radio station, coverage in the city newspaper, and fliers posted in 25 locations on campus will be needed to provide persuasive publicity. A joint letter to graduating seniors from the university and student body presidents could be useful. A donor to underwrite the cost would help the budget.

5. Strategy to be used. Use a president-to-president plea. The university president asks the senior class president for support, noting that the idea came from a senior. The op-ed piece should carry their names. If I write it, I will be ethically bound to say I'm being paid to do so. But I could draft it for their amendment and approval.

6. **Type plan.** This is a one-time use, tactical plan for a single campaign. If it is later decided to make it an annual campaign, it can be revised into a standing plan.

7. **Publics, channels and messages matched.** The immediate public consists of 5,000 graduating seniors at this university. Although there are numerous sub-publics in this group, it seems best to aim for the average student. The class consists of 2,600 women, 2,400 men. Most are from lower middle-class homes where both parents work. Eighty percent work, 60 percent full-time. Four percent are Asian, 8 percent Black, 10 percent Hispanic. Although they can afford the contribution, many have had difficult financial times in college. So a dollar still means much to them. The *Daily Collegian* is the best single channel for reaching them, since surveys show that 90 percent read it "at least part of the time." Other channels should also be used, however, as noted earlier.

8. **Schedule of activities by writer.**
   a. Review, complete research by May 1.
   b. Draft plan.
   c. Get plan approval by May 2.
   d. Complete first draft and coordinate with Office of University Development by May 4. Make necessary revisions.
   e. Duplicate and send copies of revised draft to university and senior class presidents by May 6. Make necessary revisions.
   f. Final copy to editor, *Daily Collegian,* by May 10.

9. **Budget**
   a. Five work days by PR writer @ $5/hr = $200.00
   b. Supervision: 0.06 work days @ $!2/hr = $ 5.76
   c. Computer time, paper and copying   = $ 5.00
                                         $210.76

10. **Measurement of objective accomplishment**
    a. Approved copy submitted on time = 10 points.
    b. Copy published by *Daily Collegian* = 20 points.
    c. Sample of 100 seniors all read it = 40 points.
    d. The 4,000 graduating seniors each gave $1 to the scholarship = 30 points.
                                                         100 points

This evaluation measure applies value to preparation, quality of writing, delivery of message and effectiveness, even though the writer does not have control over the success of all of the objective's elements. It can then be scaled proportionately. If 3,000 seniors gave, 75 percent of 30 points (22.5 points) would be awarded in that area for

TABLE 3.4. Public Relations Writer's Abbreviated Checklist

---

1. Complete the writing plan.
2. Outline and draft messages, and select visuals.
3. Coordinate each message with pertinent people.
4. Rewrite and polish each message.
5. Get final approval on each message from the client.
6. Write accompanying notes or letters and deliver each message.
7. Evaluate the effect of each message.

---

a total of 92.5 evaluation points (90 or above being excellent). If only half the random sample of seniors read the article, that area would receive 20 points for a total 80 points (80–89 being rated "good").

The Writer's Action Process

The writer now has a complete plan and is ready to write. This comes in the action portion of the traditional four-step public relations process of research, planning, action and evaluation. The writer's checklist in abbreviated form can be seen in table 3.4. It is a planning tool which allows those taking the action to follow the plan step by step, referring to the entire plan occasionally.

The Writer's Checklist

1. Complete the Writing Plan. Completing the plan means that all the research, thinking, discussion and planning are complete and a written and approved plan is now ready to be acted upon.

2. Outline and draft messages, and select visuals. Now the writers prepare their outlines and copy for all the assigned messages, matching each public to a channel. Word processors are invaluable in adapting messages for several publics. Make sure each message clearly states the central idea.

At this point you have probably given some thought to the visual aspects of your message. For more on this, read chapter 9. Writers are not necessarily expected to be artists, but they must be able to project the audio-visual elements of their messages if they are writing for radio or television.

3. Coordinate each message with pertinent people. Once the draft is completed, it must be approved by members of the public relations and client teams, as well as others who have a stake or role in it. A message on scholarships must be approved by the university scholarship office, just as a warning on drugs should be by the criminal justice or legal department. Negotiation is sometimes necessary. You would not wish to risk injury or financial damage by ignoring or bypassing such help.

4. Rewrite and polish each message. Once the message comes back with feedback, changes and approval, rewrite and polish it. Often a minor change in language for legal protection causes the entire message to go flat. Reviving may call for an extensive rewrite. Now polish the message. Once you are finished, it may not be changed again, so you want to make sure it's just right.

5. Get final approval on each message from client. Depending on the client and the importance of the message, final approval may be needed before the message is sent out.

6. Write cover notes or letters. Draft and get approvals for any covering notes or letters accompanying the messages. Then make sure each message gets properly delivered. Writers don't usually physically deliver the message. However, that action is the key to the success of the writing task, and you will want to ensure that it gets done.

7. Evaluate message effects. If your plan was put together well, you know exactly how to evaluate your writing. Follow through and make the evaluations, especially those that can be done while the campaign or program is under way. Be sensitive to messages that are no longer appropriate and need changing. For example, a well-known businessman did a requested humorous endorsement for a new product. Before the promotion could be aired, the businessman died. A quick-thinking marketing manager pulled the promotion only hours before it would have aired.

Chapter Summary

This chapter reviewed the planning process for writing in public relations. It first looked at those actions which should take place before the writing plan itself is written. These actions include preparing mission statements, organizational goals and objectives, and overall public relations goals and objectives. Mission statements are organizational statements of purpose, while goals are broad directions the organization seeks to move in. Objectives are precise, measurable, time-bound actions which move an organization towards its goals.

The planning process for public relations writing was covered step-by-step, with an example unfolding at each step. The planning process covers the problem statement, research, the public relations writing goals and objectives, strategies, and type of plan for the campaign being developed. Then the planning process matches channels and messages to each target public, schedules of activities needed to achieve the objectives, examines the campaign or program budget, and indicates how campaign success will be measured. Employing the discussed process, a plan is developed for a limited public relations writing assignment.

Finally, the writer's checklist was examined as a tool for applying the plan to the writing task. We noted that the plan should be followed as approved, but that actions must be changed whenever evaluation shows they are not working.

Writing Exercise One

Situation. You are the chief writer for a large Midwestern public relations firm. Your company just received a query from the chemical firm, Chemwest. Two years ago the company was fined $50,000 for dumping toxic chemicals into the Missouri River near Omaha, Neb. The company was also ordered to clean up its fertilizer manufacturing processes, the source of toxic materials. It has done so, but negative media coverage has grown over these two years. Marketing surveys indicate the negative image is hurting Chemwest's business. Farmers hesitate to buy Chemwest fertilizers because they "don't want to poison the water downstream." Chemwest management wants you to build an image enhancement program to "restore our good name."

Your boss asked you and your writing team to develop a writing plan for messages to meet this objective: "Build an image enhancement communication campaign that will, over the next six months, generally convince Midwest farmers that Chemwest is not dumping toxic chemicals and raise farmers' approval rating of the company by 20 percent, based on random pre- and post-campaign surveys of 500 farmers in Nebraska, Iowa, South Dakota, Minnesota, Kansas and Missouri." The boss says, "Don't worry about the budget yet; just tell me what you'd do and how you'd do it. Do the plan, and when you are ready to write, I'll give you five writers and three audio-visual experts."

Assignment. Prepare the writing plan. State any assumptions made. Provide underlying rationales, if they are not obvious.

Writing Exercise Two

Situation. You are a public relations writer for Slick Oil Company. The events noted earlier in this chapter regarding the company have taken place, George Slick has approved your plan as provided and the presentation has just been made in Santa Barbara.

Assignment. Write a 200-word news release about the event for on-line transmission to *The New York Times.* Presume knowledge of the mayor's speech and Slick's response. Be sure your release conforms to the plan.

Rules. The release should be neatly typed, double-spaced, error-free and photo-ready. Don't worry about press release format for this assignment. That will come later.

Food for Thought

1. Some writers say the biggest value of planning in public relations is "getting managers into the act." What is your perception and why?
2. On the surface it appears that planning adds work to the public relations writing function. How can it streamline your work in the long run?
3. In planning for a major project, you want to test a writing strategy. The idea is to publish "just say no" letters against drug abuse by 6-year-old users. But you are afraid it might backfire. Would you plan for a random survey or focus group discussions to test the idea? Why or why not?
4. What are the five biggest barriers to effective planning for public relations writing? Justify your response.
5. Some public relations practitioners maintain that they never plan before writing, yet they are successful writers. Why do you think this is so?

References for Further Study

Baskin, Otis W., and Craig E. Aronoff. *Public Relations: The Profession and the Practice.* 2nd ed. Dubuque, Iowa: Wm. C. Brown, 1988, 23–146.

Haberman, David, and Harry A. Dolphin. *Public Relations: The Necessary Art.* Ames, Iowa: Iowa State University Press, 1988, 30–51.

Lavine, John M., and Daniel B. Wackman. *Managing Media Organizations.* New York: Longman, 1988, 90–126.

Nager, Norman R., and T. Harrell Allen. *Public Relations Management by Objectives.* New York: Longman, 1984.

Nolte, Lawrence, and Dennis L. Wilcox. *Effective Publicity: How to Reach the Public.* New York: Wiley, 1984, 55–79.

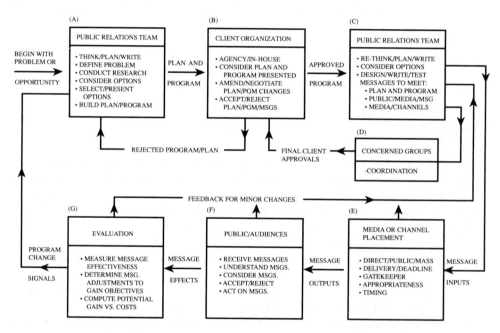

Having received the problem, the public relations team defines and conducts appropriate research. Thus begins the *think* portion of the writer's *think-plan-write* process. Gathering secondary information allows the writing team to consider what is already known that might bear on the problem. This includes, as a minimum, the nature of the client organization, the environment, background of the problem, the publics involved, and the possible messages and channels to be used.

GATHERING
SECONDARY INFORMATION • • •

Introduction

Military intelligence activities are driven by the maxim: "We only know what we know. We don't know what we don't know." For a military force, that critical missing information would easily spell disaster. In a less compelling manner, the axiom also applies to public relations information gathering. The writer needs to know all the pertinent information about a subject to be able to write authoritatively about it. Not knowing a critical piece of information could be disastrous. How can one know what needs to be known? What are the essential elements of information needed to resolve a public relations writing problem? The latter question correctly presumes that we can learn what we need to know and how to find it. The key, then, is to find a systematic way to gather and analyze information on topics we wish to write about.

This chapter is designed to assist you in gathering existing and accessible (i.e., secondary) information necessary for effectively writing public relations copy.

The Essential Elements of Information

The Writer's Organization

If your organization is different from the client organization (as when you work for a public relations agency), you must consider yours first. Some useful information includes: the mission, goals and objectives of the organization, its operating styles and philosophies, and history with the client. These are fairly constant factors and require only a periodic review once you know them. However, each time your group undergoes a major change, you'll need to update this information.

The Client Organization

You must know the client organization well to be able to serve it effectively. First, you must understand the organization's character. This is revealed in several ways. Some sources are: its formal mission statement, goals statement or charter, and background and fact sheets compiled by the public relations office. But there are other elements such as statements made by senior executives, the protocol they follow, and the philosophy and culture of the organization. For example, a corporate protocol that executives always wear suits could reveal some important client traits and preferences.

Second, you need to know the outlooks and personal philosophies of the people who share power in the client organization. This information can be learned from their biographies, speeches and decisions. Much more can be garnered from discussions with the people who know them.

Third, you need to be familiar with the organization's "stats." Is it a private organization owned by one person, a publicly held corporation, one of several holdings of a large international giant, or a charitable or philanthropic group run by an elected board? What are its total assets? How many people does it employ? What are its annual income and expenses? If publicly held, what is the value of its stock and earnings? Much of this information can be obtained from organizational literature and annual reports. If the organization is small or privately held, you may be able to get the information from management.

Fourth, you should learn as much as you possibly can about your client's products or services.

The Environment

Every situation exists in a unique environment. Environment includes all those factors outside the client organization, such as affected or influencing publics, and communications channels. The environment can also be classified along political, social, linguistic emotional and physical lines.

1. In a political environment, for example, governments may exert tremendous influence. Most communist governments state that there is no God and that religion simply conditions people to accept the ills of capitalism. Any public relations messages favoring religion might be censored in those countries.

2. Social environment can impact business in significant ways. In much of Latin America, large families are desirable to the people, even though they may encourage economic depression. Thus, programs discouraging large families would have to be planned and written very carefully. Social environment is closely aligned with the economic environment. Public relations programs which appear extravagant and wasteful are especially resented when the economy is depressed. In business, some organizations limit the cost of their annual reports during hard times.

3. Language environment is also important. Health messages beamed at Hispanic families in the U.S. need to be in both English and Spanish, because many in the audience may not understand English, and some may not know Spanish.

4. The emotional environment can be critical too. Appeals to patriotism, which are looked upon positively in times of war, may seem maudlin at other times.

5. The physical environment, such as air, ground, water and oceans, can also affect an organization and its operations. Even weather may affect the solution to the problem. A mid-winter appeal for warm clothes for the homeless may be more effective in snowbound Montreal than in sunny Los Angeles.

The Problem

Next, the public relations writer needs to understand the nature of the problem facing the client. That understanding should include knowledge of the background of the problem, its present status and dimensions, and potential future impact.

Problem Background

Exploring the background of the problem may be most critical. Find out when and how it all started. Determine the environmental and other factors that may have made it a problem. For example, when Love Canal was first used as a chemical dump, it was done legally, using accepted procedures.

Getting such information is usually simple if the problem is less than five years old. Ask the people involved, and not just the client management. For example, suppose you are asked to write a story presenting a company's side on a chemical spill. First, learn about the laws and regulations governing the issue. Then, get the perspective of the supervisors and workers who were involved. Next, talk to those who complained about the spill, or who might be affected. If the issue is being covered in the media, talk to the reporters. You are after the facts and must go wherever they lead you. Sometimes you'll find the company is at fault and needs to change its procedures. If management agrees, you can do an excellent story on that change process. If the company is not at fault, you can tell that story.

Researching the background of a problem also involves examining prior responses to solve it or prevent it. For example, in one instance, telephone operators were instructed by a manager to tell callers nothing had happened (when smoke from company grounds was visible). The strategy is to find out what the proper responses have been, and either incorporate these into the story or suggest others.

Problem Status

The next step is to find out the present status of the problem. Is anything being done now? Are there current news releases? Have company personnel been asked to make statements? Are there any ongoing actions? You'll want to incorporate these actions into writing decisions.

Now, bring your client into the problem. How do its members perceive the problem? What are its goals in relation to the problem?

Suppose a charitable organization's goal is: "To be perceived as the most trustworthy citizen of the community." The client has always acted in support of that goal. Now its executive director is accused of diverting donations to build a cabin in the mountains. Whether true or false, the accusation damages the reputation of the client organization. What does the client management now see as its most critical objectives? How do these relate to its public relations objectives? If the executive director is innocent, the operational objective might be to open his bank accounts to public scrutiny. A supporting public relations objective might be to communicate facts about the executive director's personal accounts through media to all publics aware of the accusation.

Future Impact

But what if there is no public relations response to the problem? With all the background information assembled, you need to forecast the possible outcomes. What will happen if conditions continue and you don't write the story? If you don't respond, will it "go away," as some people often hope, or will conditions get worse? For the charity problem, the answer is clear. You aren't expected to be a futurist. But, with the information on hand, you need to be able to answer these questions:

1. Are there actions outside public relations the client needs to take to resolve the apparent public relations problem?
2. What actions, including writing tasks, need to be taken by the public relations department?

The Publics

Two publics become important when you are investigating a problem—those affected by it, and those who can influence its outcome. These publics frequently overlap. Members of a city council may own land whose value is affected by the noise from your fabrication plant. They also can vote not to renew the city permit for the plant's operation within city limits.

Internal Publics

Usually, the first publics affected by the problem are those that work for and invest in the client organization. Among these are owners (if it is a private company), stockholders, board members, the president and senior corporate executives, managers, supervisors and workers. You need to know which of these publics are involved and in what ways.

External Publics

Many external publics may be associated with a problem. Some of these are affected by and affect the problem more directly and immediately. They should be your first concern.

Important external publics are those directly involved with the client organization. They might be annual contributors to your charity's fund drive who must respond to allegations of misuse of the funds. Perhaps they are suppliers who will have to lay off people when you cut production next month. Since they are directly affected by any changes in your company's activities, you should get their perspectives before shaping your message.

Mass media representatives are a critical public. Their reports can make organizations look good or bad. The U.S. mass media are so credible that people even accept their errors as gospel. Public response to these errors—which might be complaints, product returns or lack of sales—can seriously affect your organization. That's why it's critical that public relations writers provide accurate information to the media, and that any reporting errors be challenged and corrected as quickly and visibly as possible. Often, media contacts can give you valuable insights into the nature of your problem. And if you are a credible source, they will seek your input.

Government representatives are another important public. Be they federal, state or local, government agencies are primarily concerned with whether or not you violated laws, rules and regulations resulting in the problem. If you did uphold the law, they are obligated to publicly support you.

Special Interest Groups

Cause groups such as the Sierra Club, Greenpeace, Planned Parenthood, Right to Life, or Common Cause can be powerful allies or enemies in a public relations campaign. Your clients' images, operations and earnings can be severely affected by opposition from such groups. Often, however, you will find that they are willing to work with your client to resolve problems. Several years ago, a police chief had a group of blacks brought in for questioning about a crime. Although it may have been efficient, the procedure caused some people to be detained without cause, and was perceived to be demeaning to blacks. The National Association for the Advancement of Colored People protested strongly. Higher officials immediately countered the order and apologized, noting that the action was contrary to policy. The NAACP then fully supported the investigation.

Associations

There are also publics who may support and can help your position. Among these are trade and professional associations. If your client is a tour service company whose activities have been questioned, a comment that the procedures meet the standards of the National Association of Travel and Tourism can stand you in good stead.

Thus, identifying key publics and their positions is a critical step in the writing process. Be efficient. Don't devote your attention and energies to uninvolved or apathetic publics. Also, avoid getting between irreconcilably opposed publics such as Planned Parenthood and Right to Life.

Messages and Channels

Here, your concern is for the type of message and communication channel that will best deliver your message to a targeted public. The nature of the problem and its solution will determine to some extent the type of messages you will write and channels you will use. If the problem calls for image or advocacy advertising and the client organization agrees, you can use controlled channels of communications. Since you are buying space for the ad, you can place it wherever you wish, within reason. If your target public consists of top executives nationwide, you might choose magazines such as *Barron's, Business Week, Fortune,* or a business-oriented newspaper such as *The Wall Street Journal.*

Tradition suggests that you will be relying mostly on uncontrolled channels of communications. The newsworthiness of your message and how effectively you present it will determine whether or not it will be used by an editor. Even so, some media-message-public combinations are especially effective. Because they are complex, business and scientific messages fit the print mold best. American youth are best reached by radio or television. Public service announcements must often go to radio and television, since newspapers are under no obligation to provide free space.

Where Do I Find the Information?

You can get a great deal of the information discussed so far from either primary or secondary sources. Primary information gathering techniques, such as the interview, survey and experiment, are addressed in chapters 5 and 13. The remainder of this chapter focuses on some important secondary information-gathering techniques and sources.

Secondary Research

"Secondary information consists of sources of data and other information collected by others and archived in some form" (Stewart 1984, 11). Its sources include government reports, industry studies, syndicated information services, books, movies, journals and other information stored in libraries.

When you examine and analyze secondary information for your own purposes, you are conducting "secondary analysis." Since you are looking at it for your own purposes, you look for fresh angles that will shed unique light upon your client's problem.

Secondary research and analysis have a number of advantages and disadvantages (Stewart 1984, 14). On the plus side, they are less expensive than primary research and allow you to accumulate information much faster. They are also a good starting point for primary research since they allow you to explore a topic without having to make a heavy investment of resources.

On the negative side, it is possible that the original information is flawed or biased. If so, you may compound the error by building on incorrect data. Finally, by the time information is published, it may be outdated. Even in new books, findings may be two or more years old. In journals, research may be a year or more old. Thus, if you are looking at a dynamic subject, secondary information may not always be useful.

To sum up, secondary information, when properly used, is extremely valuable. It is all around you, on the radio, in the newspaper, and in your computer. You can find it in government publications, libraries, company documents, the writings and speeches of experts, and just about any other printed or recorded materials. Existing materials are a writer's treasury of information—what others have already determined that you won't have to redetermine. By using multiple sources to establish authenticity, secondary research and analysis can help you get good information economically and fast.

Secondary Information Gathering Guide

Listed below are steps to help you systematically gather information for a public relations writing project. How completely you follow them will depend on your experience, the complexity of your subject, and the time and budget available. The secret is to gather the minimum information essential to effective decision making. Knowing what that minimum is, comes with experience.

Define the Problem

Determine what you know. Chapter 2 helps you think about the writing problem. Based on your knowledge and understanding of the problem, distill it down to a few key words or phrases for use with information indexes. Each time you examine a document, use those key words to locate pertinent information. For example, for a story on matadors, key words might be **matador, bullfighter, bulls, toreador** and **torero.**

A PROFESSIONAL TIP:
Research and Writing

At first thought, it might seem that research and writing have no relationship in the public relations process. Research is a management function usually done by or for people at the highest levels of a public relations department. Writing is a technical function, usually done by entry-level practitioners or by people lower in the hierarchy of a public relations program.

Yet the two cannot be separated. No public relations person should write something just for the sake of writing it. There must be a reason. A written document should be for a strategic public. It should be developed to meet a public relations objective. It should be based on knowledge of the organization for which it was written and the public relations problem at issue. If possible, it should be pretested and evaluated. All require research. If they are not researchers themselves, therefore, public relations writers must be able to work with and seek the help of researchers if they are truly to contribute to public relations as a strategic function of an organization.

In addition, writing is a crucial part of research, especially in public relations. Researchers must be able to write clear understandable reports, or no one will ever use their work. Researchers must also be able to write clear questionnaires and other research instruments, or they cannot collect accurate data.

Writing and research, in short, are two crucial, if not mandatory, skills for public relations practitioners.

James E. Grunig is a professor and chair of the public relations sequence in the College of Journalism at the University of Maryland, College Park. A dedicated teacher and prolific researcher, Dr. Grunig's pioneering contributions were recognized by the Public Relations Society of America in 1984 when he received its "Pathfinder" award for research and again in 1989 when he was named the year's "Outstanding Public Relations Educator." He is co-author of *Managing Public Relations,* a comprehensive public relations text and co-editor of the *Public Relations Research Annual.*

Check Your Own Files

Most writers keep fairly extensive subject and idea files on topics they most often write about. Any useful material you have on hand will save you some search time.

Check Client Files

Every company has a file of corporate documents: financial and other proprietary and public reports, organizational publications, records, contracts, personnel records, brochures, letters and memos. Usually client organizations also keep copies of pertinent federal, state, county and city regulations. Ask for this information. The client company is the only place you can get some of it and often it won't be mentioned or given unless you ask.

Use the Library

A large city or university library should serve your purpose. Note that some libraries have special collections, some are devoted to special subjects, yet others are designated as special repositories for U.S. government publications. Search the card catalog for those key words and subjects under "author," "title" and "subject." Review those books whose titles fit your search. Also, check the latest issue of *Books in Print* for books your library doesn't have which may be useful.

Use your key words to search pertinent journal indexes, bibliographies and catalogs. The *Humanities Index* and *Business Periodicals Index* are almost always great places to start. Search about three years back, as older information should already be in books. Check at least two good encyclopedias. There are also indexes on Ph.D. dissertations, masters' theses, popular periodicals, government publications, and media. Table 4.1 provides a partial list of directories and indexes useful for public relations research.

Conduct Computer Searches of On-line Indexes

Ask the reference librarian about an on-line computer search. The paragraph below on data-base information contains examples of on-line indexes of use to the public relations writer.

CD-ROM is the general name for a series of data bases stored on compact disks (CD) and accessed by laser readers from "read only" memory (ROM). There are hundreds of such data bases, most of which are updated monthly or quarterly. Many standard indexes, such as the *Business Periodicals Index* and *Reader's Guide,* and reference texts, such as *Grolier's Encyclopedia,* are now available on CD-ROM (Lambert and Ropiequet 1987).

If the topic is highly specialized, ask the reference librarian for the ***Directory of Directories*** or an equivalent volume.

TABLE 4.1.   Directory and Index Guides to Secondary Source Material

Alternate Press Index   (underground publications of Marxist, feminist and ethnic groups)
American Statistics Index
Applied Science and Technology Index   (radio and television)
Bacon's Publicity Checker   (publicity requirements of more than 4,700 magazines and newsletters)
Basic Books in the Mass Media
Business Index   (broadcasting, journalists, television, women in mass media)
Business Periodicals Index   (includes *Public Relations Journal, Public Relations Quarterly, Public Relations Review)*
CIS/Index to Publications of the United States Congress   (freedom of the press, public opinion, radio, television)
Communication: A Guide to Information Sources   (bibliography)
Communication Abstracts   (includes *Journalism Quarterly, Journal of Communication, Communication Research, Mass Communication Review)*
Current Contents: Social and Behavioral Sciences   (title pages of most recent issues of journals before they are published)
Current Index to Journals in Education   (CIJE) (indexes 780 journals in education)
Dissertation Abstracts International   (Area VA: social sciences—marketing, public relations. Area IA: journalism, mass communication)
Editor and Publisher International Yearbook
Editor and Publisher Market Guide
Education Index   (includes *Communication Education, Communication Monographs, Journalism Educator, Media in Education and Development)*
Encyclopedia of Associations   (names, addresses, phone numbers, leaders and publications of all U.S. associations)
Film Literature Index   (film journals and other periodicals which periodically print film articles)
Gebbie Press All-In-One Directory   (all media for PR)
Humanities Index   (most articles on print and broadcast journalism, including *Columbia Journalism Review, Journal of Broadcasting* and *Journalism Quarterly)*
Index to U.S. Government Periodicals   (journalism, public relations, radio, television)
International Bibliography   (communications: books and reading, mass media, film, press, radio, television)
Journalism Abstracts   (theses and dissertations in mass communication)
Journalism Quarterly   (annual index)
London Times Index
Longman Dictionary of Mass Media and Communication
Los Angeles Times Index
Magazine Industry Market Place
National Directory of Newspapers and Reporting Services
National Newspaper Index   (includes *Christian Science Monitor, The New York Times, The Wall Street Journal, Los Angeles Times, Washington Post.* On-line only)
National Rate Book and College Newspaper Directory
The New York Times Index
Popular Periodical Index   (includes *American Film, Columbia Journalism Review, TV Guide, Writer's Digest)*
Psychological Abstracts   (communication systems area listed, 950 journals)
Public Affairs Information Services   (includes *Public Opinion Quarterly, Public Affairs)*
Public Relations Journal   (annual index)
Public Relations Review   (annual bibliography)

TABLE 4.1. Directory and Index Guides to Secondary Source Material (*continued*)

Readers' Guide to Periodical Literature   (includes *Commentary, New Yorker, Publishers Weekly*)
Resources in Education   (RIE) (indexes non-journal literature in education—freedom of speech,
    headlines, journalism, mass media, press opinion, television, writing for publication. On-line)
Social Sciences Citation Index   (On-line)
Social Sciences Index   (*Public Opinion, Public Opinion Quarterly, Journal of Communication*)
Sociological Abstracts   (abstracts articles from 1,000 international journals. See "Public Opinion,"
    "Communication," "Mass Culture." On-line)
Standard Periodical Directory
Ulrich's International Periodicals Directory
The Wall Street Journal Index
Washington Post Index
Willing's Press Guide   (UK, Europe, Australia, Far East, Middle East)
Working Press of the Nation   (1-newspaper directory; 2-magazine directory; 3-TV and radio directory;
    4-feature writer and photographer directory; 5-internal publications directory)
World Press Encyclopedia   (overview of mass communications systems for nations of the world)
World Radio-Television Handbook
The Writers' and Artists' Yearbook   (writers, artists, photographers, composers)
Writer's Market   (requirements for submissions to most publications)

Narrow the Search

Review tables of contents, indexes and headings of the books, and scan the articles you have selected. Discard the ones which don't fit. If you have more than you can review in the time allowed, repeat the process. If you are short of material, expand your search to more indexes and go back a few more years. In other words, adapt your search to the time and resources available.

Consult Specialists

Time and money permitting, consult a specialist. Most major universities have directories of professors and researchers in residence, and their areas of specialty. You can call a university's public affairs office for this information. Also, many large public relations firms specialize in research, as do consultants. These latter advertise in professional media pertinent to their specialties. Brody (1987, 63–65) cites several of these services.

Check with Professional and Trade Organizations

See *Encyclopedia of Associations* for American associations and *Ulrich's* for international associations. For example, if you were doing research on machine tools, you might call the office of the American Machine Tool Distributors' Association for background information.

For public relations, the Public Relations Society of America Research Information Center in New York maintains books, articles, brochures, manuals, kits, speeches and bibliographies dealing with public relations. The International Association of Business Communicators performs a similar service from its San Francisco office.

Purchase Computer Data-Base Information

Buy data from a commercial information service via on-line computer. There are now almost 1,000 such services (see Stewart 1984, 91–103). Costs run from $6 to $100 per hour, plus telephone time. Some relevant to public relations are listed in: Brody 1988, "Chapter 4: Creating Knowledge," 53–72; Stewart 1984, "Chapter 6: Computer-Assisted Information Acquisition," 91–104; among others. Examples:

ADPR: the advertising and public relations library on the NEXIS information service (Mead Data Central). NEXIS also contains *The New York Times Information Bank,* and the editorial content of major news and business magazines.

DataTimes: a newspaper and newswire archive of Dow Jones News/Retrieval.

DIALOG: a collection of more than 70 international data bases, including Nielson's Media Research Services (Lockheed Information Systems).

COMMUNICATE! The Advertising/Public Relations Network: provides access to major newswires, NEWSTAB electronic clipping service, Dow/Jones News Retrieval, ABI/Inform (Magnatex Intl., Ltd.).

CompuServe Information Service: includes PRSIG (a public relations and marketing forum), provides extensive data files, on-line conference facilities and electronic bulletin boards, as well as numerous other information files.

NewsNet: incorporates the news releases distributed by *PR Newswire* and the text of some 150 newsletters.

The Source: provides information ranging from finance to travel.

VU/TEXT: (Vu/Text Information Services, Inc.) allows access to information from 35 newspapers and wire services, as well as hundreds of business and trade publications worldwide.

Assemble and Organize All the Facts on Cards or Computer Files

If you have all the information you need, go to the next step. If not, you may need to do some primary research. If you need informal information, interviews probably work best (see chapter 5). For more formal and quantifiable information, you may need to conduct a survey or an experiment or have one conducted (see chapter 13). You can also use these chapters to interpret interview, survey and experimental data you have accumulated through secondary research. Table 4.2 contains an outline for the information gathering guide.

TABLE 4.2.   Outline for the PR Information Gathering Guide

---

1. Define the problem.
2. Check your own files.
3. Check client files.
4. Use the library.
5. Conduct computer searches of on-line indexes.
6. Narrow the search.
7. Consult specialists.
8. Check with professional organizations.
9. Purchase computer data-base information.
10. Assemble and organize the information.

Consolidating the Information

Once you have gathered the information, you are ready to find out what it means and what to do about it. At this point, you'll want the public relations team to review the results of your research and help you decide on or confirm goals, set objectives, and decide on strategies and tactics. This exercise calls for subjective interpretation and judgment.

How Much Is Enough?

Research is never complete since facts change as situations unfold. But there is a point beyond which little additional information can be learned by extended investigation. Identifying this point often confounds and frustrates most beginners, as well as some experienced public relations writers.

One way to find that point is to look back at the questions that guided the research. Your research effort is adequate if you have sufficient information to: (1) answer the question as you originally phrased it, (2) answer the revised question you came up with as you progressed with your investigation or (3) discard the question as unimportant.

Suppose you were investigating the best way to promote a new product, the home videophone. It works like a telephone but has a camera and video screen so that each party can see, as well as hear, the other. One of your research questions was to determine the average disposable income of each public interested in and needing the $10,000 purchase. During your research, however, you learned that income would not be a factor. The rich would use it for entertainment. And those who could use it at home for business might buy it, regardless of cost. Therefore, disposable income would not be a factor in initial purchases.

Answering the questions means doing so with some certainty (you are almost never absolutely sure). That means that each piece of new information you accept must be verified by at least two independent sources. Another way to be confident about the adequacy of your research is when you realize that you have "turned the corner." This is when you discover that any new effort turns up evidence you already have and cites references you have already studied.

How much research is enough also depends on the time and the funds available. Unfortunately, these are the most limiting factors in any public relations research. Sometimes, deadlines limit research. When the boss tells you that the corporation has a new president, starting tomorrow, and wants the information released to the media tonight, you may not have time to do much research.

To summarize, your research must end in time to attack the problem and do so within budget and time constraints specified by the client. You hope to have answered all the questions and turned the corner by then, but must recognize that often that is not the case.

Selecting the Data

Once your information is organized and analyzed, you are ready to decide what information you will include. If you have been allowed the freedom, you may well have hundreds of pages of research information available. You don't expect either the public relations team or client management to read it all. Although you will want to keep everything as backup information, what you present will be limited to the most pertinent information.

Use information which best answers these questions, based on the traditional problem-solving process:

1. What is the problem? How and when did it begin? What is its present status? Who was and is involved from the client organization and affected or affecting publics? What are the geographic and organizational constraints of the problem?

2. Why did the problem occur? What are the known facts and the underlying assumptions? Are there useful precedents?

3. What could have been done to prevent the problem or minimize its consequences to less than the present condition?

4. What will be the consequences if no further action is taken? What goal should guide you in proposed actions? What feasible objectives in support of this goal can be undertaken now? Of these, which are most urgent and can be expected to be most effective? What publics can be expected to support or oppose your objectives and what can be done to optimize or neutralize their efforts? What might the public relations writing components of these actions be?

Summarizing the Information

Now you summarize your problem definition and research with the help of the public relations team. This summary should be written out, and then may be used for decision making.

The steps in the information summary follow the sequence of steps (1) through (4), just covered. Pare down or beef up sections, depending on the circumstances. If members of the public relations team and management all belong to the same organization, items on organizational background and people can be limited. If the problem is new and relatively unknown, include adequate detail so that the reader needs no other reference. But a complete summary should include a reference section so that others might check your sources for additional information or verification.

The information summary does not finalize the goal and objectives, but proposes them. It may become evident in the planning process that some objectives are not feasible for reasons unknown to the writer. There also may be alternative goals or objectives which were not considered possible, but which later information renders necessary.

Chapter Summary

This chapter discussed the role of information gathering in the public relations writing process. Research helps reduce uncertainty. The authors presented secondary information-gathering techniques as part of the overall research effort to understand a problem.

Asking what is and what is not known, the chapter developed essential elements of information in studying a problem, i.e., information about the writer's organization, the client organization, the problem environment, the nature and scope of the problem, the publics involved, message and media or channels, and opinion leaders in the problem area.

The beginning writer's public relations information gathering guide was discussed in 10 steps: (1) definition of the problem, (2) checking personal files, (3) gathering client information, (4) use of the library, (5) computer on-line index searches, (6) narrowing the search, (7) consulting specialists, (8) questioning professional associations, (9) considering computer data-base information, and (10) organizing the information gathered.

Overall, information gathering is seen as the first important step in considering goals and objectives for solving public relations problems through the writing process.

A Writing Exercise

Situation: You are a speech writer in the public affairs office of a major public university in New York. It has just been discovered that three university undergraduates have contracted AIDS. None is expected to live more than two years. Since the students entered your school as freshmen and are now seniors, it is strongly suspected that they contracted the disease after arriving at the school. All three are males and live in the university's dormitories. Two have been suspected of homosexual activity in the past.

The university president wishes to give a speech in four days to all students who live in the dormitories. Her plan is to convince the students to abstain from sex due to the "frightening reality of AIDS." The president is an Hispanic, 66 years of age, whose academic work has been in linguistics. Her father was a surgeon and her mother a teacher in a private school. She is by nature quiet and retiring, but has been an effective president since being elected four years ago.

She wants a speech draft to meet her purpose. But your boss, the director of public affairs, wants you to start at the beginning with fact gathering and give him a written summary. He is not at all sure that either the president's plan, her public or her channel is appropriate. "Let's give it a full shake," he says, "and see what falls out."

Assignment: Conduct information gathering necessary to solve the problem. Avoid interviews, surveys and experiments at this time, as they may create a sense of panic. Gather all the information you can on the AIDS issue published in the last six months and provide your boss a written summary in accordance with this chapter. Your summary should run between four and five pages, plus references.

Food for Thought

1. Why do you think some scholars regard information gathering via secondary information not to be true research? What is your opinion?
2. The authors of this book say that public relations writers should be a part of the thought, research, decision-making and planning behind their work. Do you agree or not? Justify your position.
3. What are the relative advantages and disadvantages of on-line computer information gathering, compared to consulting with reference librarians?
4. Most organizations with public relations problems strongly resist paying for any research related to their problems. Why do you think this is true?
5. What do you think is the most difficult aspect of information gathering? Why is that so?

References for Further Study

Barzun, Jacques, and Henry F. Graff. *The Modern Researcher.* 3rd ed. New York: Harcourt, Brace, Jovanovich, 1977.

Baskin, Otis, and Craig E. Aronoff. *Public Relations: The Profession and the Practice.* Dubuque, Iowa: Wm. C. Brown, 1988, 100–123.

Brody, E. W. *Public Relations Programming and Production.* New York: Praeger, 1988, 53–72.

Brody, E. W. *The Business of Public Relations.* New York: Praeger, 1987, 62–85.

Cantor, Bill, and Chester Burger, eds., *Experts In Action: Inside Public Relations,* 2d ed. New York: Longman, 1989, 241–245.

Cutlip, Scott M., Allen H. Center and Glen M. Broom. *Effective Public Relations,* 6th ed. Englewood Cliffs, N.J., 1985, 199–220.

Lambert, Steve, and Suzanne Ropiequet. *CD ROM.* Redmond, Wash.: Microsoft Press, 1987.

Leedy, Paul D. *How to Read Research and Understand It.* New York: Macmillan, 1981.

Newsom, Doug, and Bob Carrell. *Public Relations Writing: Form & Style,* 2nd ed. Belmont, Calif.: Wadsworth, 1986, 37–56.

Pavlik, John V. *Public Relations: What Research Tells Us.* Newbury Park, Calif.: Sage, 1987, 16–30.

Sietel, Fraser P. *The Practice of Public Relations,* 3rd ed. Columbus, Ohio: Merrill, 1987, 111–134.

Stewart, David W. *Secondary Research: Information Sources and Methods.* Beverly Hills: Sage, 1984.

Wilcox, Dennis L., Phillip H. Ault and Warren K. Agee. *Public Relations: Strategies and Tactics.* New York: Harper & Row, 1986, 130–147.

Wimmer, Roger D., and Joseph R. Dominick. *Mass Media Research: An Introduction,* 2nd ed. Belmont, Calif.: Wadsworth, 1987.

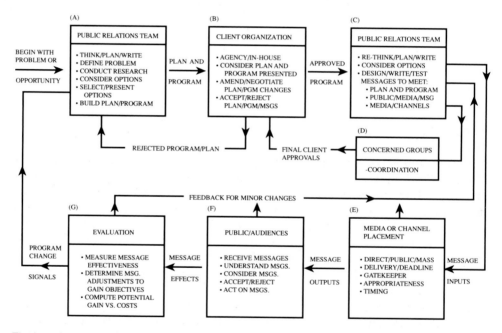

(A) PUBLIC RELATIONS TEAM

BEGIN WITH
PROBLEM OR

OPPORTUNITY

- THINK/PLAN/WRITE
- DEFINE PROBLEM
- CONDUCT RESEARCH
- CONSIDER OPTIONS
- SELECT/PRESENT
  OPTIONS
- BUILD PLAN/PROGRAM

PLAN AND

PROGRAM

(B) CLIENT ORGANIZATION

- AGENCY/IN-HOUSE
- CONSIDER PLAN AND
  PROGRAM PRESENTED
- AMEND/NEGOTIATE
  PLAN/PGM CHANGES
- ACCEPT/REJECT
  PLAN/PGM/MSGS

APPROVED

PROGRAM

(C) PUBLIC RELATIONS TEAM

- RE-THINK/PLAN/WRITE
- CONSIDER OPTIONS
- DESIGN/WRITE/TEST
  MESSAGES TO MEET:
  - PLAN AND PROGRAM
  - PUBLIC/MEDIA/MSG
  - MEDIA/CHANNELS

REJECTED PROGRAM/PLAN

FINAL CLIENT
APPROVALS

(D) CONCERNED GROUPS

-COORDINATION

FEEDBACK FOR MINOR CHANGES

(G) EVALUATION

PROGRAM
CHANGE

SIGNALS

- MEASURE MESSAGE
  EFFECTIVENESS
- DETERMINE MSG.
  ADJUSTMENTS TO
  GAIN OBJECTIVES
- COMPUTE POTENTIAL
  GAIN VS. COSTS

MESSAGE

EFFECTS

(F) PUBLIC/AUDIENCES

- RECEIVE MESSAGES
- UNDERSTAND MSGS.
- CONSIDER MSGS.
- ACCEPT/REJECT
- ACT ON MSGS.

MESSAGE

OUTPUTS

(E) MEDIA OR CHANNEL
PLACEMENT

- DIRECT/PUBLIC/MASS
- DELIVERY/DEADLINE
- GATEKEEPER
- APPROPRIATENESS
- TIMING

MESSAGE

INPUTS

The interview is a key research tool for public relations writers. It allows them to conduct original research quickly and informally, as well as to verify and expand on secondary research.

INTERVIEWING FOR PUBLIC RELATIONS WRITING

Introduction

"The interview is probably man's oldest and most often used device for obtaining information" (Kerlinger 1966, 467). The ability to interview is a required skill for all journalists. Interviewing is also one of the fastest and most effective ways to get new information. If a department store burns down, the reporter quickly interviews key people (store managers, clerks, fire fighters, police) and witnesses (customers, delivery people, passersby). Based on their accounts, the journalist pieces together as much of the story as possible by the publication's deadline.

Public relations writers use the interview extensively too, most often as a research vehicle. The public relations approach to interviewing may be formal, as when an organization's founder is interviewed for a feature story on a company's 50th anniversary. Or, it may be informal, as when the writer asks colleagues' opinions on a new promotional concept. Regardless, the interview is a key tool for the public relations writer.

Information

As you learned in chapter 4, we gather information from both primary and secondary sources. The interview is a primary source of information, delving often into the thoughts and actions of people. It helps add the human dimension to your writing by allowing

A PROFESSIONAL TIP:
Interviewing

While interviewing is a learned skill, there are people who also have been born with the talent of interviewing. These people turn out to be negotiators, counselors, writers, executives, and even con artists, successful hostesses, and consumer psychologists.

Adroit interviewing involves more than just asking the H and five W's questions. And the results certainly can glean more than age, rank and serial number.

A truly-skilled interviewer will go where no one has gone before, asking the one question never posed, interpreting a pause or a raised eyebrow or a jittery foot as a signal to go further still. Sometimes an interviewer doesn't say a word; instead, he will use silence as the biggest question of all. A very smart interviewer will simply ask a question it is presumed others have asked, but haven't.

Why learn how to interview with skill, precision and compassion?

Without interviews, how would we learn what makes our heroes tick? How would we know what products people like? How would we understand why a person becomes a public official? How would we know which company is the better one to work for? How would we learn if our messages are received? How would we know which movie to see? How would we find out what makes a child cry?

Interviewing takes place throughout the day in all manner of situations, large and small. Knowing the skill—and appreciating the art—of interviewing can mean the difference between working and living in a world, and understanding the world we work and live in.

Wilma Mathews, ABC, is manager of public relations for AT&T Network Systems. She is a Fellow of the International Association of Business Communicators and author or co-author of numerous articles and books.

you to record not only words but tone of voice, dress, gesture and demeanor. It enables you to probe, ask questions about things you don't understand and change the direction of the interview as you progress.

Say you are asked to write a publicity release on a new product called "Ladies Aide." The product is a small self-protective electronic device the size of a ball-point pen. At the press of a button, it emits a high-pitched tone audible for 100 yards and activates police radios over a two-mile radius. It was designed by a woman engineer after she had been attacked while leaving her office. You have been given two brochures and a technical treatise written by the inventor. You think it is a great idea, but that the name is "a loser." You also have many questions. How much does it weigh? How long do the batteries last? Does it affect pacemakers? What is its psychological impact on the user? Think how much more effective you could be if you could discuss the product with the inventor. That is part of what public relations interviewing is all about.

When the Interview Is Most Useful

There are generally three purposes for conducting interviews:

1. They can be used to help plan further research. For example, during communications audits, researchers generally interview members of the organization's management first. Based on these interviews, they design questions for all employees.

2. Writers often base stories solely on interviews, because there is no time for any other research.

3. Interviews support other research, such as information from books, articles and reports. Most public relations interviews fit the third category. It is rare, however, for public relations writers to base articles on single interviews.

Some Definitions

Most tend to think of the interview as a meeting involving two people, one asking questions, the other responding. That is usually the case, but there are many variations. It may or may not be done in person. It may involve more than one interviewer or more than one respondent. And it may be conducted casually or formally.

Let's define a few terms that are critical to this discussion. The **interview** is a question-and-answer session between one or more interviewers and one or more respondents. The **interviewer** plans and schedules the communication, and asks the questions. The **respondent** or **interviewee** answers the questions.

The **structured interview** closely follows a script and is used for formal research. The **unstructured interview** is an informal conversation and offers considerable flexibility.

Unstructured Interviews

For the most part, public relations writers and researchers use unstructured or non-standard interview procedures. The interview is planned and questions are written in advance. But the interviewer is free to change, add or delete questions, to probe in-depth or pursue leads triggered by the respondent's answers.

Variations in the nonstructured interview abound because each person puts a distinct flavor into the interview process. From the several types of unstructured interviews, we will note two of direct interest to public relations writers.

The Information Gathering Interview

Most public relations interviews are conducted simply to get information that only the respondent knows. Or, the interview may be the best way to get information in a hurry from an expert. The interviewer is looking for facts or perceptions to support arguments or story lines. For example, a public relations writer working on a campaign against cigarette smoking might interview an official from the National Institutes of Health to get the latest statistics on smoking-related deaths.

The Personal Interview

Here the interviewer hopes to learn facts about respondents, get their attitudes on certain people, places, things, actions and ideas, and obtain useful quotations. Public relations writers use the personal interview frequently when writing feature stories on senior staff members of client organizations as well as for other human interest stories. An example might be an interview with an employee whose avocation is aluminum-can sculpture.

Methods of Interviewing

While the type of interview reflects its purpose, the interview method indicates the way in which it is carried out. The many methods available for interviews reflect their flexibility as information gathering tools.

Person-to-Person

This method lets the interviewer take advantage of personal closeness. People's dress, grooming, gestures, touch and facial expressions all add to the richness of the information. More than half of what people communicate comes from visual and nonverbal signals. The tone of voice often says much more than the words. So does action. How often have you heard a professor ask students to express their views in class, then appear annoyed when they do so?

TABLE 5.1.   A Week's Interview Schedule for a Public Relations Writer

---

Interviews for Overseas Families Project

Week of March 6

Monday, 9 a.m.: Personal interview with CEO in Tokyo on concept: one hour.

Monday, 1 p.m.: Personal interview with finance director in Tokyo on savings to company from having managers move families to overseas plant locations, thus extending length of stay at location: 30 minutes.

Tuesday, as able: Telephone interview with production director in Tokyo on total productivity of managers in short versus long overseas stays: 30 minutes.

Wednesday, 9 a.m.: Personal interview with Alpha Plant manager in Seoul on pluses and minuses of longer in-country tours by managers: one hour.

Wednesday, noon: Group luncheon interview in Seoul for views of overseas managers: two hours.

Wednesday, 3 p.m.: Personal interview with Mayor of Inchon in Seoul on impact on local economy and social accommodations: one hour.

Thursday, 10 a.m.: Personal interview in Kunsan with Bravo Plant manager on pluses and minuses: one hour.

Thursday, 2 p.m.: Personal interview with Mayor of Kunsan in Kunsan on impact on local economy and social accommodations: one hour.

Friday, 4 p.m.: Group interview with management wives in Tokyo on pluses and minuses of family tours: two hours.

The person-to-person method can be used for almost any inquiry, provided that each party is prepared. And it is most effective for gathering in-depth information. Often known as the "elite interview," this technique allows coverage of a wide range of issues and helps the interviewer gain a thorough understanding of the respondent.

For information gathering interviews, we usually select "key informants" who are knowledgeable leaders of government bodies, publications, broadcast groups, schools, religious groups, companies, labor organizations or cause groups. Specialists also serve as key informants. Thus, engineers, professors, librarians, chemists and public relations practitioners might be called upon to provide facts and perspective for a writing project.

Public relations writers who plan feature articles on a subject generally favor the person-to-person in-depth interview. It is difficult to capture the essence of a person without hearing and observing the respondent, allowing extensive time for open-ended responses and sidelights. This kind of interview requires comprehensive research and at least two hours with the interviewee. A sample week's interview schedule for a writer working on a special project is shown in table 5.1.

TABLE 5.2. Tips for Telephone Interviews

The telephone interview merits the following special considerations:
1. *Identify yourself.* Since respondents can't see you, take special care to let them know who you are.
2. *Be brief.* At one time telephone interviews were kept short, in part because of the cost of the call. Today, the respondent's available time is the limiting factor.
3. *Speak loudly and clearly.* Many senior respondents have some hearing loss. Make sure to speak slowly and loudly enough, and pronounce and enunciate your words carefully. Avoid words which sound ambiguous.
4. *Use continuity cues.* Indicate that you are following the discussion by an occasional "I see," "yes," or "go on." Don't allow long silences. If you need time to copy the response, say so.
5. *Keep questions short.* Write your key questions out in advance. Keep them brief and clear. Test them verbally to make sure they can't be misinterpreted. Record and listen to them to make sure you aren't biasing the answers by the way you ask the questions.

Telephone

The telephone and person-to-person methods are similar, with some significant differences. Because of speed, convenience and economy, informal telephone interviews are often used. Although the casual observer might see them as simple conversations, public relations writers tend to structure interview calls based on research and planning. Secondary research prior to these calls averages about two hours, and the calls average about 30 minutes.

The telephone interview saves time since it eliminates travel and reduces interview time. Because it is not face-to-face, respondents will sometimes reveal sensitive information which they might not give in person. It can be easy to record, allowing interviewers to transcribe responses directly into computers or word processors without disturbing respondents. Also, telephone responses get psychological priority from some, especially when the calls are long distance.

But telephone interviewers cannot see their respondents and thus lose important nonverbal feedback. And, although it takes about the same preparation time as a person-to-person interview, the shorter interview time and lack of visual cues mean less information per hour of effort. Normally, the telephone interview is selected when the personal interview is not possible. But it is an effective research tool when time is short or several people need to be contacted for brief amounts of information. (See table 5.2 for tips).

Computer

An interview method which developed largely during the mid-1980s places interviewer and respondent at computer terminals connected by telephone modems. This has the advantage of live interaction. It also allows the person being interviewed to consider questions in print, type out proposed answers, review them and make changes, then transmit the answer. More than one interviewer can take part. For example, dozens of practitioners interviewed public relations leaders Edward Bernays, Pat Jackson and others during the 1980s on the CompuServe PR Link network. On the negative side, participants are denied visual communication, and the interviewer lacks the certainty that the response is that of the respondent.

Audio or Video

Often, interviewers cannot be with their respondents, or reach them for telephone interviews. A useful vehicle for willing respondents in this case is the audio or video response interview. The interviewer proposes questions by letter, memo or phone to the respondent who answers via audio or videotape. In some cases, a stand-in reads the questions and the respondent answers, both being recorded on tape. Clearly, although the videotape requires more effort by the respondent, it provides more information and is preferred by the interviewer.

Although a useful substitute for in-person or telephone interviews, audio or video responses lack spontaneity. By allowing the respondent to plan and rehearse, the immediacy and spontaneity of the live interview are lost. Also, the interviewer's opportunity to ask follow-up questions is denied.

Perhaps the ultimate in this mode is the live electronic interview, using television cameras at each end, linked through coaxial cable or satellite. Cost limits its use by the public relations writer, but it can be especially useful during fast-breaking crises when an organization's survival may be at stake.

Written

A less desirable interview method consists of written questions from the interviewer, which the respondent answers in writing. Still, this is a useful last resort for public relations writers, so long as it is not represented as a personal interview. It has all the faults of audio and video responses, however, and takes longer to complete. Also, written questions tend to get diverted to staff members for answers "approved" by the respondent.

Special Types of Public Relations Interviews

Several types of interviews are used frequently in public relations. Two are mentioned here: focus group and feedback interviews.

The Focus Group

The focus group is a unique case of the 5–10 person group interview. Practitioners use focus groups to generate or test ideas, set the stage for survey research, preview communications and discover the views of specific publics. Planning is critical to effective focus group discussions. Goals and specific objectives of each discussion must be clearly defined in advance.

The focus group consists of a facilitator and at least one person from each public relevant to the topic being researched. The facilitator (sometimes called "discussion leader" or "moderator") guides the group through a discussion of the topic, making sure to cover all the planned topics, and getting the perspective of each participant on each topic. A focus group may be recalled periodically to see how its views have changed or to determine its perspective on new subjects. For example, a toy maker might meet with a focus group of boys and girls of various ages and backgrounds each year to get their reactions to new toys.

Clearly, it is important for the facilitator to understand the process and be able to guide discussions effectively. Public relations writers do not often serve as moderators, but do often have groups set up, present issues, observe discussions and use what they learn in their written messages.

Broadcast and Print Feedback Interviews

Public relations writers sometimes conduct brief personal or telephone interviews to find out how effective certain messages have been. Let's say that an editorial comment on real estate development which you drafted for your CEO got published in the "op-ed" section of yesterday's newspaper. You might use one of several available random telephone dialing procedures (see chapter 13) to call 50 or 100 readers. Your questions might read like this: (1) Did you read yesterday's *Chronicle?* (2) Did you happen to see the article on the op-ed page titled, "Slow Growth Means No Growth?" If "yes," (3) Did you read that article or any part of it? If "yes," (4) Did it help you understand the issue?

The Interview Process

Successful interviewers outline their plans well in advance. Some do it in their heads. Beginning interviewers should plan on paper. While the amount of planning varies with the complexity of the interview and the experience of the interviewer, there are certain basic components. A sample interview plan outline listing these is included in table 5.3.

Preparation

Three steps would be completed before the interview begins: (1) conducting research, (2) making the appointment and follow-up communication, and (3) determining the interview strategy and questions. See table 5.4 for steps in the interview process.

TABLE 5.3.   A Sample Interview Plan Outline

1. Preparation
   a. Research
   b. Appointment letters and calls
   c. Interview strategy and questions
   d. Appropriate dress
   e. Equipment
   f. Transportation

2. Pre-interview preliminaries
   a. Early arrival with tools
   b. Ground rules set
      (1) Interview participants and length of interview
      (2) Subject areas agreed on
      (3) Portions on and off the record
      (4) Use of audio or video recorders
      (5) Respondent access to copy

3. Beginning the interview
   a. Rapport established
      (1) Current events
      (2) Mutual acquaintances
      (3) Mutual interests
   b. Easy-answer opening questions
      (1) Background facts
      (2) Organizational facts

4. The interview proper
   a. Necessary facts
   b. Beliefs, attitudes, opinions and feelings
   c. Projections for the future

5. The interview conclusion
   a. Stop on time
   b. Complete open answers
   c. Set up call-back
   d. Get a concluding statement
   e. Take everything you brought
   f. Remember last-minute points
   g. Leave the "door open" for follow-up

TABLE 5.4. Steps in the Interview Process

1. Thoroughly research the subject. Determine whether or not an interview is necessary.
2. Select the most appropriate interview respondent or respondents.
3. Schedule the interview with the respondent. Establish the date, time, place and type of interview.
4. Conduct additional necessary research on the respondent.
5. Establish an interview strategy. Consider questions to be asked. Complete an interview plan outline.
6. Conduct the interview, using agreed rules.
7. Review interview notes and amend as necessary. Confirm questionable points and get needed additional information from respondent.
8. Integrate interview notes with other research. Confirm interview facts through additional sources.
9. Apply integrated research to appropriate writing.

Conducting Research

Having stated the problem, the public relations writer should examine the available secondary research information before considering a survey. An interview is in order when the writer needs: (a) information in a fast-changing environment, such as a crisis; (b) information on a new corporate location or a new product; (c) background for a feature about people; or (d) interpretations and explanations from experts which will add credibility and human interest to the story.

Selecting the Respondent

Making the appointment requires that the writer first select the respondent and learn his or her background. Respondent choice is usually determined by the interview need. A personality profile usually means that feature subjects, as well as their friends and associates, will be interviewed. To write about the employee-of-the-year for the organization's newsletter, you will need to interview that person. To write about events that you did not witness, you will need to interview those who did.

Limited selection is needed in interviewing authorities. For example, a story on the city government requires interviewing the mayor, city manager or members of the city council. A story on the plans of a corporation could best be built on an interview with its president.

While picking expert respondents, choice is limited by cost, expertise and availability. The United States Surgeon General is clearly an expert on health conditions in America, but may not be available. Not knowing how to find the right expert, you should consult: (a) anyone in field, (b) a reference librarian or (c) a publication such as *The Encyclopedia of Associations.*

Normally, a great deal is learned about respondents before they are selected. Position, qualifications, general availability and personality should be understood before contact is made. These can be learned from published or organizational biographies, or by contacting associates of the respondent.

The Communications Support Group
1315 Harbor Blvd.
Austin, Texas 78745

January 19, 1991

Sam M. Jones
154 Briar Street
Roosevelt, Texas 78739

Dear Mr. Jones:

I am writing to request an interview with you on behalf of the Roosevelt Foundation. The foundation, located in Hyde Park, New York, is preparing an historical report on "The Impact of Franklin Delano Roosevelt on the American Society." Our company, as the attached letter shows, is authorized to represent the foundation in Texas in order to gather information for the report.

Roosevelt, Texas, presents one aspect of the FDR impact in our state. As one of the town's founders, a former mayor and a lifetime resident, you have important information on the town which no one else can provide. I hope to come to Roosevelt next week and spend a couple of hours interviewing you. I will call you shortly to see if this is possible. If it is, we can then discuss a time and place for the interview.

Thank you for your consideration. I am eager to be your partner in recording an important part of America's history.

Sincerely,

Billy Ray Jones, APR
Group Writer
enc: ltr.

▶ **Figure 5.1.** A sample interview request letter

Contacting the Respondent

Getting the interview often requires persuasion and negotiation. Many people are flattered to be asked for an interview, or believe they have an obligation to accept. But interviews and preparing for them require considerable time when done properly. And they tend to place the anxious and ignorant in a bad light. So it is often difficult to get an interview appointment.

One approach for setting up the interview involves several steps:

Write a letter asking for the interview and explaining its purpose. Use the company letterhead to legitimize the request. A sample interview request letter is shown in figure 5.1.

TABLE 5.5.   Telephone Interview Request Checklist

1. Identify yourself. Provide credentials, if necessary.
2. Refer to your letter of request and the organization you represent. Don't expect that your letter will be remembered. Most people who merit interviewing get lots of letters.
3. Review the subject of your research. Review why an interview with him or her is important to the success of your project.
4. Negotiate the appropriate interview type, place, date and time. Set ground rules for the interview, if the respondent desires.
5. Leave a telephone number through which you may be reached during the interval between the call and the interview. Traveling writers are difficult to contact.
6. Express your appreciation, whether you get an interview scheduled or not.
7. Write and dispatch a confirming note immediately. It can avoid misunderstandings and "lock in" the interview.

After allowing sufficient time for the letter to arrive, phone and request the interview. Some people avoid callers they don't know, so don't give up too soon. Use an intermediary, if necessary. Unless you are experienced, have a checklist covering the points you wish to make during the call. A sample is provided in table 5.5.

Once you make contact, make the prospect aware that you are informed on the subject. Repeat why his or her participation is important. Be prepared to negotiate the date, time and place. Whether you succeed or not, don't forget to say "thank you." The number of people who do forget might surprise you.

The day after the call, send a follow-up note restating essentials of the interview and any special materials you've requested. If the interview was refused, make it a "thanks anyway" note. Sometimes people change their minds.

In your log book or running notes, record all contacts with prospective interviewees. When you have several stories running at once, it is easy for an interview or follow-up to be missed.

Determining Interview Strategy and Questions

Pre-interview strategy includes determining the kind of interview appropriate for the occasion, setting guidelines for the questions and selecting types of questions.

Determining the Kind of Interview

As noted, which interview process you use depends on an agreement with the respondent, based on availability, resources, time and objective. All things being equal, the person-to-person, unstructured, information-gathering interview is preferred. It gives interviewer and respondent the most flexibility and the greatest opportunity for exchange of information.

Setting Guidelines for the Questions

Experienced interviewers prepare few precise questions, preferring instead the flexibility of an unstructured exchange. However, beginning public relations writers should prepare comprehensive sets of questions which should (Kerlinger 1966, 473–75; Kornhauser and Sheatsley 1959, 546–74):

1. Be necessary and relate to the subject (except during the introduction and conclusion).

2. Be ones the respondent is qualified to answer.

3. Be clear and unambiguous. Don't use long or multi-part probes, except for written questions requiring written answers. Break a complex question down into a logical series of single-point questions.

4. Be free of bias. Loaded questions have no place in public relations interviews, whether positive ("You do support ERA, don't you?") or negative ("Is the company still cheating on taxes?"). Avoid biases from unstated assumptions. "Should salaries be frozen for the next decade?" implies that other economic conditions will not change.

5. Be neither too general nor too specific. CEOs should not be expected to be familiar with organizational trivia. Likewise, line employees should not be expected to know the corporate master plans.

6. Not be too personal, unless the interview calls for it. When it does, give the respondent fair warning of your intent.

7. Follow a logical progression. Don't ask about childhood, then senior professional positions, then undergraduate education. Move questions from small to large, youth to old age, or local to regional to national. Progress from the known to the unknown.

Considering Types of Questions

Here are some types of questions to consider using or avoiding in public relations interviews:

1. The dichotomous or close-ended question allows the respondent only one of two possible answers, such as "yes" or "no," or "true" or "false." Interviewers seldom use this type, except as a preliminary for follow-up questions.

2. The fixed alternative is similar to the dichotomous, but allows more than two possible responses. Using it, you might ask: "Please answer the following questions 'yes,' 'no,' or 'I don't know.' "

3. The scale question is used for ratings. "On a scale of one-to-ten, 10 being best and one being worst, how would you rate the president's performance thus far?"

4. The open-ended question allows respondents to answer in whatever manner they choose. If you asked, "What do you think of public relations in China?" you might get a short answer or a lengthy response. This approach is valued by public relations writers seeking interpretations, reactions and explanations. Some variations include:

The *funnel* is a series of open-ended questions that progressively become more specific. Example:

Question 1: "What do you think about the growth of international public relations over the next five years?"

Question 2: "What do you see as the public relations growth pattern in the United States during that time?"

Question 3: "Will public relations in New York State parallel the U.S. pattern or set a course of its own over those five years?"

The *inverted funnel* question series works in reverse, moving from the specific to the general. It is a useful procedure to get people such as scientists, who are prone to give precise responses, to open up.

5. The follow-up question may be planned or spontaneous. Its purpose is to get additional information about some answer the respondent has given. There are several types of follow-up questions:

The *probe question* pushes deeper into the subject than the respondent's original answer, or moves the questioning into an unexplored area (divergence).

Example: "You say you favor the death penalty for murder. What about euthanasia?"

The *extension question* does not necessarily go deeper into the subject. It simply asks for additional information. Simple urgings such as "Go on," or "What happened next?" usually suffice to extend the answer. Sometimes silence will do it.

The *redirection question* is used to change the line of questioning. Perhaps you learn that the respondent cannot answer the question adequately. You would like to move on to something more productive. Sometimes you can be quite frank about it. At other times, however, you may need to be more indirect: "Thank you. That's a unique observation. Now I'd like to shift to a similar subject that requires a different outlook."

The *explanation question* is a follow-up that many beginning interviewers avoid to their detriment. When you don't understand an answer, just say: "Could you expand on that answer? I need some clarification." Far better to have the respondent think you shallow in conversation than for the world to see it in print.

Pre-Interview Actions

Several considerations are necessary for the pre-interview period—the day of the interview or the evening before—if the interview is to go smoothly.

Arrive fully prepared and early. Nothing crimps a session more than an interviewer who arrives late and harried. Make sure you have all the necessary tools, such as notebook, pen and recorder.

Make sure of the ground rules. Know who will be present, who will take part, the subject agreed on and whether recording is acceptable. Know the generally accepted rules for being "on the record" and how they apply. "On the record" means that everything said is publishable. "Indirect quotation" means that responses may be attributed to the respondent, but not quoted verbatim, "Background" means a response may be used and attributed to someone in the respondent's organization, but not to the respondent by name. "Not for attribution," sometimes called "deep background," means responses may be used, but without attribution. "Off the record" means that the information is provided to help the interviewer understand the subject, but it may not be published in any form. "Pre-publication review" means the respondent may see and comment on copy emanating from the interview before it is published.

Beginning the Interview

Establish a rapport as soon as possible. Respondents are often more nervous than interviewers. What gets published about them can significantly help or hinder them. If the respondent questions your authenticity, show some identification. Establish a common bond in a neutral area such as sports, organizations, hobbies or work to break the ice.

Make your first questions easy to answer. Factual questions about the respondent's background get the interview started well. But don't overdo it by asking questions that you should already know the answers to.

Often the interviewer uses the beginning period to get background information not available elsewhere.

The Interview

Outline the key questions you plan to ask. Beginners usually write them out completely, along with logical follow-ups. It is usually best to move the questions from the concrete to the abstract:

1. **What:** Ask for necessary facts about:
   a. **The respondent** (personal history, missing dates, education, chronology of employment, family).
   b. **The respondent's behavior** (media attention, buying habits, voting behavior, work hours, recreation, hobbies).
   c. **Others** (family, work associates, friends, superiors, subordinates).
   d. **Situations and actions** (work load, political campaign involvement, salary, important events).

2. **Why:** Ask about beliefs, attitudes, opinions, and feelings:
   a. **What objective factors** seem to influence these (what has been read, heard or seen; events participated in; people).
   b. **What emotional factors** seem to influence these (emotional needs, overall outlook on life, general disposition).

3. **What next:** Projections for the future. Here, give the respondent an opportunity to be expansive about the subject. What will (or may) happen in the future? What should be done to help it happen or keep it from happening?

The Interview Conclusion

The conclusion calls for six basic actions by you:

1. **Offer to stop at the appointed time:** "I see my time is up. I'd like to continue, but I'm sure you have other appointments." That way you are ready to continue or quit, as the respondent desires.

2. **Make sure you have all the answers you need** or ask to be able to call back later.

3. **Give the respondent an opportunity to close.** Ask for a concluding statement: "If you had one final piece of advice to give students studying public relations today, what would it be?"

4. **Review the outcome.** Make sure the respondent knows how you plan to use the interview.

5. **Take what you brought.** A recorder left behind means extra work.

6. **Get the final points.** Sometimes comments made in parting, after your notebook is put away, are the most important points made.

A Plan for No Plan

Having a sample interview plan outline on hand is useful, even if you don't get time to fill it out. Occasionally, an interview opportunity arises on the spur of the moment. In the event that you are one of those people who doesn't fashion questions easily, table 5.6 provides a useful tool.

It is based on the premise that you know *why* you are conducting the interview. As you will recall from earlier in the chapter, interviews are generally conducted to plan research, support ongoing research or form the basis of a story. Most immediate interview opportunities relate to the last purpose. If a person in a key position in the organization, or of significant accomplishment is available, you don't want to pass up the opportunity. Having decided why this interview is important, you may refer to table 5.7 for some generally effective questions.

Useful Interview Practices

Once you have made the necessary preparations, conducting the interview itself can be a pleasure. Don't be concerned if you are nervous. You will quickly become engrossed in your project and forget your anxiety. Some useful points:

TABLE 5.6.   Questions for a Spur-of-the-moment Interview

1. I wanted to interview you because _____ . How important is this issue/subject/event to you, your organization and society as a whole?
2. How would you say that your life experiences and education have prepared you to deal with or discuss it?
3. Who are the key people you know who are involved in the issue/subject/event? What can you tell me about them?
4. What are the pros and cons of the issue/subject/event? What is your position?
5. If events don't unfold as you think they should, what are some of the possible consequences?
6. What should have been done beforehand to make present conditions most favorable?
7. How do you expect things to change regarding the issue/subject/event in the near future? What are the main implications of those changes?
8. How do you think I could use this interview to get the most useful published article for my organization?
9. The publics I expect to reach on this issue/subject/event are _____ . What do you think my message to them should be?
10. My interview subject aside, what is the most important thing on your agenda today? How does it relate to public relations?

Keep a Record

Take notes and record the session (with permission). Experienced interviewers sometimes take one- or two-word notes of responses, then use the notes later to reconstruct the interview. But memory is no substitute for what was actually said. And misquoting can be disastrous.

Keep your questions or interview plan outline separate from the notes you are taking. You need the questions close at hand. Use a personal shorthand system for taking notes. While people speak at more than 100 words per minute, few can write at half that rate.

Maintain a Positive Attitude

Maintain a friendly, positive and open attitude. Don't be judgmental in word or gesture. You are there to find out what respondents think or know. Don't let respondents be biased by what they think you want them to say.

Listen

Some interviewers don't listen to responses because they are nervous or are concentrating on what they plan to ask next. Concentrate on the response to see how to shape the next question, especially where an unplanned follow-up probe may be of value.

Follow the Leads

When a respondent provides a new thought or a glimpse of a different self, the interviewer is often given an added dimension for the story. While listening to an actor who played stupid thugs and very much looked the part, an interviewer suddenly heard chess terms. By simply asking, "Do you play chess?" he triggered a brilliant discussion of the game and a much more interesting story.

Make the Ending Count

End the interview on time unless the respondent wishes to continue. Summarize it in one or two sentences. Then ask the respondent to add to or amend your summary. Finally, turn your recorder off, close your notebook, express your thanks and prepare to leave. But don't rush off. Many a great quotation has been picked up at this relaxed time. Table 5.7 contains an example interview which shows how much of this discussion can be used in actual situations.

Compiling the Information

The transcript of an hour's interview will yield some 30 pages of double-spaced typed copy, usually more than you can use for the article planned. Now comes the critical task of pulling out the useful parts, verifying, integrating the material with what you already know, and writing the story.

Getting It Down

Make sure you have accurately recorded the important points. If you cannot find a record of a point, your respondent may still remember what was said. Don't stop until you've been through the entire set of notes and are confident that you've got it all.

Skimming Off the Cream

Next, look for the most useful material and "skim off the cream." The richest cream may be the quotations. If you have memorable ones, you will want to capture them precisely. Other key items are the answers to your specific questions, key points and your respondents' summaries.

Verifying Information

Unfortunately, some respondents remember incorrectly. Others consider an interview unimportant and may not worry about precision. Still others may provide the information you ask for, but not be familiar with its details, since it is handled at other

TABLE 5.7.   A Sample Interview Transcript

Note: This interview transcript demonstrates several interview strategies and tactics discussed in the chapter.

Interview

Q: Mr. Chase, I appreciate very much your taking time for this interview. As I told you on the phone, we're building interview files on important communications professionals at Cal State Fullerton.

A: Am I being flattered?

Q: Not really. But you were at the top of my list. As I said, we're going to put together several volumes of these interviews for students to read. We think they can learn a lot from them. Now, I asked to interview you on your career and opinions on public relations and you said OK. You agreed it would be all on the record too. Do you mind if I tape record?

A: No. That's fine.

Q: I see you got your bachelor's degree in history. I was a history major before I switched to PR. I have to confess that I found history incredibly boring. I guess you liked it, though.

A: Well, I may not have been so certain at the time, but I am a great believer in liberal arts to give the student a broad base of knowledge. History was great training because the discipline of historical research is very similar to market research in terms of the thinking process required.

Q: Mr. Chase, you started this firm in 1966. Now you have almost 200 employees just two decades later. How has the field of public relations changed since then?

A: The basics, the fundamentals are the same. There have been lots of technical changes. But I believe the single major difference is the growing involvement of PR professionals in the broadcast media. The industry used to be focused only on the print media. Now we have to deal with broadcasting.

Q: How do you mean that?

A: Well, we used to rely on print entirely for publicity, for example. Now we use broadcast PSAs, we get our clients on talk shows and we produce video news releases . . . that sort of thing.

Q: I see. Are there other changes worth listing?

A: A growing understanding on the part of clients of what public relations can and cannot do has caused us to alter tactics. People are learning that PR is no magic cure-all. It doesn't varnish or cover up the truth. Good reporters won't let you. A lot of very good public relations people have experience as reporters. Coming from the press side, they have an understanding of what is of news value and what is not. One of the worst things you can do is to assume you can use the press. Reporters know when they are being used.

Q: I don't understand. How do PR people try to use the press?

A: One way is by pushing something that should be an ad as legitimate news and trying to get it published free. You might get away with it once. But anyone who thinks he or she can use the press on an ongoing basis is in for a lot of trouble.

Q: Don't big companies have their own public relations departments?

A: Yes, but sometimes the advertising and public relations work is just too big a job for their staffs to handle. For some, we fill in on special projects. For others, we take on specific functions. Carl's Jr. [a fast-food chain], for instance, has its own public relations staff that handles one whole segment of its work. We do advertising and public relations relating to the stores. For some, we do it all. Many firms that don't have PR staffs find the cost of building one internally prohibitive, compared to using our service.

Q: You provide a rather complete service in advertising and public relations. How about research?

A: We have our own marketing research division. Occasionally we hire additional people for information gathering, but we mostly do it all. Today there's a tremendous amount of secondary data available if you know where to look. We begin with a thorough search and analysis of this secondary data. Then our staff does any primary research that's needed.

TABLE 5.7. A Sample Interview Transcript (*continued*)

Q: Is management generally receptive to PR recommendations?

A: I think more and more they are. Most managers are willing to sit and listen. They want to know the best way to handle a situation. But PR has to be there with the right advice. An example of this enlightened management/professional PR combination happened a few years ago after an accident off the California coast. A major oil drilling firm lost a boat and crew. Reporters rushed to the company headquarters for the story. The head of the PR department, an ex-editor, gave them a detailed explanation of what he knew. He discussed the possible causes of the accident. He was open and cooperative and answered all questions. You need management support to be able to do that. As a result, the media got their stories and the PR director and his company were commended for their cooperation . . . in print by a few.

Q: Now I'd like to get your opinions on the public relations career field. What are the major talents and skills necessary for success?

A: First, you need to know how to communicate, especially in writing. Second, and most importantly, you need to know how to think . . . to think through problems. You need not only a knowledge of business, but a knowledge of people. To solve problems, you need to know what is on people's minds and what's important to them.

Q: What about working under pressure?

A: Very important. Not too long ago we had a crash project to help a major land development company explain a complex issue on land leases. There was a heated dispute going on and the company wanted a settlement and wanted it quickly. Our job was to summarize the issue for press and homeowners in a way that could be understood. In a matter of days we put together a comprehensive presentation, including press kits, slide shows, speeches and releases. Our communications worked. That's another skill you need in PR: taking a very complex issue and translating it so that people will understand the message. We convey information and give general definitions. That's really what our job is all about.

Q: Well, finally, I'd like to ask what has been your greatest challenge in working in the field of public relations?

A: On what day? Public relations is a very exciting business. And taxing. I've gotten my gray hair out of it. I find new challenges every day. There are always problems . . . no, not problems. It's better to say "opportunities." I guess I'd have to say that each day is my greatest challenge. That's what makes it interesting.

Q: Well, thanks so much for your time and patience. I think all our students will learn a lot from this interview, because you make everything so clear. For me, it was exciting and informative . . . a great experience.

Thanks again.

A: It was my pleasure. Good luck on your project.

Source: An interview with Cochrane Chase, chairman of the board, Cochrane Chase, Livingston & Company Inc., Newport Beach, Calif. Interviewer: Mary Eileen Monahan, communications major, California State University, Fullerton. Class assignment, 1985, 15-minute interview. Used with permission.

levels. While it is proper to use respondents' opinions given to you in the interview, you must cross-check facts for accuracy and completeness just as you would any other story material. Notes which just don't make sense should be double-checked with the respondent first.

Integrating the Information

Once you are comfortable with the interview information, integrate it with the other data you have gathered for the story. While there may be some contradictions, most of the information should fit together smoothly. When it does not, you need to verify again. Once it all fits, you are ready to write your story.

Using the Information

Your interview was conducted to meet a unique writing need and you hope to use it for that. But there are several other uses of strong interviews:

Evaluation. Interview data can be used to evaluate the reliability and validity of other information, and vice versa.

Filing. Public relations writers can seldom afford the luxury of interviewing someone without having an immediate need for certain information. But information from interviews can be filed for later use also.

Facts and outlooks. One of the main purposes of interviews is to quickly get the latest accurate and authoritative information on a subject from a credible authority. Yours may be the latest from an expert on the subject.

Memorable quotations. We remember great quotations because someone recorded them. You can never be sure when one will pop up in an interview. Quotations can most often be looked for in certain areas: (a) Humor: "Rumors of my death are grossly exaggerated" (Mark Twain); (b) The Nature of Mankind: "The only thing we have to fear is fear itself" (Franklin D. Roosevelt); (c) Prophecy: "I have a dream" (Martin Luther King Jr.); or (d) Challenge: "Ask not what your country can do for you" (John F. Kennedy).

History. Interview transcripts are often valuable historical records. Interviews with prominent public relations practitioners and organizational heads who use public relations are well worth saving.

Research. Interview materials are sometimes useful research data. Interview records of public relations case studies are useful for review. Parallel experiences of leaders in a field, records of which have been preserved, are often starting points for theory building.

Reports. Writers are often called upon to write reports for an organization's internal use, based on one or more interviews with key members of the group. These may be in the form of separate assessments, or comprehensive evaluations, compiled by combining data from several interviews. Such reports let top managers see how individuals and groups view management concepts.

Speeches. Often a writer, charged with drafting a speech for a senior member of an organization, bases the content on an interview with the speaker. The interview helps determine the topic and the speaker's basic outlook. The writer then researches a subject which fits the speaking occasion and drafts a speech which reflects and supports the speaker's views.

Chapter Summary

This chapter examined the interview as a primary information gathering tool for the public relations writer. The interview is a planned discussion, with one or more interviewers asking questions which are answered by one or more respondents. Public relations writers most often use information gathering or personality interviews. Although interviews may be conducted in several ways, the telephone and personal interviews are the most valued and frequently used.

Careful interview preparation is a major factor in effective interviews. The interviewer must conduct research on the subject, the respondent and the respondent's organization. Then the public relations interviewer persuades the potential respondent to grant an interview. Next, questions are designed, ground rules set up and the interview planned.

The interviewer directs the session to get the desired information, taking advantage of new opportunities for information or attitudes revealed by the respondent. The interviewer is attentive and responsive, but not evaluative.

Information is compiled immediately after the interview to ensure accuracy. It is then integrated with secondary source data to get the most complete information possible.

Finally, this chapter reviewed uses of public relations interview material. Predominant uses are for facts and informed opinions, organizational reports and personality features.

A Writing Exercise

Discussion: In order to function effectively as a professional public relations writer, you must be able to completely plan, arrange, conduct and use interviews. Practice designing and asking questions with others involved in a similar assignment. Critique each others' questions. Are the questions clear? Are they pertinent to the subject being discussed? How can you make them better? Were you able to summarize the respondent's words? Don't go to the next step until you feel competent to compose a logical and appropriate set of questions, ask them with clarity, consideration and authority, and accurately record the responses.

Assignment: You have been assigned to write an interview-based feature. It is to be published as a new feature called "People in PR" being established in *Public Relations/Public Affairs Quarterly.* Your specific tasks assigned are to:

1. Conduct comprehensive research on an active public relations practitioner.
2. Prepare and turn in a complete interview plan outline on that practitioner.
3. Obtain a one-hour personal interview with that professional.
4. Conduct the interview, following the guidelines provided in this chapter.
5. Write and turn in a 7–10 page, double-spaced, feature based on that interview and your other research. Attach a brief bibliography to the feature, indicating all the sources used in your research. You should have at least four sources.

Unless told otherwise, use the following general outline for your feature:

1. Identity of the public relations practitioner
2. Sketch of the practitioner's organization
3. Description of the practitioner's youth and education
4. Description of the practitioner's professional experience
5. Discussion of the practitioner's present activities
   a. Professional
   b. Family
   c. Service
   d. Recreational
6. Discussion of a major project the practitioner has completed
7. The practitioner's personal perspective on the future of public relations

Food for Thought

1. Some people make excellent interview subjects. Their responses are lively. They use examples, tell stories, remember details and always answer the question asked. Others are evasive, noncommunicative, boring and so brief that they are almost not worth your while. What do you see as the qualities and skills that an effective respondent ought to have?

2. If you could interview anyone alive in the world today, whom would you pick? Why?

3. Some people take great care as respondents to give you precise information, without error. Others may be careless or purposely lie. What are the most effective ways for you to determine a respondent's credibility?

4. Research may be categorized as either secondary source, interview, survey or experiment. Which of these methods do you think is the most useful for public relations, overall? Why?

5. Some writers develop comprehensive features without even interviewing their subjects. Others spend months with respondents before they feel competent to write about them. If there were no limits, what do you think would be the optimum interview time you would want to spend with the U.S. Secretary of State in order to understand him well enough to write a personality profile on him for *People Magazine?* Justify your recommendation.

References for Further Study

Biagi, Shirley. *Interviews That Work: A Practical Guide for Journalists.* Belmont, Calif.: Wadsworth, 1986.

Brody, E. W. *The Business of Public Relations.* New York: Praeger, 1987, 172–184.

Cohen, Paula Marantz. *A Public Relations Primer: Thinking and Writing in Context.* Englewood Cliffs, N.J.: Prentice-Hall, 1987, 49–58.

Hohenberg, John. *The Professional Journalist,* 2nd ed. New York: Holt, Rinehart and Winston, 1969, 305–318.

Kerlinger, Fred N. *Foundations of Behavioral Research.* New York: Holt, Rinehart and Winston, 1966, 467–478.

Kornhauser, Arthur, and Paul B. Sheatsley. Appendix C: "Questionnaire Construction and Interview Procedure," in Claire Selltiz, Marie Jahoda, Morton Deutsch and Stuart W. Cook, eds., *Research Methods in Social Relations,* rev. ed. New York: Holt, Rinehart & Winston, 1959, 546–587.

Metzler, Ken. *Creative Interviewing.* Englewood Cliffs, N.J.: Prentice-Hall, 1977.

Metzler, Ken. *Creative Interviewing,* 2nd ed. Englewood Cliffs, N.J.: Prentice-Hall, 1989.

Newsom, Doug, and Bob Carrell. *Public Relations Writing: Form and Style,* 2nd ed. Belmont, Calif.: Wadsworth, 1986, 45–47.

Newsom, Doug, and Alan Scott. *This Is PR: The Realities of Public Relations,* 3rd ed. Belmont, Calif.: Wadsworth, 1985, 254–264.

Newsom, Doug, and James A. Wollert. *Media Writing: News for Mass Media.* Belmont, Calif.: Wadsworth, 1985, 193–223.

Nolte, Lawrence W., and Dennis L. Wilcox. *Effective Publicity: How to Reach the Public.* New York: Wiley, 1984, 196–204.

Reilly, Robert T. *Public Relations in Action.* Englewood Cliffs, N.J.: Prentice-Hall, 1981.

WRITING: CRAFTING PRECISE MESSAGES

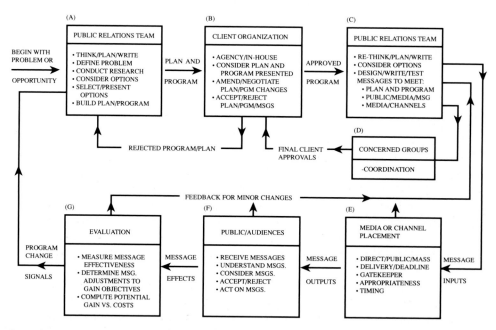

Once the plan and program are approved, the public relations writing team prepares to write the messages required. To do so effectively, they must be properly skilled and have the right tools. Considering all options, they conceive messages in the correct language, style, and approach to meet the plan's goals and objectives.

WRITING THE
PUBLIC RELATIONS MESSAGE • • •

6

Introduction

The written message is critical to all public relations activities. In fact, it is the source of almost every public communication, from press releases to *ad lib* remarks. This truth became especially evident during the summer of 1988. Americans expected that television programs and films would be canceled because of an extended broadcast and film writers' strike. But what surprised many was that several seemingly *ad lib* programs, such as NBC's "Johnny Carson Show," were also affected. Without scripted words to read, the performers could not be their best. Reruns became the order of the day.

Written preparation is valuable for all human communication. It helps speakers organize and shape their thoughts before speaking, allows writers to make clear and thoughtful proposals and provides previews and records of communication activities for others. Writing allows thought, planning, change and control. It is thus the *sine qua non* of public relations. To understand the importance of the written word, writers need to explore and understand human communication.

Some Observations on Human Communication

Planned human communication is **the systematic transfer of expressed thought from one mind to another.** Although we all communicate in unplanned ways, as when we unconsciously raise an eyebrow or use improper grammar, this discussion concentrates on "planned" communication. The thought we wish to convey is not always received and understood by our audiences. If you write, "Seven members of the Zulu tribe were killed today in South Africa," you might change the verb to "were murdered" and expect to mean the same thing. But many readers would not interpret the sentence the way you intended it.

Human communication is unique. Although most animals and plants seem to communicate, scientists believe that humans alone think in the abstract, plan for future events and combine sounds into complicated structures (Berko, Wolvin and Wolvin 1977, 5). We also use an open language system, whereas most animals use closed systems. We can say, "I'll have a New York cut, rare, please," or "Just an avocado salad, please," when we are hungry. But a dog can only bark. And one of the great gifts (sometimes frustrations) of the human language concerns the many ways in which we can say the same thing.

When humans write or speak, they reveal themselves. The accuracy, tone, values, perceptions, intelligence and sincerity of the writer are often revealed in a simple paragraph. Since public relations writers often compose messages for others to communicate, they must take care not to let their tones and perceptions appear to be those of the persons who will deliver the messages they write. This is not a simple task. Many times we don't realize how consistent our language patterns are. With the help of computers, researchers have compared texts through comprehensive content analysis and found remarkably consistent patterns in widely differing works by an author (Holsti 1969, 70–80).

Although humans communicate through all five senses, written communication must depend solely on the sense of sight. Thus, having a written communication received, understood and acted upon favorably is more difficult than when communicating using other senses. Also, reading and writing require high levels of psychomotor coordination which don't even begin to develop until several years after a child has learned to speak. Many never master reading and writing skills. It is estimated that one-third of all adults in the U.S. cannot read street signs or sign their names.

Writing as a Communication Process

Like all human communication, writing and reading are extremely complex. But following through a simple communication model can help you understand the process (DeFleur and Dennis 1988, 14–23).

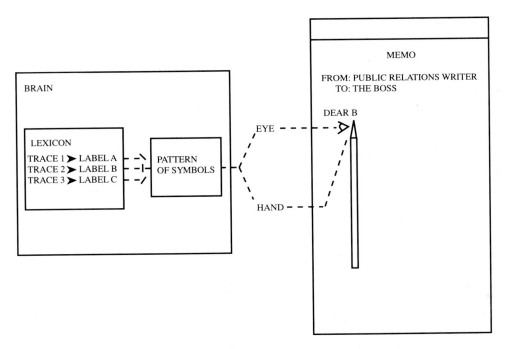

▶ **Figure 6.1.** Writing a memo. Each of us apparently has a lexicon or dictionary of matching memory traces and symbols. In order to write, we locate the configuration of traces which conforms to the thought we wish to express. We then assign labels to elements of the thought, and convert these to symbols for communication and record these patterns of symbols through eyes and hands for the reader to interpret.

Suppose you, a writer, wish to write your boss a memo about a speech you are drafting for her. Based on the meaning you intend, you pull out a mental concept of the appropriate symbols, or labels from among the billions of trace configurations stored in your brain (see figure 6.1).

Your mind and body then convert these symbols into words on paper, which you hope will be meaningful to your boss. You sign the memo (a separate communication process) and send it. When your boss looks at it, she converts the symbols back into meanings through the process of reverse labeling (see figure 6.2).

These meanings are then combined and she interprets what your words mean. The more psychologically, socially, culturally and linguistically you and the boss are alike, the fewer distractions and perceptual problems she has while reading, the greater the likelihood that what she understands will be what you meant.

Some scholars think the brain works like a computer as it goes through millions of symbol-to-meaning comparisons in its "dictionary," trying to get the right meaning of the received word combinations. Since we believe that every life experience is stored in the brain, it's no wonder the system is imperfect.

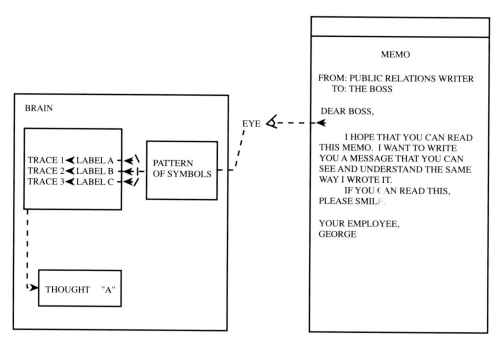

► **Figure 6.2.**   Reading a memo. Having received a message, the reader begins a process approximately reverse to that of the writer. Perceiving symbols on paper, the reader applies meaning to the symbols through his or her lexicon of mental traces. These are then combined and the result interpreted to provide a thought.

Writing doubly complicates communication because it distances receiver from communicator, making feedback and clarification difficult. This enhances the probability of error. Yet this same characteristic makes distribution easier.

Writing the public relations message, then, is difficult, complex and prone to considerable misinterpretation. Yet, having written it, the writer extends the power and flexibility of the communication process.

Essentials of Public Relations Writing

Public relations writing further complicates the writing process because the skilled writer must be able to effectively write about many subjects (e.g., AIDS, new products, personalities, issues), for many clients (e.g., corporations, charities, government agencies, politicians) and channels (personal conversation, memos, speeches, radio, television, film, print). But there are some universal skills and properties that are fundamental to all public relations writing. Several of these are discussed elsewhere in the book. Here we'll note those dealing with qualifications and tools.

Qualifications

The effective public relations writer has a sound liberal arts education. Most students acquire this through the general education programs of their universities. Accredited public relations programs require students to take about three-fourths of their courses outside communication, mostly in the liberal arts. Some writers are self-taught and educate themselves by reading. In either case, the search for knowledge never ends.

Professional writers constantly update their knowledge by voraciously reading books, professional journals, newspapers, articles, published speeches and materials from radio, television and film. Often such books and programs have caused revolutionary changes in society. Harriet Beecher Stowe's *Uncle Tom's Cabin* speeded the end of slavery in the U.S. Rachael Carson's *Silent Spring* made the environmental movement popular. Ralph Nader's *Unsafe at Any Speed* helped launch the consumer movement. U.S. network television coverage of the North Vietnamese Tet Offensive in 1968 caused millions of Americans to stop supporting U.S. involvement in Vietnam. Exposure to such information positions public relations writers to anticipate societal change and help their clients move with it, rather than against it.

Such knowledge also helps public relations writers understand the intellectual environment of the times. They may not always want to write at the highest intellectual level, but that is where great ideas come from.

Public relations writers should also understand the value of professional education and training. This education should never end. Writers, no matter how skilled, need occasional seminars and workshops to help polish their work. You might wish periodically to take courses and gain professional experience in newspaper, radio, television and motion picture writing. All of these could make you a better writer. And it is important that you are able to write for all these channels.

Tools

Having the proper tools is essential to effective writing. Competent writers in public relations require a fairly standard set of working tools (Nolte and Wilcox 1984, 97–101; Estrin 1987, 8–9). Fundamental to good writing are a thesaurus, a style manual and a dictionary. If you are using *The Associated Press Stylebook and Libel Manual,* it is important that one dictionary on hand be *Webster's New World,* since it is that stylebook's authorized sourcebook.

A few specialty references are mentioned here. Depending on your writing area, you may need the *Dictionary of Foreign Words and Phrases, Merriam-Webster's Sports Dictionary* or the *Dictionary of American Slang.*

You will also want an annual report, policy statements and pertinent publications of every client you write for, as well as a file of current journals, magazines and newsletters which concern the client's business. For public relations itself, you'll probably want to keep a file of publications such as *Communication World, Public Relations Journal, Public Relations Quarterly, Public Relations Research Annual* and *Public Relations Review* in your library. Further, you'll need at least one book each on public relations basics, research, writing and your own specialty within public relations. There are also many valuable media directories which you'll need (see, for example, Nolte and Wilcox 1984, 255). Finally, you'll need a copy of the *Professional's Guide to Public Relations Services* or an equivalent source. As you'll see in chapter 11, you may often contract out for public relations writing and other support.

You will also want to build your own information files of ideas, releases you have written, clippings, fact sheets, biographies, area laws affecting client communications and articles on subjects you might need to write about.

Few writers can afford all these references. But some organizations are willing to pay for at least the most important ones. And, in the long run, you'll want to have your own copy of most of them, purchasing them one at a time as the need or opportunity arises.

Actions

There are also essential considerations on how public relations writers should pursue their trade. They must be able to put themselves in the place of their clients, then think and write from the perspectives of those clients. They also must target specific publics. The journalist normally writes for a single generalized audience (all newspaper readers in Albany) and fashions a story but once. But the public relations writer must learn to adjust the same basic message to several publics through several channels. For example, a Red Cross information message may appear in a brochure for patients, a corporate newsletter article, a public service announcement for young adults on drive-time radio and a video news release for cable TV. In each case, the same basic message must be adjusted to a different mass medium and audience. Finally, the public relations writer's message must often go through several criticisms and approvals before it is received by an audience. All these controls on activities help reinforce the criticality of the public relations message.

Results of Public Relations Messages

This commentary is on the general effectiveness of public relations writing. In chapter 12 we will look at ways to measure the effectiveness of specific messages. Often the field is seen in extremes. Whenever sales and profits are low in some organizations, public relations people are the first to be laid off, indicating a senior management belief that their efforts are not critical. To the contrary, others see public relations as a process for persuading people to undertake things they would not otherwise do.

In truth, public relations writing is nearly always effective, but seldom startling. Julius Caesar's writing in *Acta Diurna* helped convince Romans of his greatness. Ben Franklin's writings helped bring about the American Revolution and freedom for the colonies. P. T. Barnum's stories convinced people to come to his circus. Ivy Lee's press releases about John D. Rockefeller's generosity helped change the oil man's image. Franklin D. Roosevelt and John F. Kennedy (with the help of speech writers) made Americans believe in themselves. Today we can expect that "over time good public relations will have a positive effect on profits or organizational success" (Haberman and Dolphin 1988, 12), but that immediate response may be hard to measure.

There are a few ways we can make useful inferences, however. One is by increasing employment. There are about 172,000 public relations and publicity writers employed in the U.S. today, nine times as many as in 1950 (Cutlip, Center and Broom 1985, 59; U.S. Department of Labor statistics). Secondly, those making use of public relations writing are, by and large, more successful than those who are not. Third, it has been estimated that up to 10 percent of local news in newspapers and 7 percent of broadcast news comes from public relations releases. If publicity is the intent, American mass media help the public relations writer achieve success.

Some Direct Results of Public Relations Messages

Direct results of public relations writing are difficult to measure. In the first place, it is difficult to tell what part of the public relations campaign contributed what portion of the campaign's success. Secondly, since we practice public relations in an active and ever-changing world, we cannot easily tell what portion of our successes are attributable to the public relations campaign and what part to outside factors. One might truly believe, for example, that an information and persuasion campaign was the primary factor in a reduction of gang-related killings in Los Angeles. But if the reduction of violence coincided with a 30 degree drop in 100+ summer temperatures, one could not be sure. Nevertheless, some positive results can, in good part, be credited to public relations writing. Here are four examples:

1. Stung by complaints in 1983 that increased prices for natural gas were causing the poor to go without heat, Oklahoma Natural Gas implemented its "Share the Warmth" campaign (Newsom and Scott 1985, 335). Messages invited each customer to contribute toward the bill of some person who could not afford to pay. The appeal was made in the climate of the "new federalism," with its emphasis on the private sector assuming charitable obligations formerly held by the government. Response was overwhelming.

2. Northeast Utilities and Carl Byoir & Associates Public Relations won a 1982 Public Relations Society of America Silver Anvil award for a campaign to get customers to participate in energy conservation projects (Nager and Allen 1984, 169–170). The campaign resulted in energy savings equal to the cost of 281,000 barrels of oil.

3. Speeches, prepared responses to questions, a public information handbook, PSAs, newspaper announcements and a film were used by the nonprofit La Mancha Group in Texas to find "hidden" handicapped children and get them to public schools (Newsom and Scott 1985, 373–378). Considerably more than 10,000 handicapped children were found.

4. The Bell System found that its employees recalled, on an average, about 36 percent of articles in three issues of its weekly newspaper. One article on employment office hiring scored 56 percent in this unaided recall study (Tirone 1977, 29).

Public relations writers' messages often get broadcast and published and get the desired results. However, considerable effort is needed to better quantify these results, so that management will be able to effectively measure the writer's contribution to the organization's success (see chapter 12).

Taming the Beast

Writing is an unusual process. When one begins to write, it is difficult to know what to say or how to say it. Words and phrases which roll off our tongues look strange when we commit them to paper. After a bit of practice, however, the ideas flow smoothly and sometimes effortlessly into prose. Then the problem becomes the fact that the words seem to control you, rather than the other way around. You have probably read about writers who seemingly lost control of their plots and the characters in novels. Something similar happens to public relations writers. We tend to slip into regionalisms, slang and informality. While each of these is often useful, we want to control when we should use them, not give in to our subconscious selves. It takes mental concentration and practice for us to tame the writing beast in us. What follows are some techniques which may assist you in the taming process.

Use Operational English

"Operational English" is a special use of "Standard American English." Standard American English is that which is used in literature and print, taught in school and used by most U.S. newspapers, magazines and broadcasters. Nonstandard English is language that is influenced by foreign languages, regionalisms, slang and special language. "Ain't" is in the dictionary, but it is nonstandard, so we do not use it. If you said, "I am totally going with you, actually," most of your friends would understand and accept a touch of "Valley," but an English-speaking visitor from Siberia might be confused. If you listened to a recording and said, "That's bad," some people could tell from the tone of your voice whether you really thought it was bad, or were speaking

A PROFESSIONAL TIP:
Learning to Be Your Own Editor

The one thing I've always been grateful for in my 30 years of corporate communication work has been the training I had in writing. As a freshman at Hamilton College, I was treated to the most rigorous writing experience anyone can imagine. Each paper was reduced to a mass of red-inked comments from a man named George Nesbitt. He was relentless. No mechanical error, no nonsequitur, no careless reference ever escaped his gaze. For weeks I feared and hated the man. But, God, could he teach freshmen to write!

For the next three years, I carefully avoided any course he had taught. What I could not avoid was the compulsion he forced on me to check and recheck, to rewrite, and to criticize my own thinking mercilessly. That one miserable required course was doubtless the first stone in the foundation of my career in communication. Wherever you are, George, I owe you.

Roger D'Aprix, ABC, is vice president and human resource communication consultant with Towers, Perrin, Forster & Crosby, an international management consulting firm. D'Aprix has more than 30 years experience as a consultant and communication manager with Xerox, General Electric and Bell & Howell. He has authored five books on employee communication issues, including *Communicating for Productivity,* and in 1978 was named a Fellow by the International Association of Business Communicators, the highest honor a member can receive.

"Jazz" and meant that you were favorably impressed. But most may not. Here are some nonstandard English variants you should normally avoid in writing for public relations, but might wish to use for a specific purpose. See how many you recognize:

Black English
Bush Talk
Hootch Talk
Jazz
Southern
Sunbear
Tex-Mex
Valley

Operational English is standard American English that avoids stilted usage. You have noticed that advertising often uses nonstandard English, in part to avoid sounding stilted ("Winston tastes good like a cigarette should"). As public relations writers, we tend to avoid the "good grammar or good taste" dilemma by using standard English that is neither stilted nor awkward. Note these examples:

Example One:
Correct Standard American: Neither they nor I am pleased with the score.
Correct Operational: They are not pleased with the score, and neither am I.

Example Two:
Correct Standard American: The team went to their homes.
Correct Operational: Members of the team went to their homes.

Example Three:
Correct Standard American: There is a dog, three cats and a tropical fish in the burning house.
Correct Operational: A dog, three cats and a tropical fish are in the burning house.

Example Four:
Correct Standard American: He is the only one of the Kappas who have thanked me.
Correct Operational: He is the only Kappa who has thanked me.

Example Five:
Correct Standard American: Every freshman, sophomore, junior and senior was present.
Correct Operational: All freshmen, sophomores, juniors and seniors were present.

You would probably not have selected the standard American versions of the above examples. But if you came across them and checked them in a grammar text, you might have been tempted to leave them, since they are all grammatically correct. The purpose of operational English is to use correct language which is also smooth and normal.

Formal and Informal Operational English

Like standard American English, operational English can be formal or informal. Formal English uses only proper words. It avoids slang, contractions and colloquial expressions. It should be used in essays and formal reports. It is a more precise usage than informal English.

Informal English allows contractions, colloquial expressions and slang, when these will be clearly understood by readers. It resembles spoken English and is more casual. It is used in very informal writing found in some broadcasting and print. Here are two examples:

Example One:
Informal: Let's get together and brainstorm that.
Formal: Let us meet and discuss that idea thoroughly.

Example Two:
Informal: Buzz me when you're free. We'll do happy hour.
Formal: Call me if you are not engaged Friday afternoon. We can meet at the bar and relax over drinks.

Public relations writing uses both informal and formal English. And, although grammar stresses avoiding using both in the same work, some informal usage is almost unavoidable (Dornan and Dawe 1987, 214). With operational English, one must use slang, regional expressions and jargon with great care. This is to avoid confusing the reader. If you wrote a memo to your boss which said, "One journalist didn't like my response and came totally unglued," he might or might not follow your meaning. In parts of the South, you might leave no doubt as to your intentions if you said, "I'm fixing to go." But the public relations writer can't usually count on an all-southern audience.

Operational English also avoids formally correct archaic and obsolete words, unless they are to be used for a special purpose. "Alack" is listed in the dictionary as an expression of regret, but is archaic and most of your readers would have to look it up to determine its meaning, or guess at it. Either way, you would lose clarity by using it, except in special cases. By the same token, "cote" once meant "to pass," but that meaning is now obsolete and you would not want to use the word at all. Chapter 7 discusses the specific use of informal language, such as jargon and technical language. It also covers writing we wish to avoid at all costs, such as that which reflects sexism, fuzzy thinking, puffery and pretentious language.

Use of Writing Techniques

Certain writing techniques are used with great care in operational English.

1. **Neologisms** are seldom used because they consist of words and phrases so new to the language that they are not yet generally known. For example, you might use "Watergate" in a political writing because it is in common use, but avoid "Irangate" because it is not. "Gridlock" would be acceptable to most American readers, but "time warp" might not be.

2. **Loaded words** are words that evoke either positive or negative responses in many people and must be used with full knowledge of that potential. For example, "emaciated" means abnormally lean, a condition many women desire for themselves. But if you wrote that your corporate president was a "tall, graceful and emaciated woman," you would be using loaded language, since emaciated currently means "horribly thin" to many in the U.S. Comparisons of positively and negatively loaded words give you an idea of how this tool may be used or misued:

Positive	*Negative*
I am plump.	You are fat.
I am persuaded.	You are brainwashed.
I receive a stipend.	You get a handout.
I belong to a club.	You are part of a gang.
I am economical.	You are a skinflint.

In operational English we use only **idioms** which are well known to the publics we address. Idioms are phrases which have meanings not revealed by the combined definitions of their words. If you wrote that your CEO was "cool as a cucumber" during a crisis, most publics would understand. But if you said that he had "gone off the deep end," they might not.

3. **Figurative language** must also be used with caution in operational English. It can be effective with the appropriate audience, but confusing to others. If you wrote that using a new computer-controlled lawn mower "is like falling off a log," your Japanese readers might fail to see the connection implied by that **simile. A metaphor** makes such a comparison indirectly. If you write in a company brochure that "your first day with the company will remind you of your first day of school," you will create differing impressions, since not all students enjoyed that experience.

4. **Personification** is a useful tool. "The first time you sail this new ship, you will like its intelligence as it climbs over the waves and leaps to catch the wind" is a sentence which converts a boat into an intelligent friend.

5. **Hyperbole** allows you to create a useful exaggeration. If you wrote that "America's acceptance of Bush's Star Wars proposal marks the beginning of World War III," you might not be certain that the outcome would be so tragic, but you would be letting people know of the gravity with which your political client viewed the situation.

6. In public relations writing we often find it necessary to use **euphemisms**—words or phrases substituted for ones which seem too harsh for the situation. Operational English sanctions such a use when it serves the purpose without distortion. "Street person" might be a more pleasant way to refer to someone called a "beggar" or "bum," for example. The public relations writer must take care not to use euphemisms to alter reality—a charge frequently made. It may make the client's management feel better to say that "100 employees of the Gromet Company were afforded pre-retirement release," but it can't change the fact that they were either "laid off" or "fired." You may make some people happy by calling the person who picks up garbage a "sanitation engineer," but the title would be technically incorrect unless that person operated or supervised the operation of engines or technical equipment.

7. Operational English requires that usage be logical in accordance with the **Western system of logic.** Sometimes public relations writers are pressed to accept logical fallacy in writing copy. Such pressure must be resisted.

One of the most frequent logical breaches in political writing is called **ad hominem.** The ad hominem argument attacks the person of the opponent, rather than the position represented. "George Bush was born with a silver foot in his mouth" implies two things. One of these is that a person born to wealth cannot be an effective president.

Association implies that something is worthy because of someone associated with it. "President Reagan supported the United Charities and so should you," may help get donations, but it doesn't necessarily follow that you should contribute.

Bandwagon is a kind of association fallacy in which the association is "everybody." If you write that "everyone in the company subscribes to the *New World News,*" you are asking the reader to "get on the bandwagon," so he or she won't risk isolation from the group.

Either/or arguments are useful. It is true that "your body must take in fluids or you will die." But a false either/or is dishonest. George Santana's prophecy that "those who cannot remember the past are condemned to repeat it" is not completely true, although it contains a great deal of truth.

The **false analogy** contains kernels of truth. The writer first reminds you how two things are alike. He or she then projects a similarity that may not be true. "People are like machines. They need energy to operate. If treated too roughly, they will break down. All human moving parts should be replaced periodically." This carries the parallel between people and machines one step too far.

The **non sequitur** stipulates a conclusion that does not necessarily follow from the premise. "You should contribute to Amalgamated Charities. Last year 50,000 Americans who did not contribute died. If you want to live, give now."

Overgeneralization reaches a conclusion from inadequate evidence. Example: "In 1980, more than 1,000 corporations had public relations staffs of 20 or more persons. In 1985 only 500 corporations had staffs that large. Corporate public relations is doomed."

Oversimplification makes conclusions based on noncritical evidence, ignoring more important facts. "Effective public relations writing requires technical precision in spelling, abbreviation, capitalization and punctuation. If you master these skills, you will be an effective public relations writer." The latter statement ignores other requirements for the effective writer.

A **post hoc** argument presumes that because one event follows another, the first causes the second. Example: "When we had a corporate newsletter, employee morale was high. After we discontinued the newsletter, employee morale plummeted. Newsletters cause high employee morale."

Practice Word Control

Another way to "control the beast" in our writing is to practice word, phrase and sentence control. Give yourself some limitations that will give you a challenge in producing effective text. Once you have mastered such a limitation, move on to another, returning to it occasionally. Note the following example and analyze it. Then read the instructions that follow the example. Did you figure out what the instructions would be by reading the text?

EXAMPLE ONE:

Dear Friend:

Bill can't walk. He has no feet. He was born that way. But he wants to play ball just like his friends. Can he do that? Yes! There is a way! Fleet Feet helps kids get new feet. The feet are not as good as real feet. But they work. Kids who wear them can run and play.

You can help Bill and lots of kids like him. Take this note home to your mom and dad. Ask them to write a check to "Fleet Feet." Send it to me. I'll make sure it gets there. It will help kids with no feet get Fleet Feet.

Don't wait. Do it now! Bill wants to play so much. Then one day you'll see this kid play ball. And you'll see that he has Fleet Feet. And you'll know you helped make his dream come true. And Bill will love you. How do I know that? I'm Bill. Thank you.

Your Friend,
Bill Bare
Box One
New York, NY 10000

The assignment for the above exercise was:

Instructions: Write an appeal for 9-year-old Dallas school children to contribute to Fleet Feet, a worthy charitable cause which provides artificial feet for children. Use informal Operational English. Write only one-syllable words that 9-year-olds will know. Use no commas, semicolons, colons, dashes or quotation marks. Make all sentences less than 11 words long.

But short words and sentences don't have to mean simple writing. Here is an example. It comes from the Gospel of St. John, as written for the King James version of the Bible:

Example Two:

In the beginning was the Word. And the Word was with God, and the Word was God.

The same was in the beginning with God.

All things were made by him; and without him was not made anything that was made.

In him was life; and the life was the light of men.

And the light shineth in darkness; and the darkness comprehended it not.

In the above passage, the words and sentences are reasonably short. And the language is relatively simple. But note the mystical nature of the passage and the complexity of its thought. Some thoughts can only be simplified so much.

Example Three:

Harold G. Gainesville owns and runs Calnihon, a U.S.-Asian trading company worth $600 million. He plays handball daily. Six feet tall, he looks trim at 201 pounds. His handsome face is accented by a scar. That and a slight limp are reminders of a World War II bomber mission which won him a Purple Heart. He speaks expansively, gazing through blue eyes: "I am Calnihon. I built it from scratch after the war."

Noting the company's present size, he says he'll double it in the next decade, repeating his Asian success in Latin America. "This will be America's top trading company before I'm done," he boasts.

The assignment for the above exercise was as follows:

Instructions: Describe Harold G. Gainesville in 100 words or less. The description is for a personality capsule in the new expansion brochure the company is producing.

Base your description on these notes:

Gainesville is sole owner, president and CEO of Calnihon, a $600 million trading company which owns two ships and 10 cargo planes. The company exports California agricultural products to Japan and imports small electrical appliances from the Orient. Gainesville started the company in 1945 after returning from military service in World War II. He was a B-29 pilot and flew 55 bombing raids over Japan.

Gainesville is exactly 6 feet tall, weighs 201 pounds. At age 68, he still keeps his body in shape by playing handball daily. He looks trim and fit. He has a fair complexion. His gray hair was once blond. His face has wrinkles and there are age spots on his hands. He is wearing a dark blue suit, with a white shirt and red and blue striped silk tie. His shoes are black alligator leather. His desk is a large traditional executive style made of Philippine mahogany. The walls of the office are off-white. Their only decorations are an Oriental painting of Japan's Mount Fuji and a traditional American painting of the Golden Gate Bridge.

His eyes are blue and he sports a California tan. There is a burn scar on his left cheek and he walks with a slight limp, both the result of an anti-aircraft shell exploding in his B-29 cockpit. He received a Purple Heart for that mission. His smile is infectious and he is still strikingly handsome. He speaks aggressively, like the "take charge" kind of person he is. "I am Calnihon," he boasts. "I built it from scratch after the war. I bought one worn-out plane, using my GI Bill, repaired, loaded and flew it myself. I never knew if the office would be there when I got back from a trip. But Vera kept the creditors off our backs. It was scary but, God, it was exciting. And we made it."

Gainesville turns to the photographs on the desk. They consist of a picture of his wife and separate photos of four sons and their wives. "The boys are all out of college and doing well now," he says. "I tried to interest them in Calnihon, but they said they didn't want to be clones of me. I lost Vera last year. Cancer. It's not the same without her. Calnihon is all I have left."

Gainesville confidently revealed his plans to double the size of Calnihon in five years, repeating his Asian trade success in Latin America. "This will be America's top trading company before I'm done," Gainesville said. He indicated that he expected to head Calnihon until his death. "I want to die in the saddle," he said. "What do I have to retire for? I may be around another 20 years."

Practice your own beast-taming exercises. Determine your weakest area and work to improve in it. It may be illogical sequences, puffery, long sentences, passive voice, regionalisms, nonstandard usage or one or more of the areas cited in this chapter. You know best where you need to work. Practice your writing every day. Learn to control the beast.

Chapter Summary

In this chapter we reviewed some basic considerations which must be made in writing the public relations message. First, we looked at the importance of writing to communicate, especially all forms of public relations communication. Examining human communication, we considered its uniqueness as an open system of communication and the limitations placed on a writer attempting to communicate through print.

What is known of the mental-physical process of writing was sketched in order to reinforce the complexity of the task. Essential skills of public relations writing examined were: qualifications, tools and actions.

The general purposes of public relations writing were discussed. The writer addresses the client on its publics, and vice versa.

Results of public relations writing noted were actions, growth in numbers of PR writers required and windows of opportunity kept open for public relations writing in mass media.

We then looked at ways to control the writing product. Operational English was seen as standard American English which avoids stilted usage. For public relations purposes, it was seen as accepting both formal and informal styles and avoiding or following careful usage of special techniques such as neologisms, loaded words, similes, metaphors, personifications and euphemisms. It also was described as following Western logic.

Finally, techniques were discussed and demonstrated to practice word, phrase and sentence control. The complexity of writing for public relations requires an understanding of several writing techniques and close adherence to rules of proper usage.

A Writing Exercise

Situation. Harold G. Gainesville, CEO of Calnihon, has just received notice that he will be awarded the annual Japan-American Friendship Trophy in Tokyo next week. The trophy is awarded each year by the Government of Japan to the Japanese or American citizen who has done the most to enhance the friendship between the two nations during the previous year. The trophy will be presented by the emperor.

Assignment. You are a writer in the public relations division of Calnihon. Drawing on the above information and that presented earlier in the section on Gainesville, prepare a 200-word release ($+/-$ 20 words) on the announcement for submission to the *Los Angeles Times.*

Follow these rules: (1) Make all sentences active voice; (2) Use no more than two commas; (3) Make no sentence longer than 15 words; and (4) Do not use any three-syllable words.

An Editing Exercise

Assignment. Examine each of the following sentences. Then convert each into informal "operational English," as discussed in this chapter.

1. Every text, reference book, journal, anthology and index was stacked on my library shelf.
2. Mr. Reagan was the only one of the senior citizens present who have remained calm about the tax increase.
3. There is a Frenchman, two Germans and three Poles taking part in the World War II remembrance ceremony.
4. The group produced their dossiers and began to read them.

5. Neither they nor I am going to accompany the CEO to the stockholders' meeting.
6. If a person wants to succeed in a writing career, he or she needs to be able to express himself or herself both verbally and through writing to his or her significant others and relevant publics.
7. If one wishes to succeed in a military career, one must pursue one's dreams through education and experience to one's final destiny of general officer.
8. The term "Indo-European" is expressive of the geographical extent of this extensive family of languages.
9. To exemplify this design, the reader may consider an extension proposed as an illustration of the concept of the equal pay for equal work.
10. When estimating missing values for a table of numbers, it should never be assumed that the estimated value is, in fact, equal to the value which would actually be obtained in the cell containing the missing observation.

Food for Thought

1. In this chapter we note that plants and animals "seem to communicate." Presuming that plants do communicate, describe the public relations approach the giant sequoias might take in modern America to ensure their survival. Write a PSA to be aired by U.S. radio stations, pleading the redwood cause from the perspective of the sequoias.
2. Go back 4,000 years in time. Print has just been invented. But it is only possible to carve messages in stone with a chisel, an expensive and painstaking task. As the Babylonian director of agriculture, what reasons would you give the king to convince him to publish your bulletin on crop plantings and pest control?
3. If you worked for the Ford Motor Company, how would you go about justifying the purchase of a complete reference book set for your public relations division to your boss?
4. You are a public relations writer for a cancer prevention group in Miami. Last week you wrote and distributed a release stating that Cuban Americans have a higher incidence rate of breast cancer than any other group. The health editor of the *Miami Herald* ran the story, based on your information alone. It has caused quite an uproar in the Cuban community. Now you learn that the information was incorrect. Your health researcher misplaced a decimal point. The Cuban breast cancer incidence is 0.010 percent higher than all other groups, not 10 percent higher, as you stated. The difference between groups is statistically insignificant. How will you approach the editor to try to regain his confidence?
5. Suppose you have prepared the image-building television ad for a university whose president could not tolerate Beatles' music. It was an excellent ad. How would you go about trying to persuade him to let it be used?

References for Further Study

Becker, Samuel L. *Discovering Mass Communication,* 2nd ed. Glenview, Ill.: Scott, Foresman, 1987.

Berko, Roy M., Andrew D. Wolvin and Darlyn R. Wolvin. *Communicating: A Social and Career Focus.* Boston: Houghton Mifflin, 1977, 3–25.

Bivins, Thomas. *Handbook for Public Relations Writing.* Lincolnwood, Ill.: NTC Business Books, 1988, 225–254.

Cutlip, Scott M., Allen H. Center and Glen M. Broom. *Effective Public Relations,* 6th ed. Englewood Cliffs, N.J.: Prentice-Hall, 1985.

DeFleur, Melvin L., and Everette E. Dennis. *Understanding Mass Communication,* 3rd ed. Boston: Houghton Mifflin, 1988.

Dornan, Edward A., and Charles W. Dawe. *The Brief English Handbook,* 2nd ed. Boston: Little, Brown & Co., 1987, 212–244.

Epstein, Jay. *News from Nowhere.* New York: Random House, 1973.

Estrin, Herman A. "Effective Tools of Writing." *Community College Journalist* (Winter 1987): 8–9.

Flesch, Rudolf. *The Art of Readable Writing.* New York: Harper & Row, 1974.

Fowler, H. Ramsey. *The Little, Brown Handbook,* 3rd ed. Boston: Little, Brown, 1986, 399–461.

French, Christopher W., ed. *The Associated Press Stylebook and Libel Manual.* New York: The Associated Press, 1987.

Grunig, James E., and Todd Hunt. *Managing Public Relations.* New York: Holt, Rinehart & Winston, 1984.

Haberman, David A., and Harry A. Dolphin. *Public Relations: The Necessary Art.* Ames, Iowa: Iowa State U. Press, 1988.

Hayakawa, S. I. *Language in Thought and Action.* New York: Harcourt Brace Jovanovich, 1978.

Hayakawa, S. I. *Through the Communication Barrier.* New York: Harper & Row, 1979.

Holsti, Ole R. *Content Analysis for the Social Sciences and Humanities.* Reading, Mass.: Addison-Wesley, 1969.

Martin, L. John, and Anju Grover Chaudhary. *Comparative Mass Media Systems.* White Plains, N.Y.: Longman, 1983.

McGuire, William J. "Nature of Attitudes and Attitude Change," Gardner Lindzey and Elliott Aronson, eds., *Handbook of Social Psychology,* 2nd ed., 3. Reading, Mass.: Addison-Wesley, 1968, 136–314.

Miller, Don E. *The Book of Jargon.* New York: Macmillan, 1981.

Nager, Norman R., and T. Harrell Allen. *Public Relations: Management by Objectives.* New York: Longman, 1984.

Newsom, Doug, and Alan Scott. *This Is PR: The Realities of Public Relations,* 3rd ed. Belmont, Calif.: Wadsworth, 1985.

Newsom, Doug, and James A. Wollert. *Media Writing: News for the Mass Media.* Belmont, Calif.: Wadsworth, 1985.

Nixon, Richard M. *R.N.: The Memoirs of Richard Nixon.* New York: Gosset & Dunlap, 1978.

Nolte, Lawrence W., and Dennis L. Wilcox. *Effective Publicity: How to Reach the Public.* New York: Wiley, 1984.

Pavlik, John V. *Public Relations: What Research Tells Us.* Newbury Park, Calif.: Sage, 1987.

Pei, Mario. *Weasel Words: The Art of Saying What You Don't Mean.* New York: Harper & Row, 1978.

Pei, Mario. *The Story of the English Language.* New York: Simon & Schuster, 1972.

Professional's Guide to Public Relations Services (annual). New York: Weiner.

Pye, Michael. *Everyday Japanese Characters.* Tokyo: Hokuseido Press, 1977.

Ray, Michael L. "Marketing Communication and the Hierarchy of Effects." Peter Clarke, ed., *New Models for Communication Research. Annual Reviews of Communication Research,* 2. Beverly Hills, Calif.: Sage, 1973, 147–176.

Roget's International Thesaurus, 4th ed.

Strunk, W., and E. B. White. *The Elements of Style.* New York: Macmillan, 1978.

"Two-Thirds of U.S. Adults Read Dailies." *Presstime.* June, 1984, 38.

Tirone, James S. "Measuring the Bell System's Public Relations." *Public Relations Review* 3:4 (1977):21–23.

Webster's New World Dictionary, Second College Edition.

Zissner, William. *On Writing Well.* New York: Harper & Row, 1980.

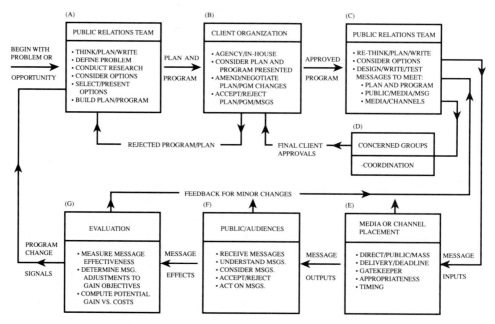

(A)		(B)		(C)
PUBLIC RELATIONS TEAM		**CLIENT ORGANIZATION**		**PUBLIC RELATIONS TEAM**

BEGIN WITH PROBLEM OR

OPPORTUNITY

(A) PUBLIC RELATIONS TEAM
- THINK/PLAN/WRITE
- DEFINE PROBLEM
- CONDUCT RESEARCH
- CONSIDER OPTIONS
- SELECT/PRESENT OPTIONS
- BUILD PLAN/PROGRAM

PLAN AND

PROGRAM

(B) CLIENT ORGANIZATION
- AGENCY/IN-HOUSE
- CONSIDER PLAN AND PROGRAM PRESENTED
- AMEND/NEGOTIATE PLAN/PGM CHANGES
- ACCEPT/REJECT PLAN/PGM/MSGS

APPROVED

PROGRAM

(C) PUBLIC RELATIONS TEAM
- RE-THINK/PLAN/WRITE
- CONSIDER OPTIONS
- DESIGN/WRITE/TEST MESSAGES TO MEET:
  - PLAN AND PROGRAM
  - PUBLIC/MEDIA/MSG
  - MEDIA/CHANNELS

REJECTED PROGRAM/PLAN

FINAL CLIENT APPROVALS

(D) CONCERNED GROUPS

-COORDINATION

FEEDBACK FOR MINOR CHANGES

(G) EVALUATION
- MEASURE MESSAGE EFFECTIVENESS
- DETERMINE MSG. ADJUSTMENTS TO GAIN OBJECTIVES
- COMPUTE POTENTIAL GAIN VS. COSTS

PROGRAM CHANGE

SIGNALS

MESSAGE

EFFECTS

(F) PUBLIC/AUDIENCES
- RECEIVE MESSAGES
- UNDERSTAND MSGS.
- CONSIDER MSGS.
- ACCEPT/REJECT
- ACT ON MSGS.

MESSAGE

OUTPUTS

(E) MEDIA OR CHANNEL PLACEMENT
- DIRECT/PUBLIC/MASS
- DELIVERY/DEADLINE
- GATEKEEPER
- APPROPRIATENESS
- TIMING

MESSAGE

INPUTS

To be effective, public relations messages must concentrate on several principles. Messages need to be technically and semantically perfect. They should be as brief and as simple as possible to carry the message content. They should be interesting and forceful, truthful, and absolutely accurate. Yet, with all these limitations, public relations messages must properly advocate the client's purpose.

BASICS OF EFFECTIVE
PUBLIC RELATIONS WRITING

Introduction

The written word is at the heart of the creative and persuasive process in public relations. From it spring news releases, speeches, letters, memos, and radio and television commentary. Not surprisingly, the ability to write is the most marketable skill of the person seeking a job in public relations.

Because the written word is crucial to public relations, this chapter addresses problems of structure, usage and style commonly encountered by public relations writers. Along the way, it also provides guidelines to help you write clearly, concisely and competently. Once you begin your own publication, it's OK to develop your own style as long as you remain consistent.

In general, writing for public relations can be organized around six principles:

1. Technical perfection
2. Semantic perfection
3. Short and simple
4. Interesting and forceful
5. Truth and accuracy
6. Client advocacy

We will examine these in the remainder of this chapter.

A PROFESSIONAL TIP:
Communicating Concisely

The ability to communicate in writing authoritatively and concisely is critical to the practice of public relations. In some instances, it may be the only point of contact with media, clients or management. Your writing represents you, the way you think and express yourself. Since it also represents your client or your company, it must be clear and persuasive to accomplish its objectives.

Barbara W. Hunter is president of Hunter MacKenzie Cooper Inc., a New York public relations firm. A past president of the Public Relations Society of America, she was formerly vice chairman of Ogilvy and Mather Public Relations and president of D-A-Y Public Relations.

Principles of Public Relations Writing

Technical Perfection

By technical perfection, we mean two things: that public relations writing be grammatically correct; and, that it abides by the guidelines of *The Associated Press Stylebook and Libel Manual.*

We endorse the AP stylebook as the authoritative companion volume to this text for three reasons:

One, as public relations writers, you will spend much time composing messages for the mass media. The AP stylebook contains writing guidelines which are followed by most major newspapers and wire services. Two, it will help you develop a consistent writing style. Three, it will give you recognized guidelines for developing stylebooks for clients when you enter the profession.

When using the stylebook, remember it is designed primarily for print messages. The broadcast media require style adjustments which are discussed in chapter 9.

Spelling

A humorous 1988 ad for a fax machine showed a distraught corporate executive surrounded by a flock of birds yelling: "Geese! Geese! I said send the lease." But the crisis created by the misspelled word did not last long. The executive was able to salvage the situation by asking for and getting the lease on his fax machine.

Unfortunately, not all mistakes lead to happy endings. After 200,000 copies of the March 21, 1983, issue of *Time* magazine had been printed, the letter "r" was found missing from the word "control" on the cover of the magazine. The magazine's editors stopped the presses, corrected the misspelled word and destroyed the faulty covers. The cost: $100,000 to put the "r" back in "control" and a delay of a day for 40 percent of the magazine's newsstand copies (Goldberg, 1984).

Why this fanatical pursuit of an error that many people may not even notice? *Time* magazine's editors realized, as you should, that their credibility as professional communicators depends not only upon the facts but also the language of their stories. Getting either wrong could easily lead to a reputation as a "careless" or "incompetent" communicator. Public relations writers whose credibility is thus diminished are of little value to their clients.

Another reason to watch your spelling is that the English language is full of similar-sounding words that have entirely different meanings. Examples of such words are:

naval	navel
adapt	adopt
discreet	discrete
canvas	canvass

A spelling error can transform one word into the similar-sounding other, change the meaning of message, and confuse or mislead the reader.

While all spelling errors are damaging, none is as lethal to the reputation of the public relations writer as the misspelled proper noun or the name of a product, a company, a service or a person. It is unlikely that you will continue to work for client **Smythe** when you insist on spelling his name **Smith** or **Smieth.** Bear in mind that the more uncommon the name, the greater the likelihood is that you may misspell it.

Even worse are the legal implications of such an error. You could libel an innocent person because of a spelling or typographical error.

For example, assume that John P. Doe and Jon P. Doe are both members of the Public Relations Society of America. John Doe is convicted in a U.S. District Court of mail fraud. The PRSA expels him from its membership and asks you, a staff writer, to prepare a media release. Because of a typographical error, your release reads: "**Jon** (not John) P. Doe was expelled from the PRSA following his conviction . . ." Whatever the reason for the error—carelessness, fatigue or oversight—you have not only tarnished the reputation of an innocent man, but opened yourself and the PRSA up to the possibility of a libel suit (also see chapter 14).

The only way to avoid spelling errors is by repeatedly proofreading copy. Nevertheless, recognizing that English is a difficult language to spell, we offer some spelling tips in table 7.1.

Punctuation

Often public relations writers may run into difficulties because they are unable to accurately place a punctuation mark in a sentence. When should commas, colons and semicolons be used? What is the difference?

The following segment offers some guidelines for using common punctuation marks.

1. **Comma:** A comma is used to separate different ideas expressed within a sentence. **Commas are properly used to separate short and simple independent clauses.**

Right: He observed, he approved, he bought.

Wrong: He observed he approved he bought.

Commas are placed before conjunctions in complex sentences containing lengthy independent clauses.

Right: The company president asked for a budget summary, selected budget statistics, and a folder in which to place the documents.

Wrong: The company president asked for a budget summary, selected budget statistics and a folder in which to place the documents.

A comma is unnecessary before a conjunction when the independent clauses or series are short and simple.

Right: The president's speech was short, simple and sweet.

Wrong: The president's speech was short, simple, and sweet.

TABLE 7.1.   The "I Wish I Could Spell" Helpline

Poor spelling is a serious but avoidable handicap that can be overcome through hard work. Here are some suggestions to help you along the way.

Work on your spelling an hour or two each day. Consistency is the key to overcoming the spelling handicap. Mere good intentions and occasional haphazard spelling work do little good.

Don't ever guess at the spelling of a word. Look it up in a dictionary. Then let your senses play with the word. Visual memory works well for some people. Try it. Imprint your memory with the picture of the word. Look at the individual letters and then the shape of the word. For others, spelling out a word aloud may help. Try that too. Spell out each word individually—several times if necessary—until the word is imprinted in your memory, e.g., i-n-t-e-g-r-a-t-e.

Try breaking up a word into syllables. It is often easier to spell a word when you divide it up into parts. For example, splitting the word "procrastinate" into "pro-cras-ti-nate" makes it easier to spell.

Identify words that you usually have trouble spelling. Keep a log of such "trouble words." Practice spelling these words until you have mastered them.

Use memory aids such as "sound inventories" and "spelling rules." These are designed to help the poor speller. For example, remember that only two words in the English language end with a **"yze."** These are **analyze** and **paralyze.**

Then, there is the doubling principle which is rather easy to apply. If a word ends in a single consonant preceded by a vowel and if that word is accented on the *last* syllable, the consonant is doubled when adding an ending that starts with a vowel. However, if the stress or accent shifts away from that last syllable, doubling does not take place.

Consider the word "prefer." It ends in the consonant "r," which is preceded by the vowel "e." The word is also accented on the last syllable: pre-fer. Thus, when you add an ending such as "ed" or "ing," both of which begin with a vowel, you double the consonant. Thus, "prefer" becomes "preferred" or "preferring."

There is also the golden IE rule for those who have trouble remembering whether the word "conceive" is spelled with an "ie" or an "ei." The IE rule is that nearly always for the sound of the long "e" in English, "i" precedes "e" (siege, believe, yield, piece), except after "c," when "e" comes before the "i" (conceive, ceiling, receive). There are, of course, a few exceptions: "either," "neither," "leisure," and "weird." When the sound is a long *a,* the "e" precedes the "i," as in **"neighbor," "vein," "weigh"** and **"sleigh."**

Finally, have others check your spelling for you. If you use a computer, the chances are that you have a spell-check program. If not, install one. Also, where proper nouns—names of people, products and companies—are concerned, you can't be too careful. So, run a spelling check on such words—once, twice, thrice—until you are satisfied that you have them correctly spelled.

Two types of independent clauses may be found in a sentence. One kind—also called a *restrictive* or *essential* clause—cannot be removed from a sentence without altering the meaning of the sentence itself. **Commas are not needed to set off such clauses.**

Right: The documents that the chairman asked for are still missing.

Wrong: The documents, that the chairman asked for, are still missing. (Removing the clause "that the chairman asked for" would change the meaning of the sentence.)

Commas, however, are needed when the public relations writer is dealing with non-restrictive or nonessential clauses. These are clauses that can be removed from a sentence without altering its basic meaning.

Right: The chairman, who is from Ireland, is an excellent financial manager. (Removing "who is from Ireland" does not alter the basic meaning of the sentence.)

Wrong: The chairman who is from Ireland is an excellent financial manager.

Commas are used to separate a string of adjectives preceding a noun when these adjectives are equal in strength or meaning.

Right: An open, generous Irishman, our company president . . .

Wrong: An open generous Irishman, our company president . . .

However, a comma is unnecessary when the last adjective in such a string of adjectives clearly outweighs the preceding ones.

Right: affordable blue chip stock (The adjective "blue chip" becomes a part of the noun "stock.")

Wrong: affordable, blue chip stock

Commas are used to introduce complete, single-sentence quotes within a paragraph.

Right: The company president said, "After losing money for three years, our company finally made a profit this year."

Wrong: The company president said "After losing money for three years, our company finally made a profit this year."

Commas are not used when the quotation within a paragraph has more than one sentence. Instead, a colon is used.

Right: The company president said: "After losing money for three years, our company finally made a profit this year. It was all due to the dedication and hard work of our employees."

Wrong: The company president said, "After losing money for three years, our company finally made a profit this year. It was all due to the dedication and hard work of our employees."

Commas should not be used to set off partial quotations.

Right: The company president attributed the success of the company to "the dedication and hard work of the employees."

Wrong: The company president attributed the success of the company to, "the dedication and hard work of the employees."

Commas are used to set off a person's age, qualifications or title when such information is used in a sentence.

Right: John Henry, 42, was appointed U.S. ambassador to Chile.

Wrong: John Henry 42 was appointed U.S. ambassador to Chile.

Right: John Jones, Ph.D.

Wrong: John Jones Ph.D.

Right: John Jones, vice president of finance, . . .

Wrong: John Jones vice president of finance . . .

Note that a comma is not needed when the title precedes the name of the person it belongs to.

2. **Colon:** This punctuation mark is generally used to introduce a quotation of more than one sentence.

Example: The account executive said: "We think several things are wrong with your company's present image. Let's first take a look at your logo . . ."

It is also used to introduce a series or list of ideas. Note that the first word following the colon should be capitalized only when it is a complete sentence or a proper noun.

Example: The chairman's request included the following items: an executive summary of the budget, a partial listing of key budget statistics, and a copy of the annual report.

Colons are also commonly used in expressions of time to separate the hour from the minutes:

Right: The board meeting convened at 2:15 p.m.

Wrong: The board meeting convened at 2.15 p.m.

Wrong: The board meeting convened at 2=15 p.m.

Wrong: The board meeting convened at 2-15 p.m.

However, when time is reported on the hour, neither the colon nor the decimal points following the colon is necessary:

Right: The board meeeting convened at 2 p.m.

Wrong: The board meeting convened at 2:00 p.m.

Colons are also used in expressions of ratios:

Right: The ratio of hydrogen molecules to oxygen molecules in water is 2:1.

Wrong: The ratio of hydrogen molecules to oxygen molecules in water is 2/1.

3. **Semicolon:** This punctuation mark falls somewhere between a period and a comma in its ability **to separate different clauses or elements in a complex sentence.** It is especially favored when such sentences contain segments that must also be set off by commas.

Example: The chairman visited our textile mill in Los Angeles, Calif.; followed it up with a quick dash to our cannery in Sioux Falls, S.D.; and spent a few days with our company's mine operators in Boise, Idaho.

4. **Hyphen:** The hyphen is commonly used to **link compound modifiers that precede a noun.**

Right: third-quarter earnings
growth-oriented economy

Wrong: third quarter earnings
growth oriented economy

Hyphens are also used to separate words that look awkward when linked to prefixes.

Right: De-emphasize

Wrong: Deemphasize (The two vowels "ee" make for an awkward combination.)

5. **Apostrophe:** There are several conventions regarding the use of the apostrophe that the public relations writer must heed.

For one, it is used to indicate the possessive case of nouns and pronouns. When we wish to say, for example, that the responsibility belongs to the finance director, we could write it as, "The finance director's responsibility." For plural forms or words ending in the letter "s," we don't follow the apostrophe with another "s." For example: "The Jones'," or, " . . . the educators' position . . ."

Simple enough, except that when dealing with possessive forms of pronouns such as, "yours," "hers," "its," no apostrophe is necessary.

Right: **Its** (meaning the painting's) value doubled overnight.

Wrong: **It's** (meaning the painting's) value doubled overnight.

The apostrophe is also used to indicate plural forms of certain things like alphabets and numerals. Examples given by the AP stylebook include:

Right: **p's** and **q's**

Wrong: **ps** and **qs**

Right: the three **R's**

Wrong: the three **Rs**

However, the apostrophe is omitted from other plural forms such as temperatures: "The high **80s;**" and abbreviations: **"IOUs," "VIPs."**

Another use of the apostrophe is to indicate contractions and omissions.

Example: I **won't** do your job for you.

Won't is a contraction of two words, namely, "will not."

Example: The stock market crash of **'87.**

In this example, the first two digits of the number denote the year 1987.

The apostrophe is also used when indicating the decade.

Example: The **'90s** promise exciting times.

However, most students of public relations seem to stumble while deciding whether a contraction or a possessive suits their purposes best. Particularly irksome is the pair "it's" and "its." A common error with such pairs of words is to use the contraction as a possessive and vice versa.

Right: **It's** (contraction of the two words, "it" and "is") against the law to drink and drive.

Wrong: **Its** (possessive, meaning belongs to it) against the law to drink and drive.

You wouldn't say, *"Belongs to it* against the law to drink and drive," would you? Likewise,

Right: **Its** (possessive, meaning belonging to the company) greatest assets are **its** (possessive, again meaning this is something that belongs to the company) employees.

Wrong: **It's** (contraction of the two words, "it" and "is") greatest assets are **it's** (contraction of the two words, it and is) employees.

Again, you wouldn't write, "**It is** greatest assets are **it is** employees," would you?

When in doubt, it is a good idea to write it out as we have done in the preceding examples. The chances are you will be able to figure out whether something makes sense or not.

Syntax

We are now in an area of grammar that causes continuing grief to most writers of English. The following represents a sampling of some rules that pose recurring problems for the public relations writer. It would work to your advantage to examine and learn the remaining rules from any of the books on style and usage that have been mentioned in this and other chapters.

1. Agreement of subject and verb: As a rule, subjects and verbs must agree in person (first person, second person and third person) and number (singular and plural).

Example: Since he has not been able to boost the productivity of the company as he promised, President **John Doe** (singular subject) **has decided** (singular verb) to resign from the company.

However, there are some exceptions that the public relations writer must be sensitive to. For instance, know that there is a peculiar breed of nouns called "collective nouns." Examples of such nouns are: cast, team, committee, faculty, crew. When you encounter a collective noun, there are two ways of handling it. In one case, the collective noun in question needs to be treated as a unit. In such a case, you would treat it in the singular and mate it with a singular verb.

Example: **The crisis planning group** (collective noun treated in the singular) **was meeting** (singular verb) in the conference room when news of the chemical spill broke.

In the second case, you would treat the collective noun as a plural entity by focusing on the activities of individual members within the group identified by the collective noun rather than on the group itself. In such cases, you would link the collective noun to a plural verb.

Example: **The ground crew** (collective noun treated in the plural) **were divided** (plural verb) in their opinions as to exactly what caused the crash.

The public relations writer faces another exception to the subject-verb agreement rule when he or she comes across the "irregular plural" noun. Such nouns look misleadingly singular but are actually plural and therefore require plural verbs. Commonly-encountered irregular plurals are nouns such as "data" (datum is singular) and "media" (medium is singular).

Right: The **mass media** (irregular plural) **have been** (plural verb) traditionally disdainful of the public relations profession.

Wrong: The **mass media** (irregular plural) **has been** (singular verb) traditionally disdainful of the public relations profession.

Right: The **data** (irregular plural) **were** (plural verb) misleading.

Wrong: The **data** (irregular plural) **was** (singular verb) misleading.

It is estimated that more than half of the public relations practitioners in the United States work in business, industrial and commercial settings (Cutlip, Center, and Broom 1985, 60). Since such practitioners may write technical copy, a comment about the grammatical convention for handling weights, measures and prices is both appropriate and necessary. Simply put, such nouns are treated as singular; thus they require singular verbs.

Right: Representatives of the Pentagon protested that $400 (the subject) **was** (singular verb) too high a price to pay for a hammer.

Wrong: Representatives of the Pentagon protested that $400 (the subject) **were** (plural verb) too high a price to pay for a hammer.

Right: **Six tons** (subject) of sound equipment **hangs** (singular verb) from the rafters of the auditorium.

Wrong: **Six tons** (subject) of sound equipment **hang** (plural verb) from the rafters of the auditorium.

2. Agreement of noun and pronoun: Often sentences are so constructed that we use a noun in the first part of the sentence and replace it with a pronoun for subsequent references. When we do this, we must make sure that a singular pronoun replaces a singular noun, and a plural pronoun replaces a plural noun.

Right: I found these **quarterly reports** (plural noun) by the water fountain where you may have left **them** (plural pronoun).

Wrong: I found these **quarterly reports** (plural noun) by the water fountain where you may have left **it** (singular pronoun).

Right: The **company** (singular noun) has **its** (singular pronoun) headquarters in Rome, Italy.

Wrong: The **company** (singular noun) has **their** (plural pronoun) headquarters in Rome, Italy.

3. Modifier maladies: Modifiers are words and phrases that are inserted into sentences to clarify or elaborate upon ideas already expressed in such sentences. They may cause grief to the public relations writer in one of two ways.

First, the writer may consciously or unconsciously insert a modifying word or phrase without completing that portion of the sentence which contains the main idea. The result is a fragmented sentence.

Example: The company president, **who is a native of India** (modifying clause).

The "who is" part could have crept into the sentence for one of two reasons. For one, the writer may have simply meant: "The company president is a native of India." In this case, the modifier was either carelessly or unconsciously placed in the sentence. Or, the writer could have genuinely intended "who is a native of India" to be a modifying clause. In this case, he or she simply forgot to insert the main idea of the sentence. For example, the writer may have meant: "The company president, who is a native of India, has no problems relating to American business executives." Whatever the reason for the modifier in the original sentence, the reader is left with a partial sentence that arouses his or her curiosity but does not make complete sense.

Another kind of problem is created when the writer places a modifier in a part of the sentence it does not belong in. In such cases, the wayward modifier ends up modifying something it was never intended to. Such a modifier is called a "dangling modifier."

Example: **As an immigration officer,** I would like your opinion about the amnesty program.

Wait a minute. Am I, an immigration officer, asking you for your opinion about the amnesty program? Sounds like I am, when what I am really interested in is the opinion of you, the immigration officer. Unfortunately, the dangling modifier wanders into the wrong part of the sentence and changes its meaning in unintended ways. Moving the modifier restores the original meaning to the sentence.

Right: I would like you, **an immigration officer,** to give me your opinion of the amnesty program.

4. Faulty parallelism: This notion is best illustrated by the following:

Example: The president **said** (past tense) that the drug-abuse campaign **was** (past tense) successful and **helps** (present tense) the company maintain a positive image.

The writer started the sentence in the *past* tense, but quickly and for no apparent reason moved into the *present* tense in the second half of the sentence. Thus, the writer constructed a sentence that was inconsistent or "not parallel." This problem is known to grammarians as "faulty parallelism."

Moving everything into the past tense in the above example makes the tense units in the sentence consistent, and, therefore, parallel.

> *Right:* The president **said** (past tense) that the drug-abuse campaign **was** (past tense) a success and **helped** (past tense) the company maintain a positive image.

Public relations writers are most apt to make such errors in sentence construction when they try to rephrase direct quotations in indirect speech form.

People are more casual when they speak. As such, their speech patterns are less likely to be fettered by grammar. Because the spoken word tends to violate grammatical rules, the public relations writer must take extra care to make sure that written versions of speeches, conversations and statements are consistent and parallel.

Usage

This section addresses some common problems in usage the public relations writer is likely to encounter, while offering guidelines for dealing with them. Most of these conventions are adapted from the AP stylebook. We strongly urge you to examine this stylebook very carefully for the remaining guidelines.

1. Capitalization: We know, both by instinct and grade school training, that proper nouns—the names of people, streets, cities, countries—must be capitalized. But then we blunder into words that seem important enough and, therefore, worthy of capitalization. But we can't decide. So, we play it safe and capitalize. The result in most pieces of writing is a random scattering of unnecessarily capitalized words.

Proper nouns must always be capitalized. However, capitalizing a common noun such as "company" is necessary only when such a noun is being treated as part of the proper name of a company.

> *Example:* The Corrugated Company of Illinois opened. . . .

However, when such a common noun is used by itself, use lower case. Often, public relations writers capitalize common nouns such as "company," "president," or "manager" to please clients.

> *Right:* The Corrugated Company opened its sixth plant in Waterloo, Iowa. The company will be making . . .

> *Wrong:* The Corrugated Company opened its sixth plant in Waterloo, Iowa. The Company will be making . . .

The same convention generally holds true for titles of company personnel as well. Capitalize only when the title precedes the name of the person the title belongs to and is not separated from the name by a comma.

Right: <u>V</u>ice <u>P</u>resident for <u>R</u>esearch and <u>D</u>evelopment John Moody . . .

Wrong: <u>V</u>ice <u>P</u>resident for <u>R</u>esearch and <u>D</u>evelopment, John Moody . . .

Wrong: <u>V</u>ice president for <u>r</u>esearch and <u>d</u>evelopment John Moody . . .

If you must separate the title from the name with a comma, treat the title as a set of common words and lower case it. In such cases, it is common practice to place the title after the name of the person.

Right: John Moody, <u>v</u>ice president for <u>r</u>esearch and <u>d</u>evelopment, . . .

Wrong: John Moody, <u>V</u>ice <u>P</u>resident for <u>R</u>esearch and <u>D</u>evelopment, . . .

And never, as is often done, hyphenate "vice president."

2. Abbreviations: The English language is constantly evolving. The abbreviated term is a significant part of this evolution, with terms being added to the language daily. The most used today are **acronyms,** words formed from the first letters of two or more words.

Sometimes, the acronym is a result of a search for powerful and meaningful symbols. An example of this is "MADD." These four letters are not only the abbreviated form of "Mothers Against Drunk Driving," but are also a compelling symbol of the rage felt by members of the organization toward drunk driving. When this is the case, the full form may be built around the acronym rather than the other way around.

Often, acronyms come about because we want to avoid repeatedly using long terms. Thus, we use "ASAP" instead of "as soon as possible." We pass around IOUs, resent the CIA, watch the CBS Evening News, and reach out and touch people dear to us through AT&T's long-distance telephone service. There is nothing inherently wrong about using abbreviations. On the contrary, because we all know what these abbreviated symbols stand for, we can talk to each other in delightfully short sentences.

However, there are other acronyms that are peculiar to the institutions in which we work. How many times have we heard something like this: "Hi Sam. Looks like JD likes the RAW proposal after all." Such acronyms may make sense to people who work in the same institution. However, they may not be as readily recognizable in wider social circles. As such, they may need some explaining.

How must abbreviations and acronyms be handled? According to the AP stylebook, prominent acronyms such as CIA or FBI don't need to be spelled out at all. The acronym is adequate for all references.

For lesser-known acronyms, two conventions may be followed by the public relations writer:

When writing for external publics, the acceptable practice is to spell out the full form on the first reference. The abbreviated form can then be used for second and subsequent references. For example:

> **The television networks look to the Centers for Disease Control [first reference] in Atlanta, Ga., for accurate and authoritative information about AIDS. It is not unusual for CDC [second reference] officials to be interviewed live on television.**

Note that the familiar acronym AIDS is used on first reference instead of the unfamiliar *acquired immune deficiency syndrome.*

When writing for internal audiences, acronyms, especially those relating to the organization itself, can be used on all references. This guideline comes from the assumption that internal audiences would have a greater degree of familiarity with institutional acronyms than external audiences might. The following example is taken from a story in the California State University newsletter, *Stateline:*

> **The CSU [first reference] Board of Trustees has named two CSU [second reference] faculty members as this year's outstanding professors . . .**

Other abbreviations of interest to the public relations writer are for tags like "corporation," "company," "limited" and "incorporated," which frequently are part of company names.

If these words appear at the end of a company's name, then they may be abbreviated as follows (AP stylebook):

Full form	*Abbreviation*
Corporation	Corp.
Company	Co.
Companies	Cos.
Incorporated	Inc.
Limited	Ltd.

Thus, "The Walt Disney Company" could be written as "The Walt Disney **Co.**" Likewise, "American Broadcasting Companies" as "American Broadcasting **Cos.**"

When the words "incorporated" and "limited" appear at the end of a company's name, a common tendency is to place a comma between these words and the rest of the company's name. According to the AP stylebook, this is an unnecessary practice. Our text will show a comma preceding Inc. only if we are quoting from an original source that shows it that way.

Right: Estee Lauder Inc.

Wrong: Estee Lauder, Inc.

Right: Lego U.K. Ltd.

Wrong: Lego U.K., Ltd.

The possessive forms of these tags are generally as follows:

Abbreviation	Possessive Form
Co.	Co.'s
Cos.	Cos.'
Corp.	Corp.'s
Ltd.	Ltd.'s
Inc.	Inc.'s

However, when such corporate tags appear in any other part of the company's name, their full form must be used.

Right: Corporation for Public Broadcasting

Wrong: Corp. for Public Broadcasting

Right: Centers for Disease Control

Wrong: Ctrs. for Disease Control

To summarize, the term **technical perfection** was chosen with sound reason. There is no place in public relations for technically flawed writing. Such writing reflects poorly not only on the writer but also on the client he or she is serving, ultimately affecting the credibility of both.

Again, we wish to caution you that there are several aspects of grammar and usage that this segment did not touch upon. Explore and know these on your own, or with the help of an instructor. Apply them to your writing assignments. Only then can you assure yourself and your clients clean, error-free public relations copy.

Semantic Perfection

The Right Word

Disregarding any of the language guidelines explained so far can interfere with the meaning of a public relations, or any, message. However, the notion of semantic perfection goes beyond structural considerations into the meanings of the words themselves. It concerns the search for the word with the right meaning for what we want to say to our audiences.

For example, how about the executive who heaps "fulsome praise" upon his boss in the hope of getting a prized assignment? Should he be surprised when the boss gives the job to a sincere fellow worker instead?

On the surface, fulsome gives the appearance of a warm and wholesome word; hence, a worthy partner to praise. In reality, though, it means insincere, loathsome, disgusting and offensive to the senses. Hardly the way to win friends and prized jobs.

Fulsome is one of many deceptive words in the English language. Some are confusing because they give false appearances, as fulsome does. Other words are confusing because they sound alike and are close to each other in spelling. Take the words "naval" and "navel." Naval refers to a navy. Navel, on the other hand, refers to the little depression on our bellies that we know as the "bellybutton."

Or, how about the words, "masterful" and "masterly"? Masterful is the word commonly used to describe a person who is domineering. Yet, the word is often, and mistakenly, used to describe a skillful or powerful speech, for which the appropriate word is "masterly" (Cutlip, Center, and Broom 1985, 278).

Likewise, words like "biennial," "biannual," "semiannual," "bimonthly" and "biweekly" are semantic bogs the writer is very likely to get mired in. Just what do these terms mean? How different are they?

The word "biannual" translates into "twice a year" and means the same as "semiannual." "Biennial," often confused with biannual, means "every other year." "Bimonthly" translates into "every other month," while "biweekly" means "every other week."

Table 7.2 contains more such pairs of words and phrases.

TABLE 7.2.   Look-Alike Words

Can you tell the difference?

straight	strait
allude	elude
ravaged	ravished
disparate	desperate
principle	principal
bussed	bused
block	bloc
fliers	flyers
flout	flaunt
marshall	marshal
compose	comprise
censure	censor
counsel	council
affect	effect
canvass	canvas
cannons	canons
aide	aid
flounder	founder
averse	adverse
peddle	pedal

Lastly, there are some words that threaten semantic sense because they mean one thing popularly, another professionally. Take the words "assault" and "battery." To the lay person, they may appear no different from each other. In fact, they're often used interchangeably to describe violent confrontations in which there is physical contact. In a legal sense, however, no such contact takes place in an assault; there is merely the threat of violence. Conversely, when violent physical contact does take place, the law not only recognizes it as assault, but also as battery.

These seemingly fine distinctions are important not only from legal and semantic standpoints, but also because of their ability to color our perceptions of people and events.

Social Sensitivity

1. Downers: Walter Lippmann (1922) observed that people carry mental pictures of the realities around them in their heads. These pictures are what guide human behavior. Lippmann further suggested that the pictures themselves, however irrational and farfetched they may be, are more powerful than objective reality in guiding our actions.

The power of words to affect reality comes from their ability to generate images far more complex than their dictionary meanings. When these images are negative, they wreak havoc upon our egos and sense of worth even though they may not be based on fact. When they are positive, they make us feel good. Thus, to most blacks, the word "negro" is not simply an indicator of race but an emotional narrative evoking complex images of bondage and suffering. On the other hand, the words "black," and more recently, "African-American," symbolize pride. There are positive and negative words like these for every race on earth. Caucasians bristle at being called "honkies," just the way Jews take offense at being called "hymies."

Implications for the public relations writer are that words are not to be used lightly. A mere consideration of their **denotative** or dictionary meaning is not sufficient. The writer must also be sensitive to the emotional colorations or **connotative** meanings of the words. Such sensitivity is especially necessary when writing about the elderly, the infirm and the disabled.

Sometimes, it is easy to recognize offensive words. Sometimes not. Knowing that words can create painful realities, how can the public relations writer sensitively deal with the language of disability? Figure 7.1 offers some solutions.

2. Sexism: Few language issues in modern times have stirred as much controversy as "sexism." Our language is rich in masculine words and terms. Some look forward to the daily visit of the "mail**man**," would rather not deal with "sales**men**," worry about a shortage of "**man**power," and despair about the future of "**man**kind." Such terms are obsolete in a world where women outnumber men. Besides, they are also offensive to the large numbers of women who work alongside men in American businesses and factories.

Watch your language!
No No's for the media regarding the disabled.

AFFLICTED—Very negative and a definite downer! Person *who has* or *is affected by* is much better.

CEREBRAL PALSIED—Sounds like an inanimate object instead of a person. Why not *person* or *people with cerebral palsy?*

C.P.—OK to describe the condition but NOT a person. This puts all people in a neat little package and deposits them in a file drawer. Please use *who has* or *who have cerebral palsy* when referring to people.

CRIPPLED OR CRIPPLER—This paints a mental picture no one wants to look at.

DISEASE—Cerebral palsy is NOT a disease. People with cerebral palsy are as healthy as anybody else. Better to say *condition.*

DRAIN AND BURDEN—We wouldn't touch these two words with a 10-foot pole. *Added responsibility* is much better.

POOR—Physical handicaps have nothing to do with how wealthy someone is. Love and self-esteem are priceless qualities. A person's character determines the richness of his or her life.

SUFFERS FROM—If someone with a disability is independent and copes with life as well as most of us, then this phrase definitely doesn't apply.

UNFORTUNATE—What's unfortunate is that this word is often used to describe people with physical disabilities. Don't offend with this one.

VICTIM—A person with physical disabilities was neither sabotaged nor necessarily in a plane, train or car crash. There's no way to rephrase this turkey.

WHEELCHAIRBOUND—Leaves the impression that the *wheelchair user*—a better descriptive term—is glued to his or her transportation.

This List is provided as a public service.

Your help is needed to keep people with cerebral palsy—or with other disabling conditions—from sounding pitiful, inhuman or like beings from outer space in your stories.

People with cerebral palsy and other disabilities have the same rights as everyone else in this world—the right to fall in love, to marry, to hold down a competitive job, to acquire an adequate and appropriate education. Above all, they have a right to self-esteem.

Please insure these rights by referring to the disabled in terms that acknowledge ability, merit, dignity. In turn, we hope your readers and listeners will follow suit.

For a fact sheet and other information on cerebral palsy, contact:

Public Relations Department
United Cerebral Palsy Associations, Inc.
66 East 34th Street
New York, N.Y. 10016
(212) 481-6344

UNITED CEREBRAL PALSY
Improving the Quality of Life for the Abled and Disabled

▶ **Figure 7.1.** The language of disability. Copyright © 1987 United Cerebral Palsy Associations, Inc. Reprinted with permission.

Can the woman who delivers mail still be called a "mailman?" As society changes, so must language. The challenge for the public relations writer is to search for labels that do not violate the equality between men and women. Douglas Ann Newsom (1986), a public relations educator and author, prefers using the neutral "mail carrier" instead of "mailman;" and "salesperson" instead of "salesman."

Likewise, even if it violates the AP stylebook, it is more desirable to use:

"workers" or "humanpower" instead of "manpower"
"ego" instead of "male ego"
"large" or "big" instead of "man-sized"
"homemaker" instead of "housewife"
"synthetic" instead of "man-made"
"the human race" instead of "mankind"
"chairperson" or "chair" instead of "chairman"

The use of masculine labels is one source of sexism in language. Sexism can also result from the conscious or subconscious use of the masculine pronoun as the preferred "generic" pronoun. Take, for example, the following sentence:

The successful manager always acts as a coach and a cheerleader to the people who work under <u>him</u>.

The writer of this sentence apparently not only assumes that all managers are men, but also, and more insidiously, that all successful managers are men. This connotation can be neutralized in one of two ways. For one, the feminine pronoun could be used every time a masculine pronoun is used:

The successful manager always acts as a coach and a cheerleader to the people who work under <u>him</u> or <u>her</u>.

Alternately, the sentence can be recast in the more neutral plural form. This form is generally preferred since it eliminates the need to deal with awkward gender pronouns.

Successful managers always act as coaches and cheerleaders to the people who work under <u>them</u>.

Finally, sexism can occur when the language used to compare men and women is not parallel. The words "men" and "women" are roughly equal in tone and temperament. Therefore, they provide for balanced comparisons when used side by side in a sentence:

Right: **Men and women can peacefully coexist in the workplace.**

This balance can be upset when the words describing either men or women are cute, euphemistic, patronizing or downright contemptuous:

This is a <u>gentlemen's</u> club. <u>Women</u> are not welcome.
You <u>girls</u> take it easy. I'll have the <u>men</u> come in and clean up.
I would like the <u>men</u> to line up to my right and the <u>ladies</u> to my left.
I am a <u>woman</u>. You are a <u>boy</u>.

Such unequal comparisons are insidious because they psychologically undermine the people they are aimed at.

To summarize, the public relations writer must take special pains to avoid sexist and other kinds of offensive language. Sometimes, **his** or **her** efforts may result in **his** or **her** writing awkward sentences. Better awkward prose than insensitive elegance. Operational English, however, aims at the best of both worlds—proper usage which reads well. It is not easy, but with time, effort and training, the public relations writer will be able to construct sentences that are not only sensitive but graceful.

Short and Simple

The Simple Word

Avoiding fuzzwords: The public relations writer's mission is to make sure that audiences get, read or hear, understand, and accept messages that are important to the client. This process hinges upon the clarity of the message. Unfamiliar words (see table 7.3 for such "fuzzwords" and their simpler forms) rob messages of their meaning and prevent audiences from responding intelligently. Most people do not rush to a dictionary every time they come across unfamiliar words. Typically, readers may ignore the words or give them their own meanings. Either way, the sense of the message is lost.

Because they interfere with the clarity of the message, difficult and unfamiliar words are of little use to public relations writers. As a rule, writers are better served by simple, familiar and easy-to-understand words.

Dealing with Jargon

One type of fuzzword that is an important part of the public relations writer's language environment is "jargon." This is a collective term for words that are specific to a particular audience or industry. "Baud," "microchip" and "byte" are among many words that were added to the English language following the invention of the computer. They are familiar to those who work in the computer industry. They make perfect sense to the computer buff. But they may not make sense to those people who do not use or understand computers.

TABLE 7.3. Fuzzwords versus plain talk

sortation	sorting
stringent	tough, severe, tight
fabricate	lie
commodious	roomy
notate	note
abbreviate	shorten
indicate	show
endeavor	try
judicious	wise
utilize	use
mitigate	soften
deficiency	lack
summarization	summary
inundate	flood
draconian	cruel
reticent, taciturn	silent
origination	origin
aggregate	sum, total
coagulate	thicken
luminous	bright

Since most public relations writers cannot escape having to deal with jargon, it is important to develop some strategies regarding its use.

First, the writer must become familiar with institutional or professional jargon. The ideal would be to develop a guidebook which includes popular meanings and synonyms for each word in the jargon of the client institution. The guidebook could also be used to help others within the client organization cope with the jargon in a consistent manner.

Second, the writer must learn when and when not to use jargon.

When to use jargon: It is economical, efficient, necessary, even desirable to use jargon when dealing with people who have no trouble understanding it. Doing otherwise may hurt the precision and clarity of the message. Professional audiences such as engineers, scientists and doctors, to name a few, are appropriate targets for jargon. However, before using jargon, public relations writers must make sure that the jargon is both appropriate for and understandable to their audiences.

When not to use jargon: It is unwise to use jargon when dealing with audiences that may have difficulty understanding it. Edward Thompson, editor-in-chief of *Reader's Digest,* is the author (undated) of "How To Write Clearly" from the International Paper Company's series on the printed word. He recalls the following sentence written by one of Franklin D. Roosevelt's speech writers:

"We are endeavoring to construct a more inclusive society."

"Inclusive society" sounds like jargon a sociology professor might use; if so, hardly representative of the type of person FDR was trying to reach. Also, "endeavor" and "construct" are uncommon synonyms of "try" and "build," respectively. Thompson notes that FDR rewrote the sentence into this winner:

"We're going to **make** (rather than construct) **a country in which no one is left out** (an inclusive society)."

If it becomes necessary to use jargon in messages aimed at lay audiences, writers must provide simple explanations the first time they use it.

For example, when public relations writers use the term "artificial intelligence," they may follow it up with this explanation:

Artificial intelligence is the ability of a machine such as a robot or a computer to imitate human actions or skills such as problem solving, decision making, perception and learning.

Cultural jargon: When we think of jargon, we generally think of technical and scientific terms. Cultures, too, can generate their own language. The public relations writer, composing messages for audiences from other nations, must be careful to avoid cultural jargon those audiences may be unfamiliar with. For example, it does not make much sense to provide "a ballpark estimate" to a customer from a country where baseball is not played.

The Readable Sentence

The second ingredient in the recipe for good, clear writing is the readable sentence. In general, the assumption is that the shorter the sentence, the more readable it is likely to be. Conversely, the longer the sentence, the less readable it is likely to be.

In January 1986, seven astronauts, including school teacher Christa McAuliffe, perished when the space shuttle Challenger exploded shortly after it was launched. Later that year, the National Council of Teachers of English faulted the National Aeronautics and Space Administration for the following explanation about the controversial decision to launch the space shuttle:

The normal process during the countdown is that the countdown proceeds, assuming we are in a go posture, and at various points during the countdown we tag up the operational loops and face to face in the firing room to ascertain the facts that project elements that are monitoring the data and that are understanding the situation as we proceed are still in the go direction ("Speaking English," 1986, A21).

From the public relations writer's point of view, what is wrong with this utterance? The first problem and its solution should be obvious from a reading of the previous segment on the simple word. The sentences are riddled with NASA jargon. What, for example, are "operational loops," "go posture" and "face to face in the firing room?" Eliminate them. Use simpler substitutes that the audience can understand. If "go posture" means "the decision to go ahead with the launch still stands," say so.

The one-idea sentence: The second problem with the NASA statement is its length. It is too long and wordy for one sentence. Most people do not use 66-word sentences in everyday conversation. It is not likely that they will be able to easily grasp the many thoughts that are expressed in the NASA statement.

The solution is to separate the different ideas expressed in the sentence; then build sentences around each of these ideas. As a rule, it is desirable to limit a sentence to one or two related ideas. To the best of our understanding, the NASA statement includes the following ideas:

— A decision to launch the space shuttle must be made (go posture).
— Once the decision is made, the countdown begins.
— During countdown, there are officials monitoring all of the key factors (project elements) necessary for a successful launch.
— If they notice something wrong, these officials confer (face to face in the firing room), stop the countdown, and, if necessary, call off the launch.
— If they are satisfied that things are all right, the countdown continues until the shuttle is launched.

Conceivably, the revised version could read something like this:

> **Once the launch is approved, the countdown begins. During countdown, officials in the firing room continuously monitor and evaluate all critical factors necessary for a successful launch. If they have serious doubts about anything, the countdown stops and the shuttle is not launched. If they are satisfied that everything is in order, then the countdown proceeds until the shuttle is launched.**

Though the public relations writer ends up with almost as many words in the overall message as before, its ideas are no longer crowded into one sentence. Instead, they are fed to the audience in four relatively short and manageable sentences.

To summarize this section, simple words framed in short sentences generally make for the most readable copy. It would, however, be a mistake to push this rule to the extreme and produce an endless stream of short sentences (Read 1972, 103):

Such writing is choppy, dull and uninteresting. The good writer strives for variety. There is nothing wrong with the occasional long sentence when it is properly constructed. The reading difficulty comes when all sentences are long and many of them are improperly constructed.

Thus, public relations writers must be concerned more with the overall readability of their copy than with having identically short sentences. According to readability expert Robert Gunning (1968, 51), if the average length of the sentences in a message is more than 16 words, it is probably not very readable. The four sentences in our version of the NASA statement contained eight, 19, 16 and 18 words. Since it averages about 15 words a sentence, this statement qualifies by Gunning's standards as a fairly simple message that makes easy reading.

Measurement of Readability: Gunning is one of many persons who have tried to reduce the notion of readability to mathematical formulas.

Readability formulas generally serve two purposes:

— They are diagnostic tools writers can use to figure out how complex or simple their writing is.

— They also provide guidelines for evaluating what level of message complexity is appropriate for different audiences. From the earlier discussion of jargon, it is clear that words considered difficult by one audience may be considered simple or even simplistic by other audiences. Consider the following set of three sentences:

The little girl looked at her mommy (seven words).
The little girl smiled at her mommy (seven words).
The little girl hugged her mommy (six words).

These short sentences contain simple, everyday, mostly monosyllabic words, and are generally written to the level of a child in the first grade.

However, older children who have a greater command of the language might find these sentences "simply" constructed, preferring instead: "The child looked at her mommy, smiled, and then hugged her" (11 words). Still monosyllabic; but now the words are arranged in one sentence instead of three.

The child psychologist, on the other hand, might find all of this too "simplistic," instead preferring, "The child established eye contact with her mother, registered approval by smiling, and then physically bonded with her." The sentence has now grown to 18 words. Also, its words are increasingly polysyllabic and we see the presence of psychological jargon such as "bonding."

These examples demonstrate the idea that the more educated people are, the greater the level of sentence and word complexity they will be able to handle. Going much below the level of acceptable complexity may offend the audiences. Going much above may place the message beyond their understanding. Thus, the public relations writer may justifiably use longer sentences and difficult words such as "bonding" when communicating with psychologists, but not when talking to school children.

Based on audience research, public relations writers must know what kind of people they are writing to. Given this, the readability formula helps them determine whether a message is too complex, too simple or just right for the audience (see table 7.4).

TABLE 7.4.   Readability and Listenability Formulas

Flesch Reading Ease Formula

One of the most widely used readability tests, the Flesch Formula is essentially based on the complexity or ease of words and the length of an average sentence in a sample of words.

To apply the Flesch Formula, as revised by Powers, Sumner and Kearl (1958), the following steps need to be taken.

Step 1: Pull a sample of 100 continuous words from the message you wish to test.

Step 2: Count the number of sentences in this sample of 100 words. A sentence is any string of words ending with a period, a colon, a semicolon or a dash.

Step 3: Divide the total number of sentences into 100 (the number of words in the sample) to get the average sentence length (ASL).

Step 4: Multiply ASL by 0.0778.

Step 5: Count the number of syllables in the 100 words.

Step 6: Multiply the figure you obtained in Step 5 by 0.0455.

Step 7: Add the figures from steps 4 and 6.

Step 8: Subtract 2.209 from the figure you obtained in Step 7 to obtain the readability score (R).

If you obtained a readability score between 5.5 and 6.5, your writing is as simple or complex as most stories in a daily newspaper or a magazine like *Reader's Digest*. Scores lower than 5.5 indicate simpler forms of writing such as may be found in pulp magazines or children's literature. Scores higher than 6.5 indicate progressively more complex forms of writing such as may be found in intellectual magazines or academic journals.

You must, however, note that many such 100-word samples need to be analyzed before you can get stable readability scores.

Abstracted from Richard D. Powers, W. A. Sumner and B. E. Kearl. "A Recalculation of Four Adult Readability Formulas." *Journal of Applied Psychology* 49 (1958):104.

Cloze Procedure

Developed by Wilson L. Taylor in 1953, this procedure analyzes the meaning difficulty of a message instead of looking at syllable counts and sentence lengths. As Taylor describes it:

This procedure also might be likened to a polling method with experimental controls. It asks members of a population sample to demonstrate how well they understand the meaning of a mutilated version of what some writer wrote by having them (the sampled members) vote on what the missing words should be. The passage whose deleted words are most often (and correctly) "written in" on the "ballot" is elected most readable (1953, 417).

To apply the Cloze Procedure, the following steps must be taken.

Step 1: Choose a passage containing 250–300 continuous words from the message you wish to test.

Step 2: Pick a random starting point in the text and replace every fifth word with a blank space. Here's how a typical passage looks after the blanks have been placed in it:

At first blush, it seems (random starting point) reasonable to assume that _____ of us would have _____ difficulty communicating in the _____ language. It is the _____ language many of us _____ as babies and learned _____ children. It is the _____ we use to learn _____ the world around us. _____ is also the language _____ use to talk about _____ world to those around ___ .

Step 3: Give the message with the blanks to a sample of people from the audience the message is ultimately intended for.

Step 4: Have the subjects read the mutilated message and fill in the blanks.

Step 5: Count the number of times the blanks are replaced with the correct words.

The higher the count of correct substitutions, the more readable the message is.

Abstracted from Wilson L. Taylor. " 'Cloze Procedure': A New Tool for Measuring Readability." *Journalism Quarterly* 30:4 (1953): 415–433.

TABLE 7.4.   Readability and Listenability Formulas (*continued*)

Fang's Easy Listening Formula

This formula is simpler to use than most readability formulas. Also, unlike most formulas, which are oriented toward print messages, the ELF is designed to test broadcast messages.

To apply the ELF, the following steps must be taken:

Step 1: Take a broadcast script you wish to test.

Step 2: For each sentence, count the number of syllables per word, less one. For example, take the sentence, "Mary had a little lamb." Ignore "had," "a" and "lamb," since these are one-syllable words. Subtracting a syllable from these words would leave us with nothing. The word "Mary" has two syllables. When you subtract one syllable from this word, you are left with a syllable count of one. Likewise, the word "little" has two syllables but a syllable count of one. Therefore, the count is two for the sentence.

Step 3: For each sentence in the script, add up all the syllables you counted.

The ELF score for the sentence, "Mary had a little lamb," is two.

Step 4: Add up all the ELF scores and divide by the number of sentences in the script. This leaves you with the average ELF score for the script.

In general, the higher the score, the more complex and difficult to read the message is.

Abstracted from Irving E. Fang. "The 'Easy Listening Formula.'" *Journal of Broadcasting* 11:1, (Winter 1966–1967): 63–68.

There are generally two types of readability formulas. The first kind is structural and reduces readability to some combination of average sentence length and number of syllables in a message. One of the best known formulas of this type is Rudolf Flesch's (1948) **Reading Ease Formula** (see table 7.4). The Gunning Fog Index and the Farr-Jenkins-Patterson formula are other examples of similar readability formulas.

The second type of formula attacks the readability issue through meaning difficulties rather than structure. An example is the **Cloze Procedure** (see table 7.4), which requires readers to fill in the blanks in a passage that is given to them. Content readability is then essentially determined by the number of blanks the reader successfully fills in.

Researcher Carl Denbow (1975) found that these formulas work equally well for measuring the "listenability" of copy written for radio and television. However, there are specific formulas like Irving Fang's **Easy Listening Formula** (see table 7.4) for measuring the simplicity and phonology of spoken materials such as speeches, and radio and television scripts.

Finally, it must be noted that readability formulas are not intended as devices for judging the overall quality of writing. It would be a mistake to use them as such.

Interesting and Forceful

So far, we have talked about the virtues of the simple word and the readable sentence without explaining how you can combine these in interesting and impactful ways.

The public relations writer's messages must not only be simple and readable, but also interesting and forceful. This segment deals with some common aspects of writing that interfere with the force and clarity of public relations messages. It also provides some guidelines for dealing with such obstacles to good writing. You can achieve a stronger writing style by applying its lessons.

Our discussion centers around the following themes:

1. Lean messages
2. Concrete messages
3. Active messages
4. Positive messages
5. Message unity
6. Human interest

It is rare for public relations writers to compose interesting and forceful messages on the first try. The chances are that they may have to edit and re-edit messages several times in order to achieve this.

In the process, writers may use one of two editing approaches. They may entirely delete the offending portions of the message:

Original copy: It has come to my attention that we need to think of a more creative approach.

Edited copy: (Strike "It has come to my attention that" and "to think of") We need a more creative approach.

Or, they may *rewrite* portions of the original message to make it read better:

Original copy: The products you see here will be produced as part of our relationship with XYZ Company, one of the leading microchip manufacturers in this country.

Edited copy: These products (The products you see here) will be jointly produced (produced as part of our relationship) with a leading microchip manufacturer (one of the leading microchip manufacturers in this country), XYZ Company.

1. Lean Messages

Most writers are prone to the word excesses noted above. Their messages are cluttered with unnecessary words and phrases. Of such words, Read says:

Unnecessary words are like weeds in a garden. They compete with the needed words, sap sentences of vitality, and may choke out the message entirely (1972, 118).

From the public relations writer's perspective, such words have another and over-riding disadvantage. They are expensive because they occupy costly space in publications.

a. Redundant words: Here the sentences are fattened because the writer uses two or more words with the same meaning in a sentence. For example:

Original copy: The public relations writer prepared two separate versions of the press release.

There is no point in writing two versions of a press release if they aren't separate and distinct from each other, is there?

Edited copy: The public relations writer prepared two versions of the press release.

Original copy: The company is facing a bad crisis situation.

Any crisis is a bad situation. So why not say:

Edited copy: The company is facing a crisis.

b. Puff words: These are adjectives and adverbs that appear in persuasive messages to make things and people appear bigger or better than they really are. Quash such words. They are unnecessary. Besides, they give public relations writing a bad name.

The point about quashing puff words is best illustrated by the following sentences from a column written by public relations practitioner Hugh Wells (1982, 8):

It is absolutely (adverb), entirely (adverb) necessary (adjective).
It is absolutely (adverb) necessary.
It is necessary.
Notice the nice icy quality of the unadorned adjective. The lady means it. She isn't pussyfooting. The masher has been quashed.

If the connection between the Wells example and public relations puffery is not clear, how about the following sentence from a product press release:

Original copy: A remarkable (adjective), advanced (adjective) skin-like (adjective) fabric covering . . .

Cut out the first two adjectives. They are vague and could be applied to anything. You wouldn't be putting out a press release if the product was not "remarkable." Out with it. "Advanced" makes sense only if there are other "beginner" versions of the product floating around. It is also what all manufacturers like to think of their products. Kill it. Now, "skin-like" is a specific description of the product. It gives a better sense about the fabric covering. Keep it.

Edited copy: A skin-like fabric covering . . .

This phrase is now as tight as a drum.

c. Empty phrases: Pompous and often useless phrases also are sentence fatteners the public relations writer must watch out for. Consider the following sentence.

Original copy: The public relations writer presented her client with a bill in the amount of $200.

Can $200 be anything other than an amount of money? And, why presented? It is not a gift. Say instead:

Edited copy: The public relations writer gave (presented) her client a bill for $200.

The rewritten sentence is not only four words shorter, but reads better. To demonstrate that sentences get better with each edit, let's try again:

Re-edited copy: The public relations writer billed (gave a bill for) her client $200.

The client had better pay up. Having lopped off seven words to reach the heart of the message, the writer now means business.

Chopping sentences down can be fun once you get the hang of it.

2. Concrete Messages

The words and expressions that make the best sense in any piece of writing are those that are concrete, or specific and down to earth. The earlier discussion on puff words showed that concrete adverbs and adjectives make more sense in public relations copy than do vague adverbs and adjectives. The same holds true for nouns.

Picture the weather report on the evening television newscast. The weather expert tells you there is heavy precipitation in the South (the map behind shows "rain"), moderate precipitation in the Midwest (the map behind shows "snow"), and precipitation in the Northeast (the map behind shows "sleet").

Unless the weather forecaster knows something we don't, it makes more sense to say "snow," "rain" and "sleet," which are concrete noun forms of the abstract noun "precipitation." Besides, that's the only way ordinary people know weather.

The moral for the public relations writer: when faced with a generic noun, always search for a more concrete alternative. It makes more sense to the reader.

3. Active Messages

Just like nouns, adverbs and adjectives, verbs too can affect the energy levels of a sentence. When they are active and working, they add to the vitality of the sentence. When they are inert and listless, they rob the sentence of its vitality.

a. Active Verbs: Sentences that use "active" verbs are called "active voice" sentences. Such sentences are more direct and forceful than sentences using "passive" verbs ("passive voice" sentences). For the most part, the active verb is the preferred alternative.

Use: The managers <u>voiced</u> (active voice) concerns about the safety proposal.
Instead of: Concerns about the proposal <u>were voiced</u> (passive voice) by the managers.

Somehow, in the latter version, the managers don't seem as concerned as before; therefore, they may not be taken as seriously.

b. Inert Verbs: These are abstract verbs that are sentence weakeners. Examples are "has," "have" and "is." Such verbs are best replaced with more energetic verbs. Take this example:

The company president, Joe Morley, <u>has</u> a liking for hard-working employees.

Replacing the inert "has" with the more active "likes" adds punch to the sentence. It also shortens the sentence by three words.

The company president, Joe Morley, <u>likes</u> hard-working employees.

Likewise, "Management indifference **is** frequently a cause of worker apathy," should be rewritten as, "Management indifference frequently **causes** worker apathy."

4. Positive Messages

Negative sentences are those that tell you what didn't happen rather than what did; what isn't rather than what is. Such sentences usually contain the word "not." They are usually weak and ambivalent and are best replaced with positive sentences. Take this negative sentence:

Employees who are <u>not</u> happy are unproductive.

It hesitates to come right out and say the employees are unhappy. On the other hand, the positive form below is more assertive and powerful, and leaves less doubt about the employees' state of mind than the negative version did.

<u>Unhappy</u> employees are unproductive employees.

According to style experts William Strunk and E. B. White (1972, 15), some negative phrases to watch out for are "**not** honest," "**not** important," "did **not** remember," "did **not** pay any attention to," and "did **not** have much confidence in." These negatives have one-word positive forms. Can you figure out what they are?

Lest public relations writers be tempted to eliminate the word from all of their sentences, we note that there are few words more powerful than "not" in a statement that is a denial. As such, it may be appropriate to use it in such sentences.

For example, there is a greater sense of finality when one says, "I did not do it," rather than "I **deny** doing it," or, "There is no truth to the allegation that I did it."

5. Message Unity

So far, we have talked about things that can be done to individual sentences. Sentences do not stand alone. Usually they are strung together with other sentences to express ideas. The more complex an idea is, the more words and sentences are needed to express it. An improper arrangement of sentences does as much damage to the meaning of an idea as the improper arrangement of words within a sentence.

The common practice is to use "transition" words and phrases to link sentences expressing related thoughts. If the proper words or phrases are used, continuity of thought and expression results. When the transitions are improper or not there at all, the sentences fall apart into confusing fragments. Take the following example:

> **The XYZ company today announced the election of Mark P. Morley to the position of president and chief operating officer. Marty B. Marley has been chairman, president and CEO. In anticipation of his retirement, Marley, who remains chairman and CEO, has elected to delegate the president's role to Morley.**

This passage breaks down at the point where the second sentence begins. We know that Morley has been elected president. But suddenly, without warning, we are forced to deal with a mysterious Marley who also appears to hold the same position. Note that the similarity of names adds to the confusion. We don't know from the present arrangement of the sentences what the relationship is between Morley and Marley.

The problem is created because there is no adequate transitional word, phrase or sentence. Adding such a phrase makes the message clearer:

> **The XYZ company today announced the election of Mark P. Morley as its president and chief operating officer. MORLEY SUCCEEDS MARTY B. MARLEY, who . . .**

The connection between the two executives is now clear.

6. Human Interest

When most people complain that a message lacks human interest, they may mean that the message does not talk about people. Public relations writers can satisfy such needs by generating stories about real people for their clients.

Or, the expression "lacks human interest" may mean that the message is impersonal and written for someone else, not us.

Public relations writers can head off such complaints by using personal pronouns in their messages. Examples of these are "I," "you," "we," and "us." Such pronouns establish personal bonds between the communicator and the audience.

On the other hand, use impersonal pronouns, such as "them" and "they" sparingly. These are cold expressions that push the communicators and their audiences farther apart. Take this example:

Employees can make the difference.

There is a hidden third-person "them" in the sentence that the employees will soon pick up on. Who are these employees? Could the message be talking to someone else in the company? It is easy for the employee to push the message away and stay uninvolved. But that is not what good public relations writers want. They like the employee to know: "Hey! **We're** talking to **you.** You can make a difference." Suddenly, by using the personal "we" and "you," the message comes alive for the employee, who now thinks, "Gee! Management thinks I, Tony Amaretto, can make a difference." The reader is hooked.

Personal words are especially desirable when the public relations writer is developing messages for familiar, localized or clearly identifiable audiences such as employees, community organizations and customers. Thus, they are effective devices to use in staff memos, community speeches and letters to customers.

The personal form is also suited to certain writing forms such as features, and to conversational media such as radio and television.

The impersonal pronoun or word has its own uses and must not be discarded by the public relations writer. It is often effectively used in the writing of straight-news messages such as one sees in a newspaper.

Truth and Accuracy

A guiding principle in all public relations writing is a respect for truth and accuracy. Under no circumstance can public relations writers deviate from this principle. To do so can cost the client legally or in lost credibility. Here are some things you can do to protect the integrity of your public relations message.

Be certain of your facts. Never speculate about the facts of your message before you send it out. Have your message checked for accuracy by others. Also make sure that it is the whole truth. Half-truths, even if they carry accurate information, are misleading and therefore unacceptable. Remember, once the message goes out, it cannot be recalled. It stands, errors and all.

Don't simply define, explain. The public relations writer is morally and professionally responsible not only for getting information across to audiences, but for making reasonably sure that they will understand its content.

Make sure your message is on firm legal footing. Again, you either know or you don't know. Never speculate. When in doubt, consult the client's legal department.

Put yourself in the shoes of the reader. Ask yourself if there is anything in your message the reader might find insensitive or offensive. Most of all, ask yourself if what you have written is fair to your reader.

Watch your typos. Remember that "little" spelling and typographical errors have an insidious effect upon the impact of any message. Errors distract the reader from the message the public relations writer is trying to convey. They are also symptoms of carelessness. If professional writers are careless with words, they might be careless with the facts as well. Either way, the effect on the public relations message and the writer's credibility is negative. Such a writer is also worthless to the client.

Illustration. Information, no matter how accurate it is, is of little use to audiences if they cannot understand its content. Take numbers, for example. Few things can be more precise than numbers. When we say there are 26 letters in the English alphabet, we mean just that; not 24 or 27, but 26.

Because of their precision, numbers impress people. Thus, we think a person who says, "I am 100 percent certain," is more credible than someone who says, "I am sure." Marketers recognize the persuasive power of numbers. Hence, they try to tempt us with beef that is "20 percent leaner" and products that are "30 percent more reliable" than last year's.

But, numbers can be problematic too, especially when they are big or contain decimals and fractions. Explaining such numbers to audiences poses a challenge to the public relations writer. A useful device for explaining or **illustrating** numbers is the analogy. Take, for example, the story in *Popular Science* (October 1987, 63) about a trillion-watt burst of energy produced by a laser device at the University of Rochester's Laboratory for Laser Energetics. Recognizing the inability of many readers to understand large numbers, the editors of *Popular Science* offered the following explanation:

> For a trillionth of a second, the device emitted an incredible trillion watts of power. That's 1,000,000,000,000 watts. To put that into perspective, take the entire electrical-generating capacity of the United States and double it.

The reader, who may have no idea what a trillion is, now begins to understand the enormity of it. Table 7.5 shows other ways of illustrating large numbers.

Client Advocacy

Lastly, public relations writers are not passive conduits for the passage of information meant for public audiences. They are champions in the causes of their clients. Their actions must thus benefit the clients.

TABLE 7.5. What's a Trillion? Here Are Some Clues

WASHINGTON—President Reagan has proposed the nation's first federal budget to exceed $1 trillion.

The president has asked Congress to approve a budget of $1,024 trillion for the fiscal year beginning Oct. 1, 1987.

What's a trillion?

It is a thousand billion. It is a one followed by twelve zeros. In Reagan's budget proposal, it looks like this:

$1,024,000,000,000.

In a speech to Congress on Feb. 18, 1981, Reagan sought to put so large a sum in comprehensible terms.

He said it would take a stack of thousand-dollar bills piled 67 miles high to equal $1 trillion. By comparison, he said, a stack of thousand-dollar bills four inches high would be equal to $1 million.

A trillion is enough to give $250 to every man, woman and child in the world.

It represents nearly a quarter of the gross national product—the value of all the goods and services produced in the United States in a year.

In miles, a trillion would represent 5,376 round trips to the sun.

Copyright 1987 Associated Press. Reprinted with permission

By doing all of the things discussed in this chapter, the public relations writer contributes to the well-being of the client. But client advocacy goes a few steps further. It involves providing active communication support for protecting and furthering the legitimate causes of the client. Figure 7.2 provides an excellent example of client advocacy.

Public relations writers who cannot espouse their clients' causes have no business representing them. If a client's cause is less than legitimate, the public relations writer must no longer represent the client. If the client wishes to peddle information for unethical purposes, then the public relations writer should withdraw his or her support. But when writers are convinced of the integrity and legitimacy of their clients' causes, then they are duty bound to protect those clients' interests with every word they use.

Chapter Summary

In this chapter, we focused on the six principles of effective public relations writing. These are the need for: technical perfection; semantic perfection; brevity and simplicity; interesting and forceful language; truth and accuracy in what the writer has to say; and, lastly, advocacy of the client.

It's Time We Talked.

The Price of Silence.

Two years ago when "unintended acceleration" stories about Audi 5000s began appearing in the press and on TV, we believed that as an engineering company, the best way to respond would be through scientific analysis. In the end, we felt the facts would speak for themselves.

Our silence not only offended our loyal customers but also prejudiced potential customers against us.

Our lack of a vocal response to our accusers was perceived by many as a sign of weakness, or worse yet, as an admission of guilt. Neither could be further from the truth.

The Truth.

In our investigation over the last two years we have studied every technical system in our cars, individually and in combination with other systems. Independent experts have also analyzed the Audi 5000.

No one has found a design flaw or malfunction of the vehicle or any part thereof that explains the incidents of alleged "unintended acceleration."

A highly regarded, independent research organization also conducted studies on those systems that have come under attack by our detractors and has concluded: "[Our] analysis did not reveal a design malfunction nor safety defect in the Audi 5000 C2 and C3 cars (1978-1986) which would cause an 'unintended acceleration' incident, (i.e., simultaneous vehicle acceleration and loss of braking effectiveness)."

Automotive Experts Agree.

A recent in-depth study by *Road & Track* (February 1988) also supports these conclusions.

At the same time various independent and respected motoring journalists, including racing great Mario Andretti, columnist Patrick Bedard of *Car and Driver*, and Chris Economaki, editor and publisher of *National Speed Sport News*, to name but a few, have expressed less detailed but similar points of view when defending Audi's position to their readers.

Audi Leads The Way For Safety.

As our own investigations and those of others continued it seemed appropriate for Audi to share our learning with both foreign and domestic car manufacturers. The phenomenon known as "unintended acceleration" has plagued the auto industry since the introduction of the automatic transmission.

By being in the spotlight Audi was also in the forefront of identifying preventive measures that could help reduce the number of incidents. One such safety device was our Automatic Shift Lock. Its introduction in 1986 was received as a positive measure to an ever growing industry problem.

By requiring all drivers to do what comes naturally to most, that is, put their foot on the brake pedal when shifting out of Park into Reverse or Drive, the Shift Lock helps avoid inadvertent application of the wrong pedal.

Japanese Manufacturers Follow Audi's Lead.

The Japanese Automotive Manufacturers Association (J.A.M.A.) has recently (December 1987) recommended that its 13 member companies install automatic shift locks in all Japanese made cars with automatic transmissions. U.S. manufacturers are considering similar solutions.

Entire Auto Industry To Benefit.

As *Road & Track* stated and others would agree, "Audi's automatic shift lock can reduce 'unintended acceleration' in all cars with automatic transmissions."

As the concern about unintended acceleration grows, and more and more manufacturers are plagued by this phenomenon, the leadership Audi continues to show in identifying the causes should go a long way to solving our industry's problem.

Among The Safest Cars In The U.S.

Identifying the causes of unintended acceleration and providing workable solutions is just one aspect of our total commitment to safety. Our pioneering work in front-wheel drive, our mastery of all-wheel drive Quattro drive and our early recognition of the benefits of Anti-lock Braking Systems (ABS) to driver control have all contributed to creating cars that do extremely well in the real world of day-to-day driving.

In-depth analysis of national accident statistics by the Highway Loss Data Institute (HLDI), a non-profit service organization, confirms the fact that the Audi 5000 is among the safest cars in the United States.

It is our hope that the information presented above will help you form your own opinions about our car's safety and Audi's integrity. We thought it important that our side of the story be told. And we thank you for reading it in its entirety.

By speaking out we've also begun to speak with you. It's a dialogue we intend to continue.

Audi

The 1988 5000 S

▶ **Figure 7.2.** Client advocacy. Reprinted with the permission of Audi of America.

You now know the importance of writing that is technically and semantically flawless. The public relations profession demands no less than perfection—the right word in the right place, expressions that are socially sensitive; sentences that are grammatically correct, simple and readable; and, ideas that are unified by sentences linked together by proper transition phrases. You know too that simple writing need not be dull writing. You understand that by avoiding generic nouns, and abstract and passive verbs, you can breathe life into your words.

Lastly, you know you must be an advocate of your client. Your professional mission is to communicate honestly, accurately and meaningfully to that client's publics. Honesty and accuracy do not, however, mean much if your audiences do not understand your words. Hence, the inclusion of the third attribute of understandable communications. We have shown how there may be a communication breakdown when you are dealing with, for example, large numbers. People do not ordinarily have the capacity to meaningfully visualize and interpret large numbers. Your responsibility as a public relations writer is to take such difficult concepts and translate them into understandable terms. Our discussion on "illustration" offers some insights into how you may do this.

Disregarding any of these principles of sound public relations writing will lead to sloppy, inaccurate and misleading messages that will hurt your credibility and damage your client's reputation. Errors can also be costly, both for you and your client, if they libel innocent people.

To summarize, if there is a moral to this chapter, it is that there is no such thing as a "small" error in public relations writing. Every error is a major error because it may cost you and your clients time, money and reputation.

Writing Exercises

1a. *Situation:* You are the staff writer for the public affairs department of the University of Higher Learning, Someplace, Calif. Your superior, the university's vice president for public affairs, asks you to edit the following rough draft of a news release. In completing this exercise, please keep in mind your mission to produce technically and semantically perfect copy. Watch out for spelling errors, socially insensitive words and jargon. If you encounter long sentences, chop them down to manageable size. Replace difficult words with simple ones. Break the story into readable paragraphs. Rearrange the elements in the story with an eye for unity. You will need a dictionary and *The Associated Press Stylebook and Libel Manual* to complete this assignment.

Copy to be edited: John P. Doe, a professional in writing and Public Relations for more than 20 years, joins UHLS as a full time faculty member in the school of journalism. Doe, author of two books, former speech writers to three top air force officials, a military public affairs officer for fourteen years says the job is a "dream come true."

Although he holds a Doctorate in Communications and has recently retired from the military service Doe has been teaching night courses in communication. Commenting on the appointment, Dean Dempsey, Vice President for University Appointments, said: "Doe epitomizes the kind of manpower this university needs to grow into a great learning institution." Asked about his most frightening moment as a military public affairs officer, Doe replied without the slightest hesitation that it was trying to explain to 150 angry Japanese newsmen how a united states navy submarine had rammed and sunk a Nipponese fishing boat. Doe will teach public relations principles and writing.

1b. Using the Flesch Reading Ease Formula, compute a readability score for the above passage. What type of audience is it aimed at? Next, compute the readability score for your edited copy. Compare the two scores. Give five reasons why you think your copy reads better than the original.

2. Some of the following words are misspelled. Others are spelled correctly. Identify and correct the misspelled words without the help of a dictionary. Once you are done, check the dictionary to see how many you got right.

embarass	rhythm
hemorrhage	quarel
accomodate	silouette
inoculate	querulous
occurred	sattelite
seperate	scheduel
priviledge	relevent
laison	reccomend
supercede	seige
council	sking

3. Chopping sentences can be fun once you get the hang of it. Try your pruning skills on the following sentences. You may use either the deletion or reconstruction technique. Also, watch out for and modify appropriately, words that are socially insensitive.
   a. The company made a profit owing to the fact that the market conditions were good.
   b. Management made the mistake on two separate occasions.
   c. I would like to bring your attention to the fact that your company salesmen are rude and discourteous to paying customers.
   d. To get a job in public relations, you must know the basic fundamentals of writing.

4. Simplify the following sentences:
   a. Management's decision was predicated on the assumption that an abundance of money was forthcoming.
   b. During the preceding year, the company operated at a financial deficit.

c. The conclusion ascertained from a perusal of pertinent data is that a lucrative market exists for the product.

d. They acceded to the proposition to terminate business.

Food for Thought

1. Some would argue that it doesn't matter whether a sentence is grammatically correct or incorrect as long as it succeeds in getting a message across. Based on your understanding of the material in this chapter, how would you respond to this assertion?

2. We have talked about how words can color our images of the things and people around us. Place yourself in the shoes of a spokesperson for the Israeli government. Generate three reasons why you feel justified in saying that "an Israeli was murdered," and that "an Arab was killed" in the context of a shooting incident. Now place yourself in the shoes of a spokesperson for the Arabs and provide three arguments to refute the reasons you gave as an Israeli spokesperson.

3. In this chapter, we have argued that you must serve clients whose causes are just and honorable. How would you determine the integrity of your client's cause? Prepare a list of questions you think will provide answers to your questions about the integrity of the client's cause.

References for Further Study

Cross, Donna W. *Word Abuse: How the Words We Use Use Us.* New York: Coward, McGann and Geochegan, Inc., 1979.

Cutlip, Scott M., Allen H. Center and Glen M. Broom. *Effective Public Relations,* 6th ed. Englewood Cliffs, N.J.: Prentice-Hall, 1985.

Denbow, Carl J. "Listenability and Readability: An Experimental Investigation." *Journalism Quarterly* 52 (1975):285–290.

Fang, Irving E. "The 'Easy Listening Formula.' " *Journal of Broadcasting* 11:1 (Winter 1966–1967):163–68.

Flesch, Rudolf. "A New Readability Yardstick." *Journal of Applied Psychology* 32:2 (1948):221–233.

French, Christopher W., ed. *The Associated Press Stylebook and Libel Manual.* Reading, Mass.: Addision-Wesley, 1987.

Goldberg, M. Hirsch. *The Blunder Book.* New York: William Morrow and Company, Inc., 1984.

Gunning, Robert. *The Technique of Clear Writing.* New York: McGraw-Hill, 1968.

Lippmann, Walter. *Public Opinion.* New York: Macmillan (original edition, 192), 1961.

Newsom, Douglas A. "Despite Progress, Sexism in Language Still Persists." *Public Relations Journal* (August 1986).

Pierce, John R. "Communication." *Scientific American* 227:3 (September 1972):31–41.

Powers, Richard D., W. A. Sumner and B. E. Kearl. "A Recalculation of Four Adult Readability Formulas." *Journal of Applied Psychology* 49:(1958):104.

Read, Hadley. *Communication: Methods For All Media.* Urbana Champaign, Ill.: University of Illinois Press, 1972.

"Speaking English in Disguise." The *Orange County Register,* (November 22, 1986), A21.

Strunk, Jr., William and E. B. White. *The Elements of Style.* New York: Macmillan, 1972.

Taylor, Wilson L. " 'Cloze Procedure': A New Tool for Measuring Readability." *Journalism Quarterly* 30:4 (1953):415–433.

"Trillion Watt Moment." *Popular Science,* (October 1987), 63.

Wells, Hugh. "How to Pick Up a Widow." *Public Relations Journal* (October 1982), 8.

Yardley, Jonathan. "The Increasing Irrelevance of Writing." *The Washington Post.* December 8, 1986, D2.

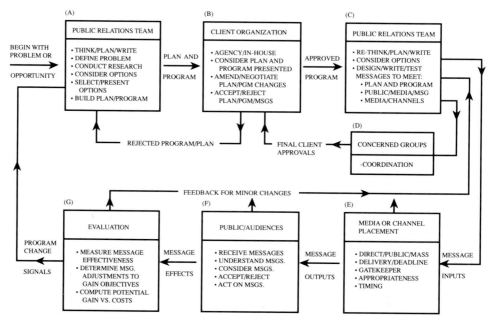

(A)		(B)		(C)
PUBLIC RELATIONS TEAM		CLIENT ORGANIZATION		PUBLIC RELATIONS TEAM

BEGIN WITH PROBLEM OR

OPPORTUNITY

PUBLIC RELATIONS TEAM (A)
- THINK/PLAN/WRITE
- DEFINE PROBLEM
- CONDUCT RESEARCH
- CONSIDER OPTIONS
- SELECT/PRESENT OPTIONS
- BUILD PLAN/PROGRAM

PLAN AND

PROGRAM

CLIENT ORGANIZATION (B)
- AGENCY/IN-HOUSE
- CONSIDER PLAN AND PROGRAM PRESENTED
- AMEND/NEGOTIATE PLAN/PGM CHANGES
- ACCEPT/REJECT PLAN/PGM/MSGS

APPROVED

PROGRAM

PUBLIC RELATIONS TEAM (C)
- RE-THINK/PLAN/WRITE
- CONSIDER OPTIONS
- DESIGN/WRITE/TEST MESSAGES TO MEET:
  - PLAN AND PROGRAM
  - PUBLIC/MEDIA/MSG
  - MEDIA/CHANNELS

REJECTED PROGRAM/PLAN

FINAL CLIENT APPROVALS

CONCERNED GROUPS (D)

-COORDINATION

FEEDBACK FOR MINOR CHANGES

EVALUATION (G)
- MEASURE MESSAGE EFFECTIVENESS
- DETERMINE MSG. ADJUSTMENTS TO GAIN OBJECTIVES
- COMPUTE POTENTIAL GAIN VS. COSTS

MESSAGE

EFFECTS

PUBLIC/AUDIENCES (F)
- RECEIVE MESSAGES
- UNDERSTAND MSGS.
- CONSIDER MSGS.
- ACCEPT/REJECT
- ACT ON MSGS.

MESSAGE

OUTPUTS

MEDIA OR CHANNEL PLACEMENT (E)
- DIRECT/PUBLIC/MASS
- DELIVERY/DEADLINE
- GATEKEEPER
- APPROPRIATENESS
- TIMING

MESSAGE

INPUTS

PROGRAM CHANGE

SIGNALS

To meet the plan's goals and objectives, public relations writers need to be skilled in writing appropriate messages for numerous print publications, using varying styles. These include newspaper and magazine copy, position papers, letters and memoranda, formal plans and reports, and brochures.

WRITING PRINT MESSAGES . . . 8

Introduction

Public relations writers wear many hats. Their ability to write for diverse media and audiences makes their jobs complex, challenging and unique. Our objective here is to focus on common types of print messages public relations writers generate. These are:

1. Media releases
2. Media alerts
3. Photo captions
4. Backgrounders
5. Position papers
6. Business letters
7. Memos
8. Reports
9. Plans
10. Brochures
11. Personality profiles
12. Features stories
13. Image advertisements
14. Issue advertisements

What can you do to make such messages count? This chapter addresses some strategies and skills you need to write effective print messages.

The customary word of caution: This is not a stand-alone chapter. It keys into concepts discussed elsewhere in the book, including the chapters on style, law, research and evaluation, critical thinking and planning, organizational communication and its management, and writing theory. Its pervasive importance can be seen in blocks A, B and C of figure 2.1, The Public Relations Writing Process Model.

Media Releases

Media releases are the most frequently used means of communicating information about an organization to external audiences. They usually inform the mass media about, among other things, material developments in a company (see chapter 14); other organizational events such as anniversaries; and crises such as a breakdown in a utility company, a plane hijacking, or an oil-well fire (Newsom and Carrell 1986, 135–143).

Thus, media releases are a useful source of information for the media. Public relations educator Bill Baxter (1988, 222) quotes an Oklahoma editor as saying, "If the releases stopped coming, we would miss a lot of stories, many of them good, . . ."

Editors' Concerns

Despite their usefulness, media releases often reflect poorly upon the thinking and writing abilities of public relations professionals. In several polls (Honaker 1978; *Editor and Publisher* 1979; Baxter 1988; Gentry 1986), editors have severely faulted public relations writers for:

Puffery. Editors believe that public relations writers generally sacrifice newsworthy information to make room for advertising puffery (Honaker 1978, 17).

Inappropriately focused stories. Public relations writers often distribute generic releases to as many media outlets as possible. Editors dislike receiving cloned messages, preferring instead releases with a local news angle of interest to their immediate readership: "With a few exceptions, we pitch all releases unless they have some local angle—city or state. A few national releases might give us an idea for pursuing a medical or educational feature, but rarely" (Ibid.).

Good news neurasthenia (Awad 1985). Here, the public relations writer deals in complete and accurate public information only in positive and upbeat situations.

Bad news phobia. According to editors polled by the *Washington Journalism Review* and the University of Missouri business journalism program, bad news often is treated casually as non-news, buried deep inside a media release, or softened or misrepresented (Gentry 1986, 38–40).

Poor writing and editing. Forty percent of the newspaper editors surveyed by the National Newspaper Association said media releases required some rewriting, 50 percent said the releases required fairly heavy to extensive rewriting, while the remaining 10 percent said that a total rewrite was the rule (*"Editors Polled,"* 1979, 30).

A PROFESSIONAL TIP:
Clear Writing Succeeds

The brightest idea dims with poor writing. The most masterly conceived public relations program drowns in overblown jargon. Reporters delight in pinning the worst examples onto their bulletin boards as the clients' money evaporates. Clear writing succeeds; clear writers triumph. John Keats said it well: "Fine writing is next to fine doing."

Norman G. Leaper, ABC, is president of the International Association of Business Communicators. He has held a number of corporate communication positions and worked as a consultant for a San Francisco-based communication consulting firm. He served in a number of IABC volunteer positions at all levels before being hired as president in 1984.

Length. Half of the Oklahoma editors polled by Baxter (1988) thought that most media releases were too long and cumbersome.

Content and Style Guidelines

Since editors decide whether a media release gets used or not, their observations about the shortcomings of this public relations tool are important to the writer. In essence, well-written media releases have a good chance of being used. Poorly written releases are a source of annoyance and often get tossed out. Norman Leaper, president of the International Association of Business Communicators, explains in the Professional Tip: Clear Writing Succeeds.

Public relations writers can improve the quality of their releases by keeping in mind the following factors:

Develop a nose for news: Generally, newsworthy information contains one or more of the following characteristics:

1. **Public Impact:** The larger an event (in terms of money, space, or other variable), and the more people it affects, the more newsworthy it is likely to be. Thus, a plant closing attracts media attention because of its effect on the unemployment levels and economy of a community. By contrast, the elimination of a 25-worker section in a company for similar reasons is not as likely to generate such interest.

2. **Prominence:** Names make news. The more prominent a person, the more newsworthy the person's involvement in an event becomes. Thus, "a local banker's embezzlement is more newsworthy than a clerk's thievery, even when the clerk has stolen more" (Mencher 1984, 64).

3. **Proximity:** People generally are interested in, and affected by events in their immediate environment. Therefore, look for the local angle. For example, the release in figure 8.1 is more likely to interest readers in North Dakota than readers in New Mexico.

4. **Human Interest:** Such events involve conflicts between people and institutions, odd and bizarre situations, and extraordinary acts of compassion or courage. By the same token, organizations' involvement in community activities are also likely to generate reader interest; thus, such stories are attractive to editors. People are the focal points of human interest stories.

5. **Timeliness:** The mass media operate on the principle of immediacy. They try to give their audiences news about events that are happening now. "No matter how significant the event, how important the people involved, news value diminishes with time" (Mencher 1984, 62). The moral: The event your release talks about must be current. If you are not writing about a current event, Masel-Walters (1984, 26) suggests looking for a new angle to renew interest in the story.

6. **Currency:** At any given point in time, certain issues dominate social consciousness. For example, in the early-to-mid '80s, society was concerned with child kidnappings and abuse. This led to media interest in any activity relating to the subject. Thus, companies helping locate missing children during that period were able to command media attention because of the importance and currency of the topic.

Masel-Walters (1984, 26) concludes:

When you are deciding whether to arrange an interview, issue a press release, or stage a press conference, determine whether your story meets these criteria, and do so from the general public's point of view. While an event may be of great importance to those involved with your business, it may be of no importance to the rest of the community. If this is the case, save the story for the company newsletter. To do otherwise would only irritate reporters now and cause them to ignore your big stories in the future.

SOURCE IDENTIFICATION

RELEASE DATE

Chevron Corporation
Public Affairs (415) 894-2978, 894-4440, 894-4581, 894-4746
P.O. Box 7137, San Francisco, CA 94120-7137

News

Chevron

FOR IMMEDIATE RELEASE

BISMARCK, N.D., August 21 -- The University of North Dakota's Chinook Salmon
Research Program landed a big one here today: a 22-foot Tiara Pursuit Model 2200,
donated by Chevron U.S.A. Inc.

DATELINE

Accepting the fully equipped outboard and trailer on behalf of the program were
Dr. Thomas Clifford, president of UND, and North Dakota Governor George Sinner.

The $24,500 vessel, christened "Research 1," will serve as flagship of the research
fleet deployed by UND scientists to aid development of the freshwater Chinook salmon
fishery on 200-mile-long Lake Sakakawea.

During dedication ceremonies for the research vessel on the Missouri River at
Marina Bay, Mandan, N.D., Jim Baroffio, regional vice president for exploration, land
and production of Chevron U.S.A. Inc., told representatives of UND and the state Game
and Fish Department, "We believe it's important to support programs which contribute to
environmental and recreational goals."

Baroffio pointed out that sport fishing, in addition to being an important
recreational pastime, can offer substantial economic benefits to North Dakota.

Citing figures showing that Michigan generates nearly $600 million annually from
non-resident fishing revenue from its Chinook salmon fishing program, he suggested that,
"North Dakota waters have the forage base and the potential to do even better."

The Denver-based Chevron executive concluded his remarks with a personal
request of the UND researchers. "Please invite me back when the program develops
some thirty-pounders."

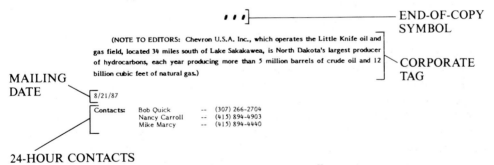

END-OF-COPY
SYMBOL

(NOTE TO EDITORS: Chevron U.S.A. Inc., which operates the Little Knife oil and
gas field, located 34 miles south of Lake Sakakawea, is North Dakota's largest producer
of hydrocarbons, each year producing more than 5 million barrels of crude oil and 12
billion cubic feet of natural gas.)

CORPORATE
TAG

MAILING
DATE

8/21/87

Contacts: Bob Quick   --   (307) 266-2704
             Nancy Carroll   --   (415) 894-4903
             Mike Marcy   --   (415) 894-4440

24-HOUR CONTACTS

▶ **Figure 8.1.** Example: media release format. © 1987 Chevron U.S.A. Inc. Reprinted with
permission.

Use accurate and well-researched facts. For more about this, see chapters 4, 5 and 13.

Ensure that the information in a media release is truthful and balanced. This means telling it as it is, even when the news is bad.

Keep your release brief, fair, simple, readable, and free of errors, trivia and other clutter. In the accompanying article, Lyle Erb shows the public relations writer how to shorten and simplify a release:

The Press Release
by Lyle L. Erb

This press release, admirable in its brevity, can be briefer still. Properly double-spaced on one page, it leaves no room between the letterhead and the text for the editor's instructions to the printer-the slug. It reads:

> PC World Communications, Inc. is pleased to announce the appointment of Margaret O'Reilly as Western Advertising Manager of <u>PC World</u> magazine.
>
> "I am extremely excited to be joining <u>PC World</u>," explains Margaret. "It will be a real joy working for the #1 IBM personal computer magazine, and for the worldwide leader in computer magazine publishing."
>
> "We are indeed fortunate to have someone with Margaret's expertise joining us as <u>PC World</u> continues to grow, and as we continue to put a heavy emphasis on marketing orientation," explains Associate Publisher Jim Martin. "Margaret never seems to run out of innovative methods and fresh ideas. We are especially pleased by her enthusiasm and energy."
>
> Margaret comes to <u>PC World</u> from a similar position on *DIGITAL REVIEW.* Prior to that, she was Marketing Training Manager and earlier Major Accounts Manager at Spectra Office Concepts, a Bay Area office products distributor for Ricoh of America.
>
> Margaret, her husband Paul, and their son Justin make their home in San Ramon, California.

In the lead, why "pleased to announce"? Make it simply "announces." Titles standing alone or following a name are not capitalized. They are capitalized, providing they are bona fide titles, only when preceding the name.

Here and lower in the story the name PC World is underscored. You shouldn't tell an editor what style to use for names of publications by underscoring, capitalizing, or quoting. Let him mark his copy according to his own style. It's easier than deleting yours.

Almost any editor of a general interest publication that I know would delete grafs two and three. The quotes are obviously phony. (See "The Case Against Fatuous Attribution," Writer's Notebook, PRQ [*Public Relations Quarterly*] Winter 1983.) In both quotes, its "explains someone." Why "explains"? Why not simply "said"? And why the inverted construction?

Throughout, the subject is called simply "Margaret." If she had been a man, would the writer have been so folksy on a first-name basis?

Although PC World is underscored, DIGITAL REVIEW is all caps. (I read it "digitalis"—all that energy in the quote.) And "before" is simpler than "prior to." Again, titles standing alone need not be capitalized. Since there is no dateline, what Bay Area is meant?

The last graf, however, needs the most fixing:

"Margaret, her husband Paul, and their son Justin make their home in San Ramon, California."

Unless Margaret is polygamous, the name Paul should be set off by commas. If Justin is an only son, his name also should be set off by commas. These are nonrestrictive terms. If they were restrictive (without commas) as written, they would mean that Margaret has more than one husband and more than one son.

Conform to the style guidelines in *The Associated Press Stylebook and Libel Manual.*

Make sure your release is free of libelous and other legally treacherous content.

And, finally, tailor your release to the editorial needs of a publication. Different media have different information needs. For example, a financial newspaper editor might be interested in the financial details leading to worker layoffs, and the costs and expected benefits of the action. On the other hand, an editor of a general daily newspaper might be interested more in the human and social side of the issue.

The advent of the computer as an electronic editing tool has made it easy for the public relations writer to generate different versions of a release for different types of media. Take advantage of it.

You can learn more about the editorial needs of different publications by reading a few issues and familiarizing yourself with their content, and by asking editors and reporters.

Leads

The battle for an editor's attention is usually won or lost in the first paragraph or two of a media release.

An effective lead performs at least two important functions. It bares the soul of the story to the editor. It also persuades the editor to look longer and deeper at the release, thus increasing its chances of being used.

Public relations writers try to interest editors and readers in their releases with two types of leads: "direct" and "delayed."

The **direct** lead highlights the most important news element in the story. It is usually used in press releases signaling material and other hard-news developments in a company. Here are some examples of direct leads:

> **SOMEPLACE, Calif.— The University of Higher Learning will receive a $1.5 million government grant to develop a physician assistant program in its nursing department.**

> **LOS ANGELES—The Futuristic Aerospace Co. received an order for 20 FAC-311 civilian jet aircraft here today.**

> **SAN FRANCISCO, July 29—Chevron Corp. today announced that Richard L. McGannon has been elected a vice president of the company, responsible for worldwide oil and gas production . . .**

> **NEW YORK—The Futuristic Biomedical Co. today gave $75 million in research funds to the State Technological University.**

Sometimes, direct leads are written to provide a gist of the information in the release. When they do, they are known as "summary leads."

> **DALLAS—In a bid to save $500 million annually, the Fastwheels Corp. will shut down nine of its auto plants nationwide and lay off 16,000 workers.**

Unorthodox variations of the direct lead are the "direct quotation" and "question" leads. The former may be effectively used when the people being quoted are easily recognizable or are popular heroes, such as Chrysler's Lee Iacocca. Here is an example of a "direct quotation" lead:

> **LOS ANGELES—"We are the transport company of the 21st century," said Futuristic Aerospace Corp. President John P. Smart, after learning that his company had won the $10 billion "hypersonic" jetliner contract.**

Question leads may be used when the company is trying to allay public fears about some issue. The question-and-answer format ensures that everyone understands what issue or issues are being addressed. It is also effective because it arouses the reader's curiosity.

Let's assume that a famed columnist advises her readers to stop drinking decaffeinated coffee because it causes cancer. Your company, the Crown Coffee Corp., finds itself compelled to defend its decaf coffees against what it feels is an unfair charge:

> **CITY OF HYPERTENSION, Calif.—Does drinking decaffeinated coffee cause cancer? Not if the coffee has been decaffeinated with fruit extracts, said John P. Knowall, chief scientist for the Crown Coffee Corp.**

Delayed leads often appear in feature releases used to announce soft news and human interest stories. They are designed to get attention through clever word play. The actual news usually follows in the second paragraph.

This example of a delayed lead (also see figure 8.1) appeared in a feature release prepared for Ronald McDonald House by the Los Angeles-based public relations firm, Gelman & Gray Communications Inc.:

> **ORANGE, Calif.—When the earth moved today at 379 Batavia, it wasn't an aftershock of Southern California's big earthquake last fall.**
> **More than 30 children being treated for cancer and other serious illnesses were joined by some 200 city officials, dignitaries and supporters in breaking ground for the new Orange County Ronald McDonald House . . .**

Likewise, a release depicting Disneyland as a "unique" experience, began with the line, "Few words in the English language are more overused than 'unique.'"

Regardless of their form, leads must be short and pithy, usually never more than about 30 words: "Long leads occupy so much of the narrow newspaper column that they appear forbidding (Mencher 1984, 136)." Some features of unattractive leads are, "useless attribution (see accompanying article), cluttering detail and compound sentences . . ." (Ibid).

The Name Game and the Art of Clear, Simple Writing
by Hugh Wells

Why does the lead in almost every news release include the name of a top executive?

The Amalgamated Blackboard Co. will build a new plant in Erasure, Pa., according to Vice President in Charge of Manufacturing Robert J. Amalgamated.

Newspapers inevitably erase the name anyway. So it reads:

The Amalgamated Blackboard Co. announced yesterday it will build a new plant in Erasure, Pa.

We know. Using the exec's name is good politics. But just as often it's done out of habit, and the executive most likely wouldn't notice and wouldn't care if the name were omitted. Yet few writers want to jeopardize their careers by being the first to drop the boss's name.

Little items of style, however, may be the difference between getting published or getting scrapped. They may be the minor irritations that will turn off an assistant city editor or a grumpy city room reporter.

Often the attribution doesn't make sense anyway. The Amalgamated Blackboard Co. is going to build a plant. That doesn't need attribution. It's a simple fact. (On the other hand, if Amalgamated doesn't think the mayor is doing a good job, that's different. It's an opinion, and you'd better attribute it to someone.)

A more logical way to insert the name is to put it in the second paragraph, using a direct quote from the executive.

"The new plant should be the most modern in the entire state," said Robert J. Amalgamated, vice president in charge of manufacturing.

(Notice that we've put his long title in lower case and after his name, where it flows naturally. Some writers seem wedded to the title-first approach, probably with the false notion that it gives greater emphasis and dignity. But it's often awkward and contrary to newspaper style.)

Some very large corporations have such close-knit managements that their executives even speak in unison:

"Profits in the dried-milk industry evaporated this year because of a reduced cat population," said Curdle Milk's Chairman Rudolph T. Jones and President Rupert S. Smith.

We can imagine them saying, "Are you ready, Rupert?" "Yes, Rudolph. A-one, a-two, a-three, go."

These simultaneous recitals often occur in releases about annual profit-and-loss statements. If the release is repeating the words of the chairman's and president's letter to stockholders, then it's better just to say so.

Profits in the dried-milk industry evaporated this year because of a reduced cat population, Curdle Milk executives said today. In a statement issued by Rudolph T. Jones, chairman of the board, and Rupert S. Smith, president . . .

The executives' names wil probably evaporate anyway if the release is printed in the newspapers, but at least the company's top managers don't look like Tweedle Dum and Tweedle Dee.

© 1984 Public Relations Society of America. Reprinted with permission from the October 1984 issue of *Public Relations Journal.*

Body Copy

The body of the release usually builds upon the lead by providing additional facts, details and perspective. These are arranged in an inverted pyramid fashion, where each succeeding fact or detail is relatively less important than the one preceding it.

Take the release about decaf coffee causing cancer. The rest of it could be written thus:

Knowall was responding to recent speculation that decaffeinated coffee is cancer causing.

The company decaffeinates its "Alert" and "Safe" brand coffees using ethyl acetate, a harmless substance found in bananas and pineapples. It also uses a water process where caffeine is washed out of the beans with hot water.

Knowall warned consumers to look out for coffees that have been decaffeinated using the chemicals trichloroethylene and methylene chloride.

These chemicals, known to cause cancer in laboratory animals, have not been used by Crown since 1975. "We don't want to risk our customers' health," said Knowall.

The locally-based Crown controls about 30 percent of the $10 billion decaffeinated coffee market.

The last paragraph in the above example is called a corporate tag. This is a "stock sentence or paragraph about the company, mainly for identification purposes" (Caldwell *et al.* 1985, 2). Here are some examples of corporate tags (also see figure 8.1):

The San Francisco-based McKesson Corp.'s businesses include McKesson Drug Co., one of the largest wholesale drug distributors in the nation; Armor All Products, automotive appearance products; and McKesson Water Division, bottlers of Alhambra Water in Northern California, and Sparkletts Water in Southern California.

Rockwell International Corp., builder of the Air Force's B-1 bomber, has 37,000 workers in California and is Orange County's largest private employer.

While corporate tags are normally used as conclusions, they can be split up and creatively interwoven into different parts of the release. For example, this story places the corporate tag in the lead:

> **SANTA MONICA, Calif.—Wickes Cos. Inc.,** *the furniture and home-improvement retailer,* **said Thursday that it will sell its lumber business . . . (The** *Orange County Register,* **April 22, 1988, E3).**

A final word about body copy. Public relations writers tend to overuse quotations in their releases. Use those which are legitimate and lend authority to the release. Avoid empty quotations that simply occupy space and are included to please company executives. And, when you do use a quotation, make sure it is short. The way to deal with important, but long and awkward quotations, is to paraphrase them down to manageable length.

Format Guidelines

Once you have thought out your release, arrange it in a consistent and acceptable form. The typical press release format contains the elements noted in figure 8.1:

1. **Page size and color:** Always type your releases on standard white 8.5″ by 11″ paper.

2. **Margins:** Be generous and leave wide margins, at least an inch all around. Also, start the body copy about one-third of the way down the page. This gives editors room to edit the release and add specifications for typesetting.

3. **Spacing:** For the same reason, double, even triple space body copy.

4. **Length:** Never more than a page and a half. If your information warrants lengthy treatment, break it up into supporting fact sheets and backgrounders to accompany the release.

5. **Source identification:** Identify whom you are writing the release for, i.e., your client, by name and address. Usually, companies use special release stationery that contains this information (see figure 8.1). If not, type it, single-spaced, in the top left corner of the page.

6. **Contact:** This is the person editors can talk to if they want to follow up on the information in a release. Include the full and formal name of this person and a 24-hour telephone number, single-spaced, in the top right corner of the page.

7. **Mailing date:** This is the date on which the release is mailed out. It usually appears in the top left quarter of the page just under source identification.

8. **Release date:** This is the date on or after which an editor can publish a release. Most releases, especially material releases, are marked **FOR IMMEDIATE RELEASE.**

Sometimes, the writer may place time restrictions on the use of a release. This is usually written in as **NOT FOR USE BEFORE (TIME [specify Eastern, Central or**

Pacific time]) (DATE); or **EMBARGOED FOR RELEASE UNTIL (TIME), (DATE);** or **FOR RELEASE (DATE) OR AFTER.** The newspaper is not legally bound to adhere to this release date, however.

The release date is usually placed in the top right quarter of the page just under contact information.

9. **Dateline:** Always indented and in caps, the dateline shows the city or town the release originated from. Cities like New York and Chicago are nationally familiar and can stand alone in the dateline. Less familiar cities must be accompanied by the abbreviation of the state they are located in. For guidelines on datelines and state abbreviations, see the AP stylebook.

10. **End-of-page symbol:** For multiple-page releases, write **-more-** centered at the bottom of all but the last page.

11. **End-of-copy symbol:** Type **-30-** or ###, centered at the end of the release.

12. **Slugs:** In the top left corner of the second and succeeding pages of a multiple-page release, place the following slug line:

The name of the company (e.g., Crown Corp.)
A clue about the topic of the release (e.g., Caffeine and cancer)
Mailing date (e.g., 06–04–90)
Page number

Slug lines help editors piece releases together should pages get separated, a common problem around deadline time.

13. **Miscellany:** Some other tips. Don't write headlines for your releases. Editors prefer to write their own. Also, never split a paragraph between two pages. And, finally, make sure your release is cleanly typed, follows the style of the publication you're writing for and is letter perfect.

Crisis Release

Crises are fast-moving, unpredictable and potentially lethal emergencies for companies. Because of the rapidity with which they unfold, crises leave public relations writers little time to think and plan. Nevertheless, at such times they are expected to generate releases, speech scripts and other materials for use with publics such as the mass media and company employees.

Thus, crises pose special challenges for the public relations writer. The key to dealing with crises is preparedness. Public relations writers can do this by researching (for more about this, see chapter 4) and writing—during non-crises times—backgrounders, fact sheets and abstracts that they can readily use during crises on the following topics:

1. **Key company operations that are prone to crises.** The organization's product or service line is a strong indicator of likely crises. For example, if you are working for a chemical company, you may want to prepare for a toxic spill; if you are working for an oil company, the likely crisis may be an oil spill or fire.

2. **Company memos and reports pointing to shortcomings in the company's operating procedures which could result in crises.** For example, in December 1984, more than 2,000 people in Bhopal, India, died after breathing the poison gas, methyl isocyanate that had escaped from Union Carbide's plant there. Two years before, the company put out a largely ignored report which warned about safety problems in the Bhopal plant that could cause a serious accident (Fink 1986, 172). Such documents clue writers in on possible areas of concern they may need to research and prepare for.

3. **Biographical and other data on key company executives, spokespersons, specialists and other personnel capable of answering media questions for each potential problem area.**

4. **Other companies' crisis responses,** including examples of media releases.

5. **Dummy copies of media releases for different classes of crises your company might face.** These would serve as models for actual copy you would write in a crisis.

For content, meticulously follow the material information disclosure guidelines listed in chapter 14. They apply for crisis releases as well.

Also, never speculate about the cause of a crisis, the extent and costs of damage done, or the ownership of blame or responsibility. If the crisis is an accident in which people are killed or injured, do not volunteer any information about them—names, addresses, occupations or job descriptions—until after their families or next-of-kin have been notified.

Marketing Support Releases

Two kinds of releases may be written in support of a company's marketing and sales program. The first is the **product release,** writing for which is discussed in chapter 14.

The other is the **testimonial release.** Here, writers publicize unsought testimonials that enhance the reputation and desirability of their clients' products. Such testimonials may be offered by organizations such as consumer groups and independent product testing agencies. For example:

> **DALLAS, June 14—The Stats 'n' Such research firm today named Fastwheels Corp.'s "Swift" car as number one in customer satisfaction.**

The guidelines for writing acceptable product releases apply to testimonial releases as well. Writers must be careful not to exaggerate the conclusions of the independent agency. Where surveys are reported, sample sizes, sample selection procedures, and the survey method used must be specified. Such data help audiences evaluate the quality of the information (also see chapter 13). Thus, continuing the Fastwheels release:

> **According to the firm, 40 percent of 500 owners randomly surveyed nationwide by telephone said that they were happy with their "Swift" automobiles.**
>
> **By contrast, only 25 percent of 500 owners were happy with the car ranked second, CARCO's "Vengeance."**
>
> **One hundred models were similarly evaluated in the survey, which had a margin of error of +/-6 percent for each sample of car model owners.**

Likewise, list the details of the testing procedures if you are publicizing the findings of a testing agency. Should the details be too technical and cumbersome, simplify and highlight the most important details. You could also offer the actual test report or survey to anyone wanting it.

Media Alerts

A media alert, sometimes known as "editor's advisory" or "fact sheet," is an announcement about an upcoming event. It usually tells the editor the name of the event (e.g., the Great American Smokeout), where and when (date and time) it is going to take place, who is going to be there doing what, and some perspective (Why is it important for the editor to send a reporter to the event?).

The format for a media alert is quite flexible. Some writers choose a memo format (see figure 8.2). Others may use the less formal question-and-answer format:

WHAT: Inauguration of Healing Hospital's "CanSurvive" program for cancer patients.

WHO: Former U.S. Surgeon General C. Everettt Koop, M.D., to preside; keynote speeches by former First Lady Betty Ford and actress Ann Jillian.

WHERE: 33 Hope Street (corner of Hope and Survival streets).

WHEN: Friday, Aug. 19, 5 p.m.

WHY: To demonstrate you can fight, beat and survive cancer, and to provide support groups for cancer patients.

Regardless of how they are written, media alerts must always contain a source identification, contact name and telephone number, and mailing date, guidelines for which have been discussed in an earlier segment on format guidelines.

Photo Guidelines

Photographs frequently accompany media releases. Editors value photos because they attract readers, add a visual dimension to the news, and help improve the appearance of their newspapers.

Photographs need captions to guide the reader through their content. The responsibility for writing such captions usually falls upon the public relations writer.

Effective captions generally follow the style rules discussed so far (also see style requirements for photo captions in the AP stylebook). They are simple and brief. They avoid details obvious from the photograph, focusing instead on what is not evident: who or what the people or the objects in the photographs are, what they are doing or

PACIFIC MUTUAL

MEDIA ALERT

To: ASSIGNMENT / BUSINESS / HEALTH EDITORS

From: Geno Effler
           Public Relations Manager
           (714) 640-3014

Date: September 28, 1987

Corporate and Public Affairs

Subject: KIZER, CDC TO ADDRESS BUSINESS LEADERSHIP TASK FORCE
           ON AIDS EDUCATION IN THE WORKPLACE OCTOBER 6

CALIFORNIA DEPARTMENT OF HEALTH SERVICES Director Kenneth W. Kizer,
M.D., will be joined by a representative of the U.S. Centers for
Disease Control (CDC), Atlanta, GA, to discuss AIDS education in the
workplace with members of the Business Leadership Task Force on AIDS
and Alcohol & Drug Abuse, a consortium of some two dozen leading
Orange County companies, on **Tuesday, Oct. 6 at 10 a.m.** at Pacific
Financial Plaza, 700 Newport Center Drive, Learning Center, Newport
Beach. **Members of the media are invited to participate.**

DR. KIZER AND THE CDC REPRESENTATIVE also will be available for
questions following the program at about 11 a.m.

THE TASK FORCE MEETING is being held in conjunction with the
month-long national AIDS public education program, "American Responds
to AIDS," sponsored by the CDC in October.

PACIFIC MUTUAL, in cooperation with the Task Force, has produced and
distributed **free-of-charge** to more than 10,000 California
businesses a comprehensive resource manual, "Facilitating AIDS
Education In the Work Environment," designed to encourage and assist
business in creating AIDS education programs in the workplace. The
64-page manual is underwritten by the Pacific Mutual Foundation and
Pacific Mutual, a member of Pacific Financial Companies.

U.S. SURGEON GENERAL C. Everett Koop, M.D., has praised the manual by
stating that it is "comprehensive and well designed and will
facilitate industry efforts to contain the spread of HIV infection."
Dr. Kizer added: "I applaud the Orange County Business Leadership
Task Force for accepting the challenge of publishing this manual and
for demonstrating the leadership and foresight necessary to combat
this disease."

COPIES OF THE MANUAL WILL BE AVAILABLE AT THE MEETING

PLEASE RSVP TO PACIFIC MUTUAL
CORPORATE AND PUBLIC AFFAIRS, (714) 640-3014

Pacific Mutual Life Insurance Company
700 Newport Center Drive
Newport Beach, California 92660
Telephone (714) 640-3014
Member Pacific Financial Companies

▶ **Figure 8.2.** Memo format for media alert. Copyright © 1987 Pacific Mutual Life Insurance Co.
Reprinted with permission.

intended to do, and other background and perspective. Good captions also tell their stories in the present tense, using action verbs and active sentences. Direct quotations are desirable if they are short and provide relevant information.

Two kinds of captions are important to the public relations writer. The first is a news caption, the second a feature caption.

1. News captions are written for hard news photographs. They generally include the "five W's and H" elements of a news story. If the photograph is about people:

> Follow a standard order when identifying groups. "From left to right" normally is understood and does not have to be written. "Top to bottom" and "front to back" are logical order, but need to be explained. If one person is more important than the rest in a group shot, give the name and then the rest in logical order. In crowd shots, identify the group. If one person [in the group] plays an important role, tell the purpose of the group and then give attention to the central figure (Caldwell et al. 1985, 33).

Following is an example of a news caption (also see accompanying insert).

> **WASHINGTON, June 14—MANDATORY AIDS TESTING BEGINS—Thomas Kitkat, president of the candy company Sugarcoat Corp. takes the nation's first workplace AIDS test under the new mandatory AIDS testing law. (Photo by John P. Doe, Sugarcoat Photo Lab.)**

ELEMENTS OF A CAPTION

TUSTIN, Calif. [(1) dateline] JUNE 14—IT'S SUPERPLANE [(2) overline]—The first

hypersonic jetliner rolls out of Futuristic Aerospace Corp.'s assembly plant. Flying 10

miles high at 5,500 mph, the plane can transport 200 passengers from Tokyo to Los

Angeles in 55 minutes [(3) caption]. (Photo by John A. Shutterbug, Futuristic Corp. Photo

Division [(4) photo credit].)

---

2. Feature captions are written to explain human interest and other soft news pictures. Such captions usually highlight unusual or interesting aspects of the photograph that are not readily apparent. The following caption might, for example, accompany a Rockwell International photograph showing construction of the space shuttle *Columbia.*

> **DOWNEY, Calif., June 14—A main engine is guided into the tail of the space shuttle *Columbia*. The shuttle's engines burn a mixture of liquid hydrogen and liquid oxygen, using 60,000 gallons a minute during takeoff. (Photo by John P. Doe.)**

Once you have composed your caption, format it properly. As a rule, include a dateline, a headline (also called a cutline or overline) to draw and hold the editor's attention and a photo credit.

Backgrounders

Often, media appetites for news cannot be satisfied by mere media releases. Editors and reporters may want to dig deeper into the facts to: learn more about the organization; clear doubts they may have about a release; look for unique and exclusive story angles; ferret out additional story opportunities; and better interpret an organizational news event for their readers.

Public relations writers satisfy editorial needs for perspective by putting out backgrounders on a variety of organizational topics. Simply put, these are no more than detailed fact sheets about different aspects of an organization's people, products, technologies, operations and events.

Sometimes, backgrounders are used to support the main story in a press release. At other times, they are used to meet independent requests by the media for information about an organization.

Backgrounders are useful internally as well. They serve as reference guides and information bases for organizational personnel (including public relations staff) for writing speeches, and for preparing media interviews and press conferences. Thus, backgrounders ensure that the information disseminated about an organization is consistent and accurate, no matter who gives it out.

Content Guidelines

1. Backgrounders generally are single-topic or single-theme documents. If many significant people, products and technologies are involved in an event, write a backgrounder for each of them.

2. They are meticulously researched and painstakingly accurate. Research is the key to writing effective backgrounders. If the information is flawed, errors could carry over to other documents that are based on the backgrounder. Chapter 14 outlines some of the major legal consequences of distributing inaccurate data about an organization.

3. They are almost exclusively based on fact. Opinions are rarely used in backgrounders. The exceptions are when these come from experts to clarify or legitimize some fact presented in the backgrounder. When expressing opinions, state the name and qualifications of the person making them. Avoid empty opinions. They devalue backgrounders.

4. They contain one or more of three types of information: background or historical information; current information, including statistical data; and a summary of the implications of the information, i.e., what does it all mean?

5. Finally, the information sources a backgrounder is based on must be carefully documented and cited. This may take the form of bibliographies or footnotes.

Citations serve two purposes. They help establish the authenticity of the information given in the backgrounder. They also help readers wanting to further pursue specific points dig deeper into cited documents.

If, for aesthetic reasons, you do not cite sources in your backgrounders, be prepared to produce such documentation should a reporter or editor ask.

Format Guidelines

Backgrounders can take many forms. Sometimes they are written as collections of interesting and important facts. For example, the Fun'n' Frolic amusement park might put out the following backgrounder.

Backgrounder: Interesting Food Facts

On an average day, Fun'n' Frolic visitors consume:
   11,300 hamburgers
   7,000 hot dogs
   11,800 orders of fries
   7,600 ice cream bars and popsicles
   14,000 cans of soft drinks

At other times, backgrounders are written as more formal reports (see figure 8.3). In such cases, the facts can be arranged either chronologically—this is often so with backgrounders on persons and topics with a great deal of historical information—or in the order of importance, as in a news release.

Regardless of the format, backgrounders must be clearly identified in a slug line appearing at the top of the document (see figure 8.3).

Finally, as with everything you write, compose your backgrounders in simple, clear and understandable English. Translate corporate jargon and technical details into everyday speech. By following these conventions, you can make sure your backgrounders make sense no matter how sophisticated your audience.

THE CHALLENGE:
TO FLY A
HUMAN-POWERED
AIRPLANE
FROM ENGLAND
TO FRANCE

AIRCRAFT
DESIGNED
AND BUILT BY
PAUL MAC CREADY,
PASADENA,
CALIFORNIA.
SPONSORED BY
THE DU PONT
COMPANY

BACKGROUNDER: Bryan Allen

Bryan Allen, 26, chief pilot of Gossamer Albatross
human-powered aircraft, was born October 13, 1952, at Visalia,
Calif. He received his Bachelor of Science in biology in 1974
from California State College at Bakersfield.

Since 1977, Allen has devoted his time and considerable
muscular effort to ground training and practice flights with the
Gossamer aircraft. Ground training consists of bicycle riding
and exercise on the Ergometer which applies load to typical
bicycle pedals and crank, while indicating the operator's speed
and horsepower output.

At six feet and 137 pounds, Allen possesses the strength/
weight ratio that human-powered flight presently demands.

At Tulare Union High School, Bryan Allen won the annual
Bicycle Day track race three years in succession and competed
with the cycling club at Cal State for two years. Then hang-
gliding called. He and two partners invested $300 in a kite and
taught themselves to fly.

Media Contacts:
Jack Conmy, The Du Pont Company, Wilmington, DE 19898 (302) 774-6695/Stanley Fields, Hill and Knowlton, Inc., (212) 697-5600

▶ **Figure 8.3.** Example of backgrounder. Copyright © The Du Pont Co. Reprinted with permission.

- 2 -

```
        While the "horsepower output rating" is seldom a re-
quirement of famous pilots, in Allen's case it is all-important.
He can sustain .35 HP for more than two hours.


                            #      #      #
```

▶ **Figure 8.3** (*continued*)

Position Papers

A position paper, as the name implies, clarifies an organization's opinions about some important issue. Good position papers share all of the characteristics of good backgrounders, but with a difference. They are always heavy on opinion. Because they are in many ways similar to backgrounders, position papers are sometimes called "issue backgrounders."

While writing a position paper, the writer must be additionally careful to:

1. Provide the reader with both sides of an issue. Stacking the deck with one-sided information will make the reader suspicious and skeptical about the contents of a position paper and devalue its credibility. In general, the best strategy is to acknowledge opposing viewpoints and then refute them using credible and well-researched facts.

2. Summarize clearly the client's opinions of and position with respect to the issue in question. This is usually done towards the end of the document in a clearly marked section.

3. Treat the reader as an intelligent consumer of information. Position papers that talk down to, insult or preach to an audience are self-defeating.

4. Use a slug line on the title page that says "position paper."

Figures 8.4A and 8.4B contain the opening and closing pages of a 24-page position paper that Kaiser Aluminum distributed in support of its battle for equal time on ABC television's *20/20* program.

Business Letters

Letters are the mainstay of an organization's communication efforts. They are the means by which companies feed information about themselves to diverse audiences, and learn about their clients' needs, complaints and praises. Letters are also used to persuade people to support causes, issues, products and services important to organizations.

Public relations professionals write many of these letters for their clients. Hence, it is important for you to know what a good business letter looks like, contains and does.

PERSPECTIVE

Contents

At Issue: Access to Television addresses the question of whether corporations should have access to television in order to buy paid commercial messages on issues and ideas. The access question places two fundamental First Amendment rights on a collision course: the right of free speech versus free press rights.

While the issue is a relatively recent one on the American scene, it is also a matter of growing concern. An increasing number of companies are seeking to communicate their goals and aspirations to the public, in addition to participating in the solution to some of this country's problems, such as energy, inflation, productivity, taxation, environment, government regulation, and unemployment.

As the following pages will show, the broadcasting field —and television in particular—is a uniquely 20th century phenomenon, a technology for communication which has grown up overnight, and is unparalleled in history. Efforts to govern or regulate broadcasting, an industry which couldn't have been anticipated by the framers of the Constitution and Bill of Rights, have been difficult and evolutionary, especially since granting one person the right to use the airwaves automatically excludes all others who might want to use that same channel.

The government has been trying to stimulate a diversity of opinions and viewpoints on the air, primarily through the Fairness Doctrine promulgated by the Federal Communications Commission. Corporations, and others who have attempted to air their views in recent years, have been turned down by the television networks, which cite that same Fairness Doctrine as the reason for their refusal.

Thus, the public does not have the opportunity to hear what business — a significant, contributing force in today's society — might have to say on the pressing issues facing this country as it enters the extremely uncertain Eighties. This issue is now of concern to members of both Houses of Congress who themselves are wrestling with how to insure both free speech and free press in our increasingly complicated society.

The purpose of this publication is to look at the development of television; review the laws, regulations, and rulings which have evolved to govern it; and examine the issues surrounding the controversial idea of corporate access.

Finally, it will focus on an area of reasonable compromise in this complex conflict, a compromise which will protect television's freedom of the press and at the same time allow corporations, and others, access to its valuable airwaves. Most important, the solution will provide the public with more, not less, information than it presently receives.

AT ISSUE: ACCESS TO TELEVISION was written and published by Kaiser Aluminum & Chemical Corporation. It is the fifth in a series of AT ISSUE publications examining issues of importance to the corporation and the nation.

The publication is written for a nontechnical audience to represent as fairly and concisely as possible the major positions and concerns relating to the issue. Information contained in the publication has been taken from public testimony and published sources, as well as from individual research. Any misrepresentation of the facts of the issues or of any individual's or group's position is unintended.

August 1980

KAISER ALUMINUM
& CHEMICAL CORPORATION

Television sets progressed swiftly from a curiosity, providing a status symbol for the most affluent homes, into a common household item. Today, more than 76 million American homes have at least one television set, a means of instant communication without precedent in the history of the world.

▶ **Figure 8.4A.** Position paper – opening. Reprinted from *At Issue,* 1980, by permission of the copyright owner, Kaiser Aluminum & Chemical Corporation.

VIEWPOINT

The proper role of television in a democratic society is being debated increasingly and more heatedly as the enormous impact of such a powerful medium is being realized by the American public.

Kaiser Aluminum & Chemical Corporation believes that the television networks have primary responsibility for recognizing their obligations as a mature business serving the public interest, and that the industry itself should be the moving force in accomplishing reforms.

As this brief study has shown, there is nothing which has preceded television which can rival its sheer power as a means of mass communications, nor its immediacy, its impact, and its ability to influence and educate people. Consequently, regulations by the Federal Communications Commission, legislation passed by Congress, and court decisions regarding television have developed in an evolutionary fashion in reaction to the emerging technology, without any precedent as a guide.

It is clear, however, that at present the decision of who will have access to television rests primarily with television itself. Because of today's structure, decisions relating to a national audience are made almost exclusively by ABC, CBS, and NBC.

With this basic structure, there are four options available to correct the existing situation:

1. Seek legislative redress through a change in the laws which would provide "limited right of access."

2. Seek to change the laws to provide that broadcasters may not reject material simply because it's controversial.

3. Seek regulatory redress which would eliminate the Fairness Doctrine — or exempt commercial time from Fairness Doctrine application — to remove fear of economic loss from the broadcasters.

4. Seek neither legislative nor regulatory redress, but rather work with broadcast management itself to secure the necessary changes in their policies which would allow issues-oriented and/or controversial material to be accepted.

Accordingly, Kaiser Aluminum & Chemical Corporation believes that networks should allow the widest possible access, subject to libel and good taste, for the purchase of commercial air time for the expression of opinions, ideas, and viewpoints. Only by being exposed to a diversity of views will the American public have the ability to choose an ultimate course of action in its own, and therefore the nation's, best interests. If television is not responsive to this need for fairness and balance and does not provide access itself, then regulators and legislators may make the decisions for it, using one of the first three options. That is not the way this issue should be resolved.

Kaiser Aluminum believes that the proper and most effective way to achieve this diversity of views is through the fourth option, by working directly with broadcast management, and through the arena of public opinion, to secure these basic changes in television policy. This responsibility rests with businesses and corporations, politicians and policy-makers, students and educators, and individual citizens.

There is too much at stake by failing to provide for a diversity of views and a balance of facts on television. As Fred Friendly said, "What the American people don't know can kill them."

One of television's finest hours was the journey to the moon. An estimated 723 million people in 47 countries — more than one-fifth of the world's entire population — watched as man first set foot on the moon.

24

▶ **Figure 8.4B.** Position paper – closing. Reprinted from *At Issue,* 1980, by permission of the copyright owner, Kaiser Aluminum & Chemical Corporation.

Parts of a Letter

A standard business letter contains eight elements (see figure 8.5). These are:

1. Source identification, or the formal and complete name and address of your client. Often, this information is engraved or printed on your client's stationery or letterhead. If not, type it flush left and single-spaced at the top left corner of the page.

2. Letter date, or the date on which the letter is written, and preferably mailed. It should appear between the source and receiver IDs on a letterhead, or below source ID on a plain sheet of paper. It should be written thus: January (never abbreviate the month) 14, 1991 ('91 is not acceptable).

3. Receiver identification, or the name, title and address of the person the letter is being sent to. Type this information flush left and single-spaced two spaces below the letter date.

4. Salutation: This is "simply the formal written equivalent of 'Hello' or 'Good morning' " (Sheff and Ingalls 1961, 25). Type it flush left two spaces below the receiver ID. The salutation ends with a colon and ranges from the impersonal (Dear Madam, or Dear Customer) to the formal (Dear Mr. Smith), the casual (Dear Elizabeth), and the personal (Dear Charlie). The choice of salutation depends upon the tone and nature of the letter, and the familiarity of the reader to the writer.

5. The body of the letter is generally single-spaced with two spaces between paragraphs.

6. The complimentary closing statement: Most business letters end with "Sincerely yours," or simply "Sincerely." Other acceptable complimentary closes are "Cordially" and "Respectfully yours," Less formal letters are likely to close with phrases such as "Best regards" or "Best wishes."

Regardless of the phrase used, always capitalize the first letter of the close and follow the last letter with a comma. The close always stands alone, flush left on a line of its own.

7. The signature block begins flush left five spaces below the complimentary close. On a letterhead, it includes the name and title of the person writing the letter. When the letter is typed on a plain sheet of paper, the title of the letter writer is treated as part of the source ID, and is therefore unnecessary in the signature block.

The space between the complimentary close and the signature block is used for the letter writer's signature.

8. Reference: This part of the letter contains: the initials of the secretary typing it (see figure 8.5), the names and titles of other people receiving copies of the letter, and the notation "enc." if the letter is accompanied by other materials. Reference information usually appears flush left two spaces below the signature block.

Crown Coffee Corporation
33 Cardiac Arrest Lane   ①
City of Hypertension, CA 00000

January 14, 1991 ②

Dear Buffy
c/o The Editor   ③
The Daily Scoop
12 Newsprint Alley
City of Hypertension, CA 00000

Dear Buffy: ④

I have been reading your "Healthwatch" column since 1969. I can't thank you enough for all you have done to educate people about some dangerous chemicals in our food.

However, it is not true that all decaf coffees are cancer causing as you suggested in your column, "Cancer in a Coffee Cup" (January 10). Since 1975, many companies have been decaffeinating their coffee beans with fruit extracts. We at Crown use ethyl acetate, a harmless substance found in bananas and pineapples. We are also experimenting with a water process in which we flush out the caffeine from the beans with hot water.

Your readers, however, should be aware that some manufacturers still decaffeinate their coffees with trichloroethylene, a chemical known to cause liver cancer in mice. Methylene   ⑤
chloride is another possible carcinogen that is sometimes used to manufacture decaf coffee.

How can you find out which coffee is safe? My advice is, read the label of contents. If chemicals like trichloroethylene and methylene chloride show up on it, the coffee may pose a cancer risk. If it says fruit extracts or hot water, you can be rest assured you are drinking cancer-safe coffee.

Also, if you have any more doubts about decaf coffee, its contents or the way it is manufactured, call our toll-free hotline. We will be happy to answer any questions you or your readers may have. The number is 1–800–4–DECAFF.

Sincerely, ⑥

John P. Knowall, Ph.D. ⑦ ①
Chief Scientist

jk/jp ⑧

▶ **Figure 8.5.** Composing a letter. A standard business letter must contain a complete identification of the source ①; mailing date ②; identification of the letter recipient ③; salutation ④; a body containing the letter's main points ⑤; complimentary close ⑥; signature block ⑦; and reference information ⑧.

Content and Style

1. Write your letters in simple and understandable English. Remember, the readers are not as involved in the message of your letter as you are. Having other things to do, they are not likely to waste much time on a letter they have difficulty understanding.

2. Be personal, casual and conversational. You can do this with personal pronouns (see chapter 7) and contractions ("we'll" instead of "we will," "can't" instead of "cannot").

3. Use attention-grabbing language. A dull letter is an unread one. Regardless of what you have to say, you need to persuade the reader to look at and attend to your letter. This isn't easy, especially since people are inundated with hundreds of pieces of junk mail.

You can wrest the reader's attention by making the message interesting. A common strategy is to arouse the reader's curiosity with a question:

> **"Are you angry about the high costs of health care?**
> Another strategy is the teaser:
> **Soon the only place your children will see the California condor may be in a picture book.**

An emotional plea can also be effective. (See figure 8.6 for a pitch letter that uses an emotional lead.)

Another way you can win your readers' attention is by tailoring your message to their special needs. For the most part, people want to know what's in a letter (or anything) for them. Consequently, they pay attention to any information with personal and professional benefits.

Assume you want your employees to participate in an AIDS awareness and education program. Your letter might read:

> **You know that we may all soon face the reality of working beside someone who has AIDS.**
> **What can you do to lessen your risk for the illness? And, what can we all do to make life bearable for fellow workers who contract AIDS?**

4. Build upon the benefits of your message. Having caught your readers' attention, involve them in the message by telling them something useful they didn't know before. The AIDS letter might continue thus:

> **With this in mind, we have produced for your benefit a 40-minute videotape on "AIDS in the Workplace."**
> **The videotape tells you in simple language what AIDS is, what some easily recognizable symptoms are, and what you can do to minimize your chances of getting it.**
> **You will also get the advice of five experts on how you can deal with a fellow worker who might have AIDS without any danger to you.**

GELMAN & GRAY

COMMUNICATIONS, INC.
LOS ANGELES · SAN FRANCISCO · PORTLAND

January 22, 1988

Ms. Carole Chouinard
"Hour Magazine"
5746 Sunset Blvd.
Los Angeles, CA 90028

Dear Carole:

"Sometimes you need someone to talk to, or hug...and someplace just to cry." Laura Suzuki knows the needs of parents whose children suffer from a life-threatening illness. Her five-year-old son, Nicholas has leukemia.

Families like the Suzukis, who regularly travel four-and-a-half hours from Lompoc to Childrens Hospital of Orange County (CHOC), will soon have access to a "home-away-from-home" during their child's stay in the hospital. On Friday, February 12, ground will be broken in Orange County for the Orange County Ronald McDonald House, a home where families of seriously ill children can stay while their children are being treated at Orange County hospitals.

Like many families whose children require treatment for cancer, cystic fibrosis or neonatal intensive care, the emotional and physical demands placed on family members can be tremendous.

"It's difficult for these families to provide the support needed by the child when their basic needs, -- sleep, a shower and a good meal -- are not being met," says Dr. Geni Bennetts, director of the Hemotology/Oncology Department at CHOC and president of the board of trustees for the Orange County Ronald McDonald House.

As with the more than 100 Ronald McDonald Houses worldwide, the Orange County house will provide emotional support to parents and siblings of sick children who also benefit by knowing the family is close by. Since 1974, the houses have eliminated costly hotel bills, while providing a secure place to stay -- a place where additional strength and stability are received from other resident families in similar situations. Fundraising efforts to build and maintain the new house are already underway.

818 West Seventh Street, 4th Floor, Los Angeles, California 90017 · (213) 688-7200 · FAX (213) 688-7289

▶ **Figure 8.6.** A pitch letter with an emotional lead. Copyright 1988 Gelman and Gray Communications, Inc. Reprinted with permission.

Page 2

Dr. Geni Bennetts and other community leaders are available for
interviews in preparation for the groundbreaking celebration. We
believe these resources will interest your viewers. We'll
contact you soon to determine your interest. In the meantime,
should you have any questions or would like additional
information, I can be reached at (213) 688-7200.

Sincerely,

Allison Farnsworth
Assistant Account Executive

AF/

▶ **Figure 8.6.** *(continued)*

5. Spur your readers into action. Certain kinds of letters are wasted if they do not motivate the reader into taking positive action. Continuing the above example:

> **So, take a few minutes to ask your supervisor for a copy of the videotape. Then, take it home, keep it and view it at your convenience.**
> **And, when you are done, if you still have questions, call 1–800–4–AFRAID. That's our hotline. We won't ask your name, but we will have an expert answer all your questions.**

Here, the writer provides readers with easy decision and action choices. Since not much effort is involved, the employees may actually take the company up on its offer.

In an informational letter (see figure 8.5), action choices may be as simple as making a phone call for additional information.

6. Empathize with your readers. Show a concern for their problems. Especially avoid embarrassing them if your letter deals with sensitive subjects. The above example demonstrates such tact.

7. Highlight important points. Thanks to computers and laser printers, you can emphasize important parts of your letter by boldfacing them or using color. But don't overdo this. Too much boldface or color makes a letter garish.

8. When you have to give out bad news, spit it out in the first paragraph or two. The best strategy is to start off with an empathy statement, give the bad news next, followed by an explanation and some action choices for the reader, as in the following example:

> **Thank you for applying for a place in our teen astronaut's program. We received applications from 900 excellent candidates such as you.**
> **We could pick only 25 teens for the program. Regrettably, you weren't among them. The major factor against your selection was a negative rating on the "alpha" test. As the enclosed report shows, your scores on the other tests were satisfactory or excellent.**

We have another selection round coming up in six months. Please write or call 1–800–123-4567 if you want us to keep your application on file. Regardless, we'd like to wish you the best of luck in your future endeavors.

For good-news letters, use a similar approach, but substitute a congratulatory lead for the empathy beginning.

9. Make it letter-perfect.

10. Make it easy on the eye. You can do this by providing generous margins, and showing lots of white space through short paragraphs.

Memos

Memos, short for memoranda (singular, memorandum), are notes used only for internal communication, i.e., for the people working within organizations. Their audiences range from a few managers to large groups of employees. Chapter 10 focuses on the strategic aspects of memo writing. Here we address the technical aspects.

Content and Style

Any topic that is important or relevant to an organization and its employees or members can be the subject of a memo.

Good memos resemble good letters in many respects. They are precisely focused, clearly and cogently written, and either inform or motivate their readers.

There are, however, some differences. For example, because their audiences are familiar with company abbreviations, memo writers can safely use these on first reference. For the same reason, institutional jargon is also permissible in memos.

Parts of a Memo

1. Title: Memos are usually typed on special stationery containing the company name and logo, and the legend "memorandum." If you have to type your memo on a plain sheet of paper, center the word at the top of the page.

2. Reference information: This includes, in order, the date the memo is written and sent, the name and title of the receiver (if the audience is a group, use a group label), the name and title of the sender, and a headline-like indication of the topic of the memo:

MEMO

Date:	**January 14, 1991 (01/14/91 is also acceptable.)**
To:	**John P. Knowall, chief scientist (If the audience is a group, say, for example, "All employees.")**
From:	**Peter J. Doe, vice president, public relations**
Subject:	**Response strategies to counter "Dear Buffy" column**

3. The body of the memo provides additional information, suggestions, and, if necessary, a call for action. Continuing the above memo:

> **We need to respond to Dear Buffy's charge this morning that drinking decaf coffee causes cancer.**
> **The best way we can do this is by emphasizing that we use harmless fruit extracts to decaf our "Alert" and "Safe" brand coffees. We may also want to mention the experimental hot water process.**
> **At the same time, I think we need to educate our consumers about carcinogens that are used to decaf other coffees in the market.**
> **Let's meet at 2 p.m. in CCG-42 to draft a letter along these lines to Buffy. My recommendation is that this letter carry your name and signature to enhance its credibility.**

4. Sender's initials: When the sender is satisfied that the memo is ready to be sent to its destination, he or she must initial or sign it in the space above sender name and title. This act legitimizes the memo and its contents.

Reports

Reports are records of company actions and accomplishments which are distributed to a variety of internal and external audiences. Among these are: government agencies, professional associations, stockholders and the financial community, employees and management groups.

Parts of a Report

1. The title page: Every report must have a title page consisting of the name or title of the report, the date of the report, the name and title of the author(s), and the organizational group the report is generated for.

If the report is intended for external audiences, the title page must also contain the name and address of the company, and copyright information, if any.

REPORT OF THE 1990 HALLOWEEN
SAFETY FINGERPRINTING CAMPAIGN
By
John P. Doe
Vice President, Public Relations
The Child Safety Foundation
23 Haven Street, Sometown, Somestate 00000

November 20, 1990

Copyright © 1990 The Child Safety Foundation

2. Narrative or the body of the report: As with everything, there is a wrong way and a right way of writing the body of a report.

Ineffective narratives are poorly written accounts of poorly organized facts. They list activities rather than explain accomplishments, focus on trivial details, and do not leave readers with a perspective of events and activities. They are often repetitive and verbalize details already clear from the tables and figures which frequently accompany reports.

By contrast, good narratives are cogent, well written and stimulating, and do the following things for their readers: They:

a. Highlight important accomplishments.

> **The Foundation's annual Halloween children's fingerprinting campaign was conducted on October 31. Three hundred children, between ages 3 and 10, were fingerprinted at the Mainplace Mall with the assistance of the Sometown police and fire departments.**

b. Explain how the activity fits in with the "big picture," or the overall mission and goals of the organization.

> **This is the sixth such campaign since 1984 when the Foundation was established in the wake of a national scare about missing and abused children. Its primary goal is to help create a safe environment for children through public education.**

c. Measure accomplishments against objectives. Without such comparisons, readers of the report will have trouble deciding whether an action is successful or not. For example, assume you are told that a company made a profit of $5 million. Is this good news or bad? It depends. If the company expected to make $3 million but made $5 million, it is indeed good news. If the company expected to make $10 million, then the news is not so good. If the company made a profit of $12 million the year before, the $5 million figure is definitely bad news.

Continuing the Foundation report:

> **By fingerprinting 300 children, the 1990 campaign exceeded its target of 150 children by 100 percent.**

d. Measure current accomplishments against past performance. One of the functions of a report is to bridge the past with the present.

> **This figure represents a significant increase over the 1989 campaign which resulted in the fingerprinting of 125 children.** (You may want to include a graph showing how many children were fingerprinted during each of the years since the campaign was started.)

e. Give the good with the bad by objectively explaining the success or failure of your actions.

> **The success of the campaign can be attributed to two factors.**
> **First, the issue of child safety has been weighing heavily on people's minds since the much-publicized John P. Doe Jr. kidnapping September 28.**
> **Second, the 1990 campaign effectively addressed two dominant problems that research showed could prevent parents from bringing their children in to be fingerprinted. These were: the toxicity and messiness of fingerprinting ink.**

To calm parents' fears, fliers were distributed around town assuring them that the inks were colorless and nontoxic. The messages were repeated in radio and television public service announcements.

A survey of the 300 parents at the fingerprinting site showed that 80 percent decided to have their children fingerprinted after reading the information on the fliers.

On the negative side, the response of the city's Alpasian immigrant community was discouraging. A post-campaign survey of the 200 heads of households in this community showed that 90 percent did not (and would not) have their children fingerprinted for fear that this information would go into a permanent police record and possibly be used against them.

According to Professor Joseph Couch, a specialist on Alpasian affairs at the local College of Higher Learning, only criminals are fingerprinted in Alpasia. He added that a majority of Alpasians bring these negative associations with them to the United States. This would account for their unwillingness to have their children fingerprinted.

f. Provide recommendations for future actions based on what you have learned from this experience:

Future campaigns can overcome this barrier by assuring Alpasian parents that they would be given the only set of fingerprints taken to keep and take to the police if a child was missing.

g. Provide other supporting information, such as costs of the activity (compare actual costs against projected costs) and personnel involved.

h. Conclude with a summary. Wrap up the report with a short summary of the action(s) explained in the report:

Overall, the 1990 fingerprinting campaign succeeded beyond expectations. The only disappointment came from the poor response of the town's Alpasian community. This could have been avoided had the community's fears been investigated and understood at the research phase. These concerns are now known and understood. By incorporating this knowledge, future campaigns can be assured of greater success.

3. Visual support: Many report writers add a visual dimension to their reports by including charts, graphs and photographs. These not only make reports attractive, but also visually highlight important pieces of information.

A final word on reports. As with everything else, make sure your report is cleanly typed or printed and letter-perfect. How a report looks may make the difference between whether it is read or not.

Plans

Plans are blueprints or guides to future activities. Like reports, they must be clearly and cogently written, and:

—explain the objectives of a planned set of activities;
—relate the objectives to the overall goals and philosophy of the client organization;
—list the activities necessary for accomplishing each stated objective;

—estimate the costs (personnel and material) of each activity;
—specify the deadlines for each activity;
—detail contingency and backup actions for each activity; and,
—provide a method for evaluating the success of each activity.

For a more detailed discussion on how to develop and write plans, review chapter 3.

Brochures

Brochures are well-designed and produced pieces of literature used to support an organization's marketing, promotional and other plans.

Any event or subject of importance to the client organization can be the topic of a brochure. Brochures are also flexible documents that are well able to accommodate a variety of writing styles to suit a variety of objectives.

While writing brochures, follow the rules of style addressed in this book. Additionally, investigate and understand the brochure's uses and its actual and potential audiences before you begin to write. Also, find out how much space you are going to be given for body copy. Then, fit your words into the space.

Brochures are visually oriented. They often contain photographs, drawings and other illustrative materials. Familiarize yourself with these so your copy complements the illustrations.

There are two kinds of brochures: informational brochures and feature brochures. **Informational brochures** are functional and use a simple, direct, no-nonsense style of writing. They are written to the understanding levels of their audiences. Figure 8.7 is an example of an informational brochure written specifically for children. It uses very simple language set in large type. Notice the way body copy is complemented by cartoons.

Feature brochures, on the other hand, use colorful and descriptive language. Figure 8.8 is a feature brochure containing interesting historical and other information about humans' attempts to fly.

The following segments provide some guidelines on how feature copy, including those for brochures, can be written.

Personality Profiles

So far, we have been talking largely about functional writing styles. Often, public relations writers are required to compose messages that not only inform but entertain. Such writing, called feature writing, is designed to stir our emotions, stimulate our senses and imagination, and arouse our passions and interest.

Frequently, these compositions are about the people who work with us. They are sold to newspapers and magazines as human interest stories, drama in real life if you will, and make up the content of most company magazines.

Feature stories rely on a writer's particular view of reality. As such, they may take on as many forms and shapes as there are writers:

> Just as witnesses to an accident rarely remember the same details, feature writers select different elements of a scene to report. One might discover an interesting individual; another might observe a revealing exchange between several people; the third might focus on the overall scene without choosing any particular element in it. The choices are largely subjective, but a (writer) learns how to make them with an eye toward the best story material (Rivers and Smolkin 1981, 80).

Thus, while we cannot provide you with a feature-writing formula, we can advise you about some choices open to you while writing features.

Features that focus on a person are called "personality profiles." Like every other form of writing, they have a beginning (a lead), a middle (a body), and an end.

Leads

Public relations writers can choose from among several types of leads to begin their features. Among these are:

1. Contrast lead: Here, the writer juxtaposes two contrasting elements for enhanced effect. *Time* magazine (Aug. 12, 1985, 16) started an arms smuggling story thus:

> **To his colleagues, Army Lt. Col. Wayne Gillespie seemed a straight-arrow soldier, a West Point graduate, . . .**

Six lines down the same paragraph, the story line reads:

> **But, according to FBI agents who arrested him last week, he was also part of a seven-member smuggling ring that conspired to ship antitank missiles to Iran, . . .**

Movie and rock stars like Michael J. Fox and Michael Jackson come to mind when we think of Pepsi. A similar contrast between this high-stepping and frenetic image of the company and its calm chief executive is presented in the lead of this profile ("Liz Claiborne" December 1987, 37):

> **For the chief executive of an aggressive and fast-moving company, D. Wayne Calloway, 51, is remarkably laid back. Colleagues know him as an analytical and unflappable manager who rarely raises his voice in meetings.**

2. Direct quotation lead: Sometimes, writers try to hook their readers with quotations. These are effective when they are short, pithy, moving and otherwise memorable. Democrat Ann Richards, in her keynote address at the 1988 Democratic National Convention, roused her audience by saying that Republican presidential contender George Bush was born with a "silver foot in his mouth." The quotation was a natural lead for several newspaper and television reports the next day.

A word of caution. Avoid long quotations, no matter how strong the temptation to please your client. They turn readers off.

Telephone Tips for

KIDS

Dear kids:

This is for you. It's a few things you should know about using the telephone. Things like:

- Using your telephone to **get help.**
- **Answering calls.**
- **Making calls.**
- **What calls cost extra money.**

Your Mom and Dad will help explain anything you don't understand. And keep this handy in case you need it. After all, it was written for you!

When the Telephone Rings:

Sometimes when you answer the telephone you can't be sure who you're talking to. Find out! Always ask:

"**Who's calling, please?**"

If you don't know who the caller is, don't answer questions they may ask, like:

- "Where do you live?"
- "Is your Mom or Dad home?"
- "When will they be back?"

Or any other questions. It's best to tell these people:

"**Who's calling? May I take a message?**"

That's all you have to say.

If you answer the telephone and you don't like what you hear: strange noises, scary talk, or maybe nothing at all; it's OK to hang up the telephone. You know that the telephone is not a toy to play jokes with. You don't use it that way, and you don't have to listen to other people who do.

How to Call for Help

Knowing how to use the telephone is the quickest way to get help fast. But it's tough trying to remember a telephone number if you're in a hurry or excited, so make it easy on yourself. Be prepared. Open this paper up and make a list of your most important emergency telephone numbers. Your parents will help you. Then keep this list by the telephone, so it will be handy. Remember, _____ call 911 to get _____

A special thanks to the following members of our advisory group:

Tom Cecil
State Department of
Consumer Affairs

Mike Groza
Consultant on Arts, Education
and Human Services

Susan Lange
State Department of Education

Dorothy Leonard
California State PTA

Olivia Martinez and
Estella Morris
California Association for
Bilingual Education

Pat Mohr
Children's Lobby

Emilio Nicolas, Jr.
KUVT-Channel 14

Thom Peters
Santa Clara Valley YMCA

Jim Richards
California Collaborative for Youth

Margie Swartz
American Civil Liberties Union

Jim Vidakovich
Children's Television Workshop
Far West Region

When There's a Babysitter in the House:

Make sure to ask your parents to leave a telephone number when they go out. Then keep that number by the telephone where you can see it. You'll feel better knowing how to reach your parents if you need to, and so will they. Also, make sure the babysitter sees your list of emergency numbers. That way, your babysitter will be prepared for anything, just like you.

Playing it Safe:

The telephone is one of the safest things in your house to use, but it's not a toy. To be safe, remember:

- Keep the telephone away from water.
- Try not to use the telephone during a lightning storm unless you have to.

Calls that Cost Extra Money:

Some of the calls you can make cost extra money each time you call. These calls have numbers that start with 976, 1, 0, or 411. You should ask your Mom and Dad before you make one of these calls. After all, they have to pay for them, and no one likes a surprise in their telephone bill!

There are some special telephone numbers that you can use to find out about things like baseball scores and TV shows. These numbers all start with 976 and they all cost extra money. Remember to ask first.

Tips for Making Calls:

It's a good idea to ask your Mom or Dad if you can use the telephone. They will tell you how long you can talk. Don't talk a long time, because other people may want to use the telephone or call you.

▶ **Figure 8.7.** Informational brochure for children. © 1989 Pacific Bell. Reprinted with permission.

The Gossamer Albatross

The Dream

The Technology

The Creation

The Achievement

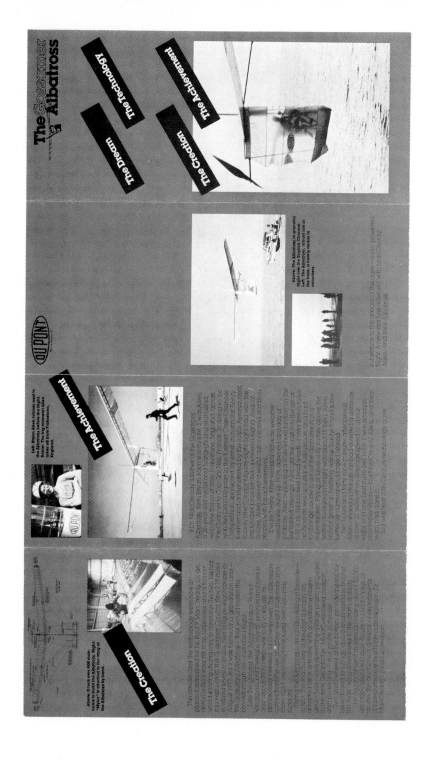

Above: The Albatross in graceful flight over the English Channel. Left: The Albatross, almost lost in the haze, is barely visible to onlookers.

Left: Bryan Allen relaxes next to the Albatross before the flight. Below: The big moment! Allen takes off from Folkestone, England.

Above: It took over 400 man-hours to build the Albatross. Right: "Mylar" is attached to the wing of the Albatross by hand.

▲ **Figure 8.8.** Feature brochure. Copyright © 1979 The Du Pont Company. Reprinted with permission.

3. Descriptive leads attract the reader's attention by their vivid imagery:

> He looked like Gary Cooper in "High Noon" standing in the middle of this sleepy old town's main street.
> Police Chief Lonny Hurlbut, 49, was wearing a black hat, an open shirt, black vest, faded jeans, cowboy boots. His .357 magnum rested in a holster hanging from his belt (Hillinger 1985, 6).

4. Teaser lead: Here, the writer tries to lure the reader into the story by making statements that make sense only when you read on:

> To say that Elizabeth Claiborne Ortenberg designs and sells sportswear misses the point (*"A Mellow Style"* December 1987, 46).

5. Dramatic lead: The writer overpowers the reader with a striking statement:

> Tipping the scale at 1,200 lbs., he is the heaviest man in the world.

> At age 22, John P. Doe is the youngest self-made billionaire in the world. Chief executive of . . .

6. Anecdotal lead: Readers love stories in which the writer tries to please them with a few tales and flashbacks:

> John Liljeberg believes that even a seemingly hopeless situation can be turned around with the proper help. The 48-year-old Louisiana developer's conviction was born 26 years ago after a near-fatal air accident.
> Liljeberg was co-piloting a twin-engine Navy plane on a routine training flight over Greenville, Miss., when . . . (*"Material Support"*, May/June 1984, 14).

7. Narrative lead: The writer tries to build reader interest by narrating a sequence of events. Jon Franklin, chief science writer for *The Evening Sun* in Baltimore, wrote this lead for a story that, in 1979, won him the first Pulitzer Prize to be awarded for a feature story:

> In the cold hours of a winter morning, Dr. Thomas Barbee Ducker, University Hospital's senior brain surgeon, rises before dawn. His wife serves him waffles but no coffee. Coffee makes his hands shake.

8. Chronology lead: Here, the writer uses time and date with telling effect:

> 11:30 p.m.
> The office building is dark except for a light in the corner office on the 12th floor.
> "The boss is working late again," mutters old Peter Vigilant, the watchman, as he makes his rounds.

9. Humorous lead: Properly written, this is one of the most effective leads. Journalism professor Richard Lentz demonstrates the use of humor in this lead for a story about an unemployed worker who waits three hours in a line before he's told he's in the wrong line. Something snaps inside the worker who goes to a nearby supermarket, buys a pie, returns, and flings it at the woman who told him he was in the wrong line.

Revenge was not only sweet for unemployed welder Nickolas H. Romain—it was loaded with calories.
And the price was right—$2.79.

Writers wishing to use humor must be careful that their barbs are not tasteless and offensive to the reader.

Body Copy

1. Synthesize observation with creative expression: People's mannerisms, the way they dress and the objects they surround themselves with say a great deal about their personalities. New journalism pioneer Tom Wolfe calls these symbols of a person's "status life" (Rivers and Smolkin 1981, 21). They also provide the fascinating little details that bring feature stories to life.

Observe every little detail you can about your subjects and their surroundings. Interviews provide wonderful opportunities for observation. See chapter five. When you walk into the room, look around. See if you can recognize an art object; make a mental note about the books on the shelves in the room; and watch your subjects as they go about their business.

Having recorded an observation, synthesize it with words into a creative expression. Use detail for effect. Jon Franklin, whose work we introduced in the section on leads, describes Dr. Ducker's actions as he sits in the lounge, contemplating a dying patient, and waiting for the end:

> **He lays the sandwich, the banana and the Fig Newtons on the table before him neatly, the way the scrub nurse laid out instruments.**

Charles Hillinger's description of Police Chief Hurlbut is another example of how visual detail can be used in a feature.

2. Use color words and expressions: Words have the power to change human perceptions about objects. Use them wisely to plant vivid images about your subjects in the minds of readers.

Author Donna Cross (1979, 125–126) demonstrates the power of language with these contrasting descriptions of a secretary named Nina:

> **Nina, in the anteroom, was seated at her typewriter. Her slender fingers played lightly over the keys. Her blonde hair fell softly to her shoulders. Occasionally, she paused to gently flick one stray lock off her forehead. Her white skin shone with a translucent delicacy.**

Now the negative description:

> **Nina, in the anteroom, was sitting at her typewriter. Her skinny fingers moved across the keys. Her bleached hair hung limply to her shoulders. Occasionally, she stopped to push one messy strand back from her forehead. Her pasty skin was shiny and one could see the blue veins underneath the surface.**

These descriptions attract us to, or repel us from, Nina. Similarly, we shush ourselves and bite our fingernails as we are led into the operating room in Jon Franklin's story about the brain surgeon:

> **A small sensor has been threaded through her veins and now hangs in the antechamber of her heart. Dr. Jane Matjasko, the anesthesiologist, connects the sensor to a 7-foot bank of electronic instruments. Wave forms begin to move rhythmically across a cathode ray tube.**
>
> **With each heartbeat, a loudspeaker produces an audible popping sound. The steady pop, pop, pop, pop isn't loud, but it dominates the room.**

3. By the same token, use positive words in descriptions, not negative ones. Remember, public relations features and profiles are never intended to denigrate or insult people.

4. Show people doing things. There is nothing better than action to keep a feature moving.

5. Use direct quotations. Let your characters do the talking. Present events and happenings through the eyes of the people you are writing about. Being a bystander, you cannot hope to duplicate their emotional and intellectual reactions to events better than they can. Tom Wolfe calls this "interior monologue" (Rivers and Smolkin 1981, 21). For example, *Time* magazine ("Death at the Bronx Zoo," August 12, 1985, 21) captured a father's sadness about the death of his daughter, an animal keeper at the Bronx Zoo, who was killed by a Siberian tiger.

> **Robin's death marked the second time that tragedy had struck the family: In 1969, a son died in a freak accident. Said Sol Silverman, 62: "It's a lot of loss. Seeing my son and daughter lying next to each other in the cemetery was very difficult."**

While following the above guidelines, be sure to avoid:

a. Overwriting. If you try too hard for effect, you may blow it. Keep it down to one, at best a few anecdotes or quotations to illustrate the points you are trying to make.

b. Getting bogged down in background. You can lose your readers by feeding them too many details. Look for highlights, oddities, idiosyncrasies, not a day-by-day or a blow-by-blow account.

Endings

Individual writers have their own ways of ending a profile. You can end with a summary, an anecdote or "a revealing or insightful quotation, or a striking statement that stands on its own as a culmination to the build-up of the article" (Rivers and Smolkin 1981, 78).

Finally, remember that feature writing, while it is a subjective representation of reality, does not give you the license to produce fiction. As with everything else you write in public relations, make sure your features are carefully and thoroughly researched and grounded in fact.

Subject-Matter Features

Public relations writers not only develop features about people, but also about the products, technologies and events of their client organizations. These are loosely called "subject-matter" features to distinguish them from personality profiles.

Generally, subject-matter features share many of the style qualities of personality profiles. They can be colorful, often use visual detail, and present objects in an interesting light to readers. Thus, many of the guidelines presented for writing personality profiles are appropriate for subject-matter features.

Additionally, the writer may do the following things to enhance the effect of a subject-matter feature:

1. Highlight the unusual. If you are writing about a product or technology, give readers an idea of its unique and unusual applications. For example, Stouffer (1960, 108–112) made an ordinary product like paper interesting to his readers by dwelling on trivia such as throw-away paper bathing suits (a novelty then), paper "so strong that, even when soaking wet, it could be run over by a tank . . . without falling to pieces" (Ibid, 108), and wallpaper "that will not only paste itself on, but will kill flies and keep itself clean" (Ibid).

2. Illustrate the difficult. Often, the scientific and technical aspects of products and technologies are complex and difficult to interpret for the reader. Public relations writers may achieve this by illustrating such details (see chapter 7 for more about illustration) through analogies.

3. Bring people into the story. Behind every product, technology or event is a person or a team. And, where there are people, there is always some anecdote that brings a human-interest dimension to products and technologies. Quote, for example, the people involved with the product. Have the people who are going to use it (or have used it) say what they think about it.

Likewise, talk about the people participating in events.

4. Look at the subject matter from the perspective of the reader. Look for angles to connect the reader to the feature. Write to the level of your audience. The Stouffer feature on paper succeeds in giving the kind of information children like. After all, it was written for *Reader's Digest Junior Treasury,* a collection of stories for children.

Lastly, to repeat an earlier point, features are not licenses to write fiction. Make sure your features are grounded in fact.

Image Advertising

The next weapon in a public relations writer's arsenal is the ability to write advertising copy.

Public relations professionals use advertising to achieve three objectives: to enhance a client's social reputation, to persuade people to support some cause or issue dear to the clients, and as a marketing support tool.

Advertising that is used to show a client off as a good citizen is called "corporate image," or simply "image" advertising. It achieves this objective by showing the client as a constructive partner in an issue that is dear to society.

Figure 8.9 shows one of many actions Chevron Corp. is taking to protect our environment, an issue that has dominated societal consciousness since the 1970s.

The **headline** teases the reader into wondering about the connection between the golden eagle and a power line. The **body copy** picks up where the headline leaves off by detailing a thoughtful action taken by a thoughtful company to protect the golden eagle from coming to harm by landing on a power line. The last element in the ad is the company signature, or **logo.** The logo identifies the oil company, Chevron, as the protector of the eagle.

Among other social issues that image ads can successfully tie client organizations to are:

1. Efforts to hire women, minorities and handicapped persons.

2. Participation in socially-beneficial programs. For example, McDonald Corp.'s highly-publicized Ronald McDonald House provides a "home-away-from-home" for relatives of cancer patients in Australia, Canada, Europe and the United States.

3. Efforts to improve the quality of education. IBM Corp. ties its efforts to provide needy schools with teachers drawn from among its own employees to its image as a leader in education.

Likewise, public relations writers can enhance their clients' reputations by showing them as hardworking, intelligent, progressive and honest.

Issue Advertising

When advertisements are used to build support for some issue or cause dear to a client organization, they are called "issue" or "issue advocacy" ads. Figures 8.10 and 8.11 contain calls for support for opposing views about the subject of gun control.

Both ads use the traditional ad layout of a headline, body copy and a logo.

Sometimes, however, the body copy of an issue ad can be written as an editorial (see figure 8.12). When this is done, it is known as an "advertorial," or an ad written like an editorial. Writers must make sure that advertorials are boxed and clearly identifiable as ads. Chapter 14 addresses some legal consequences of a failure to do this.

Regardless of how it is written, the body copy of an issue ad must clearly state the issue being addressed, the client organization's view of the issue, supporting evidence, a plea for public support, and a call for action.

Different kinds of appeals can be used to muster public support for a client's point of view. A commonly-used appeal is fear. The National Rifle Association ad in figure 8.10 plays on people's fear of being victimized by criminals to support its plea for the right to bear arms. The Handgun Control ad (see figure 8.11), on the other hand, tries to scare its audience with references to cop killers and armed criminals at large.

Fear and other emotional pitches are rarely used in advertorials, which, like editorials, instead appeal to logic and reason (see figure 8.12).

The eagle and the powerline.

This Golden Eagle could land in trouble. The high point he seeks to rest on could be a 13,000-volt power line. But, fortunately, he lands unharmed.

Wooden platforms above the power lines now protect the eagle. They were designed and put there by a lot of different people whose jobs brought them to this remote area in Wyoming — people who worked together to keep the eagle above danger.

Do people really reach that high to protect a natural wonder?

People Do.

Chevron

For more information write: People Do-E, P. O. Box 7753, San Francisco, CA 94120

▶ **Figure 8.9.** Image advertising. Copyright © 1987 Chevron U.S.A. Inc. Reprinted with permission.

HOW MUCH RED TAPE IS TOO MUCH RED TAPE WHEN HE THREATENS TO KILL YOU?

According to the U.S. Department of Justice, a 20-year-old American has a 72% chance of being victimized by violent crime in his or her lifetime.

Any red tape is too much.

Why should a threatened human being be forced to "wait" weeks or months before she can acquire a firearm for legal self-defense? She has never committed a crime. She never intends to. Yet she must wait. While those who *do* intend to commit crimes do not obey the law. And do not wait.

That's why our constitution guarantees your right to own a firearm. A right that can be as precious as life itself.

Don't own a firearm if you choose not to. But never let anyone deny or delay your constitutional freedom to make that choice.

DEFEND YOUR RIGHT TO DEFEND YOURSELF.

▶ **Figure 8.10.**   Issue advertising. Copyright 1988 National Rifle Association of America. Reprinted with permission.

"Cop-killer bullets, machine guns, mail-order handguns... Has the N.R.A. gone off the deep end?"

Joseph McNamara, Police Chief
San Jose, California

❝It's my job to enforce the laws and keep the peace.

And like many of my colleagues, I used to think the National Rifle Association was on my side. After all, they supported firearm safety among hunters, targetshooters and other law-abiding gun owners.

But lately, the N.R.A.'s leaders seem to have lost any sense of responsibility.

A few years ago, for example, they lobbied Congress to allow the sale of armor-piercing bullets.

This special ammunition isn't used for hunting game. It's for blasting through "bullet-proof" vests and killing the man or woman inside—most likely a police officer.

The N.R.A. wanted to keep these cop-killer bullets legal. And that's not all. Their high-powered lobbyists also tried to make it legal to sell handguns through the mail.

I think you'll agree the last thing we need is a flood of cheap, largely untraceable handguns on the streets. But that's exactly what mail-order sales would encourage.

It took the united voice of professional law enforcement to stop the N.R.A.'s push for cop-killer bullets and mail-order handguns.

The N.R.A.'s leadership, however, seems beyond reason. Now they want to permit the sale of new machine guns nationwide. Machine guns! What's next—flamethrowers? Bazookas? It's enough to give a police officer nightmares.

The N.R.A. is also busy trying to gut state laws against carrying concealed weapons. They're fighting common-sense proposals for a waiting period on handgun sales—a basic safeguard giving law enforcement time to check for a criminal record.

They've even come out against legislation to prevent extremist hate groups from running para-military "boot camps" in our peaceful countryside.

In recent years, the N.R.A.'s leadership has repeatedly ignored the objections of professional law enforcement. Their actions make our jobs more difficult—and more dangerous. And they've poured millions of dollars into local elections, seeking to intimidate public officials who dare to speak out.

If you're an N.R.A. member, start questioning your leadership. If you're a citizen concerned about violence in America, please start getting involved.

Sale of cop-killer ammo would be legal if the N.R.A. had its way.

The N.R.A. has become one of the most powerful special interests in Washington. Like a loaded gun, that power must be handled with care. And should never be pointed in the wrong direction.❞

Help me fight the N.R.A.!

John Hinckley pulled a $29 revolver from his pocket and shot the President, a secret service man, a police officer, and my husband. I'm not asking for sympathy, I'm asking for your help. Tens of thousands of Americans have joined Handgun Control, Inc., for the reason I did—because, together, we can take on the N.R.A. and win. Please pick up a pen, fill out the coupon, add a check to aid our work, and mail it to me today. Thank you.

Sarah Brady

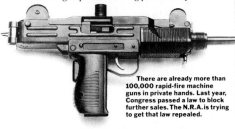

There are already more than 100,000 rapid-fire machine guns in private hands. Last year, Congress passed a law to block further sales. The N.R.A. is trying to get that law repealed.

It's time to break the N.R.A.'s grip on Congress once and for all. Here's my contribution to Handgun Control, Inc., the national non-profit citizens group you help direct:

☐ $15   ☐ $25   ☐$35   ☐ $50   ☐ $100 or $_____

☐ Tell me more about how I can help.

NAME _____

ADDRESS _____

CITY _____ STATE _____ ZIP _____

HANDGUN CONTROL

1400 K Street, N.W., Washington, D.C. 20005, (202) 898-0792

▶ **Figure 8.11.**   Issue advertising. Reprinted with permission of Handgun Control, Inc., Wash. DC, Sarah Brady, Chair.

...with liberty and justice (and free speech) for ~~all~~ *some*

It has become something of a cynical cliche to state that all men are created equal, but some are more equal than others.

Today, severe pressure is being exerted from several quarters to bend the First Amendment guarantees of free speech and make some speech and some speakers more equal than others. One bill in Congress would proclaim that it's perfectly proper to ban "lesser" speech, such as cigarette advertising, so long as more noble speech, such as campaign orations, one would presume, remain constitutionally protected. On another front, the Federal Communications Commission has voted to abolish the Fairness Doctrine, on the ground that it has, over the years, restricted the free-speech rights of broadcast journalists. Left unanswered by the F.C.C. is the question of what happens to the right of everybody else to speak and be heard on television.

The bill to ban cigarette advertising is currently the subject of hearings by the House Subcommittee on Health and Environment. The transcripts are lengthy; some are erudite legal briefs, replete with footnotes. Others are statements by professional athletes and others concerned with the health threat posed by smoking. We have no doubt that all the proponents are motivated by a desire to protect the American people—from themselves, if need be. And that Big Nanny attitude is precisely what worries us.

We are deeply concerned that once there's a precedent for protecting us against ourselves, there'll be no way of getting the censor's nose out from under the national tent. Many Americans see liquor, wine, and beer as a health threat. Once cigarette ads are banned, pressure is sure to follow to outlaw advertising for those products. Cholesterol has been linked to heart disease. There go ads for beef, cheese, and milk. Cars, too, can kill. There go the auto ads. Boating and skiing can be dangerous. There go the advertising revenues that support the travel section in your Sunday papers. (And if papers and TV net-

works lose the bulk of their revenue sources, who'd bring us the news each day? A government press?)

The point is that, in a free society, people need as much information as they can get, from all sources, to make informed choices. And when the sources of information are restricted, so is the individual's freedom of choice.

We could muster all the legal arguments against curbing the First Amendment rights of cigarette advertisers, but we'll leave that to the lawyers. As we've said, we see the overriding issue as censorship by an elite—any elite—and the domino effect such censorship, once imposed, is guaranteed to generate.

As for the F.C.C. and the Fairness Doctrine, we strongly urge the Congress to step in and mandate that all sides of a controversial issue of public importance be fairly represented on the airwaves, and not just those views held by network newspersons.

It has been stated that the Fairness Doctrine may have been necessary when there were only a few TV stations, but that cable TV, ultra-high-frequency channels, and other means of "narrowcasting" have made it obsolete. But the fact remains that vast portions of the nation—including some parts of a major city like New York—have no access to cable TV. It's also still a fact that the majority of Americans get the bulk of their news from the three major networks.

The Fairness Doctrine, properly enforced, was the only vehicle for assuring television access for minority opinions and even for unpopular opinions. In a democracy, such access is far too important to leave up to the handful of de facto censors who decide what Americans can and cannot see on the nightly news.

We maintain that voices in a democratic society—individual and corporate alike—shouldn't be stifled or filtered through Big Nanny. Whether the topic is cigarettes, or energy policy, or the latest in designer jeans, the First Amendment shield must never be lowered, or selectively applied.

Mobil®

▶ **Figure 8.12.** "Advertorial" advertising. Copyright © 1987 Mobil Corporation. Reprinted with permission.

Marketing Support

Often, institutional ads, because of their reputation-enhancing qualities, are used to support a client organization's marketing and sales efforts. Such ads highlight and tie attributes such as a company's commitment to technological excellence, trustworthiness and reliability to a specific product or service (see figure 8.13).

Chapter Summary

In this chapter, we addressed three writing forms the public relations writer must know and master. The first was informational writing, examples of which are media releases, media alerts, fact sheets and backgrounders, business letters, memos, reports and plans. For each, we provided format, content and style guidelines, and examples.

The second type of public relations writing discussed in this chapter was feature writing, or writing for entertainment. We addressed two types of features commonly expected of public relations writers, namely, personality profiles and subject-matter features. The former focuses on people, while the latter is about products, technologies and events generated by companies.

The last type of writing addressed in this chapter was persuasive writing. Here, we looked at advertising forms prevalent in public relations. In particular, we focused on image ads, issue ads and marketing support ads, their content, some appeals used to persuade people, and some examples of each.

A final word. As we said earlier, this is not a stand-alone chapter. For it to make complete sense to the student of public relations writing, it must be read in tandem with the chapters on style, law, research, planning, and theory. Good writing incorporates elements of each of these. We hope yours will.

Writing Exercises

You are the staff writer for the Child Safety Foundation (23 Haven Street, Sometown, Somestate 00000). Read through the report on fingerprinting children in the "reports" segment of this chapter. Using the information in that report, complete the following assignments:

1. Assume that the fingerprinting campaign never took place. However, you want the Foundation to get involved in such a campaign. Based on information in the report, draw up a plan or blueprint for such a campaign using the guidelines in the section on "plans" and in chapter 3. Justify the communication instruments, such as fliers, brochures or pamphlets you propose to use. Research and include these and other estimated campaign costs in a budget section.

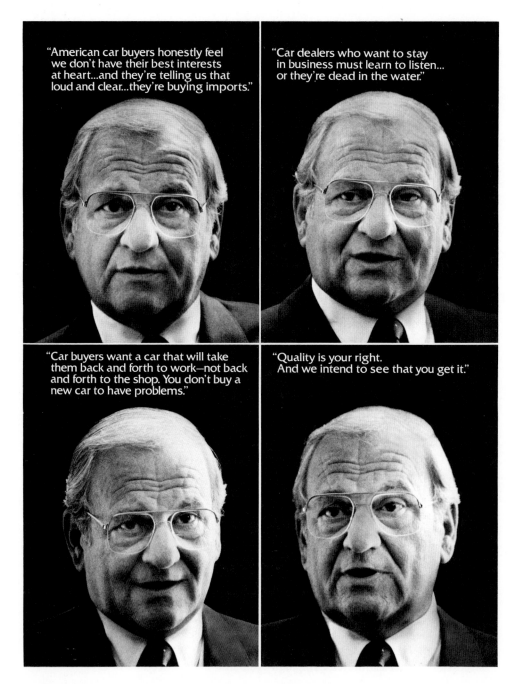

▶ **Figure 8.13.** Institutional advertising. Copyright 1990 Chrysler Motors. Reprinted with permission.

CHRYSLER MOTORS ANNOUNCES

THE CAR BUYER'S BILL OF RIGHTS

1. EVERY AMERICAN HAS THE RIGHT TO A QUALITY CAR

You want a car that will start every morning.

You want a car that will age well. And give you years of satisfaction.

You want quality. It's your right. Undisputed right.

Quality is also the first commitment of the carmaker. Without it he becomes morally and fiscally bankrupt. Chrysler has no intentions of forsaking this commitment.

Since 1980, Chrysler–with new leadership and a new resolve– initiated **Five Key Quality Programs** involving every member of the work force, every level of management. Chrysler has completed 5 million hours of worker training, enrolled 26,000 employees in quality schools and put 583 quality teams in place.

The goal: top the quality of the imports. It's an ambitious goal, but results are already showing it is within reach. Corporate quality indicators show that, over the last 8 years, Chrysler-built car and truck quality has improved 43%.

Lowest recalls. During the same 8-year period, Government records show that Chrysler has the lowest average safety recall record of any American car company for passenger cars registered for the '80 through '87 model years.

And over the last 5 years, lower than such prominent imports as BMW, Porsche and Volvo.

2. EVERY AMERICAN HAS THE RIGHT TO LONG–TERM PROTECTION

Chrysler has consistently led the industry in long-term quality protection.

In 1980, Chrysler introduced the innovative 5/50 Protection Plan. In 1987, Chrysler extended this coverage substantially on the most important part of your car, the engine and powertrain, to 7 years or 70,000 miles. It's the **longest powertrain protection** in the industry. And you also get 7-year or 100,000-mile protection against outer body rust-through.* The plan covers every car, truck and minivan Chrysler builds in North America, and now it includes '89 Jeep vehicles. 7/70, unprecedented when introduced…unsurpassed today.

3. EVERY AMERICAN HAS THE RIGHT TO FRIENDLY TREATMENT, HONEST SERVICE AND COMPETENT REPAIRS

Dealer service is the key link–the most fragile link–between the car buyer and the carmaker. It can make or break a relationship.

Chrysler understands this, better than most. And (under the direction of Lee Iacocca) has taken specific action to strengthen and revitalize this relationship. Results are gratifying.

Highest satisfaction. Chrysler owners have the highest level of satisfaction of any buyers of American cars. Higher than GM owners. And significantly higher than Ford owners.**

As Lee Iacocca says, "The next great leap forward in the car industry isn't going to happen in Detroit. It's going to happen at the dealership." One telling example: In 1981, our dealer technicians received 184,000 hours of training. Last year, 542,184 hours. That's an increase of almost 200%. And the result of a joint effort by Chrysler Management and the tremendous and willing commitment of over 4,000 Chrysler Motors' dealers.

4. THE RIGHT TO A SAFE VEHICLE

Safety is a right we all desire, not just for ourselves, but for our families, too. That's why Chrysler has committed enormous resources and talents to building you a safe car. And that commitment has taken hold:

…Chrysler Motors–not Ford or GM–is the first American car company to offer **air bags as standard equipment** on selected models.

…Every Chrysler-built passenger car has over 30 safety features standard for '88.

…By 1992, Chrysler will have spent 440 million dollars on testing to learn how to enhance your safety.

…Chrysler Motors has a **Safety Shield Program** from design through assembly. Safety components are identified by a safety shield, so everyone at the factory knows its importance to safety. This program guards against the malfunction of critical items such as brakes, wipers, steering systems and starters. And is one of the prime reasons why Chrysler Motors has the lowest average percentage of safety-related recalls for any American car company.

5. THE RIGHT TO ADDRESS GRIEVANCES

If you have a warranty-related problem with your dealer, you have an impartial ear ready and willing to listen to your side of the story, and this comes at no cost to you: **The Customer Arbitration Board.**

This Arbitration Board consists of three voting members: a local customer advocate, a technical expert and a person from the general public. Not one of them is affiliated with Chrysler in any way.

All decisions made by the Board include the action to be taken by the dealer or Chrysler and the time by which the action must be taken.

All decisions are binding on the dealer and Chrysler, but not on you, unless you accept the decision. The whole process normally takes no longer than 40 days.

6. THE RIGHT TO SATISFACTION

Chrysler believes there's no secret to satisfying customers. Build them a quality product. A safe product. Protect it right–with the longest powertrain warranty in the business. Service it right. And treat them with respect. It's that simple.

And Chrysler is doing exactly that. The proof is coming from you, the customer.

J.D. Power and Associates, one of the most respected research organizations in the industry, surveyed over 25,000 owners of 1987 passenger cars for product quality and dealer service. The results: Chrysler Motors has the **highest customer satisfaction** of any American car company–**two years running**–for overall product quality and dealer service. **

Chrysler believes it's our job to satisfy your needs. We have the obligations…you have the rights.

"QUALITY IS YOUR RIGHT. AND WE INTEND TO SEE THAT YOU GET IT."

Lee Iacocca

CHRYSLER MOTORS

CHRYSLER·PLYMOUTH·DODGE
DODGE TRUCKS·JEEP·EAGLE

*See these limited warranties at dealer. Deductibles and some restrictions apply. **J.D. Power and Associates 1988 CSI Customer Satisfaction with Product Quality and Dealer Service for 1986 and 1987 domestic cars.

2. Write a one-page press release for use by *Kidweek,* a monthly magazine aimed at children between ages 5 and 10. Visualize a picture that you would like to send along with the release and write a 35-word caption for it.

3. Visit your local police station. Gather the facts and write a one-page backgrounder or fact sheet on each of the following topics:
   —The ink (or inks) used for fingerprinting.
   —How the fingerprints help police track missing children.
   —Tips for parents on completing and storing the fingerprint sheets.

4. Assume that your town's mayor and his staff are ignorant about the magnitude of the missing children problem. Write the following to enlighten the mayor:
   —A backgrounder on how serious the missing children problem has become. Research and include statistics on missing children between 1984 and 1990.
   —A pitch letter persuading the mayor to lend support for the campaign.

5. Prepare two issue ads urging parents to get their children fingerprinted. Use a fear appeal in the first of these. Appeal to reason in the second.

6. Assuming that the campaign has been successfully completed, write a memo circulating the news to your colleagues in the Foundation.

Food for Thought

You care for children and are horrified by tales of missing kids. You desperately want to do something to make the world safer for children. You are convinced that fingerprinting kids is the best way of doing this.

Your past campaigns to persuade parents to get their kids fingerprinted failed miserably. You feel a big scare is needed to get the parents motivated.

With the best of intentions, you decide to plant false information about missing children in the media. You also plan a fake kidnapping to scare your audience.

Think about this awhile. Then write a 150-word rationale, stating three good reasons why you shouldn't do what you plan to do.

References for Further Study

Awad, Joseph F. *The Power of Public Relations.* Westport, Conn.: Praeger Publishers, 1985.

Baxter, Bill. The news release: "The Ideas Whose Time has Gone" in Ray E. Hiebert, ed. *Precision Public Relations.* New York: Longman, 219–223.

Caldwell, Mary P., Elizabeth B. Dickey, Ann H. Herlong and Elnora W. Stuart. *Public Relations and Persuasion Writing,* 2nd ed. Minneapolis, Minn. Burgess Publishing Company, 1985.

Cross, Donna W. *Word Abuse: How the Words We Use Use Us.* New York: Coward, McCann & Geochegan, Inc., 1979.

"Editors Polled on Acceptability of News Releases." *Editor and Publisher.* November 10, 1979, 30.

Erb, Lyle L. "The Press Release." *Public Relations Quarterly,* 30:3 (Fall 1985):32.

Fink, Steven. *Crisis Management: Planning for the Inevitable.* New York: AMACOM, 1986.

Gentry, James K. "Business Editors Rate the Best and Worst of Corporate PR." *Washington Journalism Review* 8:7 (July, 1986):38–40.

Hillinger, Charles. " 'Cowboy Cop' Has a Look of the Past and Town Loves It." *Los Angeles Times,* June 10, 1985, 2–6.

Honaker, Chuck (1978). "When Your Releases Aren't Working." *Public Relations Journal* March 1986, 16–19.

"Liz Claiborne." *Business Month.* December 1987, 46.

Masel-Walters, Lynn. "Working with the Press: Strategies for the '80s." *Public Relations Quarterly* 29:3 (Fall 1984):24–27.

"Material Support." *Du Pont Magazine.* 78:3 (May/June 1984):14–16.

"A Mellow Style." *Business Month.* December 1987, 37.

Mencher, Melvin. *News Reporting and Writing,* 4th ed. Dubuque, Iowa: Wm. C. Brown, 1984.

Newsom, Doug and Bob Carrell. *Public Relations Writing: Form & Style.* Belmont, Calif.: Wadsworth, 1986.

Rivers, William L. and Shelly Smolkin. *Free-Lancer and the Staff Writer: Newspaper Features and Magazine Articles.* Belmont, Calif. Wadsworth, 1981.

Sheff, Alexander L. and Edna Ingalls. *How to Write Letters for All Occasions.* Garden City, N. Y.: Doubleday & Company, 1961.

Stouffer, Lloyd. "It's All Done With Paper." *Reader's Digest Junior Treasury.* London: The Reader's Digest Association Limited, 1960, 108–112.

Time. "Death at the Bronx Zoo." 126:6 (August 12, 1985):21.

Wells, Hugh. "The Name Game and the Art of Clear, Simple Writing." *Public Relations Quarterly,* 30:3 (Fall 1985):32.

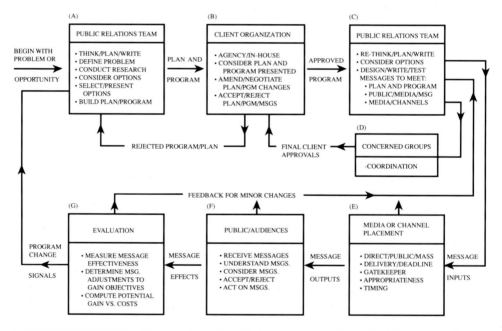

(A) PUBLIC RELATIONS TEAM	(B) CLIENT ORGANIZATION	(C) PUBLIC RELATIONS TEAM

• THINK/PLAN/WRITE
• DEFINE PROBLEM
• CONDUCT RESEARCH
• CONSIDER OPTIONS
• SELECT/PRESENT OPTIONS
• BUILD PLAN/PROGRAM
	• AGENCY/IN-HOUSE
	• CONSIDER PLAN AND PROGRAM PRESENTED
	• AMEND/NEGOTIATE PLAN/PGM CHANGES
	• ACCEPT/REJECT PLAN/PGM/MSGS
		• RE-THINK/PLAN/WRITE
		• CONSIDER OPTIONS
		• DESIGN/WRITE/TEST MESSAGES TO MEET:
		  • PLAN AND PROGRAM
		  • PUBLIC/MEDIA/MSG
		  • MEDIA/CHANNELS

BEGIN WITH PROBLEM OR OPPORTUNITY — PLAN AND PROGRAM — APPROVED PROGRAM

REJECTED PROGRAM/PLAN — FINAL CLIENT APPROVALS

(D) CONCERNED GROUPS — -COORDINATION

FEEDBACK FOR MINOR CHANGES

(G) EVALUATION	(F) PUBLIC/AUDIENCES	(E) MEDIA OR CHANNEL PLACEMENT
• MEASURE MESSAGE EFFECTIVENESS • DETERMINE MSG. ADJUSTMENTS TO GAIN OBJECTIVES • COMPUTE POTENTIAL GAIN VS. COSTS	• RECEIVE MESSAGES • UNDERSTAND MSGS. • CONSIDER MSGS. • ACCEPT/REJECT • ACT ON MSGS.	• DIRECT/PUBLIC/MASS • DELIVERY/DEADLINE • GATEKEEPER • APPROPRIATENESS • TIMING

PROGRAM CHANGE — SIGNALS — MESSAGE EFFECTS — MESSAGE OUTPUTS — MESSAGE INPUTS

Effective public relations writers must also be able to prepare copy for radio, television, and motion picture media channels. We live in a world of sight and sound. Many of today's visual generation read little. Public relations writers need to know which aural and visual channels each key public attends to and be able to reach these listeners and viewers.

WRITING FOR SOUND AND SIGHT . . . ▼

9

Introduction

The language of public relations is rich in references to the printed message. Words like "press release," "press agentry," "house journal," "newsletter"—common to modern-day public relations discourse—have progressively become a part of the profession's print heritage ever since 1643. This was the year Harvard University published *New England's First Fruits,* "the first of countless public relations pamphlets and brochures" (Cutlip, Center and Broom 1985, 24).

The romance between public relations and the print medium is also reflected in training programs, which, even today, emphasize print communications almost to the exclusion of other skills needed by the modern public relations writer. As chapter 8 showed, a considerable portion of the writer's energies is spent composing print messages.

But, increasingly, as Frank Wylie points out in his Professional Tip, the public relations writer is called upon to generate a variety of messages for radio, television, and newer media, such as videotex and teletext. Our objective is to help you write effective copy for such media. We also include a discussion on speech writing. Like broadcast communication, speeches are aimed at the eyes and ears of the audience, and thus belong in this chapter.

In keeping with the spirit of the book, we do not intend this to be a stand-alone chapter. To get the most out of it, read it along with the writing concepts and guidelines expressed in the chapters on, for example, style, writing theory, research, and organizational communication and management.

A PROFESSIONAL TIP:
Sound, Sight, and Script

We live in a world of sound, are most affected by the medium of television, and yet we are taught to write as if the written word was all that existed or mattered. Also, we are deluded into believing that all we need to do is learn to write news style, and we can easily adapt to broadcast and speech. It is not so. Writing for the ear, placing deft emphasis on the proper sound, is an art unto itself . . . indeed the art of our present and future. And, we must also learn to write in a manner which complements the way others speak, for often we write for their presentation, not ours. When given the advantage of sound plus picture, we must realize that the script, however polished and often approved, is but a draft. When we visualize the pictures, we must be willing and able to rewrite the script . . . letting the pictures tell the story and using the words to emphasize that which is most important.

Frank Winston Wylie, APR, former president of the Public Relations Society of America and director of public relations for Chrysler Corp., is a professor of journalism at California State University, Long Beach.

Copyright © 1991 Frank Winston Wylie. Used with permission.

The Nature of Radio

Any study of radio writing style demands an understanding of the medium itself.

On April 14, 1912, broadcaster David Saranoff picked up radio signals from the *S.S. Olympic,* steaming some 1,400 miles off the east coast of the United States in the Atlantic, that the *Titanic* was sinking:

> For three days and nights, he received and transmitted messages. There was little time for food or sleep. The first reports included names of survivors. Later came the long list of casualties. Saranoff's wireless became the nation's information link with the disaster of the decade.
>
> It was also electronic media's first scoop. Newspapers took their information directly from radio. Many years later Saranoff recalled, "The *Titanic* disaster brought radio to the front . . ." (Whetmore 1985, 98).

Since those fateful days, radio has become an inescapable part of our lives. Its sounds follow us everywhere, soothing our minds with music, and alerting our senses to news around the world.

Radio is important to the public relations writer for several reasons. As the *Titanic* episode demonstrated, radio is capable of spreading news to far-flung audiences even as it is happening. Radio is a constant and continuous medium that is so easy to program that news bulletins can be flashed or repeated at will any time of the day.

Despite its ability to reach vast audiences, radio is an immensely personal medium. As Read (1972, 197–198) puts it, radio messages are not intended for "everyone out there in radioland":

We are visiting with one person or two or three persons who are listening to us on a particular radio set. The electronic system [of radio] duplicates the one-to-one sender-receiver environment several hundreds or thousands of times.

President Franklin Roosevelt recognized this strength of radio when he used his on-the-air "fireside chats" in the early 1930s to sell social and economic programs directly to his constituents (Whetmore 1985, 99).

Because it communicates solely through sound, radio is better able to stimulate the imagination and emotions of audiences. This ability was demonstrated when Orson Welles' production of "War of the Worlds" on October 31, 1938, panicked millions of Americans into believing that aliens from Mars had landed on earth.

Radio is a portable medium. Its audiences tune into it while driving, while cooking in the kitchen, and even while in the shower. Thus, radio audiences are not only far-flung, but easy to reach as well.

For the most part, radio stations are structured to serve local audiences (Newsom and Scott 1985, 216). Radio is also a selective medium in which programming choices are geared toward specific audiences. For example, all-news radio stations are usually heard by adults over 40, most of whom are men (NIH Publication No. 84–2485 1984, 10). Table 9.1 shows some types of radio stations and their audiences.

Thus, radio allows messages to be targeted at precise audiences or regions.

But radio is not without its limitations. It is, for example, unable to supplement its messages with pictures, charts and graphs, as newspapers, magazines and television are able to.

A second limitation is that people usually pay casual attention to radio programs. That is, they do other things while the radio set is on—cooking, driving, eating—that can easily distract them from a broadcast message.

Third, you cannot immediately re-listen to radio messages as you can re-read a magazine article or newspaper story. The listener who misses a message must wait until it is repeated. Even so, because of the casual nature of radio listening, the person may be preoccupied with some other activity and miss the message the second time around as well.

Lastly, because radio stations must make the most of the little time and attention their audiences give them, radio messages are short. This leaves the public relations writer, indeed any radio writer, little time to elaborate and clarify a message.

TABLE 9.1.   Who Listens to What

Station Format	*Audience*
Top-40 rock or hot hits	Teens to mid-30s
Soul or urban contemporary	Black youth, teens to mid-30s
Middle of the road (MOR)	Adults, 45 and over
Adult contemporary or soft rock	Adults, 25 to 50
Easy listening or beautiful music	Adults, slightly older than MOR listeners
Album-oriented rock	Teens to mid-30s, usually more men
Classical	Adults, usually higher income listeners
Country	Adults, 24 to 54
All-news	Adults over 40, usually more men
All-talk	Adults over 40
Religious	Adults, slightly older than MOR audience
Foreign language and ethnic	Ethnic groups; varies depending upon concentration of such populations in media market

Source: National Institutes of Health, Publication No. 84–2485, "Making PSAs Work: A Handbook for Health Communication Professionals." Reprinted April 1984.

Writing for Radio

Radio writing poses special challenges for the public relations writer because it, in effect, simultaneously addresses three audiences. These are: the audience the message is targeted at, the announcer who reads the message on the air, and those specialists who are involved in integrating sound effects into the message.

Public relations writers can satisfy the needs of all three audiences by making their messages short, simple, clear, interesting and relevant; and by including enough clues to help others involved do a better job of producing and announcing these messages.

Keep it Simple

Simplicity is the key to effective radio writing. Not only does it help to make a message clear to audiences, but also makes the job of the person announcing the message on the air a lot easier. Chapter 7 contains a more exhaustive discussion of the ways and means of making messages simple and understandable. However, some key points to remember for broadcasting are:

1. Avoid unfamiliar and difficult words. Such words confuse listeners and trip up announcers. Listeners who stop to ponder the meaning of a difficult word may miss the rest of the message.

For the same reason, avoid using foreign words and expressions unless you are certain that these words are common to everyday conversation among your audiences or absolutely essential to your story.

2. Avoid cliches, especially if you are writing a news release for use by a radio station. "These are trite and usually obscure, rather than clarify facts. Besides, as a broadcast news writer, you are to deal with factual information, and cliches are opinion statements or unsubstantiated facts (e.g., how old is 'old as the hills,' and who made the 'original judgment?')" (Broussard and Holgate 1982, 36).

3. Avoid tongue twisters, or awkward letter and word combinations. Especially watch out for "combinations in which consonants clash with one another and create a slushy or whistling 's' sound. 'Was seeking' can be rewritten as 'was looking for' and 'businesses' are also 'business firms' " (Ibid, 37).

Tongue twisters can trip up the announcer and ruin the flow of your message. Because radio messages are completely dependent upon sound patterns and intonations for the communication of meaning, tongue twisters can confuse your audience and weaken your message.

Keep it Short

Radio writing generally demands a punchy, direct style. This means short, simple sentences with a single point and few, if any, modifying clauses. Each sentence should be a bite, a snippet of the message. For the sake of clarity, be direct and literal. Never assume that the listener will remember a point you made before. Make the meaning of your message clear by, if necessary, making the connections (for your listener) between different parts of your message.

Chapter 7 included a discussion on strategies for shortening sentences. In addition to the points made in that chapter, it is useful to remember the following points in the context of radio.

If the sentences in a broadcast message are long, chances are they contain a modifying clause or two. When this is the case, the offending clause can be pulled from the original sentence thus:

> **Original: John P. Doe, VICE PRESIDENT OF RESEARCH AND DEVELOPMENT AT THE XYZ PHARMACEUTICAL CORP., today said before a congressional committee that an AIDS cure will become a reality by 1993.** (31 words.)

> **Revised: John P. Doe today told a congressional committee that an AIDS cure will be available by 1993.** (17 words). **DOE IS A VICE PRESIDENT OF RESEARCH AND DEVELOPMENT AT THE XYZ PHARMACEUTICAL CORPORATION.** (14 words.)

Instead of one long sentence, there are now two short and clear sentences. Another way of dealing with a modifying clause is to convert it into a label.

> **Original: Michael Ross, A ONE-TIME SECRETARY OF STATE, decided to throw his support to the president in a speech to the U.S. Chamber of Commerce yesterday.** (26 words).

> **Revised: FORMER SECRETARY OF STATE Michael Ross yesterday endorsed the president in a speech to the U.S. Chamber of Commerce.** (19 words.)

While short sentences are desirable in radio copy, never try to make your sentences uniformly short. Rhythm and tempo are important in radio copy because, after all, it is meant to be heard. A quick succession of very short sentences may upset the tempo of a message by producing harsh, awkward and uncomfortable staccato sounds. So, try to intelligently vary the length of your sentences so that the average sentence is about 16 words long.

Listenability: There are listenability formulas to help the public relations writer compose simple and brief radio messages. The most commonly used and well known of these is Irving Fang's Easy Listening Formula (see table 7.4).

Make it Conversational

Simple words and short sentences alone do not make for good radio copy. Keep in mind that radio is a personal medium and that good radio writing is also conversational. Public relations writers achieve this by:

1. Using personal pronouns. Pronouns such as "you," "we" and "us" establish personal bonds between the communicator and the audience (also see chapter 7). Such pronouns also convey a sense of relevance by saying, for example, "**We** have a problem," "I'd like to tell **you** what's going on in the world," and, "**You** shouldn't be drinking and driving."

Thus, a public relations writer wishing to put out the word on the traffic problems caused by the victory parade for the 1988 baseball world champion Los Angeles Dodgers might have written:

> **If *you* were thinking about driving into downtown L-A Monday, *you* might want to put it off for another day.**

Likewise, a writer for an airline wishing to motivate people to fly to Europe might say:

> **Now might be the time for *you* to take that dream vacation in Europe.**
> **Flysafe Airlines is slashing airfares to London, Paris and Geneva 40 percent . . .**

2. Using contractions. People commonly use contractions in everyday conversations. Thus, they say, "I **shouldn't** be doing this," instead of, "I **should not** be doing this."

Because radio mimics personal conversations at a mass level, it is all right, in most cases, for the writer to use contractions such as:

isn't	**wouldn't**	**won't**	**hasn't**
he'll	**she'll**	**haven't**	**he'd**

Some contractions are confusing unless they are pronounced clearly. An example is "can't" which can sound like "can" if the announcer of the message is not careful. In such instances, the writer should choose other words, or if that's not possible, to caution the announcer to pronounce the word clearly.

Strive for Vigor and Movement

As with all forms of communication, radio messages that are dull and slow are likely to be ignored by their audiences. By contrast, lively and vigorous radio copy succeeds in attracting the attention of its listeners.

Chapter 7 provided several guidelines for injecting movement into public relations copy. These guidelines—using, among other things, active and working verbs, concrete words, and simple and direct sentences—are valid for radio copy as well.

Additionally, public relations writers can weaken or strengthen radio copy by the manner in which they handle attributions.

For example, when writing for newspapers, it is common practice to credit the source of information at the end of a sentence:

> **An AIDS cure will be a certainty by the end of the decade, ACCORDING TO DR. JOHN P. DOE, RENOWNED AIDS RESEARCHER FROM THE UNIVERSITY OF CALIFORNIA, LOS ANGELES.**

Placing the source at the beginning of the sentence makes it appropriately more lively and forceful for radio:

> **RENOWNED U-C-L-A AIDS RESEARCHER JOHN P. DOE predicted that a cure for the disease will be found by 1990.**

Use a Helpful Style

In this section, the focus is on things you can do to make the announcer's task of reading your message on the air easier. Remember, even the best-written message can fall apart if it is not read properly.

1. Abbreviations confuse radio announcers. Either avoid them or provide instructions on handling them.

As a rule, avoid the following abbreviations in radio copy:

St.	**Ave.**	**Atty.**	**Blvd.**	**Jr.**
Prof.	**Dem.**	**Rep.**	**Dir.**	**Pres.**

If you are compelled to use such words, write out their full form. Thus, write "President" instead of "Pres."

But some abbreviations are acceptable for radio copy. Examples of these are "Mr.," "Mrs." and "Dr." When using them, merely capitalize the abbreviation since you want it read as a complete word, (e.g., Mr., Mrs., Dr.).

Acronyms (abbreviations formed from the first letters of a group of words), such as YMCA and WAC, can be handled in one of two ways. If the acronym is to be read as one word, type it out in capital letters with no periods (e.g., NATO, OPEC, NASA). On the other hand, if you want the letters of the acronym to be read separately, then capitalize and hyphenate (e.g., Y-M-C-A, U-N, C-I-A, A-M, P-M).

Likewise, write out the words "dollar," "cent" and "percent." Do not use the symbols.

2. Numbers are difficult to handle on the air. Write out numbers one through nine and eleven. Use numerals for the numbers 10 and 12 through 999.

For numbers greater than 999, use combinations of words and numbers. This will make the task of reading them easier. For example, instead of 1,632, write **16-hundred-32.** Also, unless the exact number is important to the story, round it off, (e.g., **one-and-one-half million** instead of 1,497,455).

If a sentence begins with a number, write it out.

When numbers are part of an address, hyphenate the numbers if you want each number read aloud (e.g., 20273 Cottage Hill Lane should be written as **2–0–2–7–3 Cottage Hill Lane).** Alternately, the number for an address such as 1672 Birch Street can be broken down as 16–72. In this case, the announcer would read it as "sixteen-seventy-two."

For days of the month, use numerals. Also follow the dates with suffixes such as "nd.," "and "st.," (e.g., **June 14th, October 31st, May 2nd).**

Write out all fractions or partial numbers (e.g., **three-point-two billion dollars,** not $3.2 billion; **three-fourths,** not 3/4).

3. Phonetically write out difficult or unfamiliar words so that the announcer does not stumble over or mispronounce them. Most broadcasters are familiar with the United Press International phonetic guide (see table 9.2). Use it (or alternately, the Associated Press pronunciation guide) to remind announcers of the proper way to pronounce difficult words. If you don't have access to such guides, any form of phonetic transcription will help, as the examples in the following paragraphs show.

The convention is to write out the phonetic transcription in parentheses immediately following the word, e.g., Mihaly Csikszentmihalya (chik-sent-me-high-ye), Milan Panic (Pah-nitch). The former is a University of Chicago psychologist; the latter the chairman of a pharmaceutical company.

4. Be selective about the punctuation marks you use. Avoid all punctuation marks except commas, periods, question marks, dashes and dots. The dots or dashes can be used in place of quotation marks.

Integrate Sound Effects

Sometimes, music and sound effects are used in radio messages. When this is done, you need to instruct production personnel on where in the script the sound needs to be integrated. Says Mayeux (1985, 43):

> Be specific in your music or sound effects notations. Always identify the exact sound effect or type or title of music to be used. Indicate how each is to be heard [up full (in the foreground), under announcer (in the background), up and then under, etc.] and how each is to be disposed of (fades out, under and then out, etc.).
>
> Be certain to note that the music or sound effect is "under" or "in the background" when a voice is to be heard over either audio element.

TABLE 9.2. United Press International Guide to Phonetic Spelling

---

Vowels

A   Use AY for long A as in mate.
    Use A for short A as in cat.
    Use AI for nasal A as in air.
    Use AH for short A as in father.

E   Use EE for long E as in meet.
    Use EH for short E as in get.
    Use UH for hollow E as in the or le (French prefix).
    Use AY for French long E with accent as in pathe'.
    Use IH for E as in pretty.
    Use EW for EW as in few.

I   Use EYE for long I as in time.
    Use EE for French long I as in machine.
    Use IH for short I as in pity.

O   Use OH for long O as in note, or ough as in though.
    Use AH for short O as in hot.
    Use AW for broad O as in fought.
    Use OO for O as in fool, or ough in through.
    Use U for O as in foot.
    Use OH for ough as in trough.
    Use OW for O as in how, or ough as in plough.

U   Use EW for long U as in mule.
    Use OO for long U as in rule.
    Use U for middle U as in put.
    Use UH for short U as in shut, or hurt.

Consonants

Use K for hard C as in cat.
Use S for soft C as in cease.
Use SH for soft CH as in machine.
Use CH for hard CH or TCH as in catch.
Use Z for hard S as in disease.
Use S for soft S as in sun.
Use G for hard G as in gang.
Use J for soft G as in general.

Finally, remember that these are but a few of the many guidelines for writing effective radio copy. Many good books on radio writing are available at your college library. Read through some of these. Given the growing importance of corporate telecommunications, their lessons can be invaluable.

The Nature of Television

In 1940, the Journal Company of Milwaukee applied for the first license to broadcast over a relatively new and unknown medium—television (Whetmore 1985, 150).

Since then, millions of Americans have been entranced with television as they have with no other medium. They watch situation comedies and game shows for entertainment; vicariously participate in steamy soap operas; and, even see and learn about distant events in their homes. It is estimated that 80 million people watched the CBS show *Dallas* to find out who shot the villainous J. R. Ewing.

Television has been hailed for its capacity to inform, excite, inspire, even terrify, as when it brought the Vietnam War into America's living rooms. Its Big Bird and Mr. Rogers have been praised for exciting children about learning. At the same time, television has been blamed for encouraging violent crime by showing a lot of it, and portrayed as a narcotic that has weakened people's capacities to read and write competently.

But love or hate television, there is no denying that it is a compelling medium which derives its power from its ability to instantaneously transmit pictures and sounds of events across great distances.

Television and radio are similar in some respects. Like radio, television brings messages into the receiver's own environment. Thus, it is personal. Like radio, it is almost everywhere. Thanks to microelectronics technology, you can carry a pocket-sized television set and receive signals almost anywhere you go. Unlike radio, television is visually compelling. Because of this feature, it is, for the most part, able to command the attention of its audiences.

Producing and transmitting television pictures requires sophisticated and expensive technology. Because of high costs, television messages are by necessity compact, their duration short. This may constrain public relations writers from elaborating and clarifying their messages in any great depth. Since the medium is dominated by pictures, it is also more suited to depicting concrete and dramatic events than it is to explaining abstract topics. Thus, television may limit the public relations writer's ability to explain complex subjects adequately.

Writing for Television

As with radio, television messages are written for three publics: the audience the message is intended for; the television personality or actor reading the message; and the technicians producing the message.

Because sound is an important component of television, its messages are, for the most part, handled like radio messages. Thus, all of the radio writing guidelines discussed earlier apply to television writing. However, the television writer is left with one additional task, that of writing for and accommodating the visual aspect of the medium.

The following strategies are intended to help the public relations writer effectively use the visual side of television.

Think Visually and Verbally

Remember, you're writing to be heard, not read. Make the words easy to listen to and recall. That means being personal and writing in an easy, conversational style. Select words you would use when talking to your friends. Say "use" rather than "utilize," "look over" rather than "peruse." Don't be afraid to use contractions. The key to successful television (and radio) writing is that it must sound right and clear. So, after you have composed your message, read it aloud to yourself and to someone else. If it sounds right, don't change it. If it sounds wrong, rewrite it until it sounds right.

As a television writer, your aim is also to make sure your words complement the pictures in your message. You can achieve this by:

Discriminating word selection: Conserve words as much as possible. Fight the common tendency to pour too many words over the visual elements. Allow viewers to think about the words, to link the words with image and sound, before pelting them with more words. Also, the words, images and sounds should be in balance, neither competing with nor overshadowing each other. For example, optimistic words about managing, even beating the AIDS disease, can be contradicted and weakened if accompanied by funeral music. The message that AIDS is not merely a gay person's problem can be contradicted by pictures of just young and obviously single men talking about the illness.

Also, do not use words that simply describe the visual. The picture does that well enough by itself. Rather, use the words to memorably explain, enhance and clarify the visual.

Provide Directions

A television message never is the work of one person. Several people are involved both in the production and reading of the message. The public relations writer must take care to provide clear and helpful directions to the others. All of the language needed for guiding the reader and the producer should be present in the script.

Directions to the announcer or actor include pronunciation guides, as well as verbal cues for handling abbreviations and numbers. (See previous section on writing for radio.)

The directions should also address variations in tone and pitch, as well as describe the facial expressions and gestures that are necessary for communicating the character of the message:

> *Verbal Cue*
> John: (angrily) Of all the dumb things!
>
> *Visual Cue*
> Susan: (her face deathly white) God! This can't be happening

Directions to camera operators and sound technicians: Without instructions from the public relations writer, these specialists will not be able to provide the appropriate visuals and sound for the message. Table 9.3 provides a selection of technical terms that are necessary for communicating with sound and camera specialists, and should be included in the script itself.

Releases for Radio

Public relations writers can profitably use radio to speedily disseminate information about their clients to large and diverse audiences.

Content Guidelines

When writing releases for radio, writers should keep in mind that:

1. They are writing to a medium and an audience that are intolerant of long messages. Radio is fast and immediate. It offers glimpses of happenings, but rarely goes into detail. Thus, the shorter the message of the public relations writer, the better its chance of being aired.

If writers are uncomfortable about writing news snippets, they can attach fact sheets offering more details about the news events in question. Such an action, while satisfying public relations writers' need for completeness and detail, also allows radio station personnel to look for other aspects of the news that may interest their audiences.

2. They are writing to local, not national audiences. The medium is both structured and licensed to serve local audiences. Being so, it better accommodates stories that have local angles. Public relations writers can capitalize on this characteristic of radio by reshaping the same body of news into several news releases, each with a unique local angle. Thus, though no one radio station will permit public relations writers to say much about their clients, the stations collectively allow the writers a tremendous scope for spreading client news.

TABLE 9.3. Everything You Wanted to Know about Television Talk but Were Afraid to Ask

The following is a partial list of terms used to guide camera and sound specialists in the production of a television message. Abbreviations used for some terms appear in all caps in the script. These are identified below in parentheses after each term. Where abbreviations do not appear, the terms are used in their full form.

Cover shot   A camera shot of all the action in a scene.

Cut   A sudden change from one scene to another.

Fade   As an audio term, fade refers to an increase or decrease in sound volume. As a video term, it refers to the transition of the picture to or from black.

Special effects (SFX or FX)   Term used to point to places in the script where sound effects (e.g., person breathing heavily, sound of car engine) need to be integrated.

Voice Over (VO)   Term signalling the introduction of an announcer's voice into the message.

Wipe   Term for an electronic effect where it looks like one picture pushes, or wipes, another picture off the video screen.

Zoom   Denotes the movement toward or away from the person or scene being shot by a fixed camera with variable focal length (or zoom) lens.

Extreme long shot (ELS)   A shot in which the camera shows a long, distant or complete view of the scene.

Wide or long shot (WS or LS)   Here, the camera moves in closer but still permits a view of most of the scene.

Medium long shot (MLS)   Here, the camera is far enough from the actor to permit a view of his entire body.

Medium shot (MS)   The camera is close enough to the person to provide a view of him or her waist upwards.

Medium close-up (MCU)   The camera moves even closer to the person and permits a view of his or her face and shoulders.

Close-up (CU)   In such a shot, only the head and neck of the subject are visible.

Extreme close-up (ECU)   Here, the face of the subject completely fills up the screen.

Single (1-shot)   A shot of just one person.

Two-shot (2-shot)   A shot of two people, as when a talk show host like Larry King is interviewing a guest.

Three-shot (3-shot)   As the term suggests, there are three people in this shot.

Group shot   A shot in which there are more than three people.

Pan   A term signaling horizontal movement of the camera. "Pan left," for example, directs the camera operator to move the camera horizontally to his or her left. "Pan right," would entail moving the camera focus to the right of the operator.

Tilt   Moving the camera vertically on its axis so that it either points and moves up or down.

Ped up   Raising the camera by working its pedestal. By the same token, "ped down" means lowering the camera by lowering the pedestal.

Dolly in   Moving a mobile camera toward the object being shot. By "dollying out," the operator moves the camera away from the subject.

Truck   Moving a mobile camera laterally. This results in both the object being shot and the camera shooting the object moving in the same direction parallel to each other.

TABLE 9.4.   Model Radio Release

Public Relations Department
The Carmel Institute of
Fashion Design
333 Fabric Lane
Sometown, CA 00000–0000

Contact: John Moneypenny
Day: (415) 000 0000
Night: (415) 000 0000

January 14, 1991

FOR IMMEDIATE RELEASE

20 seconds
8 lines

California designer nation's best ——— Throw-away lead

L-A's Peter Creative was named 1991's outstanding designer at the prestigious Carmel fashion show held in San Francisco last night.
The 32-year-old grabbed the award for a line of clothes that uses native American designs and materials.
The fashion show was organized by the 100-year-old Carmel Institute, located in Sometown, here in Northern California. (61 words.)

–30– ——— End-of-copy symbol

Take for example, the radio release in table 9.4. Let's assume that in addition to naming Peter Creative as the nation's outstanding fashion designer, the Carmel Institute honored three other designers: John Wordy of Omaha, Neb.; David Finch of Atlanta, Ga.; and Woody Graves of Seattle, Wash.

Aided by a word processor, the public relations writer can, in essence, write three more versions of the release, each individually aimed at radio stations in Omaha, Atlanta and Seattle. Conceivably, they all may read something like this:

> **Local fashion designer wins national honors.**
> **Omaha's own John Wordy (Atlanta's own David Finch; Seattle's own Woody Graves) was recognized as a top fashion designer at the prestigious Carmel fashion show held in San Francisco last night.**
> **Wordy (Finch, Graves) grabbed the honor for his outstanding designs in leather (silk, cotton) clothes.**
> **The show was organized by the 100-year-old Carmel Institute located in Sometown, Calif.**

Likewise, radio stations in Sometown could be fed details of the event itself: who was there, what happened that evening and what were the highlights.

Thus, by its very orientation toward local audiences, radio offers a versatility that public relations writers can use to their clients' advantage.

Content Organization

The typical radio news release contains two elements, namely, the throw-away lead, and the body (see table 9.4).

1. The throw-away lead: Radio is a casual medium to which audiences may be half listening. The throw-away lead is a short sentence—15 words or less—that alerts audiences to an upcoming story on radio without revealing too much of its content. If the writers do not use such a lead and plunge right into the story, their audiences may miss it because their attention is elsewhere.

Examples of throw-away leads are:

Lotto fever strikes Southern California.
E-T comes home at last.
AIDS drug maker indicted by grand jury.
Drug maker stops distribution of abortion pill.
Soviet icebreakers free trapped whales.

In essence, the throw-away lead sentence is much like a headline in a newspaper story. It calls attention to the news which follows.

2. The body: This is a short summary of the news event the public relations writer has written about. Typically, it uses as many elements of the five W's and H that characterize a news story, and is about as long as a newspaper lead. The E.T. story might continue thus:

Home videocassettes of the movie about the lovable alien, E-T, go on sale tomorrow at most Southland stores. Eleven million copies of the video have already been ordered in advance by customers.

The 19–82 Steven Spielberg movie about the lost alien became the top-earning film of all time . . . grossing 700-million dollars. Home video sales could make E-T the first movie to earn one-billion dollars. (70 words.)

Reading at an average rate of 155 words-per-minute, most radio announcers would be able to dispose of this story in 25 or 30 seconds.

Make sure your information is accurate. Remember: "Opportunities for correcting mistakes are rare in broadcasting since you can never address the exact same audience twice. All those who heard your mistake may not hear your correction" (Broussard and Holgate 1982, 86). Also, don't be fooled by the conversational nature of the medium into editorializing. Stick to the facts of the news. That's all you have time for.

Format Guidelines

While writing radio releases, follow these guidelines (table 9.4):

1. Use standard 8.5″ by 11″ white stationery or sheets of paper to write your release on.

2. Leave generous margins all around the body of the copy.

3. If your message runs more than one page, never continue a sentence from one page to the next. Also, do not break up words by hyphenating them. Remember, hyphens serve a different purpose in radio copy than they do in print.

4. Identify the source of the release in the top left corner of the page, unless you are using company stationery.

5. Include a 24-hour contact's name and telephone number.

6. Print the release date in the space just under contact information. For more tips on how to handle release dates, see the section in chapter 8 that deals with format guidelines for media releases.

7. Include a mailing date in the space just below source identification.

8. List the number of lines in your copy and the time it takes to read the message in a slug line just below the mailing date. Using a stopwatch is the most accurate way of timing a radio release. Alternately, you can count the number of words in the message and calculate how long it will take to read it at an average rate of 155 words-per-minute.

9. Mark the end of your message with the traditional -30- or ### symbols.

Video News Releases

The public relations video news release, commonly known as a VNR, is simply a news release that is recorded on a videotape and released to television stations for their use.

The '80s saw a sharp increase in the use of video releases by organizations—both commercial and nonprofit—for breaking news developments to the outside world and to their employees. Figure 9.1 demonstrates how one organization used television to tell its story.

As is evident by now, television writing, while it shares many of the concerns of radio writing, poses more complex challenges because of the added need to accommodate pictures into the script.

Video productions are also very expensive. For example, it may cost $10,000 to produce and distribute a VNR to 100 television stations (Davids 1988, 17). Because of the high costs, the writer has to take extreme care to make every word and picture count.

Spectrum

Shriners use VNRs to tell health care story

Late last year the Ancient Arabic Order of the Nobles of the Mystic Shrine (most people know them as "Shriners"), launched an all out media blitz to promote their no-cost network of 22 childrens' speciality hospitals. The blitz included a multi-part video news electronic press release kit, titled "A Heritage of Helping," a 38-US city satellite TV tour, two satellite news feeds and a nationwide high profile celebrity public service campaign featuring US film stars Burt Reynolds and William Shatner, among others.

"It may seem odd to have to use such a sophisticated approach in promoting a hospital system when the care at all Shriners Hospitals is totally without charge, but the truth of the matter is that misconceptions have long existed about the Shriners unique no-cost network of childrens' hospitals," says Michael C. Andrews, director of public relations for the Imperial Council and Shriners Hospitals for Crippled Children. "A lack of belief on the part of the public that quality medical care could actually be free of charge, and without any strings attached, lay at the heart of this non-belief."

The PR department of the Shriners developed the campaign, which, according to Arbitron research, reached nearly 100 million TV households. "The Shriners were able to communicate their story in a manner never before tried, and to fully explain that there weren't any catches to the quality health care services provided at the 19 Shriners Hospitals for Crippled Children and three world renowned Shriners Burns Institutes," adds Andrews.

▶ **Figure 9.1.** One organization's use of the video news release. Copyright © 1988 Communication World.

Public relations television writers accommodate and integrate visuals and sound into their scripts by using a split-page format. Here, the visual elements of the story are arranged in a column on the left half of the page, with corresponding sound and word elements in a column on the right half of the page. Figure 9.2 illustrates how a public relations writer can combine words, sound and pictures into a cohesive message.

Public Service Announcements

Public service announcements, or PSAs, are messages that are designed to: "promote programs, services, activities, or issues of community [or public] interest. The broadcast air time for these messages [and, in some cases, the production services] is provided free of charge by the radio and TV stations and networks" (NIH Publication No. 84–2485 1984, 1).

VIDEO SCRIPT

PRODUCTION/PROJECT __BECKMAN INSTRUMENTS_____
    Apolipoprotein Blood Test Video News Release

PAGE _1_ OF _3_

DATE _6/25/87_

VIDEO	INSTRUCTIONS	AUDIO
Wide shot of Larry Grannis (high-risk heart patient) with nurse	Sound up-full	SOT: "The males in my family... ...my days are numbered." (:12)
MS Patient with nurse	Voice-over	ANNOUNCER: LARRY GRANNIS IS ABOUT TO GET THE ANSWER TO A QUESTION HE'S
CU Patient's arm		WONDERED ABOUT FOR YEARS. EVER SINCE HIS DAD SUFFERED A HEART ATTACK AT 60,
Wide shot of nurse giving patient a shot		LARRY HAS WORRIED THAT HE TOO HAS A HIGH RISK OF GETTING HEART DISEASE.
Matte – Fullerton, California		BUT NOW, LARRY IS ABOUT TO TAKE A REVOLUTIONARY NEW BLOOD TEST DEVELOPED BY BECKMAN INSTRUMENTS IN FULLERTON, CALIFORNIA.
Wide shot of laboratory and technician		THE TEST MEASURES TWO SPECIFIC PROTEINS IN OUR BLOOD. LARRY WILL FIND OUT IN MINUTES WHETHER HE HAS A GENETIC PREDISPOSITION TO STROKE OR HEART ATTACK
CU Blood test		BEFORE CLOGGED ARTERIES DEVELOP. BEST OF ALL, HE'LL HAVE A CHANCE TO GET TREATMENT, AND TO CHANGE HIS EXERCISE AND EATING HABITS SO HE CAN LIVE A LONGER, HEALTHIER LIFE.

▶ **Figure 9.2A.**   Video news release – split-page format. Copyright 1990 Jim Ryerson Productions. Reprinted with permission.

VIDEO SCRIPT

PRODUCTION/PROJECT BECKMAN INSTRUMENTS
Apolipoprotein Blood Test VNR

VIDEO	INSTRUCTIONS	AUDIO
Matte – Cleveland Clinic		THE CLEVELAND CLINIC FOUNDATION STUDIED THESE NEW BECKMAN INSTRUMENTS
MS computer screen and test tube		TESTS, WHICH DETECT LEVELS OF SUBSTANCES CALLED APOLIPOPROTEIN A-1 AND B IN THE BLOOD. DR. HERBERT
CU Dr. Naito – Cleveland Clinic Foundation		NAITO OF THE CLEVELAND CLINIC SAYS IT IS MUCH BETTER THAN THE CHOLESTEROL TESTS DOCTORS USE NOW.
Interview: Dr. Naito	sound up-full	SOT: "We don't quite know why measuring these proteins in the blood seems to be better associated with individuals having the disease... all we know from a scientific standpoint is that it's three to five times better than cholesterol... ...as part of the general physical. (:36)
Long shot of jogger	Voice-over	ANNCR: SCIENTISTS POINT OUT THAT ONE IN THREE AMERICANS IS PREDISPOSED TO A HEART ATTACK AT AGE FORTY OR FIFTY, SO
MS People at salad bar		MAKING THIS DETERMINATION CAN ALLOW THESE PEOPLE TO MODIFY THEIR LIFESTYLE
CU Salad bar		WITH EXERCISE AND PROPER DIET TO REDUCE

▶ **Figure 9.2B.**   Video news release – split-page format. Copyright © Jim Ryerson Productions. Reprinted with permission.

VIDEO SCRIPT

PRODUCTION/PROJECT__BECKMAN INSTRUMENTS_____
Apolipoprotein Blood Test VNR

VIDEO	INSTRUCTIONS	AUDIO
CU Computer		THEIR RISKS. THOSE WHO WANT THE NEW EXAM SHOULD REQUEST AN APOLIPOPROTEIN A-1 AND B BLOOD TEST, BUT DEVELOPERS HOPE THAT THE TESTS WILL SOON BE GIVEN ROUTINELY AT BIRTH OR TO SCHOOL
MS Doctor with patient		CHILDREN. IT'S INFORMATION THAT CAN MAKE LIFE A LOT EASIER AND MORE
CU Patient		PRODUCTIVE, ESPECIALLY FOR THOSE WITH A FAMILY HISTORY OF HEART DISEASE.
		THIS IS JIM RYERSON IN FULLERTON, CALIFORNIA.

▶ **Figure 9.2C.** Video news release – split-page format. Copyright © Jim Ryerson Productions. Reprinted with permission.

Characteristics

To qualify as a PSA, a message must:

1. Originate from a nonprofit organization. Because PSAs are aired (and sometimes produced) free of cost, radio and television stations allow this privilege only to those organizations that can furnish a copy of the Internal Revenue Service's authorization granting the organization nonprofit status.

2. Normally occupy no more than 60 seconds of air time. PSAs are usually produced to occupy 10-, 15-, 20-, 30-, or 60-second time slots. Often 60-, 30-, and 10-second versions of the same PSA are sent together, thereby increasing its chance of being aired. Ten-second spots get the most exposure in heavy viewing or listening periods, particularly in big cities (Goldsmith 1986, 34).

3. Normally be noncontroversial and come from noncontroversial organizations. Broadcasters usually avoid accepting PSAs about controversial subjects such as abortion, preferring instead to address such issues in their news programs. Broadcast stations also do not accept PSAs from controversial religious and political organizations, or groups "promoting alcohol, cigarettes, or games of chance" (Ibid, 33).

Topics and Objectives

PSAs can appropriately be used to urge people not to drink and drive or play with fire, and to keep parks and recreation areas clean; in short, to address any matter or issue of public interest, or, more importantly, public benefit.

PSAs may be written with one or more of the following objectives in mind:

1. Changing or reinforcing existing attitudes. For example, a PSA may try to persuade people that everyone should be concerned about AIDS, heart disease, cancer, recycling or preserving the environment.

2. Motivating people to take specific and beneficial actions, such as wearing reflective clothing while jogging, getting pets vaccinated, and using low-flow shower-heads and water-saving devices.

3. Teaching new, important and beneficial skills. This might, for example, include things you can do to minimize damage in the event of an earthquake, or steps you can take to make your kitchen safer for your children.

Message Development

This section briefly summarizes some message development guidelines provided by the National Institutes of Health to help the public relations writer write effective PSAs (NIH Publication No. 84–2485 1984, 22). These are:

1. Keep the message simple and short.
2. Organize the message around one or two key points. Repeat these as many times as time will permit.
3. Tie the message to a slogan or theme (e.g., "Give a hoot, don't pollute").
4. Provide as much new information as time will permit. Make sure that this information is accurate and reliable.
5. Use positive rather than negative appeals where possible.
6. Use only a few characters in the PSA. Don't clutter it by having too many people say too many things.
7. Present the facts in a straightforward manner.
8. Make sure that the message presenter comes across as a credible source of information.
9. Be sure that your message is relevant to the concerns of your target audience.
10. Be sure to test alternate message appeals to see which one is most effective. In general, humor is a good appeal provided it does not offend your audience. Fear is an effective appeal too, provided you don't scare your audiences silly. In other words, too much fear is counterproductive.
11. Test a variety of formats. For example, the National Cancer Institute used a testimonial when it had a mother say: "I never thought any of my children would get cancer. So when my son did, I was frightened. But then I learned the facts . . ." (Ibid).
12. Where possible, demonstrate the actions and skills you want your audiences to take and develop.
13. When writing for television, superimpose critical portions of the message (a hotline number, the names and addresses of shelters and agencies) on the screen to reinforce the spoken part of the message.

PUBLIC SERVICE ANNOUNCEMENT

CITY OF GARDEN GROVE, CALIFORNIA

11391 ACACIA PARKWAY, P.O. BOX 3070, GARDEN GROVE, CALIFORNIA 92642

GARDEN GROVE

PUBLIC INFORMATION OFFICE: (714) 638-6623

```
Contact:  Maggie Parker, (714) 638-6766
Senior Center Supervisor

10-Second Spot

                                  SCBA #061588-529 GI

                                  Begin Immediately
                                  End Nov. 9, 1987

              FREE FLU CLINIC FOR SENIORS

     SENIORS ARE INVITED TO A FREE FLU CLINIC, NOV. 9TH AT

THE H. LOUIS LAKE SENIOR CENTER IN GARDEN GROVE.

     FOR MORE INFORMATION, CALL THE CENTER OR THIS STATION.

GARDEN GROVE:   YOU SHOULD SEE US NOW!


                        ###
```

▶ **Figure 9.3.** Ten-second announcer script. Reprinted with permission of the City of Garden Grove, Calif.

Packaging

Radio PSAs: These can take one of three forms:

- announcer scripts
- audiocassettes
- reel-to-reel tapes

1. Announcer script: This is by far the easiest form and consists of a message to be read on the air by station personnel. While preferences vary, most stations will accept and use announcer scripts. Figures 9.3, 9.4, and 9.5 contain examples of 10-, 30- and 60-second announcer scripts.

PUBLIC SERVICE ANNOUNCEMENT

CITY OF GARDEN GROVE, CALIFORNIA

11391 ACACIA PARKWAY, P.O. BOX 3070, GARDEN GROVE, CALIFORNIA 92642

PUBLIC INFORMATION OFFICE: (714) 638-6623

GARDEN GROVE

```
Contact:  Roxanne Kaufman (714) 638-6711
Recreation Supervisor

30-Second Spot

                                    SCBA #061588-529 GI

                                    Begin Nov. 5, 1987
                                    End Dec. 3, 1987


                    SONGS OF CHRISTMAS
               IN HARMONY WITH HOLIDAY SPIRIT

     SHARE THE SEASON'S GOOD TIDINGS AT THE CITY OF GARDEN

GROVE'S SONGS OF CHRISTMAS CELEBRATION, DEC. 4TH, 7 P.M. AT

THE COMMUNITY MEETING CENTER.

     THERE'S SOMETHING FOR YOUR WHOLE FAMILY AT THIS ANNUAL

EVENT.  THE CHILDREN CAN ENJOY FREE CANDY AND A VISIT FROM

SANTA WHILE YOU PARTICIPATE IN A FESTIVE SING-A-LONG.

     YOU'LL WATCH IN SPLENDOR AS THE CITY'S CHRISTMAS LIGHTS

ARE LIT FOR THE FIRST TIME.  YOU CAN ENJOY ALL THIS IN THE

SPIRIT OF THE HOLIDAY SEASON AT GARDEN GROVE'S SONGS OF

CHRISTMAS CELEBRATION.

     MARK IT ON YOUR CALENDER TO ATTEND THE SONGS OF

CHRISTMAS, DEC. 4TH AT 7 P.M.  AND BEST YET, IT'S FREE.

GARDEN GROVE:  YOU SHOULD SEE US NOW!


                      ###
```

▶ **Figure 9.4.** Thirty-second announcer script. Reprinted with permission of the City of Garden Grove, Calif.

PUBLIC SERVICE ANNOUNCEMENT

GARDEN GROVE

CITY OF GARDEN GROVE, CALIFORNIA
11391 ACACIA PARKWAY, P.O. BOX 3070, GARDEN GROVE, CALIFORNIA 92642

PUBLIC INFORMATION OFFICE: (714) 638-6623

Contact: John Bushman (714) 638-6623
Administrative Services

SCBA #061588-529 GI

Begin Sept. 24, 1987
End Oct. 19, 1987

60-SECOND SPOT

SENIOR MEALS VOLUNTEERS

THE CITY OF GARDEN GROVE IS SEEKING CARING, SINCERE AND
HARDWORKING INDIVIDUALS WITH EXTRA TIME ON THEIR HANDS.
COULD THAT BE YOU?

THE STAFF AT THE H. LOUIS LAKE SENIOR CITIZENS CENTER
NEEDS VOLUNTEER DRIVERS TO DELIVER MEALS THROUGH THE HOME
MEALS PROGRAM.

MONDAY THROUGH FRIDAY HOT LUNCHES ARE DELIVERED TO MORE
THAN 130 HOME-BOUND SENIORS. SINCE THESE SENIORS CANNOT
REGULARLY VENTURE OUT OF THEIR HOMES, THE AMENITIES OF THE
CENTER ARE BROUGHT TO THEM. BUT TO DO THIS THE SENIOR
CENTER RELIES ON VOLUNTEERS.

BECAUSE OF GARDEN GROVE'S GROWING SENIOR POPULATION,
THE DEMAND FOR VOLUNTEER DRIVERS IS GREATER THAN EVER AND
NEW ROUTES ARE FORMING ALL THE TIME. A DRIVER AND
ACCOMPANYING RIDER ARE NEEDED TO COVER EACH ROUTE
THOROUGHLY.

GARDEN GROVE'S SENIOR CENTER ASKS YOU TO COMMIT JUST
TWO HOURS A WEEK TO DELIVER MEALS AND A DOSE OF FRIENDSHIP
TO THESE NEEDY SENIORS. THE REWARDS YOU RECEIVE ARE
PROPORTIONAL TO THE HAPPINESS YOU DELIVER. HELPING SENIORS
IS ONE OF OUR GOALS, LET IT BE ONE OF YOURS. GARDEN GROVE:
YOU SHOULD SEE US NOW!

▶ **Figure 9.5.** Sixty-second announcer script. Reprinted with permission of the City of Garden Grove, Calif.

TABLE 9.5. Radio PSA Script

UNIVERSITY OF HIGHER LEARNING
DEPARTMENT OF HANDICAPPED STUDENT SERVICES
HANDICAPPED PARKING SPACES
06/14/88
30 SECONDS

	(SFX:	SOUND OF CAR DRIVING BY SLOWLY. FEATURE BRIEFLY, UNDER, THEN OUT)
VOICE		Boy, the parking lot sure is full.
	(SFX:	CAR ENGINE SOUND. FEATURE BRIEFLY, UP, UNDER, THEN OUT)
VOICE		Wow! There's a spot right by the U-C . . . Am I in luck? Darn it! It's a handicapped spot.
	(SFX:	SOUND OF CAR SCREECHING TO HALT. FEATURE BRIEFLY, THEN OUT)
VOICE		Well . . . I only have to drop off this paper to Dr. Jones . . . (HESITATES) . . . It can't hurt if I park here for a few minutes . . . can it?
	(SFX:	SOUND OF CAR SCREECHING TO HALT. FEATURE BRIEFLY, THEN OUT)
ANNCR		Can you believe that guy? Doesn't he know how hard he's making it for students like me . . . You see. . . . I'm handicapped . . . I have to use a wheelchair to get around . . . So please, if you're tempted to park in a handicapped zone, think of me . . . and my wheelchair. Thanks.

---

2. Prerecorded tapes: Whether recorded on reel-to-reel tapes or audiocassettes, these are more complex and usually use and incorporate sound effects. The public relations writer's task is to write the script showing how the words and the sounds fit into the message. Technical personnel then produce the tape by working off the script. Table 9.5 provides an example of a script for a prerecorded PSA.

3. Television PSAs: These are generally produced on 16mm film or videotapes (3/4″ or 1/2″). Regardless of the format, their starting point is the script, which is usually written by the public relations writer. This is done using a split-page format in which the audio, words and picture elements are integrated into one message by the writer (see figure 9.6).

VIDEO SCRIPT

PRODUCTION/PROJECT ORANGE COUNTY DISASTER PREPAREDNESS ACADEMY
Public Service Announcement

PAGE _1_ OF _1_
DATE 5/19/90

VIDEO	INSTRUCTIONS	AUDIO
MS Fireman on ladder, burning building	SFX: Fire truck siren and horn	
MS Man with oxygen mask, woman and firemen at rear bumper of firetruck		WOMAN: HE WENT BACK INSIDE TO TRY AND SAVE THE COMPUTER RECORDS.
CU Fireman		FIREMAN: YOU DON'T HAVE A DUPLICATE SET OF RECORDS?
Wide shot of man shaking his head		
CU "Orange County Disaster Preparedness Academy" pamphlet	Voice-over	ANNOUNCER: COULD YOUR HOME OR BUSINESS SURVIVE A DISASTER? I'M JIM RYERSON. THE ORANGE COUNTY DISASTER PREPAREDNESS ACADEMY IS A NON-PROFIT FOUR-DAY SERIES
MS burning building	Super-impose dates	DESIGNED BY EXPERTS TO HELP YOU BE BETTER PREPARED FOR THE WORST. TAUGHT BY PROFESSIONALS, THE ACADEMY WILL HELP YOU RESPOND TO THE UNEXPECTED. READY TO MAKE
MS People hosing down down burning building	Super-impose phone number	THE RIGHT CHOICES AT THE RIGHT TIME. NOW IS THE RIGHT TIME TO REGISTER. CALL FOR INFORMATION. 835-5381
CU Man, woman and fireman		MAN: I NEVER THOUGHT ANYTHING LIKE THIS COULD HAPPEN TO US.

▶ **Figure 9.6.**   Television PSA script. Copyright © 1990 Jim Ryerson Productions. Reprinted with permission.

For this script to be transformed into a PSA, it has to go through a production process, the starting point for which is the storyboard. The storyboard is an artist's rendition of how the PSA is going to look scene-by-scene. Typically, the artist may use line drawings to depict each scene in the PSA, with the relevant audio and script portions beneath each drawing. A storyboard that uses line drawings is called an **animatic.** A well-produced animatic is generally used to pretest the PSA to see if audiences will like and listen to it.

Once the producers are satisfied that the animatic tells the story to the liking of the audience, the line drawings are replaced with photographs. When this is done, the storyboard is called a **photomatic** (see figure 9.7 for an example). Using the photomatic, the producer then proceeds to shoot the final product that you see on television.

Writing for Videotex and Teletext

Two electronic methods of communication that have come into use in the past few years are videotex and teletext. Chapter 10 discusses the organizational strategies affecting the uses of these new media. Here, we focus on their technical applications.

Simply put, videotex is an electronic newspaper which can be called up on a computer terminal or television screen. Videotex is interactive because it allows audiences to make decisions about the type and extent of information they wish to see.

By contrast, teletext is an electronic message board that is not interactive. Once a message has been programmed to appear on the electronic board, there is nothing the audience can do to stop or change it. Hence, it is called a one-way medium.

Teletext calls for headline writing skills and one-line summaries of important stories or messages of the day.

Videotex offers greater challenges to the writer. It is a computer-based system capable of handling large amounts of information, and thus can accommodate newspaper-length stories. Also, because the information appears on a video screen, videotex can, to some extent, simulate television.

Thus, writers of videotex have to use a style that is compatible with both newspapers and television. To cope with this problem, the Electronic Text Center in the University of Florida's College of Journalism and Communications devised a style manual (see table 9.6) particularly suited for electronic media.

Public relations writers can effectively deal with the electronic media by writing their stories as they would for newspapers, then making the adjustments listed in the manual.

Dow lets you do great things.

The greatest gifts of all... the gifts of health...and life.

"Transplant" :30

1. MUSIC. ANNCR. (V.O.): Organ transplants are a modern miracle.

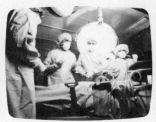

2. (OPERATING ROOM SOUNDS)

3. DOCTOR: Let's close.

4. 2ND DOCTOR: Good thing we found a donor. DOCTOR: Can you believe there was a time when people wouldn't even talk about donating organs?

5. ANNCR. (V.O.): But the need is *still* critical.

6. That's why Dow is funding a major educational effort to encourage organ donation.

7. DOCTOR: Mrs. Simpson?

8. Jenny is doing fine. She's a brave little girl.

9. (SHE SOBS AS MUSIC SWELLS.)

*Trademark of The Dow Chemical Company

▶ **Figure 9.7.** Photomatic storyboard. Courtesy of The Dow Chemical Company.

TABLE 9.6. Videotex Style Guide

Excerpts from the Electronic Text Center Stylebook. This stylebook was designed for student editors at the Electronic Text Center in the University of Florida, Gainesville, College of Journalism and Communications.

Abbreviations and Acronyms

Follow AP for all those not listed here.

The following abbreviations are acceptable in all uses and require no explanation:

AD	IRS	3-D
AWOL	LSD	TV
AT&T	NAACP	UF
BC	NASA	UFO, UFOs
CIA	NATO	USSR
FBI	OPEC	VD
GI, GIs	PLO	VIP, VIPs
IOU, IOUs	ROTC	YMCA, YWCA

Abbreviate miles per gallon and miles per hour as *mpg* and *mph* when connected to a figure: 45 mph, 30 mpg, 10–15 mph.

Abbreviate am and pm when connected to a figure, with no space after figure: 10am, 7pm, 10:23am.

Abbreviate *building, department* and *university* only when they are part of a name: County Administration Bldg, Defense Dept, Univ of Georgia, journalism dept.

Addresses

Abbreviate *Ave, Blvd, Ct, Rd* and *St* when used with a street name: 100 W University Ave, 75 NE 10th Ct, corner of Easy St and Tower Rd. Spell out all others: drive, alley, terrace, circle, etc.

Use figures for all numbers in an address, even street names: 7 5th Ave, 100 21st St.

Abbreviate compass points: 222 E 42nd St, 56 K St NW.

(Also see *Numerals.*)

Attribution

Always use *say, says* or *said.* Use said if a date is mentioned, *say* or *says* if no date is mentioned: "UF officials said today . . . " "UF officials say . . . "

If a day is not mentioned in the attribution, at all costs make sure it is mentioned someplace else in the story.

Contractions

All contractions listed in the dictionary are acceptable. However, don't use odd contractions (*would've*) if they aren't necessary. Try to trim the story somewhere else if you can.

Dates

Use *today, this morning, this afternoon, tonight,* etc. as appropriate instead of the day of the week. Rotatext is a medium of immediacy and using *today* gives stories immediacy.

Use *Monday, Tuesday,* etc., for days of the week within 7 days before or after the current date. Use the month and a figure for dates beyond this range. Avoid the redundant *last Tuesday* or *next Friday.* Let the verb signify past, present or future tense: "He finished Tuesday." "She will return Friday."

TABLE 9.6. Videotex Style Guide (*continued*)

Abbreviate the months Jan, Feb, Aug, Sept, Oct, Nov and Dec when followed by a specific date: Jan 15; April 5. "Aug 10 1984 is an important date." "February 1976 was a cold month." Note that commas are not used to set off the year in a date.

(Also see *Numerals.*)

Dollars and Cents

Always use a dollar sign and figure: $3, $23 million, $2.34, $56.6 million, $3500.

If using cents alone, spell it out: "He had 56 cents."

Ellipsis

When using an ellipsis . . . do not put spaces around it.

Use an ellipsis when condensing quotes to indicate the deletion of 1 or more words. Be careful to avoid deletions that distort the meaning. See AP stylebook for punctuation guidelines.

Fractions

Try to avoid at all costs. Use decimal point if possible: "He walked 2.5 miles." Spell out fractions less than 1: "The sailor was two-thirds of the way there." Use numerals for fractions greater than 1, linked by a hyphen: "It was over after 2–1/2 hours." "He pitched 7–1/3 innings."

(Also see *Numerals.*)

Names

Use first and last name on first reference with 3 exceptions: "Gov Graham," "Pres Bush" and all past presidents of the United States, such as "former Pres Carter." Usually "former Pres" is not needed: "John Glenn met with Jimmy Carter in Plains, Ga." However, "former Pres Garfield" is more specific than "James Garfield."

Use first and last name for all others with the titles president or governor: UF Pres Robert Marston, former California Gov Jerry Brown.

Like all other abbreviations, initials do not take periods: JC Penney, TJ Hooker.

Avoid middle initials and middle names unless it is a familiar part of a person's name: John F Kennedy, John Paul Jones. Do not use nicknames unless the person is widely known by the nickname: Bear Bryant, Magic Johnson.

Do not use "Jr," "Sr" or roman numerals (I,II) unless the person is widely known by that designation or to avoid confusion between father and son: King George IV, Hank Williams Jr.

It should be "House Speaker Tip O'Neill," not "Thomas P O'Neill Jr;" "Pope John Paul" (or "the pope), not "Pope John Paul II."

A very important exception to all this would be when identifying a person accused of a crime. Try to identify as completely as possible: "Hawthorne carpenter George R Johnson Sr, 35, was arrested today . . ."

Numerals

Use cardinal numbers (1,2,3, etc.) for all figures in all cases except when the figure is used as a pronoun or when it begins a sentence. Examples: "There were 1 or 2 things wrong." "He couldn't tell the difference between the two." "Police said 4 men were in the car." "He said that one must be prepared for the worst."

Usually when a number begins a sentence, the sentence can be rewritten: "Twenty-three passengers were aboard the ship." "The ship carried 23 passengers."

Spell out ordinal numbers (first, second, third) up to ninth. Use figures for 10th and above: "It was the third time he was arrested." "A 15th suspect was arrested today." "Second-ranked Louisville defeated Slippery Rock." Better: "No. 2 Louisville beat Slippery Rock." The 1 exception is street names, which are always numerals.

TABLE 9.6. Videotex Style Guide (*continued*)

Percentages

Use "%" when linked with a figure: 99%, 46.5%.
For amounts less than 1%, precede the decimal point with a zero: 0.7%.
Repeat "%" with each individual figure: "He said 10% to 30% may vote."
(Also see *Numerals*.)

Titles

Follow AP with the following exceptions:
Do not use "Mrs," "Miss," "Ms" on second reference.
Use "Dr" ahead of a person's name only for physicians, not for UF professors.
See *Names* section for style on "president," "governor."
Use "Supt" as the title for superintendent ahead of his or her name.
Use these abbreviations for government titles before a person's name: Atty Gen, District Atty, Gov, Lt Gov, Postmaster Gen, Pres, Rep, Sen, State Atty, Vice Pres.
Use "Det" instead of detective for police officers.
Use "Rev" instead of "the Rev" before a name.
Abbreviate "secretary" when it is a part of a government title, but not when it is used alone as a title: Commerce Sec Malcolm Baldridge, Interior Sec James Watt, UN Sec Gen Javier de Cuellar, secretary Jane Jones.
Follow AP on other religious and military titles, deleting the period on abbreviations.
Use "Prof" when used before a professor's name: History Prof James Oates, English Prof Julian Smith.

Copyright © 1985, University of Florida, Gainesville. Reprinted with permission.

Speechwriting

Public relations writers are frequently called upon to write speeches for senior company executives. The purpose of this section is not to explain the relationship between the speechwriter and the speech maker, or the politics and place of speechwriting in organizations—chapter 10 does that. In this chapter, we identify the elements and techniques of a good speech.

Good speeches are:

brief
warm, human and empathetic
forceful
lively
well organized

Brevity

The executive speech has undergone dramatic changes during the past few decades. At one time long speeches were the norm. They lasted 30 to 60 minutes, addressed many subjects, quoted the classics, and were one-time affairs. By contrast, today's speech is short—lasting 15 to 20 minutes—covers a single topic, quotes Yogi Berra and Peter Ueberroth, and is adaptable to several audiences. Remember, long-winded translates into "boring."

Public relations speech writers can ensure brevity by picking one or two main speech points and making them well:

> Speakers who try to cram a dozen points into a speech are shortchanging themselves and their audience.
>
> The mind can absorb only so much, particularly if the subject is alien or complicated, which many business issues tend to be.
>
> Take a lesson from the clergy. Most preachers wouldn't dream of delivering a sermon on the entire Book of Revelations. But they can reach the faithful by taking one verse and applying its meaning to the congregation's daily lives (Beckham 1985, 30).

Warmth

Audiences react to the speaker as much as they react to the speech. Despite his skill as a debater, Michael Dukakis, Democratic Party nominee for the presidency in 1988, was criticized for coming across as a mechanical doll, a robot with little warmth or feeling. Such perceptions may interfere with the message the speaker wants to impart to the audience.

While speechwriters cannot alter the personality of the speaker, they can help inject warmth into a speech through their choice of words and expressions. In particular, they can:

Strive for a conversational tone. Speeches are written for the ear. So if it makes a speech sound good, use contractions and personal pronouns. That's how most people speak. Resist the temptation to overuse numbers and institutional or professional jargon. Replace them with image-provoking illustrations, analogies and examples (for more about this, reread chapter 7).

Tell a good story. People relate to other people; they respond to talk about people; they are drawn to stories about people. So, talk about people when you can. Democrat Lloyd Bentsen, Michael Dukakis' running mate in the 1988 presidential election, could have talked about the statistics of drug use among youth when he addressed school children in Oakland, Calif. Instead, he read aloud a letter written to him by a 9th-grade student:

> I don't know much about you or your campaign (the letter said). But if you're running with Michael Dukakis, I guess that makes you OK.

Fair enough (said Bentsen, as the students laughed loudly. But the inner-city assembly hushed as Bentsen continued to read) I hope you make it possible for our country to become drug-free. Being a young black woman in America is hard. Day after day, I watch people slowly fading away. I walk home seeing young men and women dealing and hustling drugs (Jehl 1988, 24).

Force and Impact

Good speeches are forceful speeches. The public relations writer can help a speaker along with the following devices:

Repetition: Speechwriter and consultant Joan Detz (1987, 3) says:

If you have a good phrase, repeat it several times during the speech so you can pull the audience into the spirit of your message.

Read aloud this portion of a speech by James Robinson III, CEO of American Express, and listen to the way he repeats key phrases to make a strong appeal for the United Way.

"I'm delighted we're all together for our Centennial conference. But why are we here? Why do we volunteer our time and skills? Why do we work for United Way, or in shelters for battered women, centers for drug addicts, soup kitchens for the hungry? Why do we answer phones, ring doorbells, write letters? . . . My answers are simple. Because we don't pass the buck! We don't play ostrich! We don't say, 'Let someone else do it.' "

Triads: According to Detz (Ibid), "For some mysterious reason, the human mind is strongly attracted to things that come in threes . . . You too can use triads to capture (and keep) the attention of your audience."

The Rev. Martin Luther King Jr. demonstrated the power of the triad on April 3, 1968. His own death may have been on his mind when he said:

But I'm not concerned about that now. I just want to do God's will. And he's allowed me to go up the mountain. **And I've looked** over. **And I've seen. And I've seen** the Promised Land [emphasis added].

Later, he brought the crowd to its feet with:

With this faith, we will be able to achieve this new day, when all of God's children—black men, white men, Jews and Gentiles, Protestants and Catholics—will be able to join hands and sing with the Negroes in the spiritual of old: **'Free at last! Free at last! Thank God Almighty, we're free at last'** [emphasis added].

Liveliness

All of the devices discussed so far will move you toward writing lively and spirited speeches. There is one other device you can employ to make your speech memorable: humor. Kuperszmid (1987, 24) recalls the words of Michael Iapoce, a corporate humor consultant: "When the president (Ronald Reagan) was shot in 1981, Iapoce recalls, he immediately calmed people with remarks like, 'I sure hope these surgeons are Republicans.' And when (Lee) Iacocca announced, during Chrysler's lean times, that he would reduce his salary to just $1 a year, he assured concerned stockholders with the comment, 'Don't worry, I'll spend it very carefully.' "

A caveat about humor. It can offend, and, if it does, your speech could backfire on you. So consider humor carefully and test it before you use it.

Organization

The last major characteristic of good speeches is that they are well organized. The simplest way of organizing a speech is thus:

Greeting
Introduction & objective
    A statement about what you hope to achieve with your presentation
Body
    Main Point #1
        Subsidiary point
        Support
    Main Point #2
        Subsidiary point
        Support
Summary
    Repeat key points
    Concluding statement
Sign off

Chapter Summary

This chapter addressed several forms of writing designed primarily for the eyes and ears of an audience. It started off with a discussion of the nature and characteristics of radio and television.

From there, the chapter moved to guidelines necessary for the public relations writer to cope with radio and television. The primary focus was on simplicity, brevity and euphony (pleasant sound). In addition, this chapter addressed strategies and jargon necessary for the public relations writer to effectively communicate with sound, camera, and other technicians involved in the production of radio and television messages.

Next, the chapter addressed writing and organizational techniques necessary for composing radio and television news releases.

The second type of broadcast message addressed by this chapter was the persuasive message forms of PSAs and corporate ads.

Having discussed broadcast writing, the chapter moved into writing issues and techniques for the newer, computer-based electronic media such as videotex and teletext. Included in this section of the chapter was a style manual specially suited for writing for such electronic media.

The last genre of writing for sight and sound discussed in this chapter was speechwriting. In particular, it focused on several devices the public relations writer can use to write spirited, forceful and high-impact speeches.

A final word. This chapter is not meant to be read in isolation from other chapters. While going through its contents, your mind should relate the ideas expressed here with ideas expressed elsewhere in the book. For example, research is equally important whether you are writing print messages or broadcast copy. And the law never changes regardless of what you write. So, let those ghosts hover in your mind when you review this chapter, and, more importantly, apply its ideas to your writing.

Writing Exercises

1. In the section on writing radio news releases, the following examples of the throw-away lead were given:
"Drug maker stops distribution of abortion pill."
"Soviet icebreakers free trapped whales."
These are real stories that happened in September 1988.
Research them and then, for each lead, complete the body of a 30-second radio release.

   For the first story, assume that you are writing on behalf of the French company Greoupe Roussel Uclaf's New York office (make up an address). For the second story, assume you are writing for the National Oceanic and Atmospheric Administration in Barrow, Alaska.

2. At least three appeals are evident in PSAs written for television. The first is fear. This approach can generally be seen in PSAs aimed at the issue of drinking and driving. The second is a peer group appeal in which the communicator talks to the audience through people it can relate to. An example is the use of singer Michael Jackson to persuade teens not to use drugs. The third is an emotional appeal in which the communicator tries to make the audience feel guilty. Many PSAs aimed at getting you to donate food for the poor use this appeal.

   Write three 60-second radio PSA scripts, one using the fear appeal, the second using the peer group appeal, and the third using the emotion or guilt appeal. For each, use the topic addressed in table 9.5.

3. Pull a financial news story from *The Wall Street Journal* or the business pages of *The New York Times*. Using the information in this story, write a press release for use by the commercial XYZ videotex system servicing all of
_____ (the area you are located in). Remember, the release is composed exactly like a press release, only styled differently.

Food for Thought

You are a public relations writer for an oil company. Your firm has not been in the news for some time now. You are called to a meeting in which you are told that the company is proposing to arrange a minor oil spill and then swiftly solve it. The idea is that the action will result in some positive publicity for the company.

You are warned not to talk about this to anyone. Further, you are asked to anonymously tip the television stations when the spill occurs and be on hand to feed information to them about clean-up operations. You also know that the spill is going to take place in an area where humans are not likely to be affected.

How would you respond to this situation? Write a 100-word justification about what you plan to do, and why.

References for Further Study

Beckham, Jr., James A. "How to Make Speeches Work." *Public Relations Journal* (August 1985):29–30.

Bittner, John R. *Broadcasting and Telecommunication: An Introduction.* 2nd ed. Englewood Cliffs, N.J.: Prentice-Hall. 1985.

Broussard, E. Joseph and Jack F. Holgate. *Writing and Reporting Broadcast News.* New York: Macmillan, 1982.

Cutlip, Scott M., Allen H. Center and Glen M. Broom. *Effective Public Relations,* 6th ed. Englewood Cliffs, N.J.: Prentice-Hall, 1985.

Davids, Meryl. "Now You See Them . . ." *Public Relations Journal* (May 1988):14–20, 47.

Detz, Joan. "Writing and Editing: Five Ways to Add Style to Your Speeches." *Communication Concepts.* December 1987, 3.

Goldsmith, Margie. "How to Get Results with PSAs." *Public Relations Journal.* (January 1986):33–34.

Jehl, Douglas. "Bentsen Returns to Texas in Effort to Carry Crucial State for Dukakis." *The Los Angeles Times.* October 29, 1988, Part 1, 24.

Kuperszmid, Celia. "Corporate Jester." *Public Relations Journal* (November 1987): 24.

Mayeux, Peter E. *Writing for Broadcast Media.* Boston: Allyn & Bacon, 1985.

National Institutes of Health. *Making PSAs Work: A Handbook for Health Communication Professionals.* NIH Publication No. 84–2845, Bethesda, Md., 1984.

Newsom, Doug, and Alan Scott. *This Is PR: The Realities of Public Relations.* Belmont, Calif.: Wadsworth, 1985.

Read, Hadley. *Communication: Methods for All Media.* Urbana: University of Illinois Press, 1972.

Whetmore, Edward J. *Mediamerica: Form, Content and Consequence of Mass Communication,* 3rd ed. Belmont, Calif.: Wadsworth, 1985.

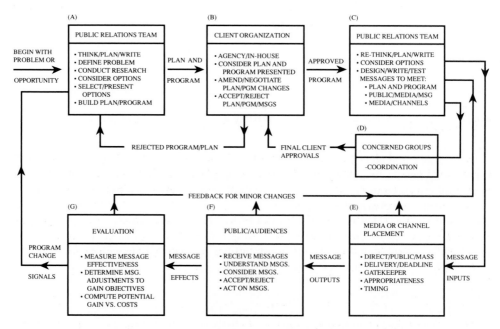

(A) PUBLIC RELATIONS TEAM

BEGIN WITH PROBLEM OR OPPORTUNITY

- THINK/PLAN/WRITE
- DEFINE PROBLEM
- CONDUCT RESEARCH
- CONSIDER OPTIONS
- SELECT/PRESENT OPTIONS
- BUILD PLAN/PROGRAM

PLAN AND PROGRAM

(B) CLIENT ORGANIZATION

- AGENCY/IN-HOUSE
- CONSIDER PLAN AND PROGRAM PRESENTED
- AMEND/NEGOTIATE PLAN/PGM CHANGES
- ACCEPT/REJECT PLAN/PGM/MSGS

APPROVED PROGRAM

(C) PUBLIC RELATIONS TEAM

- RE-THINK/PLAN/WRITE
- CONSIDER OPTIONS
- DESIGN/WRITE/TEST MESSAGES TO MEET:
  - PLAN AND PROGRAM
  - PUBLIC/MEDIA/MSG
  - MEDIA/CHANNELS

REJECTED PROGRAM/PLAN

FINAL CLIENT APPROVALS

(D) CONCERNED GROUPS

-COORDINATION

FEEDBACK FOR MINOR CHANGES

(G) EVALUATION

PROGRAM CHANGE

SIGNALS

- MEASURE MESSAGE EFFECTIVENESS
- DETERMINE MSG. ADJUSTMENTS TO GAIN OBJECTIVES
- COMPUTE POTENTIAL GAIN VS. COSTS

MESSAGE

EFFECTS

(F) PUBLIC/AUDIENCES

- RECEIVE MESSAGES
- UNDERSTAND MSGS.
- CONSIDER MSGS.
- ACCEPT/REJECT
- ACT ON MSGS.

MESSAGE

OUTPUTS

(E) MEDIA OR CHANNEL PLACEMENT

- DIRECT/PUBLIC/MASS
- DELIVERY/DEADLINE
- GATEKEEPER
- APPROPRIATENESS
- TIMING

MESSAGE

INPUTS

Writers for public relations use the same *think-plan-write* approach for organizational communication as for any other writing. Different are the specific purposes for informing, motivating, and obtaining feedback from employees. There are also unique channels used to reach organizational publics, such as annual reports, newsletters, company magazines, speeches, and corporate electronic media. Finally, the coordination and approval requires special skills.

ORGANIZATIONAL COMMUNICATION: STRATEGIES FOR INTERNAL AUDIENCES

Introduction

The company president just told his staff that he plans to retire in two months. That's three years before everyone—employees, stockholders, Wall Street, customers—expected him to step down. He's been the guiding force behind the company's surge from bankruptcy to record profits. This news is a sensitive "bombshell," to say the least. Perhaps no group will take the news harder than employees, who've looked to him as their leader. But the words must be found to tell them, to reassure them, to explain to them. This means preparing newsletter and magazine articles, a speech for the president, remarks for all his vice presidents, and a videotape script for the company's monthly news show.

So who will do this writing? That's right—you.

When you think of public relations writing, you probably imagine writing for the mass media, for community groups, for Congress, maybe even for stockholders. A common perception about public relations is that its efforts are focused exclusively on outside publics. After all, organizations need to "win over" as many influential groups as they can. Too many managers assume that internal publics, such as employees, are naturally loyal and don't need much persuading to support their organizations. And for a long time, many top executives believed that. Fortunately, things are changing.

Today, many managers realize that taking employee support for granted can hurt their organizations' performance. Damage can range from decreasing productivity and organizational loyalty, to rising absenteeism and increasing employee turnover.

One approach managers can use to build and maintain employee commitment is more and better communication.

Variously called internal communication, internal public relations, employee communication, or organizational communication, the responsibility for communicating with people employed by an organization often belongs to the public relations department. This chapter addresses the **strategic** aspects of such communication.

The Changing Face of Organizational Communication

The Impact of Effective Communication

Today, communicating with employees is a business necessity and responsibility that more managers are taking seriously. Research suggests that employees' perceptions of their communication with different levels of management can substantially affect their job satisfaction and job performance (Pincus and Rayfield 1987). The quality of communication between managers and employees can influence employees' faith in management, their acceptance of management's messages, and their emotional attachment to the organization's mission. To quote Chrysler's Lee Iacocca: "You can't motivate employees if you don't communicate with them" (Iacocca 1984, 54).

Management's Reluctance to Communicate

For years, however, the value of management-employee communication went unnoticed. Executives seemed to follow the slogan, "The less we tell employees, the better," because, "If we let workers see how we run the business, they'll only ask a lot of uncomfortable questions and, worse yet, expect more of everything."

So for many years, some managers were information misers, doling out bits of information to employees only when absolutely necessary. For example, if management planned layoffs or if the company was suffering financially, such information was kept secret until it could no longer be avoided. And, employees silently accepted management's tight-lipped communication style. Perhaps they just didn't realize they had the power to change things. But change things they did.

A New Breed of Employee Emerges

The focus of organizational communication has changed dramatically over the past two decades. These changes have been triggered by changes in society and are reflected in employees' attitudes toward work, careers, families and lifestyles. Major shifts in people's way of life—such as the influx of women into the workforce, and people living and working longer—have reshaped employees' basic values and career motivations. Whereas work and security were the typical employee's main concerns in 1960, that employee's children's key concerns in the '90s are personal accomplishment and self-fulfillment.

This evolution of employee values has forced management to respond with more sophisticated and diverse communication approaches. Thus, the demand for communication professionals with strong and diverse **strategic communication** skills has increased correspondingly.

Attitudes Toward Work

People's attitudes about work have changed substantially since World War II, altering the way managers and employees view each other and their work roles. Employees today are motivated by different kinds of rewards from their jobs than their parents and grandparents were. Whereas grandpa worked for money, his grandson may be most interested in the job that allows him the most "self-expression." Today, employees are willing to work hard, but they also expect more leisure time for themselves.

Also, employees must struggle with issues their parents never faced, such as dual-career families, single parenting, child and elder care, to name just a few. These societal shifts have permanently altered the way employees and employers view the world of work.

From Wordsmiths to Strategists

Until the 1970s or so, many organizational writers were simply told what to write, how to write it, when to write it and whom to write it for. In other words, **communication with employees was essentially top-down, guarded and heavily censored. As mouthpieces for management, public relations writers were word technicians who were not expected to think about, research or analyze the content of the messages they wrote.** They merely reworded management's thoughts into clearly understandable phrases and sentences.

During the '70s and '80s, the public relations writer's role in organizational communication began to change from wordsmith to communication strategist. This change was triggered by two concurrent trends: (1) the public relations community's rising emphasis on professionalism, training and issues analysis; and (2) organizations' increasing need for substantive and sophisticated communication with various audiences, including dynamic employee publics, in order to respond to an increasingly competitive marketplace.

As the need to communicate with different key audiences grew, so did the need for writers who could adapt their styles to a variety of media, from newsletters to video scripts to speeches. And this need was perhaps greatest inside organizations. Information-starved employees at all levels wanted, needed and demanded more and better communication between themselves and top management. Consequently, organizational writers were being given responsibility for conceiving, planning and writing management's—or, more appropriately, the organization's—messages. They evolved into independent problem-solvers with special knowledge of the communication process and a gift for expressing the written word convincingly in various print, person-to-person and electronic media.

The Purposes of Organizational Communication

As we have seen, top managers have traditionally viewed communicating with employees as a "harmless," even "fruitless," obligation. In contrast, top executives today demand that organizational communication programs contribute to the bottom line. In many cases, promotions, resources and budgets hinge on the professional communicator's ability to convince top management of the public relations program's direct contributions to meeting key objectives such as profitability or recruitment.

Most organizational communication objectives seek to strengthen the management-employee relationship and to contribute to the organization's goals. Each organization shapes its own approach to communicating with employees, depending on the business objectives it stresses. Organizational communication objectives tend to fit within one or more of three areas: informing, motivating, and obtaining feedback.

Informing Employees

A major purpose of all organizational communication is to share job-related and company information with employees. For instance, most employees are interested in the financial status of their organizations, major policy or structural changes, new products, future business directions, and top-level management shifts. All workers want information directly affecting their jobs and futures. For example, they want to know about fringe benefits, work schedule changes, training programs and salary adjustments. "People respond best to functional, 'how to' communication," says Ray Hiebert, editor and publisher of *Social Science Monitor*. "They want to know how to do their jobs better. The more simple and direct the communication, the better" (Ellis 1985, 6). Informed, knowledgeable employees will better understand their roles in the organizational scheme, feel more satisfied in their jobs, and appreciate that management cares about them as people, not just as workers.

Motivating Employees

This objective seeks to develop employees who see their personal interests as overlapping with the organization's interests. Such employees feel they are an integral part of the organization, believe in its values, and are willing to make personal sacrifices to help the organization prosper. Truly motivated employees want to better their organizations because they believe they'll get back as much, if not more, than they give. Hiebert puts it another way: "The organization has to create an environment that motivates through pride in work rather than through fear of losing a job" (Ellis 1985, 6). Communication that addresses employees' concerns and interests directly and honestly will help create motivated employees.

Obtaining Feedback from Employees

Increasingly, the purpose of organizational communication is to ask employees about their reactions, ideas, suggestions and concerns. More top managers today understand that such information can be critical in making intelligent business decisions (Pincus and Rayfield 1987). At the same time, management's asking for feedback from employees can boost employees' feelings of self-worth and enhance their support of decisions they contributed to. This "bottom-up" information exchange can break down some of the psychological barriers that often separate managers and employees. Feedback may be formal (e.g., surveys, audits) or informal (e.g., conversations, grapevine).

One point that must be emphatically repeated is that **communication objectives should always be an outgrowth of and directly linked to an organization's business objectives.** This ensures that communication efforts will contribute to achieving management's goals. These objectives should always reflect the organization's current mission.

Key Media Used in Organizational Communication

Public relations writers with responsibility for employee communication must be able to vary and adapt their writing styles to a host of internal media. This section discusses the purposes, target audiences and strategies associated with a few commonly-used print, interpersonal and electronic organizational communication media.

Print Media

Print materials rise or fall on the quality of the writing contained in them. Although many printed messages rely on and are enhanced by visual components—such as photographs, graphics and illustrations—to supplement the written message, it is the persuasive power of the writer's selection of words that distinguishes one magazine or newsletter from another.

This section discusses the strategic uses of annual reports and a few key internal print media.

A PROFESSIONAL TIP:
Writing for the Internal Audience

Inform. Explain. Justify. Sell.

No matter what message the public relations practitioner has to communicate, it must be communicated with words. Mostly written words. Clearly. Sharply. Accurately. Concisely.

That's obvious for external audiences, less so for internal. Obvious for news releases, less so for memos to the boss. Don't underestimate the importance of the written word within the organization. In the corporate environment, the justification memo, monthly program report, the annual budget request are among the written documents vital to the practitioner's success. You can't communicate outside if management inside doesn't understand your function because you have failed to communicate effectively to your bosses, your peers and others within your own organization.

Julian R. Levine is vice president of communications for the Space & Defense Sector of TRW. He has worked in public affairs and public relations for Continental Airlines, the Aerospace Industries Association, Aerojet-General and Martin Marietta Corp. He spent nine years as special assistant to the U.S. assistant secretary of defense for public affairs.

Annual Reports

The annual report is the corporation's yearly financial story. There are three types of annual reports of concern to the organizational communicator: (1) the traditional, legally-required annual report for stockholders; (2) the non-required, internally focused annual report for employees; and (3) the relatively new "highlights-only" summary annual report. Although they contain some similar information, each has a different purpose and format, and demands a different writing style.

1. The annual report for stockholders is a legal requirement of all corporations that sell stock to the public. It is first and foremost a report of a company's financial state, containing certain financial data (e.g., five-year display of key financial indicators, including a balance sheet and an income statement). The annual report must be filed with the Securities and Exchange Commission and distributed to all stockholders. Originally designed for stockholders and other potential investors, the annual report has evolved from a dry, simple, numbers-oriented document into a colorful, multipurpose, graphics-oriented corporate communication tool.

The annual report has emerged as the printed piece that tells—and shows—the company's story. Many companies print three or four times as many annual reports as they have stockholders. That's so the annual report can be used for many corporate purposes, including recruiting, marketing and image-building.

Innovative approaches have marked annual reports for years. Managements want their annual reports to be noticed and remembered. To do that, they strive for a visual treatment that "grabs." Some feature customers, others highlight employees, and still others emphasize products. For example, Genentech Inc., a biochemical research company, in its 1987 annual report had a pop-up centerfold of its new corporate headquarters on San Francisco Bay. Since 1977, Baltimore-based McCormick & Co. has made its annual reports literally "smell" with a different one of its spice scents each year. In fact, annual report producers have become so design-conscious that the reports are viewed by some as works of art. That was the case when a leading New York art museum exhibited 225 annual reports in 1988, displaying the work of some leading American graphic designers and photographers (Berton 1988).

Because annual reports are being used more and more to tell corporations' stories to key non-investment publics (e.g., customers, media), public relations writers are becoming increasingly involved in shaping and writing annual report copy. The annual report has emerged as a corporate "showpiece," being widely distributed to many key audiences.

As the annual report has evolved from a strictly financial report to a corporate communication vehicle, public relations professionals are writing much of its non-accounting copy. For example, a public relations writer may take the lead in writing the "Letter to Shareholders" from the Chairman and CEO (see figure 10.1) or the narrative sections describing a company's various divisions and units or its contributions to social programs. The effect has been that much of annual report copy today has moved from a highly formal, jargon-heavy style to a more informal, conversational style.

2. The employee annual report, which surfaced within the last 20 years, targets a single public: employees. While annual reports must comply with a number of government regulations, the employee annual report is not legally required and, therefore, can be whatever management wants it to be. Its purposes are: (a) to provide employees with vital financial information about their company; and, (b) to publicly recognize employees' contributions to the company's success in the prior year. In essence, employee annual reports serve both employees' need for information and management's desire to motivate and build trust in its employees.

A Letter to Shareholders...

For Gannett, 1983 was a year of continuing progress . . . with profits, products and people.

It was a year that saw our World of Different Voices expand internally, while at the same time our horizons for the future broadened and brightened.

Our vitality, variety and visibility all were enhanced.

The increased visibility came about primarily because USA TODAY, The Nation's Newspaper, set unprecedented circulation records and became the third largest newspaper in the country in less than one year. But even as USA TODAY heightened our visibility, excellence in all Gannett divisions sharpened our vitality and added to our variety.

The challenge—and the success—in 1983 was to pursue traditional, largely local paths, while exploring new, mostly national endeavors.

The blend of those goals worked well. Indeed, some of our local units established themselves as national showcases of local excellence.

As we increased and improved our mix of national and local objectives, our performance in three primary areas—profit, product and people—continued to carry our company forward.

Consider profit . . .

Earnings per share rose 6 percent to $2.40 from $2.26 in 1982.

Net income increased to $191,665,000, up 6 percent from $180,507,000 last year.

Revenues increased 12 percent to $1,703,646,000, up from $1,519,514,000 in 1982.

The Board of Directors approved a three-for-two stock split, the fourth since the company went public in 1967.

Quarterly dividends rose 7 percent, the 16th straight year your dividend payments have gone up.

Consider products . . .

The progress we made in our products in 1983 augurs well for future profits.

Our newspaper division, with 85 daily newspapers, continued to be the backbone of the company. Our total daily average circulation grew to about 4,800,000—by far the largest in the country.

Our newspapers continued to be recognized by readers and judges alike for their excellence. Of the more than 900 awards won by Gannett news staffers, our Clarion-Ledger at Jackson, Mississippi, won the Pulitzer Prize Gold Medal for Public Service, the second for Gannett in three years. Gannett News Service won several top national awards and many of our local papers won top state awards.

USA TODAY became what many have called the nation's most imitated newspaper in 1983. For growing thousands of readers, it is the nation's most popular newspaper too. By December, the average daily net paid circulation was 1,328,781, more than 15 percent ahead of pre-publication projections.

Our broadcast stations continued to improve operations and worked to increase market share. We acquired new stations in two splendid markets: WTCN-TV in Minneapolis-St. Paul and WLVI-TV in Boston.

Gannett's KOCO-TV in Oklahoma City won the prestigious Peabody Award, and WTCN-TV received the coveted DuPont-Columbia University award.

In radio, we now have the largest weekly radio listenership of any group in the country without a New York City station—more than 5,800,000 listeners every week. Several of our stations achieved sharply higher ratings through superior programming, including station KIIS-FM in Los Angeles, the number one station in Los Angeles out of 70.

Gannett Outdoor Advertising led the industry in public affairs projects involving domestic and foreign issues, developed more aggressive selling at the local level and produced an increase in its earnings.

Our variety of activities increased as we found new ways to fill consumer needs in this expanding and exciting information age.

2

▶ **Figure 10.1. Annual report: letter to shareholders.** Once heavy with numbers and technical verbiage, annual report copy today is increasingly more lean and conversational. This change reflects corporate America's desire to communicate more directly with individual potential investors. Public relations departments frequently are responsible for planning and managing the formation of their company's annual report—including writing of the copy.

In this 1983 annual report by Gannett Company, a diversified news and information organization, former Chairman Allen Neuharth's ''Letter to Shareholders'' reflects the stylish, inviting, expository writing style found in many contemporary annual reports.

Gannett Media Sales was formed to work with advertisers and agencies to help them take advantage of our diversity and synergistic opportunities with mixed-media and multiple-market buys in newspaper, broadcasting and outdoor.

NEWSCOPE, a satellite-delivered daily half-hour TV news program, was launched and shown in 93 markets.

MacNeil-Lehrer-Gannett Productions began daily airing of the expanded MacNeil-Lehrer NewsHour on public television.

We named a seven-member committee to study new media possibilities, part of our continuing effort to harness new technology as it unfolds, if it meets the desires of consumers and blends with our own vision.

Consider people . . .

At the very center of our performance with profits and products have been our people.

Some top management realignment demonstrated that your company's future leaders are already aboard, participating in the daily decisions and long-range planning that will continue to propel your company forward.

Throughout your company, at every level, the commitment continued to truly reflect a World of

Al Neuharth surveys Manhattan at dusk from the 32nd floor terrace of Gannett's New York City offices at 535 Madison Avenue.

Different Voices. There were 125 new opportunities in upper management in 1983; 42.1 percent of those new jobs now are held by women and 16.9 percent by minorities.

We will continue to set the pace for the communications industry, from the boardroom to the newsroom, in hiring and promoting women and minorities.

The Right Mix . . .

That mix of our people, our products and our profits made 1983 a good year.

The same policies, philosophy and style have produced the steady, uninterrupted 10-year growth record illustrated on the preceding and following pages of this report.

That 10-year period covers exactly the decade during which it has been my privilege to serve as your chief executive officer.

My associates and I believe we have built a base for an even bigger and more successful company in 1984 and beyond. We hope you, as an owner, will share with us pride in this report.

Sincerely,

Al Neuharth

Allen H. Neuharth
Chairman and Chief Executive Officer

3

▶ **Figure 10.1.** *(continued)*

Writing and producing employee annual reports frequently fall within the public relations or employee communication department's domain. Employee annual reports come in many different shapes, sizes, formats, lengths, and "looks." They differ from traditional annual reports in several ways: (a) they are light on narrative copy, and heavy on photos and personality features of employees and their individual contributions to company goals; (b) the writing style is highly conversational and informal, with references to employees, including managers, by their first names; and (c) financial information is confined to key facts only, such as sales and profit figures accompanied by simple, attractive graphics.

3. The latest innovation in annual reports of interest to public relations writers is the **summary annual report.** Recently approved by the SEC, the summary annual report is an abbreviated form of the tradtional annual report to stockholders. It was created in order to streamline and simplify the communication of financial information. Over the years, research has consistently shown that the average investor doesn't understand the detailed financial data and technical jargon contained in annual reports ("Summary Annual Reports" 1987).

The first company to use the summary report was McKesson Corp. in 1987. Written in a very readable style, the 24-page report is about half the length of McKesson's regular annual report. The financial data are compressed, colorfully illustrated and discussed in narrative form. Some companies are adapting summary annual reports to video forms.

Newsletters

The most common form of print communication from management to employees is the newsletter. As the term implies, a newsletter provides for employee audiences timely, concise, pertinent "bits" of information about the organization and issues affecting it. An organization's employee newsletter may be its most important written communication. A newsletter: (a) defines and explains the organization to employees; and (b) through its look, tone, degree of candor, and issues covered, is a window to management's view of employees and what management considers important.

The newsletter, in many ways, is like a newspaper. It is designed to deliver important information in an interesting manner on a timely basis at a relatively low cost. With news as its driving force, the newsletter is usually written in an informal journalistic or news style, emphasizing and interpreting the factual elements of a story (e.g., who, what, why, when, where and how). These stories are usually presented from management's perspective, and are designed to influence employees or help them understand the meaning behind situations or issues confronting the organization. Since space is limited, the articles are generally brief (three to eight paragraphs) and to the point (short, punchy sentences).

Public relations writers may play the role of "reporter," and rely on many of the same research tools, such as interviews and computerized data bases, as a newspaper reporter would in writing a story. The primary objectives (organizational vs. public interests) and target audiences (employees vs. public), however, differ from those of a typical newspaper reporter. Many newsletters contain a mix of news and lighter, more entertaining pieces, such as personality profiles, "how to" columns, and special reports of employee or organizational accomplishments. The "news" items in newsletters encompass a number of different topics: organizational plans and changes; new policies, products or services; information about the competition; key financial news about the organization; major personnel changes; reports on and previews of special events (e.g., seminars, classes, social gatherings); and special messages or reports from top management.

Most newsletters are one-way communication efforts from management to employees. In recent years, as managements have realized the value of feedback from employees, newsletters have increasingly been used to deliver employees' concerns and opinions to management. This is done through a variety of techniques, such as using guest experts or employee columnists, "Letters to the Editor" sections, unedited employee responses to a "Question of the Month," and results of readership surveys. Figure 10.2 shows how one company used a "Question of the Month" format in its newsletter for managers. In some organizations, such as Atlantic Richfield Co., newsletter editors and writers are given substantial editorial freedom and independence from top management so that the employee viewpoint can be openly expressed without filtering or rewording by the "bosses."

Newsletters vary widely in size (8.5" x 11" or 11" x 17"), length (usually two to eight pages), number of colors, target audiences (segments of employees), frequency (weekly, bimonthly, monthly), type of information and budget. Employee communication consultant Roy Foltz explains these variations: "The old house organ is playing a different tune, supplying different information. The old predictability is gone, and style and formats of publications are as varied as the organizations they represent" (Foltz 1985, 11).

Magazines

In contrast to the "hit and run" treatment of timely topics in newsletters, magazines give more analytical, in-depth treatment to **a few** "news-oriented" topics or issues. Newsletters present timely information, with little, if any, overt effort to persuade; magazines, on the other hand, merge that same factual information into more fully developed arguments in hopes of influencing readers' attitudes. Most organizational magazines are published bimonthly or quarterly, are professionally written and designed by staff or free-lancers or both, and are printed on high quality paper in two or more colors.

Barbara Birks

Personnel Director,
Marriott's Hunt
Valley Inn

". . . my greatest responsibility lies in my ability to set an example." It may involve something as simple as turning off a typewriter, but if I walk away even once without doing my part, no amount of talking will convince other employees of my concern for the energy shortage.

"Marriott Corporation also has the responsibility of setting an example. By developing a realistic energy policy and insisting that individuals adhere to it, we not only set an example for the entire industry but for each individual employee as well. I'm proud to say that the management team here at Hunt Valley is very energy conscious.

Dave Miller

Assistant Manager,
Hot Shoppe Cafeteria #159
Minnesota

"One of the best ways to control energy use is to be more aware of how the equipment in our shops consume energy. Information received from corporate headquarters has been very helpful along these lines.

"The corporation has encouraged all units to be more energy conscious for some time. Energy costs are right up there with wage and food costs, and there is little doubt that energy costs will continue to rise."

Tom Gimmelli

Assistant Manager, Manners Big Boy
Euclid, Ohio

"The company has energy saving programs and guidelines, but it's really up to each manager to see that conservation takes place. In our unit we have found it's the small things that really make the difference—things like turning the fryers, grills and toasters down during slack periods. We also try to keep lights off whenever possible and, more importantly, keep conservation foremost in the minds of our employees. We discuss energy saving measures at our regular safety meetings and stress the fact that when equipment is turned down or off we will not only save energy, but avoid hazards."

Ned Perry

Manager, CFS, B&I Account
Germantown, Maryland

"Working together with our client, we have already taken steps to reduce energy consumption. We've removed all of the light bulbs from our vending machines and are only using our kitchen equipment on an 'as needed' basis.

"In a company as large and diverse as Marriott, energy conservation must be left in the hands of each unit manager. My own philosophy is to keep the lid on consumption the same way I do in my home."

COUNTERPOINT

Question:

Energy costs are
skyrocketing.

What should you
as a manager, and
Marriott
as a company,
be doing to
save energy?

Dick Burlingame

Chief Engineer, Denver Marriott Hotel

"Marriott is doing more in the area of conservation than any other hotel system I know. We have a Management Training program. We upgrade equipment regularly and are backed by management's commitment to conservation.

"Locally, we are very active in energy conservation. Recently, I was elected Chairman of the Colorado/Wyoming Hotel Energy Council, which is composed of Chief Engineers from major hotels. We work closely with the Regional Federal Energy Administration, the U.S. Department of Commerce and the Assistant to the Governor for Energy Conservation. The Council's purpose is to promote development of energy conservation in hotels and ex-

change information and ideas. We also try to keep abreast of current energy legislation, utility rates and new products and programs. The energy Council also acts as an advisory group to members of the Colorado/Wyoming Hotel and Motel Association who do not have qualified energy conservation personnel on their staff."

Andrew McCauley

Assistant Manager,
CFS Health Care Services
Bowling Green, Kentucky

"Here at the hospital, we've been following a program of minimizing use of electrical equipment for quite some time. We are currently using only half of our lighting capabilities and trying to make every employee more energy conscious."

Joseph Vos

Vice President,
Sun Line Cruises, New York

"We at Sun Line are doing all we can, both here and abroad to conserve energy and fuel. Our ships always avoid going at maximum speed and have taken other steps of a more technical nature to save.

"When I make up an itinerary for one of our ships in the Carribbean, I try to have the ship arrive at its destination at the optimum hour, cruising at the minimum speed, because each additional knot means more fuel consumption."

Liz Martin

Manager of Sales,
Great America Theme Park
Gurnee, Illinois

"It's true that all Marriott employees should be aware of the energy situation, but it's up to the managers to see that something is done about it.

"One suggestion we have implemented in our own office is to take out the middle two bulbs in all four bulb flourescent units. This reduces costs and consumption without any ill effects. This could surely be done in all hallways and open areas where there is probably an over abundance of light to begin with."

9

▶ **Figure 10.2. Newsletter encouraging employee participation.** More than ever before, top executives want and seek input from employees *before* they make decisions. Two-way communication between managers and employees can take many different forms. An increasingly popular approach is putting direct questions to employees and publishing their responses—unedited—in the company-wide publication.

In *Memo,* a monthly newsletter for managers throughout Marriott Corporation, an international hotel and restaurant company, the editorial staff conducts telephone interviews with a random set of managers and reports the results verbatim. In this example, the question concerned ways to cut energy costs. Copyright © 1977 Marriott Corp. Reprinted with permission.

An example of this difference is how the issue of drug testing in the workplace would be treated in a magazine, as opposed to a newsletter. A newsletter might devote a few paragraphs to announcing and briefly explaining the company's rationale for its drug testing policy, which might include comments from the CEO and vice president for human resources. In contrast, since drug testing is an important topic that could influence the tenor of management-employee relations, the public relations writer might plan a more elaborate story for the company magazine that explores the key issues—pro and con—surrounding the topic. This story might include extensive background research, interviews with company executives, affected employees and perhaps outside medical or legal experts, and a stated conclusion or recommendation by the writer. Figure 10.3 is an example of an issues-oriented magazine article.

The quality of many organizational magazines, whether targeted for internal or external audiences, rivals commercial subscription magazines. Figure 10.4 is an example of a magazine treatment of an employee profile.

As a general rule, organizations are eager to share their messages with any interested or potentially influential publics. After all, trying to limit or control who sees or doesn't see a magazine, or any publication, is virtually impossible. Therefore, public relations writers must remember that secondary audiences (i.e., "pass-along" readers) are likely to read and react to their stories too.

The writer uses different writing styles for newsletter and magazine stories. The newsletter story is quite journalistic or "matter of fact," with few, if any, accompanying photos or graphics. But the multi-page magazine story uses a flexible, more creative writing style that weaves together material from various sources and punctuates it with absorbing, thought-provoking illustrations or photographs. Writing a magazine feature story offers the writer more latitude in selecting a format and language. It's important, however, not to lose sight of the story's purpose and accidentally drown the theme in a sea of words. For instance, introductions may be attention-grabbers of several paragraphs, language may be descriptive and complemented with adjectives. Points may also be supported with multiple sources via facts and quotations, and the writer's or organization's point of view may be woven into the article.

The Memo

Business writing—which includes memoranda, letters, reports, notes, executive summaries and so on—is not the exclusive domain of the public relations writer. All employees, particularly supervisors and managers, at one time or another must produce various forms of written communication. Indeed, many organizations today are buried in their own blizzard of paper because managers cannot write concisely and clearly. Since the public relations writer is the professional writer, the example setter, the writing trainer, we believe it important to review strategies behind the most common form of intra-organization written communication, the **memorandum** or the **memo.**

**Direct-line sales units add a new dimension
to the term "remote control"**

LONG DISTANCE MANAGEMENT

Bob Finberg used to work less than 20 feet from his boss. Now it's more like 2,000 miles. But Finberg, a second level national account manager for Continental Airlines in Los Angeles, prefers his present location.

"There's more responsibility at second level in this type of situation and that's good," he says. "There's more growth on your part when you have to manage the total job on your own."

Finberg is one of hundreds of managers in the national sales department working under the direct-line reporting structure. Direct-line means that instead of reporting to the regions, as was the case in the past, the chain of command for all sales units will now lead directly to the national sales department at headquarters.

While a primary goal of the new structure is decreasing the distance between boss and subordinate on the organization chart, in some cases it has greatly increased the distance on the map.

For many NAMs, like Finberg, it's their first experience at managing by long distance. As a market manager at headquarters last year, Finberg's desk was on one side of the room and his boss's office on the other. Next door was his boss's boss. Total distance: about 90 feet.

Today, Finberg is in Los Angeles, his boss is outside Chicago and his boss's boss is in Atlanta. Total distance: about 2,800 miles. Clearly, management styles that worked between adjoining offices may show the strain of being stretched across a continent.

"One of the problems we've experienced is that most administrative practices are predicated on third level approval and we're all second level NAMs out here," he says. "So just the fact that we don't have a district level organization creates certain problems in itself."

But managing by long distance may be less of a culture shock for some managers than it is for others. That's the feeling of Nora Pfennig Pearce, national account manager for American Cyanamid.

Pearce had worked in operations and engineering in the regions before becoming a NAM. She believes that despite some drawbacks, the NAM job offers managers a chance for greater autonomy.

"When I moved to operations and there were 40 miles between my boss and me, I felt a lot more independent than I had in engineering, where my boss, my subordinates and my peers were all co-located," she says.

"But when I became a NAM, I found that I was really running my own show. Whether the boss is next door or 500 miles away, NAMs are responsible for their own group, and they tend to manage it that way."

Although they may no longer be in the same building, or even the same state, direct-line reporting is by no means the end of the traditional boss/subordinate relationship.

A good example is the changed role of the general manager-sales (GM-S). Dennis Lukas is GM-S for the computer/office products segment. He has 14 NAMs reporting to him. Among his objectives is visiting each of them at least once every quarter.

Among other things, Lukas says, his visits to the NAMs focus on where they've been, where they are and where they're headed. Lukas reviews the NAM's sales tactics for the coming quarter, tries to anticipate roadblocks and generally get a feel for the key issues that could affect the account in the months ahead. He believes this type of control has been reponsible for the success the segment has had so far.

Perhaps the largest single change any group of managers has experienced with direct-line reporting is the amount of traveling required of the general manager-

▶ **Figure 10.3. Issues-oriented article.** Employee publications today are much more than the "babies and bowling scores" approach that characterized them 20 years ago. Employees want and expect more than "puff" pieces; they prefer substantive, professionally prepared articles on issues affecting them and their organizations.

A good example of the type of issues-oriented article contained in many internal publications appears in *Mgr.*, a magazine for managers of AT&T. Its objectives, according to the company, are to offer a "variety of viewpoints on the science of managing as well as practical information on company policies and programs." In the opening spread of this three-page article on a new company-wide management reporting system affecting hundreds of managers, the writer personalizes the issue of organizational structure while weaving together the reasons for the move and how managers are adapting to it. Used with permission of AT&T.

▶ **Figure 10.4.   Magazine treatment of employee profile.** Internal magazines may contain a number of different types of articles: (1) stories about issues affecting the organization, (2) reports about events in the organization, and (3) profiles about employees' contributions to the organization. Employee profile stories usually try to show the employee as an individual and as a member of the organization.

An illustration of a typical employee profile story appears in Marriott Corporation's quarterly employee magazine, *VISIONS*. In this story about former big band singer Bob Davis, the writer attempts to explain why Davis left show business for a new career and to illustrate why his job is important to the orgaization's success. The writing style is light and descriptive. Used with permission of Marriott Corp.

A somewhat younger Bob Davis
when he led his own orchestra
during the Big Band Days of the '40s.

by David Pincus

Bob Davis has composed his own song of life during his 48 years. He isn't the kind of guy who goes around blowing his own horn—unless it happens to be a trumpet or trombone. Back in the "big band" heydays of the 1940s and '50s, he was one of the giants of the flourishing music industry.

You're not sure you remember him? He was the guy who replaced Dick Haynes as the lead vocalist with the famous Tommy Dorsey Band. He took over for Ray Eberle with the Gene Krupa Band. He still writes music for the unstoppable Harry James. He was the leader of his own orchestra, and once replaced Frank Sinatra in one of the big bands.

Still can't place the face? Wondering what happened to him? You'll find Bob working as a flight equipment handler (FEH) at Marriott's in-flite kitchen in Las Vegas, Nevada. His life has changed. But he sought the change—and he doesn't regret it.

After 30 years on the road as a musician, singer, composer, conductor, arranger, actor and card-dealer—having begun as a seven-year-old singer on the Beverly Hillbillies radio show—Bob is honest with himself.

"Sure I miss the music industry," says the father of four and husband of 27 years. "But I had it for a long time. Now it's the young peoples' turn."

Davis is not looking back over his shoulder. He's realistic about his career, past and future. He's proud of what he's accomplished in a tough, competitive industry. He's also satisfied with the present. He walked away from the only life he ever knew with only slight hesitation.

The easy smile which creases his ruddy, sun-darkened complexion reveals his self-confidence. "The music industry became too political for me," says Bob, who has written music for Disney and several Broadway musicals. "I never had to do things politically and I wasn't about to begin." So he set out in a new direction.

Bob decided to search for a new career a couple of years ago. He wanted to remain in Las Vegas where he owns a home, and stay within walking distance of the familiar, bright lights of show business.

He first tried his hand at dealing cards at the Tropicana Hotel in Vegas. The excitement wore off quickly. "I didn't like it at all," recalls Bob. "There's no security and it became terribly boring."

Then he found his way to Marriott In-Flite's new kitchen near Las Vegas' McCarran Airport. It was the first time he ever had to fill-out a job application.

So far, the harmony between Bob Davis and Marriott has been on key. They've each met the other's expectations. "It's a whole new scene for me," says the transplanted New Yorker. "I never punched a time clock before. The exercise is great for me. There's no time to get bored."

He may have switched careers, but his lifestyle hasn't changed. He still sees many of his show business friends. He jokes about his salary as an FEHer not "quite" being the $1,500 a week he once earned as a singing cowboy with Columbia pictures. But Bob says he has never lived by the dollar. Besides, his work is steady now and he sees his family every night, not just between the endless string of one night gigs.

Nobody made Bob Davis' decisions for him. There is still a place for him in the music industry if he wants it. He left because he wanted to. His principles guided him and his determination motivated him.

No regrets either. He knows what he wants. And he knows what is important to him. His cool eyes tell you that he wouldn't have changed any part of his life.

"It's all in me, a part of what makes me what I am . . . at least I've been there," he explains with a touch of nostalgia. Bob Davis wrote his own melody in life. Not many people can say that.

It's never too late to begin a new career. Ask Bob Davis about it.

15

▶ **Figure 10.4**   *(continued)*

The memo is a brief, direct, timely written message between employees. Essentially, it is a reminder, a record, or a request. Memos are important to business because they commit words—ideas, summaries, plans, suggestions—to paper. In Lewis Carroll's *Through the Looking Glass,* the following short passage illustrates the value of the memo: "The horror of that moment," the King went on, "I shall never, never forget!" "You will, though," the Queen said, "if you don't make a memorandum of it."

Memos are usually sent from one person to another person, although they may also be used to communicate with groups as well. For instance, department managers, in order to save time and make sure that each employee receives the same message, may send the same memo to each member of the department. Generally, they are written in an informal tone. This rule, of course, will vary with the situation and the degree to which the people know each other.

Memos are used for many different purposes, and may range from the straight informational to the highly persuasive. Some of the common situations in which memos are appropriate are: (a) to share information, ideas or policies; (b) to produce a written record of a conversation, meeting or activity; (c) to avoid confusion or misunderstanding when one or more people or departments is involved with a project; (d) to indicate that the communication is neither formal, urgent nor critical (although it may be important); and (e) to convince others to take some action or to garner support for an idea or program.

A memo may be as simple as telling employees that their starting time has changed from 8:45 a.m. to 9 a.m., which requires no response. Or it may be as complex as trying to persuade the CEO to authorize $50,000 for an employee opinion survey.

The memo, or "formal note," is designed to be a brief communication. Generally speaking, it is three to five paragraphs, limited to a single page, no more than two. Many of today's organizations, such as American Golf and Dana Corp., which have declared war on the "run-on" memo, have outlawed memos of more than a page. A memo should focus on one subject or point only, with little, if any, "optional" material. The idea is to get to the point immediately and take as little of the reader's time as necessary.

Three words best describe how memos should be written: simple, simple, simple. That goes for its organization, language, sentence structure and sentence length (see chapters 7 and 8). Being simple, however, doesn't mean that preciseness, creativity and style must be sacrificed. Relying on active voice, active verbs, subject-verb agreement, and descriptive and appropriate language should be applied as diligently in memos as in any other type of written communication.

Here are a couple of examples of poorly-worded sections of memos and their more simple translations (*How to Polish Your Writing Skills* 1981):

Example One:

> We solicit any recommendations that you wish to make and you may be assured that any such recommendations will be given our careful consideration.
> *Translation:* Please give us your suggestions. We'll consider them carefully.

Example Two:

The finance director claimed that substantial economies were being effected in his division by increasing the time interval between distribution of data-eliciting forms to business entities.

Translation: The finance director said his division was saving money by sending fewer questionnaires to employees.

Technology has begun to affect the writing and sending of memos. Many organizations are installing electronic mail systems for their employees. Electronic mail, or "E-mail" as it's often called, allows employees to write and send messages (i.e., memos) via personal computers. E-mail saves time and allows immediate exchange of messages. But since the words must be read on a small computer screen, which can be tough on the eyes, messages should be brief and tightly edited.

Interpersonal Media

This book stresses the importance of written communication in effective public relations. As should be obvious by now, the number of media in which the written word dominates are many and varied. Despite the vital role of the written word in organizational communication, it is not the preferred—or most effective—form of communication. That title is reserved for the more interactive, live, face-to-face or interpersonal communication.

People respond more to other people than to words on paper. That's especially true if the person delivering the message is a believable source and addresses a subject important to the listener. In essence, interpersonal communication adds the human touch—emotional nuances, eye-to-eye contact, and immediacy—to the words comprising the message. Unfortunately, the opportunities to communicate person-to-person or person-to-group are relatively few and far between in large organizations. Most managers and supervisors simply don't have enough time to communicate personally with their employees as often as they'd like. Although most top executives try to "manage by walking around," better known as MBWA, it is the rare CEO or vice president who is able to consistently communicate "eyeball-to-eyeball" with employees (Peters and Waterman 1982). And that's where mass communication tools, such as memos, newsletters and videotapes, must serve as stand-ins for face-to-face contact.

In spite of many executives' frustration with never having enough time for face-to-face communication, most recognize the enormous impact their words can have on employees when they do (Pincus and Silvis 1987). This is true of almost any face-to-face setting, be it a small group meeting, a briefing, a press conference or a chance conversation. What managers say and how they say it, no matter if the audience is employees or stockholders, reflects on the entire organization. Therefore, a role frequently played by public relations writers is to anonymously write speeches or remarks for top-level executives. It's that role, better known as ghostwriting, we'd like to discuss next.

Speechwriting

As business leaders have sought to tell their organizations' stories, they have increasingly taken on a more visible and public communication role. Lee Iacocca, for example, gives about 60 formal speeches each year. This role may frequently find top executives in interviews with business reporters, appearing on television or radio talk shows, testifying before congressional committees or speaking to employees or stockholders. Whether the speech's target audience is inside or outside the organization, employees and stockholders will hear about it and respond to its message. As speech opportunities have grown, so too have executives' reliance on professional speechwriters ("Nobody Ever Throws Fruit at the Speechwriter" 1987). Most of the largest 500 companies in the U.S. employ full-time or part-time speechwriters. These speechwriters may be public relations staff writers or outside consultants. Nevertheless, among large organizations with many executives who give formal talks, the role of speechwriter has been elevated substantially in recent years. Salaries for experienced corporate wordsmiths range from $70,000 to $120,000; the art of penning speeches has emerged as a distinct communication specialty (Reibstein 1987).

The corporate speechwriter's life has its ongoing obstacles. For one thing, some writers of speeches have trouble gaining access to the people for whom they're writing because of the many demands on executives' time. If the relationship between the two is well established, that may not be much of a problem. But if the writer and speaker don't know each other well, the result could be many rewrites, a speech that doesn't sound like the speaker, and a rocky relationship. Another frustration can be the many "advisors," such as lawyers and accountants, who can become involved in approving a speech manuscript. Nitpicking by others and lengthy, meandering approval processes are facts of life for the corporate speechwriter.

In reality, most of the work in writing a speech occurs before the writer puts pen to paper, or fingers to keyboard. Selecting points and words comes after the writer has analyzed the following factors: (1) purpose of speech or remarks (e.g., persuade, inform, build support); (2) primary and secondary audiences (e.g., who, where, how many, position on issue); (3) physical setting (e.g., room size, time of day, placement of podium); and (4) occasion (e.g., date, reason for gathering, historical context). This information will then guide the writing process, including the appropriate title, organization, main points, language, supporting facts, and length. The key word is *appropriate*. For instance, an hour-long speech by the vice president of manufacturing on employee productivity, given in the company's 300-seat auditorium and brimming with visuals of production figures, to a group of 10 potential management recruits might be a case of overkill.

The most sage advice in preparing a speech has not changed since Aristotle's day. That is, tell 'em what you're gonna tell 'em, tell 'em, and then tell 'em what you told 'em. In other words, every speech has three interdependent parts: an opening, a body and a closing. The opening should grab the audience's attention, challenge them to think about the speaker's theme and viewpoint, and preview the rest of the speech. The body should consist of laying out the major points, supplemented with supporting material, and linked together via transitions. The closing should summarize—in memorable terms—the theme and major points, and, when appropriate, tie back to the opening.

Electronic Media

Traditionally, public relations writers responsible for internal audiences wrote mostly for publications, a little for face-to-face communication, and almost not at all for internal electronic media. That's not to say that public relations departments weren't involved with broadcast media. Quite the contrary. Preparing copy for radio and television news releases, public service announcements, opening statements at press conferences, and, more recently, video news releases, to name a few, are common assignments for public relations writers. However, writing for an organization's internal broadcast media was uncommon until the early '70s.

Over the past 20 years or so, as new technologies have entered and dominated our personal and work lives, organizational writers have also become more involved in writing for private narrowcast media. Perhaps defining terms would be helpful. Broadcast, as it is literally interpreted, means to communicate to large, broadly dispersed public audiences. In contrast, the term narrowcast, as it is often applied to organizations, refers to relatively small, geographically limited private audiences. By far, the narrowcast media of choice among organizations is video, which encompasses everything from satellite videoconferences to video annual reports to employee video magazines. To a far lesser degree, some writing is being done for limited-use media such as teletext and videotex. The thrust of our discussion will focus on the emergence of organizational video.

Organizational Uses of Video

The rise of video within organizations should not be surprising. Television has become an integral part of our lives. Research indicates that almost 70 percent of Americans get most of their news from television, and that the average college graduate spends about 40 hours a week in front of the "tube" ("Whether We Like It or Not," 1986). People today think more in visual terms because of their reliance on—and acceptance of—television as an information and entertainment medium. In response to this expanding social trend, organizations have since the early 1980s, increasingly embraced video.

Video offers organizational communicators advantages beyond its popularity and acceptability. Video appeals to the viewer's auditory and visual senses, thereby strengthening the viewer's understanding of the message. It creates a sense of reality, bringing life to the words behind the message. Also, video possesses interpersonal, face-to-face elements that can span time and distance and bring people closer together

(Grunig and Hunt 1984). And, finally, videotape allows organizations to control and standardize their messages, and then deliver them to various internal groups where and when they choose.

Corporate and nonprofit organizations' use of video has literally exploded in recent years, doubling in size every three years since 1973. In a market estimated to be almost $3 billion, the number of organizations that are producing their own internal video programs jumped from about 3,000 in 1981 to approximately 8,500 by 1986 ("Corporate/Institutional Video Market Hits $2.3 Billion" 1987). This growing reliance on video doesn't seem to be a frivolous change in communicators' strategies. Says John Budd Jr., vice president of communications for Emhart Corp.: "Corporate video today is not simply a new generation of visual aids, a souped-up method of corporate filmmaking. Video, especially non-broadcast private video, represents a new and dynamic medium of communication" (Budd 1984).

When video first came on the organizational scene, it was used mostly as a training tool because of its effective demonstration capabilities (Grunig and Hunt 1984). For example, a videotape illustrating how to safely slice carrots is much more likely to hold an employee's attention than a written manual attempting to explain and show the same thing. Over time, organizations have discovered many applications for video to internal and external audiences. Such uses include news and information, orientations for new employees, sales and marketing presentations, and credibility-building. Two examples should help illustrate the diverse and widening uses of video:

1. In 1982, San Diego Gas & Electric Company produced a 20-minute employee-orientation video—entitled "Heartbeat of the City"—because it wanted to create a "sense of belonging" between the company and its new employees. Its communication staff felt that the best way to do this was, according to John Pruyn, employee communications supervisor, to build "a groundwork of understanding of the major issues affecting utilities." In this case, that meant showing new employees the critically important relationship of gas and electricity to contemporary society. Working with an outside video production company, SDG&E wove together old film clips, slides, newly-shot video segments, and taped interviews with customers to create a fast-paced, visually-diverse videotape. It cost $40,000 and received such positive reaction from SDG&E employees that it has also been shown to influential community groups (Pruyn 1983).

2. Many organizations, such as LTV Corporation, a large steel, aerospace and energy company, have created employee video news magazines. Designed in 1980 as a supplement to its regular employee monthly newsletter, "LTV Report" is a quarterly 10–15 minute video program that "focuses on in-depth feature stories about LTV's three basic companies," says Julie Price, supervisor of employee and financial communication. Managed by LTV's public relations department, "LTV Report" is actually produced by an outside television journalism firm. It uses a journalistic style to report on what's happening in the company and is shown in employee cafeterias on a continuous basis for several days following its release (Price 1986).

Accustomed to seeing high-quality video productions on network television, employees may think less of or tune out organizational videos of inferior quality. "We have to match the quality of the material they're used to seeing on television or renting from their local video stores," says Mary Kay Oswald, account executive with a video distribution firm in Chicago. "The quality of the production has a lot to do with how it's received" (Winkleman 1987).

This stress on quality, combined with the expanding applications of video, has led many organizations—Westinghouse, Johnson & Johnson, Bethlehem Steel, Southwestern Bell, to name just a few—to develop their own video staffs and studio facilities. The initial investment can be hefty, perhaps as much as a million dollars, but as more uses are found for video, it can pay for itself quickly. A case in point is J. C. Penney, which relies on video regularly for training, marketing, and merchandising. It operates its own studio and maintains an audio-visual department staff of more than 30 people, and produces about a third of more than 50 programs a year for different departments within the company, each one costing between $2,000 and $15,000.

What is the public relations writer's role in video productions? It varies from organization to organization and from program to program. Relatively few organizations need or can afford to support all the equipment and expert systems required for most video productions. Therefore, quite often, the staff writer will work with an outside video production firm. Although frequently viewed as a specialized form of writing, the organizational writer's responsibilities may include one or more of the following:

1. A concept outline, which incorporates the major objectives, a description of the key target audiences, major points to be covered, and rough ideas for visuals.

2. A script treatment, which is an informal, yet focused, narrative explaining the direction and approach to be followed for a particular video program.

3. The script, which integrates the words (dialogue, voice over), camera shots (visual angles, props), transitions, audio (music) and the time budgeted for each segment.

As should be obvious, making a video is never a one-person operation; it demands coordinating and integrating the efforts of a number of specialists. Overseeing or managing the process is usually a member of the organization's public relations department. This person, who plays the role of an executive producer, may or may not be the chief writer. Nevertheless, it is that person who is ultimately responsible for the video's message being effectively communicated. Despite the tendency by some non-communicators to emphasize the pictures over the words in a video, never lose sight of the importance of the words themselves. The words guide, reinforce, explain, distinguish, focus, clarify, and provide the context and direction for all those involved in producing a video. Whether the organizational writer's role is primary or secondary, whether it includes scriptwriting or just concept writing, the written words are the roots from which other decisions grow.

An example of a typical videotape script is reproduced in figure 10.5. Notice the separation of the narrative on the right-hand side of the page from the accompanying visuals, times and directions on the left. Double or triple-spacing is always used for ease in reading. Frequently, the copy is put in all-capital letters for the same reason. Writing for the ear is different, and some would say more difficult, than writing for the eye.

Beckman's ASQ-HIV Test for AIDS   *Page 2*

VIDEO   AUDIO

FADE IN

1
FULL SHOT Computer art
of horizon. A
silhouette moves
forward. A number of
silhouettes then fade
on.

(OPENING MUSIC)

(Music fades under voice)

NARRATOR
The AIDS epidemic has created an urgent
demand for accurate tests to identify
infected people.

VIDEO TRANSITION
Picture recedes to 1/2
frame and flips.

2
1/2 FRAME/CLOSE SHOT
Drawing blood specimen
from arm.

The organism that causes AIDS is the
Human Immunodeficiency Virus--commonly
referred to as HIV-1. Its primary target
is the human white blood cell--the T4
lymphocyte . . .

VIDEO TRANSITION Wipe

3 PAN SHOT Sign of NIH
to building.

Scientists at the National Institutes of
Health were among the first to identify
and isolate the virus in 1983.

▶ **Figure 10.5. Example: videotape script.** All video programs must begin with the written words comprising the script—words that direct the production crew and words to be spoken by the narrator or actors. Pictures and words must work hand-in-hand. As video has become a more favored communication tool, public relations writers are increasingly involved in script writing.

These scripts integrate within a two-column format both video and audio instructions. In the opening segment of a 1988 video script designed to demonstrate how to use an AIDS test kit developed by California-based Beckman Instruments, writer Ken Lyall demonstrates the step-by-step interplay between words, sounds and images.
Copyright © 1988 Beckman Instruments. Used with permission.

Beckman's ASQ-HIV Test for AIDS   *Page 3*

VIDEO   AUDIO

VIDEO TRANSITION Slide on	
	Dr. Robert Gallo--Chief of the Laboratory of Tumor Cell Biology . . .
4 CLOSE SHOT Robert Gallo	
	ROBERT GALLO Infection of the T4 lymphocyte by the AIDS virus leads to a premature death of that cell and eventually to a marked decrease in the total T4 cell population of the infected person . . .
5 FULL SHOT Micrographs of infected T-cells mosaics on from top to bottom of screen.	
	So the person infected with the AIDS virus has an increased incidence of many different types of infections,
"HIV INFECTED T4 CELL" is superimposed.	
6 FULL SHOTS Electron micrograph zooms from infected cell showing budding of virus. "AIDS VIRUS" is superimposed	
	which take far more serious courses than they would in a person with a normal immune system.
MATCH DISSOLVE	
	(MUSIC STING)

▶ **Figure 10.5** *(continued)*

Videoconferencing

Another product of the communication technology revolution is the videoconference. A videoconference links together, via television screens, geographically-separated groups by bouncing signals off satellites. It is generally designed to be an interactive form of communication. That is, it allows live, instant communication among the parties at various national or worldwide locations. The most popular format is one-way video, two-way audio (Hattal 1984). Such a format was used effectively by Johnson & Johnson to reintroduce Tylenol following the first tampering incident in 1982. Based in New York and linked to 50 other cities throughout the U.S., the president of Johnson & Johnson was able to demonstrate to media throughout the country—instantly and simultaneously—how the newly designed, tamper-resistant Tylenol container works and then immediately answer reporters' questions (Wilcox, Ault and Agee 1989, 349–350).

Videoconference programs have been used by organizations for a variety of purposes, ranging from educational seminars and marketing promotions to news conferences and employee meetings. A videoconference, however, is not appropriate—or justifiable, given the cost—in all situations. A 30-minute video news conference, for instance, will run around $10,000. One or more circumstances should exist before making such an investment: (a) the message itself will be significantly more effective in a visual medium; (b) the audience is spread out; (c) the message is time-sensitive and needs to be transmitted simultaneously; or (d) interaction between the presenters and viewers is necessary or desired (Hattal 1984). If one or more of those factors is important to a communication scenario, then the cost begins to dwindle when you consider the cost of travel, lodging, food and employees' time to get those same people to a meeting site. The underlying value of videoconferencing, which is difficult to measure in monetary terms, is its ability to bring people in different locales together on a face-to-face and ear-to-ear basis.

As with most new technology, organizations are discovering new and different applications for videoconferencing as challenging situations arise. A case in point was United Airlines' use of a daily videoconference to update its employees during its pilots' strike in 1987. Many national and international public corporations are videoconferencing their annual stockholder meetings so that more stockholders and media representatives can participate. And as the technology moves from complex satellite link-ups to streamlined fiber optics transmission (via phone lines), costs will shrink, making it more affordable for almost any organization to hold videoconferences with its publics.

The writer's role in a videoconference may span from writing the proposal arguing for it, to the script used to direct the sequence of events and the principal speakers. At the heart of any videoconference are the messages—the words and images—exchanged between the parties. The vital point to remember is that time is at a premium, so everything must be short and sweet. The same editorial guidelines for videotapes also apply to videoconferencing. Simply put, write in bites, not mouthfuls; and be simple and straightforward, not complex and indirect.

Slide-Tape Presentations

Another type of visual impact communication is the slide-tape show, a synchronized combination of 35 mm color slides and audiotape. Although the slide-tape presentation has been losing some ground to videotape in recent years, it still has its place in organizational communication. "The multi-image slide show is still unsurpassed in its impact on people attending large meetings," explains Bill Wittich, president of Corporate Image Productions, a California-based video production firm (1988). "The big screen, flashing images and the high quality sound that surrounds an audience drive home a message like no other medium."

Slide-tape productions can be simple or complex. Much depends, as always, on situation, audience, budget and creative capabilities. For instance, the Idaho First National Bank, which started an in-house audio-visual department in 1980, produces slide shows ranging from a monthly 36-slide, one-projector show for its board of directors to a 20-minute, 24-projector annual report. "In addition to showing the annual report to shareholders, we also take it around the state for viewing by business and civic groups in the 70 Idaho communities with branch banks," says Production Manager Bill Cottle ("Corporate AV Scene Explodes" 1982).

Many organizations transfer an original slide-tape show to videotape. This allows organizations to more cost-effectively reproduce the presentation and distribute it to audiences at multiple locations. Since videotape playback equipment is standard at many organizations, employees are likely to view a taped presentation. Slide-tape shows, on the other hand, require a screen, the right kind of slide projector and a synchronizer to cue the slides to the audio tape.

The writing demands associated with slide-tape productions usually are a concept treatment and a script. The concept treatment, of course, focuses on objectives, target audiences, and message. It may also need to consider, because of the production implications, the extended uses of the presentation if, for example, it will be transferred to videotape for wider distribution. The script itself should clearly integrate short, vivid, to-the-point words (e.g., voice over, dialogue) with slides (e.g., photographs, graphics) that illustrate and explain the presentation's message. The writer must pay special attention to—and specify in the script—the integration and timing of the words and pictures. For instance, rapidly-changing slides of large, clearly distinguishable pictures, say one every two seconds, can create a sense of motion. Slides of tables or charts of information, in contrast, should remain on the screen for at least 10-to-15 seconds to give the viewer a chance to absorb the information. The writer, then, in developing the script must "visualize" the interplay between the words that are heard and the pictures that are seen.

Teletext and Videotex

At some of the more technology-advanced organizations, public relations writers are preparing copy for two "visual word display" media, **teletext** and **videotex.** Still relatively new technologies, these two forms of video communication are gradually being applied to organizational situations.

The more common of the two, **teletext,** is a "video bulletin board," displaying copy on regular television screens or on thin, horizontal screens through which the copy moves from right to left. Teletext is a one-way form of communication. The viewer controls when the information is to be displayed, but cannot send messages back through the system. Teletext is being increasingly used on cable systems, which often have a teletext channel that may include news capsules, entertainment guides, sports scores, restaurant reviews, and community service listings.

Often called "silent radio," teletext copy is also being used in public places—such as grocery stores and banks—to offer customers news and entertainment information while they wait in line. Within an organizational setting, teletext has been used primarily as an information vehicle for employees. On their computer monitor screens, for example, employees might be able to call up visual texts of the organization's telephone directory, organizational chart, and news bulletins. Some organizations have installed moving copy video displays in heavy traffic areas, such as employee cafeterias and office waiting areas, to communicate major news bulletins and updates.

Videotex is similar to teletext, but it is a two-way form of communication. In other words, the viewer can interact—that is, exchange information—with the organization by generating words on a television monitor. Many videotex users today do their banking via videotex systems right from their own living rooms. Opinion polling has also been adapted to video; the respondent may, following viewing of an advertisement or a political speech, answer questions posed on the screen. The researcher, then, gets instant feedback from thousands of viewers. These data may then be immediately tabulated by computers that are linked to the video system.

To date, organizations have used videotex for internal audiences only sparingly. That may change with time, however. Some companies have adapted it to allow employees to request particular information, such as an article from the last company newsletter or clips from the CEO's last speech to stockholders. In addition, top executives may adapt videotex to employee research projects, such as asking employees how they feel about a company policy and then getting instant feedback. Top managers who know where employees stand on an issue, such as their position on a pending labor strike, may be able to make more informed decisions that will benefit all organizational members.

Writing for teletext or videotex is the ultimate in writing brevity. Whole, complex thoughts must be boiled down to a sentence in many cases. You must first choose the single key point, the essence of what you want to say. Then, because time and space are extremely restricted, each word must precisely convey the meaning you intend.

With so few words available, each one carries that much more weight of the overall message. Copy moving across television screens that can't be recalled at will must be simple, direct and clear—if is is to be understood and remembered. Writing for these "coming media" is like writing a broadcast news script composed of snippets of information—only more so.

Potential Stumbling Blocks

Public relations writers for organizations sometimes see themselves as merely "word-crafters," responsible for taking other's thoughts and packaging them in understandable language. Not true.

Organizational writers must be concerned with more than just the words they select. In order to have those words accepted, writers must be sensitive to the forces influencing the target public's interpretation of those words.

There are potential obstacles throughout the writing process that can affect the content and style of the writer's words. We'd now like to discuss the implications of a couple of those obstacles and suggest ways to overcome them.

Message Control

Management is concerned most with the survival and progress of its organization. Sometimes, in its zealous desire to move the organization forward, management may—consciously or unconsciously—become heavy-handed, or even manipulative, in trying to influence the message writers send to employees. Some managers, for instance, incorrectly view the organization's newsletter as their mouthpiece, rather than as the organization's information vehicle. *"Mary, don't forget that you're writing for me, nobody else,"* says the dominant CEO, *"and that article had better deliver my message the way I'm giving it to you."* Since they control the communication budget, managers may at times use those purse strings as leverage over the organizational writer. *"OK, Joe, I want you to leave out that stuff about us losing money last quarter,"* threatens the vice president, *"or you'll be out of business. The workers don't need to hear that bad news from us."*

Obviously, this is a sensitive issue. In truth, management has the power to control much of the communication within its organization. It is also true that many top managers, pulled in many different functional directions, may be out of touch with their employees' feelings and attitudes—and, therefore, may not be sensitive to how employees are likely to react to particular messages or delivery styles. In other words, management's "hit-'em over-the-head-whether-they-like-it-or-not" approach may satisfy management's desire for control, but will probably cause employees to reject or tune out the message and think less of management.

When management has this urge, the organizational communicator has a role and a responsibility to try to represent both management's **and** employees' interests.

"I see your point, Mr. President," says the diplomatic writer, *"but are you aware how employees reacted at our #1 competitor when they tried it this way?"* Put another way, the organizational writer should be most concerned with the organization's best interests. As difficult as it may be, this means attempting to remain objective, reconciling what may be conflicting points of view pressed by various organizational parties. *"Well, let me get this straight, Mr. CEO. You want me to include our statement in the newsletter article but leave out Mr. Union Leader's,"* recaps the tip-toeing communicator. *"Is that fair to our employees?"* The organizational writer is, in effect, a conduit through which the various interests within an organization try to influence each other. Such a delicate balancing role calls for a continuous weighing of the facts and interests so that the most complete, accurate, objectively stated message can be shared with all.

Fortunately, many managers are realizing that the heavy-handed approach is usually counterproductive and doesn't win over many hearts and minds. Employees today know their minds and want to be treated as intelligent and discerning people. Nevertheless, writers must constantly be on guard for those who would try to influence them. *"Mary, just do me this favor, please. Slant your story this way this time and the next time you need a quick interview with John (the CEO), I'll be sure you get it,"* cajoles the smooth vice president.

One way to avoid such sticky situations is to make sure that top managers are aware of what their employees think, and how they are likely to react to certain types of communication. Synthesize key articles for management on employee values, explaining, with a short cover memo, how your organization can apply such information. Another approach is to encourage top managers to spend more time with employees, listening to their questions and concerns. Then write a story about it for the organization's publications. Still another suggestion is to get to know organizational leaders, their thoughts, preferences, and their philosophy on communicating with employees; then get them to know, trust and appreciate you, your judgment, and integrity. In that way, if and when a conflict arises, it is less likely that your motives and judgment will be questioned.

Secondary Audiences

"Mr. Editor, your words in the employee magazine say that our sales projections are looking up," snaps the angry employee, *"yet I read in the business section of the local paper that we're in trouble. Which is it?"* The baffled editor, struggling for a response, thinks to herself, *"The employee wasn't supposed to see the information in our news release."*

Unfortunately, this situation is not unusual. Audiences not targeted to receive messages often do. And if the writer hasn't considered that possibility, the result can be embarrassing or, worse yet, damaging to the organization's credibility. Writers generally write for a particular audience or set of audiences; however, they must evaluate their copy as if it will be read or heard by many other audiences as well. Because, quite often, it is. An obvious example is the employee newsletter. It is written for employees of the company, period. Nevertheless, many employees share it with their families, even friends. Some of those friends may work for a competitor.

The point is this: All organizational literature distributed to internal or external publics should be considered public information. This is because people may be members of several publics and interact with each other.

Organizational messages, regardless of the primary target audience, should be consistent in both language and tone for all audiences. Writers should put themselves in each of these audience's shoes when reviewing copy. Which publics are likely to receive this message, whether targeted or not? How will each audience likely react to this message? Will they understand the point? Will they take offense? If you don't know a specific audience well enough, find someone in the organization who does and ask him or her to read the copy. In fact, many organizations are aggressively sending their publications to secondary audiences. For example, IBM often gives copies of its employee magazines to key customers to help them understand the IBM culture better and to keep the IBM name before them. And Pfizer Pharmaceutical Co. mails its annual report to medical doctors in the U.S. to let them know about the company's new drug products.

Chapter Summary

This chapter discussed the strategic considerations—as well as some of the tactical concerns—inherent in writing for employee audiences.

It began with an overview of the varying purposes of organizational communication: (1) to inform employees about happenings in their organization, (2) to motivate employees to support their organization and its leaders, and (3) to obtain feedback from employees to help executives make decisions. Then we analyzed how employees' values, feelings toward work, and media preferences have changed over the past few decades, and what that means to organizational writers today. Next, the organizational writer's changing and increasingly sophisticated role was explored.

The heart of the chapter, however, was devoted to outlining some of the strategies behind writing for various organizational communication media. This analysis encompassed writing for three major media: (1) print, (2) interpersonal, and (3) electronic.

In addition, we also examined some of the potential practical and political obstacles facing the organizational writer. Finally, we examined issues involving management's influence on editorial content, potential snags in the approval process, and possible effects of publications on secondary audiences.

A Writing Exercise

Your company, Widgets Galore, has been facing a shrinking market for its major product line—manual typewriters—for some time. Management has tried to hold the business together by expanding into other areas, such as non-digital watches and fountain pens. Despite its best efforts over the past two years, the organization has come to a cross-roads. In order to survive, 30 percent of the current 5,000-employee workforce must be laid off. Those employees with the longest service with Widgets Galore will keep their jobs; those with the least seniority will have to go.

As the firm's top public relations professional, it's your responsibility to prepare the communication strategy to tell employees, stockholders, the media and the community of the decision. You have, of course, been part of the management team making this decision. Therefore, you're aware of management's desire to be as fair and helpful as possible to those employees it proposes to lay off.

Nevertheless, Walter Widgets, president and CEO, who succeeded his father, the company's founder, in 1965, has told you: "I want to help every one of these employees and their families make the best of this situation. Let's hire an outplacement firm to assist them in finding new jobs. Let's give them each two months severance pay. And, most of all, let's let them know how much I value their service and loyalty." Widgets has always been viewed by employees as a caring leader—at least, up to this time.

—What would be your overall communication strategy? What is the key message you would want to send?

—Draft an article announcing this decision for the monthly employee newsletter, *Widget World.*

—Draft the first five minutes of the speech that Widgets will give to all employees, telling them what's happening and how it will affect them.

Food for Thought

1. Some argue that writers are "word artists." They shouldn't have to worry about anything except the writing itself. How does that argument square with organizational communication writers?
2. An employee is an employee is an employee. Employees' main concerns are paychecks, vacation time and overtime pay. Nobody works because they want to. What's your reaction to these thoughts?
3. Every executive must give speeches or make remarks at one time or another. Unfortunately, few do it effectively. What are the ingredients to a good five-minute talk to employees?
4. Some would say that there are few, if any, real differences between writing for newsletters and magazines. Do you see any substantial differences in writing styles between the two types of publications?

5. Your manager, the vice president of human resources, wants you to soften the tone and language in a story you've written about the company being charged with discriminating against women in its hiring practices. He's concerned with how outsiders, as well as employees, will view the company. For instance, he asks that you change the word "charged" to "being investigated." What would your response be to your boss' request?

References for Further Study

Alsop, Ronald. "Line Between Articles and Ads is Fuzzy in These Magazines." *The Wall Street Journal* (September 17, 1987): 33.

Berton, Lee. "The Gallery: Annual Reports as Art." *The Wall Street Journal* (August 18, 1988): 20.

Blundell, William E. "Confused, Overstuffed Corporate Writing Often Costs Firms Much Time—and Money." *The Wall Street Journal* (August 28, 1980): 21.

Budd, John F. Jr. *Corporate Video in Focus.* New York: Spectrum Publishers, 1984.

"Corporate/Institutional Video Market Hits $2.3 Billion." *Communication World* (January, 1987): 10.

"Corporate AV Scene Explodes." *IABC News* (January, 1982): 1, 7.

Cutlip, Scott M., Allen H. Center and Glen M. Broom. *Effective Public Relations,* 6th ed. Englewood Cliffs, N.J.: Prentice-Hall, 1985, 354–390.

Davids, Meryl. "Tough Stuff." *Public Relations Journal* 43:9 (September 1987): 28–31, 63.

Ellis, Robert J. "The American Work Ethic: Does It Still Exist?" *The Wyatt Communicator* (Summer, 1985): 1–8.

Foltz, Roy G. "Communication in Contemporary Organizations." Carol Reuss and Don Silvis, eds. *Inside Organizational Communication.* New York: Longman, 1985, 3–14.

"Getting the Word Around: A Guide for Communicating in Business." Upper Saddle River, N.J.: Western Union Company.

Grass, Robert C. "Measuring the Effects of Corporate Advertising." *Public Relations Review* 3:4 (Winter 1977): 39–50.

Grunig, James E. and Todd Hunt (1984). *Managing Public Relations.* New York: Holt, Rinehart and Winston, 375–382, 414–428.

Hattal, Daniel. "Videoconferencing: Public Relations' Newest Tool." *tips & tactics,* a supplement of *pr reporter:* 22: 15 (November 19, 1984).

"How to Polish Your Writing Skills." *Business Week,* July 6, 1981, 106–110.

Iacocca, Lee. *Iacocca.* New York: Bantam Books, 1984.

Johnson, Greg. "Bottom Line on Annual Reports: Appearance Makes a Difference." *Los Angeles Times,* April 12, 1988, Part IV, 1,8.

"Nobody Ever Throws Fruit at the Speechwriter." *Business Week,* October 12, 1987, 112–116.

Norton, George P. "Corporate Advertising: Useful Tool or Ego Trip?" *tips & tactics,* a supplement of *pr reporter,* 17: 2 (January 15, 1979).

Peters, Thomas J. and Robert H. Waterman, Jr. *In Search of Excellence.* New York: Warner Books, 1982.

Pincus, J. David and Robert E. Rayfield. "The Relationship Between Top Management Communication and Job Satisfaction and Job Performance." *Communicare* 6:2(1987): 14–26.

Pincus, J. David and Donn Silvis. "How CEOs View Their Communication Roles." *Communication World* 4:12 (December, 1987): 18–22.

Price, Julie. "Employee Video Magazines." *Public Relations Journal* 42:5 (May 1986): 11,14.

Pruyn, John. "Heartbeat of the City." *Reddy News* (March/April, 1983): 12–13.

Reibstein, Larry. "For Corporate Speech Writers, Life is Seldom a Simple Matter of ABCs." *The Wall Street Journal* (June 30, 1987): 3.

Reuss, Carol and Donn Silvis, eds. *Inside Organizational Communication,* 2d ed. New York: Longman, 1985.

"Summary Annual Reports: A New Option to Improve Shareholder Communications." A Publication of Deloitte Haskins & Sells and Financial Executives Research Foundation, 1987.

"Teaching the Boss to Write." *Business Week* (October 25, 1976): 56–58.

"Whether We Like It or Not, Video is Medium of Choice for People Who Are After Information." *pr reporter* 29:9 (March 3, 1986): 1.

Wilcox, Dennis L., Phillip H. Ault and Warren F. Agee. *Public Relations Strategies and Tactics.* New York: Harper & Row, 1989.

Winkleman, Michael. "Video Age." *Public Relations Journal* (April 1987): 24–28.

Wittich, William. Personal interview, August 17, 1988.

PART

4

AFTER WORDS: MANAGEMENT AND WRITING EFFECTIVENESS

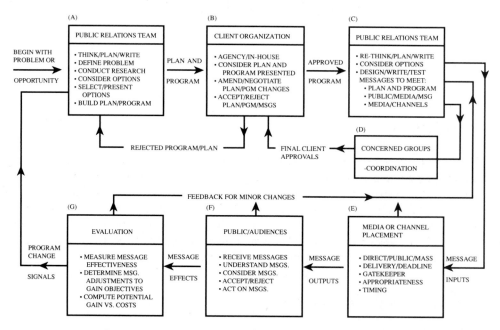

Managing public relations writing programs involves assuring the success of the entire process, from definition and research, through planning and programming, processing and delivery of the messages. It involves managing writers and writing, as well as shepherding message drafts through the minefields of coordination by interested parties. The writing manager must also be familiar with current print and electronic production techniques.

MANAGING PUBLIC RELATIONS WRITING PROGRAMS

11

Introduction

Writing copy is merely one step in the overall process of public relations writing. Thinking, planning and writing are critical to the process and have been covered in detail. But it is also the writer's responsibility to ensure the accurate and timely delivery of the complete message to the target audience. Inherent in that responsibility is moving the message through several steps involving other people after it has been written. These steps include coordination, approvals, production and distribution. In this chapter you will learn various ways to manage writing programs.

The Writer as a Writing Manager

We usually achieve public relations objectives through: (1) definition and research, (2) planning and programming, (3) action and communication, and (4) evaluation and redirection.

Managers essentially integrate four assets to meet organizational objectives: **people, equipment, facilities** and **programs.** Managing public relations writing is a more limited exercise requiring integration of the basic tools of the writer. These are: **research materials, writing equipment, talent** and **time.** Equipment and facilities are part of overall management. Although they can strongly influence reaching the objective, they are not a part of the writer's immediate responsibility and won't be discussed extensively here.

A PROFESSIONAL TIP:
Working with Senior Management

The successful public relations practitioner is many things: spokesman, researcher, planner, writer, editor, corporate conscience and, perhaps most importantly, counselor and alter ego to senior management. To earn this latter role, he or she must be among the most knowledgeable members of the company or institution and substantively involved in the policy process. True professionals work harder than their staff counterparts and share a common trait: they know how to write and are trusted to present complex policy issues clearly and concisely. The public relations counselor is truly effective when the boss says simply, "You know what I want to say."

Marv Braman is director of public relations and advertising for Lockheed Sanders Inc., headquartered in Nashua, N.H. A U.S. Air Force veteran of more than 28 years, his military public relations assignments included USAF chief of media relations, director of public affairs for the U.S. Pacific Command, and deputy assistant secretary of defense for public affairs.

Normally, public relations writers are not responsible for managing the entire message production process. But they do manage or help manage their own work, and are often called upon to manage writing and message support done by others. An effective case can be made that writers may be the best managers of their craft. The writing process is concerned with thinking, planning, writing, delivering and evaluating messages. The process begins with an idea and ends in one or more delivered messages. Of all members in an organization, its writers are best able to articulate organizational missions and goals, and are best able to evaluate how well others incorporate them. Writers also understand other writers. Thus, they can best motivate other writers to meet the organizational objectives. Finally, they know the writing process and can best tell how well each step has been followed and what changes are needed. Thus, the writer is often most qualified and knowledgeable about the copy and can best supervise the process.

Types of Writing Management Tasks

Writing management usually takes one of three forms, although it is possible to get involved in all three simultaneously. The first is managing one's own writing program. The second is managing an in-house program as part-author and coordinator. The third is managing writing projects that are contracted out to public relations firms, support groups or free-lance writers. Each has unique aspects.

Self-Management

Like it or not, all public relations writers are managers when it comes to their own copy. If that management role is neglected, the written words may be changed by others and the key message distorted. They must be "captains of their ships," keeping the copy on course, steering it through turbulent waters into safe channels. For the author is, after all, best qualified to know that the words are true and supportive of organizational objectives.

Time Management

Perhaps the first step in self-management for writers is management of time—meeting deadlines. Occasionally impractical deadlines are pressed on writers: "You can have this tomorrow, can't you, Joe?" More often, however, writers may commit to time schedules that can't be met because they overestimate their capabilities. An experienced writer should know about how much time it takes to perform assigned tasks. Table 11.1 can be used as a planning guide for those who have trouble managing time. Remember, all planning should include extra buffer time to allow for the unexpected.

Negotiating Skills

To manage their writing projects effectively, writers should also be skilled negotiators. It would be easy to say, "Sorry, boss, that's wrong and I won't do it," to an incorrect or improper chief executive officer's comment on your writing. But that kind of response is not conducive to lengthy employment. It is better to explain courteously why some things won't work out. Do not fall in love with your copy. Be willing to change it to make it better, or to accept changes that don't affect the work's quality or effectiveness. It is difficult to see your work of art become a committee treatise, but keep in mind the objectives of public relations writing.

TABLE 11.1. Average Times for Writers' Activities

The following are average times required for a first-year professional public relations writer to accomplish indicated tasks. They are useful for planning in cases where actual average writing times are unknown.

Average Time Hours:Minutes	Task to Be Accomplished
0:05	Read one page of research material.
0:15	Construct one survey/interview question.
1:39	Conduct a one-hour personal interview.
0:15	Survey one subject by phone.
0:24	Survey one subject, door-to-door.
9:30	Analyze complete research on one subject.
0:45	Prepare a one page press release.
1:20	Script one minute of a speech.
2:21	Script one minute of a plan/formal proposal.
7:18	Prepare 20 media kits.
0:32	Prepare & shoot one 35 mm slide (no art).
2:05	Set up & conduct a one-hour meeting.
4:32	Set up one 20-minute press meeting.
0:21	Coordinate one page of art/photo/layout.
2:32	Complete one page of simple layout.
0:25	Deliver one press release to a media contact.
0:10	Phone one press response to a media contact.
0:15	Mail one release to a media contact.

Technical Perfection

A surprising key to self-management is proofreading (Turner 1978). Media representatives are not the only ones to reject good news releases because of sloppy technical work. Clients often view copy containing misspellings, poor grammar or typographical errors in the same light. "It can't be very well done if the words aren't even spelled correctly," many say. One reason readers jump on writing errors is to participate in the process. Many want to help make sure anything they are associated with is well done. So, if they don't know the specific subject you are writing about, they will concentrate on what they do know—language competency.

You can help assure top quality in your copy by soliciting help from fellow writers. You are usually the only one who can verify the facts of your story. But a proven way to catch most other errors is to get at least three others to read your copy independently and initial it. Review chapter 7 for more points on correcting language.

TABLE 11.2. Steps in Managing the Public Relations Writing Process

1. *Think:* Define the problem; Conduct research; Consider options; Analyze and select options.
2. *Plan:* Build a plan and program.
3. *Write:* Write messages for each message-public-channel.
4. *Process:* Move messages through required processes:
   a. Coordinate, edit and rewrite.
   b. Client approvals obtained.
   c. Typesetting completed and approved (print).
   d. Layout designed, approved and completed (print).
   e. Visuals completed and approved (print/video).
   f. Audio/video tapes completed & approved.
   g. Printing selected, proofed, approved & bound (print).
5. *Deliver:* Completed message products delivered to intended destinations in accordance with the plan.

Controlling the Flow of the Process

Finally, self-management means seeing the project all the way through to the extent you are able. Table 11.2 lists steps in the management of the public relations writing process over which you may have some control. You will probably have an extensive role in thinking, planning and writing messages that you are assigned. You are also likely to be the agent for processing your messages through coordination and approvals. You may know little about layout, production of visuals or printing, but you will want to learn about these so that you can help influence them. Poor work by a printer, for example, can destroy the quality of your work. How you may influence these, as well as message delivery or placement, will be discussed later in the chapter.

Managing Messages for Which You Are Part-Author

You may also be called upon to manage writing jointly produced by you and others in your organization. This responsibility often falls on either the most senior or most junior public relations writer. Regardless of how it is assigned, the approach must be the same. If asked, you should advise on writing quality and technical accuracy. The primary responsibility for these functions falls on the authors of the copy; you would not want to usurp them. Coordinating editing and rewriting functions should also be handled by the originating authors. They are best qualified to verify facts, explain meanings and justify their positions. When you are asked to act as coordinator, be certain to read each author's input thoroughly so you can ask (and be able to answer) questions.

Here is an example of how the process works. Your public relations firm has landed a contract with a major record producer to launch a new rock group called "Orange Agent." OA consists of three men and three women who dress and look alike. All sing and play the electric guitar. One man also plays electric bass and one woman plays the drums. Although all are in their early 20s, their sound is rather mellow, often reminiscent of Bach, Brahms and the Beatles. They have just completed an album of their best songs. Its lead song, "Are You Me?" is already a hit and features a two-part segment in which all the men sing soprano and the women respond in bass.

OA will begin its first tour of the U.S. in six weeks. Advertising will handle a direct sales ad program on a city-by-city basis and will take care of all art. The plan calls for one newspaper and one TV feature for each market in the three weeks prior to each performance. The group is appearing in 23 cities. You are to do six of the newspaper features and coordinate the rest. Marketing will take care of distribution. There are four other writers.

Your management tasks might go something like this:

1. Assign all features, based on the desires and known capabilities of the writers. For example, if one writer is a native of Kansas City, have her do the features for that city. A unique feature is preferred for each source. But it is possible to submit the same feature in different cities, so long as it is not given to competing media.

Make sure everyone is clear on assignments, the project's goals and objectives, material on OA and first draft deadlines. Get copies of photos, recordings and videos of the group to each writer. If possible, get the group to perform for and be interviewed by the writers.

2. Review each writer's drafts as they come in for compliance with project and task objectives. Suggest changes where necessary.

3. Get the entire package of features reviewed by your firm's account executive, lawyer and the client liaison. Also get a few newspaper and television entertainment editors to preview it all. If possible, get OA members' and manager's thoughts too.

4. Request final approval by a designated member of the client organization. Since there are five writers involved, you might represent all of them to explain, defend and negotiate. Or, your supervisor may take this task off your hands. If the client CEO wishes to approve the package, it will probably be through a general briefing and discussion, rather than a reading of the entire copy. So the coordinator should be prepared for an oral presentation and discussion.

5. Make sure newspaper releases are typed and formatted properly, proofed and edited, and ready for release.

6. Review each newspaper feature with the firm's art or photo director for visual support. Decide on three or four photos or illustrations for each release. For features likely to be used as Sunday supplements, request four-color photos. Complete an agreed upon shot list. Involve other writers to the extent they are available.

7. When the photos are ready, make sure there is author-photographer agreement on the cut lines. Accept only first class photos. A poor quality photograph is worse than no photograph.

8. Match the feature releases with their photographs. Then give the complete packages to your marketing representative. Since you are dealing with features, there should be one addressee per story, so you needn't worry about making duplicates as long as you save the master copies.

Managing Outside Writing

Sometimes you may be asked to manage writing tasks subcontracted to outside agencies or consultants. All the considerations previously discussed apply in such a case. But there are a number of others you'll want to be aware of. These concern the nature of the outside agent, the contractual arrangement and the precise duties expected of you.

Public Relations Firms

Sometimes the outside agent providing you with writing support is a public relations firm or agency. If so, coordination is relatively simple. Costs are usually based on some combination of basic fee, expense reimbursement and time required to do the job. While open to some negotiation, agency costs are usually fixed well in advance. Most public relations firms provide competent writing support and meet all deadlines. Yet, a major problem with them, as with any outside support, is lack of familiarity with the client organization. Often they don't know your organization well and tend to minimize organizational research, since it doesn't contribute to their bottom lines. Additionally, agencies hire people whose experience ranges from outstanding to fair to negligible. If your organization's account is small, there may be a tendency to assign the least experienced person to work on it. As a writer-manager, you should be able to detect these weaknesses and demand that they be corrected.

Free-lance Support

Writing support may also come from free-lancers. Their capabilities, experience levels, writing abilities and fees may vary. By and large, you really "get what you pay for." The best procedure, however, is to check references, review work and develop a few good free-lance contacts you can rely upon and use them repeatedly.

Managing Communicators

What qualities do communicators have in common that makes them difficult to manage? Some say that they are "right brained," implying that their thoughts and actions are largely controlled by the artistic right half of the brain, rather than the more logical left half. They are sometimes typecast as "creative people." This label can be misleading since many of the world's most creative people are scientists and technicians. For the most part, however, communicators are intelligent, rational people who, despite differences in skills, are devoted to improving the quality of their products. While this is an oversimplification, it does give us a basis for understanding, motivating and managing them. Here are some useful guidelines which can be applied to these tasks:

Recognize their Special Expertise

Insist that they demonstrate it. Nothing frustrates communicators more than being compelled to do things that they know are beyond them or are counterproductive to effective communication. A familiar example is that of the talented company newsletter editor forced to print "grip and grin" photos of corporate executives smiling at workers while they press flesh. A top-quality communicator should be given as much freedom to operate as possible. The results will often be outstanding. The editor and staff of the *ARCO Spark* magazine are given a high degree of freedom in telling employees about their company, for example. They use this autonomy to build a publication that is highly respected for "telling it like it is," both externally as well as internally.

Insist on Support of Organizational Goals

Managers have a right to know that all members of the organization understand and contribute to the bottom line. The time has passed when art, company publications or public relations could be supported simply because someone thought they were useful, creative or the right thing to do. Management-by-objectives techniques allow us to conceive communication goals and objectives that reflect and support those of the organization in measurable ways.

Minimize Formal Requirements

Communicators work better in personal and informal atmospheres. A highly qualified speech writer turned down a promising opportunity to work for a national leader because he was told he could have no direct contact with the CEO. The writer noted that the job would deny him the thing that made speech writing worthwhile and exciting—the intellectual one-on-one with a brilliant leader. Likewise, long staff meetings and formal reports seem to stifle the artistic mind. Knowing that interpersonal communication is the most effective method, communicators prefer it. They also feel a strong compulsion to be "heard out."

Tolerate a Few Quirks

If a good art director cannot function during standard office hours, try to arrange equivalent alternatives. A corporate speech writer was allowed to go home for important writing assignments because the "office conformity and routine dampened creativity." A great advertising team may work continuously on a campaign proposal for days "to keep the juices flowing," then disappear when it is complete. To get the best out of people with the most talent, find ways to come to terms with their minor nonconformities.

Managing Non-communicators

One of the most difficult things for public relations writers to endure is the inevitable approval process required for their messages. Those involved vary by organization, message and circumstance. Generally, the more important the message, the more people become involved. Complexity is also influenced by the standing of public relations in the organization (Wilcox, Ault and Agee 1986, 66–67). Where other departments hold "command authority" or "concurring authority" over public relations, nothing can be released that they don't approve. Facing these complexities, public relations writers attempt to write well and negotiate the copy through the process, while keeping it essentially intact.

The Approval Process

If you work for a corporation, you will need to get approval or agreement from at least one or two other departments, such as legal and finance. Then one or two top executives will need to concur. If you are writing for an agency, you will need the approval of your boss, the vice president or president, the client's liaison and others directly concerned with the project.

Gaining multiple approvals often requires changes in copy. Sometimes advice from varying departments conflicts. That's where tact and diplomacy help. They count most with managers who see the work as unimportant and say things like, "I'm sorry, but I won't be able to approve the newsletter copy by your deadline. I'll get to it as soon as I can, but don't publish until I do, OK?"

Seeking approvals strikes at the egos of writers. Others with little time or energy invested want to change what the writers have devoted much to completing. But public relations writer-managers must hold their egos in check. Even though it is their draft, the final release represents the entire organization, and the CEO is responsible for it. The writer-manager is the orchestra leader who selects the music for the group and coordinates each member's contribution, but is not the producer. Constructive feedback constructively applied makes for a better product that more completely represents the organization.

Approvals also protect the writer and client organization. By reviewing material, legal counsel can preclude lawsuits caused by ambiguous or erroneous writing. Public relations writers usually have the best broadscale knowledge of their organizations. But in a large organization, no single office can be up-to-date on everything. To make sure you are right, make sure every office with a potential interest in the story reviews it for accuracy.

But there are times when you are right and the person wanting to change the copy is wrong. When that happens, explain your point until you are sure it is clear, providing supporting evidence. If the disagreeing person is your boss, you usually make your best pitch and then accept the decision. When someone tries to force you to lie or accept an erroneous conclusion, you may have to appeal the decision to a higher level. This may offend someone who will want to punish you. But if your integrity is at stake, the cost doesn't matter. You wouldn't want to work for someone who expected you to lie, anyway.

Many times the right and wrong of the issue are not clear-cut. When you are not sure, or the point is moot, give in graciously. Keep the objectives of the message in mind. Anything that doesn't defeat them is probably negotiable. Chapter 10 offers additional suggestions for managing the approval process.

Improving Coordinating Efficiency

To improve coordination, first make sure you have a standard process. Some messages, by their very natures, need comprehensive coordination. Top managers appearing before Senate committees, for example, may represent their entire industries. Other messages, such as financial statements, require fewer consultations but even greater precision. Each writer needs guidelines for determining what coordination each kind of message may require.

The Coordination Record

Use some kind of covering letter or memorandum when coordinating copy (see chapter 8 for writing guidelines). It should indicate who should see the copy, why it was written and what you hope to accomplish with it. Use sign-off approval blocks so that each recipient will know who else has seen or will see the proposed message. Include a deadline.

Managing Production Processes for Print

As a writer, you may be responsible for managing the production processes for your messages or those of others. This gives you an opportunity to influence the quality of the frame in which the picture you have painted will be presented. Since you know the effect visual support can have on print messages, you should want to take part in this process. Thus, it is to your advantage to learn production processes so you can supervise them effectively.

Contracting: Production by Others

Many corporate public relations divisions, nonprofit organizations and public relations firms contract all their production work out to professionals. This is a good way to get best quality work by knowledgeable people with sophisticated equipment and techniques. If you are not careful, it can also be a way to get shoddy work done at inflated prices. The key is to use only those who have a reputation for top quality work. You can find them in your area by asking others to whom they are contracting production work. While dealing with contractors, beware of false economies. Poor layout or printing will destroy the effectiveness of your message, which means you have saved money to no end.

If there are any artists, photographers or production people in your organization, by all means ask for their help. If there is desktop publishing available in-house, see if its quality makes it competitive with outside production. Certainly the price will be.

Build a production budget before you begin, based on estimates from three respected professionals recommended by your associates. It should include projected costs for writing, photography and design, typesetting, printing, binding, packing, shipping and taxes (Brody 1988, 175–177). If you can't afford to have the production done well, you may wish to wait.

The Essentials of Production

Most writers believe they have little to do with print production. They think in terms of a release sent out in standard format or a message whose production is handled by outside professionals. But format and visual quality can influence the success of any message, even a press release. Editors may not admit it, but they are favorably impressed by attractively laid out and perfectly-typed copy on high quality bond paper. However, most do not appreciate releases on colored paper of odd size or shape, or those that are printed in colored inks.

Good production management can enhance the quality and acceptability of most print messages through optimized visual effect. Before deciding on a format, consider the type of publication needed. That was decided in the planning stage, but it is wise to rethink before you commit yourself to expensive production costs. Sometimes, for example, the message that was planned for a simple flier turns out to be more appropriate in a brochure.

But regardless of whether you plan to market your print message through a newsletter, brochure, fact sheet, letter or other vehicle, there are certain fundamental production decisions to be made. These include the paper to be used, copy specifications, visuals included with the copy, layout and the printing process.

Paper

Publication paper can vary by finish, color, texture, cost and weight (Brody 1988, 173–175). In general, heavier paper is more expensive, looks better, prints better and wears longer. However, it does not fold as well as lighter stock paper and costs more per page to mail (Nolte and Wilcox 1984, 334–335). A hard finish—usually the result of enamel or other coating—is used for photos. Paper with a softer finish is best for publications that will be read under bright lights. This softness can be achieved by dull-finish enamel coatings or thinner matte coatings.

Newspapers normally use light inexpensive paper called newsprint. Magazines use heavier "book" paper. Most brochures, folders and booklets are printed on "book" paper. High-quality publication covers require a special paper.

White paper is generally preferred, since it is easy to read from and takes color well. It also provides the best contrast for black ink. Using standard sizes and shapes for pages is important. Odd sizes and unusual folds add to production costs, since both presses and paper come in standard sizes. Since printing requirements significantly influence paper choice, you'll want to consult with your printer on paper decisions.

The Copy

Since the copy is already written, most of the work on it is complete when you get to production. But the copy still needs managing. In a standard production process, technicians may work on your copy before it is produced. If you provide perfect copy to the typesetter in the beginning, things will go much easier. Some typesetters set exactly what you give them, errors and all. And, once the copy is set, correcting any errors can be quite expensive, depending on the contract. Matthews (1988, 110–111) cites costs of a single revision running from $20 to $300, depending on the stage of production the copy is in when the change is made.

If you must make last-minute corrections in the copy, make sure they are above the line and in ink. If the instructions get difficult to follow or the page becomes messy, take the time to retype the page.

TABLE 11.3.　Type Specifications for Print

1. Express the type size you want in "points." A point is 1/72 of an inch.
2. Specify whether you want added white space (leading) between lines.
3. Identify the name of the type family (font or "face") you want, such as **Times Roman** or **Helvetica**.
4. State the variation (style) of that type font you prefer (e.g., Light, Medium, Bold, Extra Bold, Condensed, Expanded).
5. Clarify the posture of the type (e.g., upright, called "roman," not "Roman," or slanted, called "italic").
6. Indicate whether you want the copy in all capital letters, upper and lower case, or large and small capital letters. This is called "letter composition."
7. Appointment of Space. This code shows whether you want your copy aligned with the left margin (flush left, ragged right) or aligned with both margins (flush left and right), as well as any special letter spacing you wish.
8. Stipulate the width of the line of type you wish in picas. A pica is 1/16 of an inch.

Source: J. William Click and Russell N. Baird, *Magazine Editing and Production,* 5th ed. (Dubuque, Ia: Wm. C. Brown, 1990), 227. Used with permission.

Where typesetting is done directly from a computer file, errors can be equally costly for two reasons: they are harder to detect on a computer screen than on paper and fewer people generally see computer-originated copy before it's ready for print.

Copy must be marked, either electronically or by hand (except with desktop publishing), so that the printing process can ensure the proper spacing, alignment, column width, type styles and sizes for body copy and headings (for a thorough discussion, see Click and Baird 1990, 227–235). Electronic codes vary with the system used. You might be asked to input these codes for copy in a computer-stored file, but could expect some specific training beforehand. Manual codes are standard, however. If you are familiar with the process, you will want to do your own. If not, discuss what you want with your printer and he or she will do the coding. In any case, you should have some familiarity with the coding. Complete type specifications include eight codes, though not all are always required (Click and Baird 1990, 227). See table 11.3.

A Complete Coding Example

Copy specifications might read: "Set body 8/10 Futura Medium roman c/lc, fl, × 14 picas." This means you want the text (body copy) to be set in 8-point type on 10-point tall lines, to add 2 points vertical spacing. The type you have selected is "Futura," a clean type, and you want its strokes in "Medium" thickness. You want the letters standing upright, or "roman." The printed copy should use normal capital and lower case letters (c/lc), you want the copy to be justified to the left margin (fl) and the line of print to be 14 picas wide (about two and one-third inches).

A new "Set" code is needed each time you want to change the size, style or orientation of type. That means each heading or headline needs its own code. Headline type is called "display type." The codes and measures are the same for body type and display type. However, type size of 14 points or larger is normally designated as display type. If you asked for a 10-point display type face, it might not be available. If you are using a desktop publishing program, however, it's possible you will have almost unlimited choice in type size, slant, expansion and constriction for any type font offered by the program.

You may also need to "size" the copy. Even though you planned for a certain number of words, by the time you select the page size, type sizes and visuals, you may need to trim the copy to fit the pages. This is especially true for single-page printings and brochures, where the total space is severely limited. Copyfitting seems confusing, but is easy to measure once you know the type "face" (name of the type style, e.g., Bodoni Book), the type "size" in points, the column width in picas and the length of the copy. You can roughly approximate the space you'll need for your copy by knowing that one page of double-spaced copy will take up a space one standard column width (about 2.3 inches wide) by 4.1 inches long in standard 10-point type (27 lines of copy, 65 characters wide, 10-point Helvetica, 1-point leading, 14 × 24.75 picas).

Visuals

Visuals or illustrations include everything you add to the words on a page. They normally include "line drawings" or "line illustrations" or continuous tone photographs or paintings. Line drawings are much easier to print because they are all black and white, with no shades of gray. Most visuals used are either photographs (black and white, duotones, full color), artwork (from simple black-and-white line drawings to full-color oil paintings and watercolors) or computer-made illustrations (charts, bar graphs, diagrams and maps). The more sophisticated the visual, the higher the cost and the greater chance there is of problems occurring. Visuals are an integral part of the print communication process and should be carefully planned from the outset. The writer should compose with copy, artwork, photography and the approximate appearance of the final product in mind.

Visuals are a major factor in print production, intended to accomplish one or more of five purposes: (1) attract attention, (2) illustrate a point made in the text, (3) tell a complete story with the aid of a caption, (4) tell a story in conjunction with other illustrations, and (5) give visual relief to a design (Click and Baird 1990, 184–188). When you do a feature on the new corporate president for the company magazine, the article is enhanced when you let readers see what he or she looks like. If you write that the city art museum used 25 percent of its funds on acquisitions, 50 percent on salaries, 15 percent on facility and 10 percent on administration, you can show the reader that information much better through a pie chart (see figure 11.1).

Since poorly conceived or executed visuals can have a negative impact on the message, base your decisions on professional ability, not convenience. If you can't afford

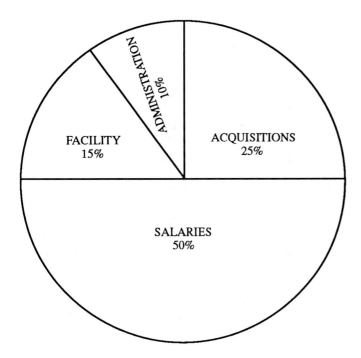

▶ **Figure 11.1.** A pie chart. "How the City Art Museum Used Its Funds." The pie chart is a simple way to help publics visualize different weights of emphasis.

good visuals, do without them. Give your photographer or artist a written description (and a sketch, if possible) of what you have in mind. Ask for a sketch or photo plan in return and a cost estimate. Most artists work by the job and most photographers by the hour or day, plus expenses. Some changes and extra photos are almost always necessary. So have an agreement with the artist on how many alterations you can make and with the photographer on what extra shots will cost. Don't overmanage. Say what you are after and then step back. The result may well be better than you could have imagined. If it isn't, then you may need to step back in.

If you are using photographs that were taken for your story, they will probably be 8″ × 10″ or 5″ × 7″ black and white glossies. Normally, photos are cropped and sized to give them better balance, focus, and to expand the subject to the space available. For example, if you had a full-view photo of a person on whom you were doing a feature, you might want to crop off the lower portion. The resulting photo would be relatively larger, letting the reader get a good look at facial expression. You would also use cropping to cut out unnecessary and distracting portions of a picture.

The cutline that goes with the visual is an important part of your business. The cutline carries a message that helps the visual support the story or provide a separate supporting message. Writing cutlines is discussed in chapter 8.

Layout

Layout is the art and craft of uniting visuals, title, headings or captions, copy and white space into an aesthetically pleasing and effectively presented message. "The layout is the plan for the finished piece" (Nolte and Wilcox 1984, 341).

As with other functions, you should begin by considering what it is that you wish your message to do. The layout should be focused on your objective, whether it be to shock, please or inform. An article on the gold rush in 19th century California might call for large, vivid photos, bold display type and strong-lined body type. A promotion for a new woman's shaver, on the other hand, might benefit from elegant type and a photograph that reveals the shaver as a thing of beauty.

Once you have thought out the possibilities and decided what you want to do, the next step is to create a mock-up or "dummy" of the finished piece. Initial dummies may be made on any size and kind of paper, but the shape of the page must be in direct proportion to the actual page envisioned. The final dummy is usually on the same paper and in the same size as the actual published page. For an example, see figure 11.2.

Printing

Good printers have busy schedules, so arrangements need to be worked out long before you need them. If you don't have a regular printer, get estimates from three or four recommended printers. Look at examples of their work within the context of your needs. If you have special requirements the printer may have to "job out," which will increase the time and cost. The less expertise you have, the more cooperative a printer you will need. This might cost more, but it is cheaper than making serious printing errors.

Most printers have standard contract forms, but costs vary a great deal, depending on what you want done. The only way to get exact costs for comparison is by providing specifications (Click and Baird 1990, 154–158). These include page size, the area of the page to be covered by type, each kind of body and display type, and the paper to be used. Color needs must also be specified, as well as illustrations. If a cover is required, the special treatment in paper, colors and size needs to be decided. A magazine or book needs to be bound by gluing, wire or stitching.

For their part, printers must provide you with **production timelines.** You especially need to know how long it will be from the time you deliver the material until you receive proofs. And there must be agreement on what role, if any, the printer takes in packaging and distributing your publication. This service adds to production costs.

Two actions need special consideration. The **"mechanical"** is the camera-ready pasteup of type and visuals made to the specifications of the final dummy. The printer photographs the mechanical to create a negative for the printing plate. The printer can make the mechanical, or you can deliver it completed as "camera ready copy." Budget and your expertise determine which. Figure 11.3 shows an example of a mechanical.

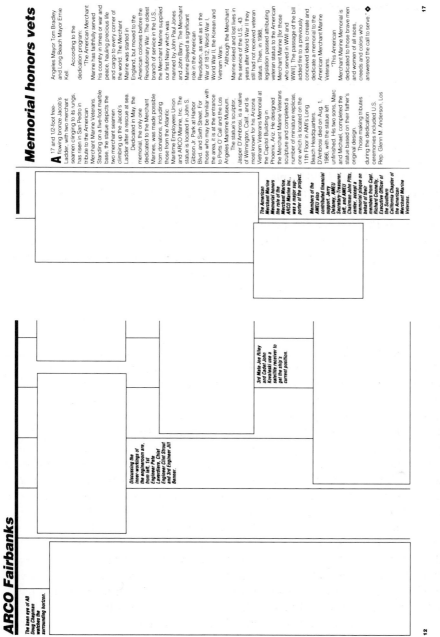

ARCO Fairbanks

The keen eye of AB Doug Chapman watches the surrounding horizon.

Discussing the inner-workings of the engineroom are, from left, 1st Engineer Pete Laverdiere, Chief Engineer Clint Strout and 3rd Engineer Jill Benner.

3rd Mate Joe Riley and Cadet John Kowalecki use a satellite receiver to get the ship's current position.

12

Memorial honors vets

A 17 and 1/2-foot free-flowing bronze Jacob's Ladder, with two merchant seamen clinging to its rungs, has risen in San Pedro in tribute to the American Merchant Marine Veterans. Standing on a five-foot marble base, the statue depicts the two merchant seamen climbing up the Jacob's Ladder after a rescue at sea. Dedicated in May, the memorial, the only one dedicated to the Merchant Marines, was made possible from donations, including those from the Atlantic Maritime Employees Union and ARCO Marine, Inc. The statue is located in John S. Gibson Jr. Park at Harbor Blvd. and Sixth Street. For those who may be familiar with the area, it is at the entrance to Ports O' Call and the Los Angeles Maritime Museum.

The statue's sculptor, Jasper D'Ambrosi, is a native of Wilmington, Calif., and is most known for his Arizona Vietnam Veterans Memorial at the Capitol Building in Phoenix, Ariz. He designed the Merchant Marine Veterans sculpture and completed a number of miniature replicas, one which is located on the 11th Floor in AMI's Long Beach Headquarters.

D'Ambrosi died on Aug. 1, 1986, with the statue left unfinished. His two sons, Marc and Michael, completed the statue based on their father's original design.

Those making tributes during the dedication ceremonies included U.S. Rep. Glenn M. Anderson, Los Angeles Mayor Tom Bradley and Long Beach Mayor Ernie Kell.

According to the dedication program:

"The American Merchant Marine has faithfully served his country in times or war and peace, hauling precious life and cargo to every corner of the world. The Merchant Marine was started in England, but moved to the American colonies before the Revolutionary War. The oldest branch of service in the U.S., the Merchant Marine supplied our first Navy which was manned by John Paul Jones and John Barry. The Merchant Marine played a significant role in the American Revolution, as well as in the War of 1812, World War I, World War II, the Korean and Vietnam Wars.

"Although the Merchant Marine risked and lost lives in the service of the U.S. 43 years after World War II they still had not received veteran status. Then, in 1988, legislation passed attributing veteran status to the American Merchant Marine [for those who served in WWI and WWII]. The passage of the bill added fire to a previously conceived idea to create and dedicate a memorial to the American Merchant Marine Veterans.

"This American Merchant Marine Memorial is dedicated to those brave men and women of all races, creeds and colors who answered the call to serve." ◆

The American Merchant Marine Memorial honors the role of the Merchant Marine. ARCO Marine Inc. was a major supporter of the project.

Members of the AMEU also contributed financial support. Jerry Delaney, AMEU Secretary-Treasurer, left, and AMEU Chairman John Pitts, center, accept a memorial plaque on behalf of their members from Capt. Richard Connelly, Executive Officer of the Southern California Chapter of the American Merchant Marine Veterans.

17

▲ **Figure 11.2.** Layout dummy. This layout is for two pages placed side by side. Note the asymmetric balance of the blocks representing visuals to be used. See Figure 11.3 for the completed work. From ARCO Marine *MariTimes*. Used with permission.

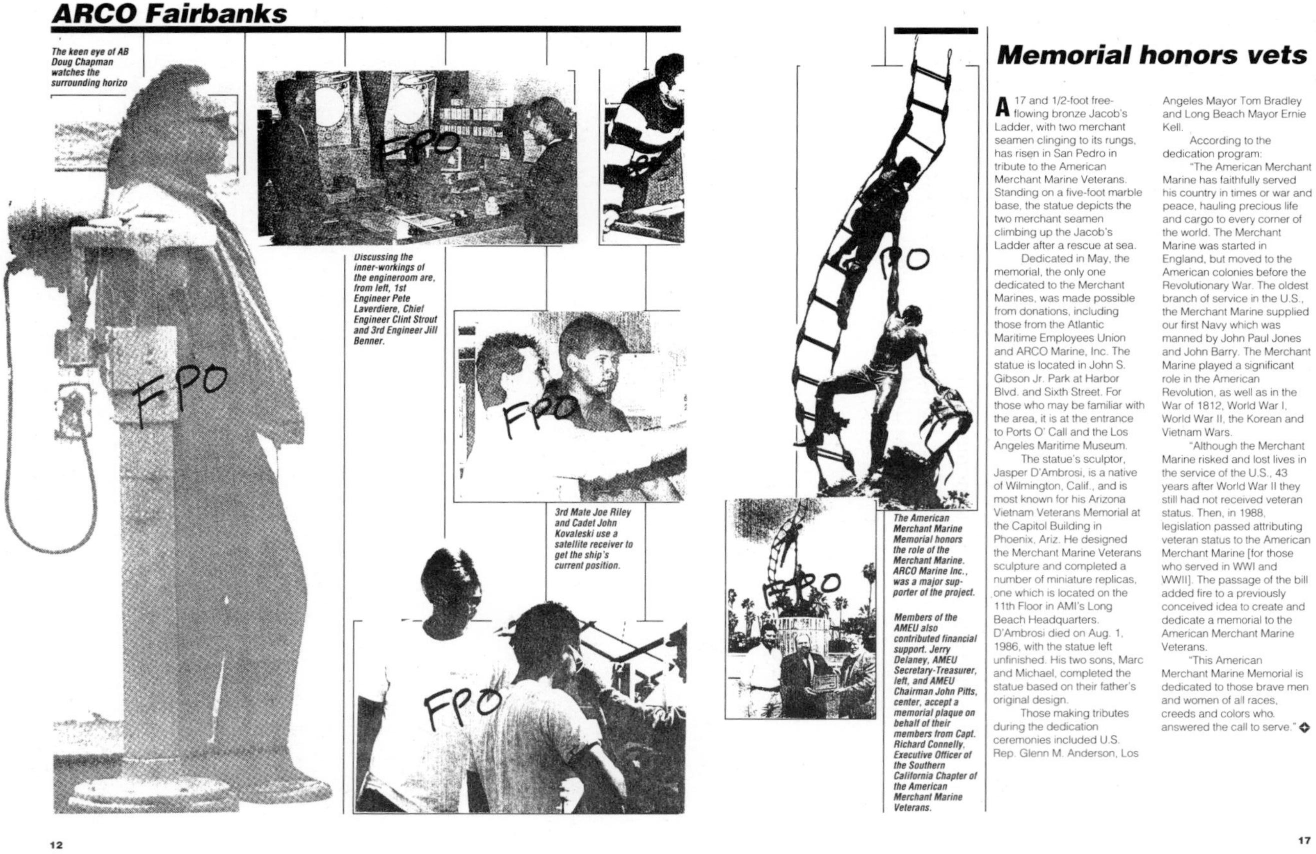

ARCO Fairbanks

The keen eye of AB Doug Chapman watches the surrounding horizo

Discussing the inner workings of the engineroom are, from left, 1st Engineer Pete Laverdiere, Chief Engineer Clint Strout and 3rd Engineer Jill Benner.

3rd Mate Joe Riley and Cadet John Kowalski use a satellite receiver to get the ship's current position.

12

Memorial honors vets

A 17 and 1/2-foot free-flowing bronze Jacob's Ladder, with two merchant seamen clinging to its rungs, has risen in San Pedro in tribute to the American Merchant Marine Veterans. Standing on a five-foot marble base, the statue depicts the two merchant seamen climbing up the Jacob's Ladder after a rescue at sea.

Dedicated in May, the memorial, the only one dedicated to the Merchant Marines, was made possible from donations, including those from the Atlantic Maritime Employees Union and ARCO Marine, Inc. The statue is located in John S. Gibson Jr. Park at Harbor Blvd. and Sixth Street. For those who may be familiar with the area, it is at the entrance to Ports O' Call and the Los Angeles Maritime Museum.

The statue's sculptor, Jasper D'Ambrosi, is a native of Wilmington, Calif., and is most known for his Arizona Vietnam Veterans Memorial at the Capitol Building in Phoenix, Ariz. He designed the Merchant Marine Veterans sculpture and completed a number of miniature replicas, one which is located on the 11th Floor in AMI's Long Beach Headquarters.

D'Ambrosi died on Aug. 1, 1986, with the statue left unfinished. His two sons, Marc and Michael, completed the statue based on their father's original design.

Those making tributes during the dedication ceremonies included U.S. Rep. Glenn M. Anderson, Los Angeles Mayor Tom Bradley and Long Beach Mayor Ernie Kell.

According to the dedication program:

"The American Merchant Marine has faithfully served his country in times or war and peace, hauling precious life and cargo to every corner of the world. The Merchant Marine was started in England, but moved to the American colonies before the Revolutionary War. The oldest branch of service in the U.S., the Merchant Marine supplied our first Navy which was manned by John Paul Jones and John Barry. The Merchant Marine played a significant role in the American Revolution, as well as in the War of 1812, World War I, World War II, the Korean and Vietnam Wars.

"Although the Merchant Marine risked and lost lives in the service of the U.S., 43 years after World War II they still had not received veteran status. Then, in 1988, legislation passed attributing veteran status to the American Merchant Marine [for those who served in WWI and WWII]. The passage of the bill added fire to a previously conceived idea to create and dedicate a memorial to the American Merchant Marine Veterans.

"This American Merchant Marine Memorial is dedicated to those brave men and women of all races, creeds and colors who, answered the call to serve." ◆

The American Merchant Marine Memorial honors the role of the Merchant Marine. ARCO Marine Inc. was a major supporter of the project.

Members of the AMEU also contributed financial support. Jerry Delaney, AMEU Secretary-Treasurer, left, and AMEU Chairman John Pitts, center, accept a memorial plaque on behalf of their members from Capt. Richard Connally, Executive Officer of the Southern California Chapter of the American Merchant Marine Veterans.

17

▲ **Figure 11.3.** The mechanical. This is the final camera-ready pasteup of type ready for the printer to photograph. Photocopies of photographs have been included for position only (FPO). It is based on the dummy in Figure 11.2. Note how the photographs lead the reader to the copy. From ARCO Marine *MariTimes*. Graphic design by Partners By Design. Used with permission.

The second key action is the **proof process.** Get an agreement on how many proofs the printer will provide and how long you will have to consider each. Most page proofs are photographically reproduced from the printing negatives. They are called "blue-lines" or "brownlines." Each proof gives you an opportunity to see how the final product will look and make needed changes. While you are in the proofing process, the printer pays for printer errors, while you pay for alterations you make.

Throughout the print production process, the writer-manager is forced to make **balanced judgments** in order to get the best possible product for the money spent. You certainly don't want to waste the client's money. But, if you have to skimp on production, skimp on the side of plainness by giving up things like visuals, color or special paper. Don't sacrifice the quality of the work. Professionally-produced publications can last a long time. But so can poorly produced ones.

Managing Audio-Visual Production

For this discussion, audio-visual communications will include live radio broadcast and audiotapes, live television and videotapes, motion pictures, filmstrips, sound/slide presentations and multimedia presentations.

In the past, broadcasters sometimes accepted and used amateur material when its purpose was to support worthwhile causes. Today, however, few stations will accept any program material not of broadcast quality, regardless of its purpose. Professional writers would not want it otherwise.

Audiotape

We normally market messages for radio in two ways. One is by **providing a release** to the radio station or its marketing group. The station then uses its own talent and production staff and facilities to broadcast the message either live or tape delayed, amending it as desired. A 30-second PSA for a local charity could be produced this way.

Alternatively, we may **provide a program idea** and outline, or possibly a complete script to a station for consideration. If the station decides to produce the message, its personnel then take over the production, with public relations playing an advisory role. An example of this might be the appearance of the president of the local chapter of Stop Terrorizing Our People on a half-hour public affairs radio program to explain the S-T-O-P campaign.

There are times, however, when you and your client believe that the radio station should be furnished with **a complete broadcast-ready program.** These could include corporate non-product advertisements, PSAs, responses to editorials, or special programs for clients. You may have people qualified to produce these programs. If so, by all means let them do it. If you have the experience and training, you may wish to follow through to ensure the quality of your message. If not, you should contract out to a professional producer, while maintaining some supervisory control.

The **elements to coordinate** for producing broadcast-ready tapes are diverse. You will need to know the **format** preferences of the station. At one time, you could count on fitting a 26-minute audiotape into a 30-minute program. Today, you'll need to check with the station as to length and number of possible break points.

Second, it's useful to have a **recording studio.** Audiotapes can be produced in ordinary rooms or outside. You would only want an outside recording if you needed to reproduce sounds essential to the message. Ordinary rooms can cause sound problems, such as echo or deadness. And you need the proper recording equipment. You can record an audiotape with a simple and inexpensive recorder, but it won't have high quality sound. Since you don't want to go to the trouble of producing your own audiotape unless it has a good chance of being aired, the recording studio is usually a worthwhile investment.

In most cases, you'll also need to hire **"talent"** (announcers and actors for speaking parts), sound effects and music, as well as purchase audiotapes on which to make copies of the recording to send to selected radio stations. And, unless you have the expertise, you'll need to hire a professional director to mastermind the taping. If the recording is an ad, you'll also need to buy air time from the stations. For public relations advertisements, it's often best to have advertising people coordinate the production, since they have the contacts and the media selection expertise.

Videotape

Many of the points made about radio and audiotapes also apply to television and videotapes (or video discs). The writer-manager's involvement in video production normally does not go beyond making sure that the messages are properly integrated into the storyboards (see chapter 9). The expertise and expense required to produce a good quality videotape are normally beyond the capabilities of most writers.

Although technical complexity dictates that nothing is really simple in television, the simplest such effort you might be involved with would be a television PSA. Some large stations have special facilities that they will make available to you free of charge. Television production costs are very high, so if such an opportunity arises, use it. Advocacy messages may also be station-produced. For example, a two-minute editorial that you write in support of nuclear power could be produced by a television station with your client's CEO as spokesperson.

If you have to do your own production, you will want to hire a producer, unless you are experienced. Public relations specialists primarily use videotapes for organizational communications and video news releases. In either case, the viewing public will likely compare your production with the high-quality commercial television they see every day. If your productions are to be viewed favorably, they must be of high quality.

You, as the writer-manager, may be asked to coordinate videotape production for a client. If so, you can separately contract out each element of the production. You may write or supervise the script. Then you may rent a production studio and hire your own talent and production team. Generally, however, you will be better off contracting with a production studio for everything but special talent and the script. There are a number of independent television production studios in every major city. Ask colleagues about the quality of their work. Review some work each has produced. Get three or four estimates. Then, when you get the best combination of quality work and cost, stick with it.

Video News Releases

Sometimes called video newsclips or TV newsclips, video news releases are video-tapes about news involving clients that are produced for television news programs by public relations practitioners. They usually run for 30–90 seconds. The client benefits from the release by being identified, but without appearing to promote itself or advertise its products (Seitel 1987, 237–238). The television station benefits by getting video that might be costly to produce or impossible for it to obtain independently. Today, VNRs are almost entirely produced by independent production companies and cost sponsors about $3,000–$6,000 each. The public relations writer-manager may conceive the VNR, write the script and coordinate the production, but production specialists are necessary to ensure that the release can match or exceed broadcast quality standards.

Your job as writer-manager is to produce top-quality videotape at a reasonable cost. The product must be truly newsworthy. Sponsor identification must be subtle. For example, if your client is a beer company, you might produce film of an auto race and brief interviews with some drivers. The only sponsor identification might be the company's name on the side of a passing race car. If the sponsor identification is overplayed, the VNR becomes a commercial and won't be used on a news program.

Finally, you don't have to be a technical expert to spot production flaws. Hot or dark spots reveal poor lighting. Scratchy sound usually comes from poor recording equipment. Echoes may mean that the speaker's microphone isn't working, and the audio is being picked up by another mike. Dead time means that editing is called for. A camera on speaker A for more than an instant when speaker B is talking means you either must edit-in from the second camera or reshoot the scene. You may not be aware of all the technical implications, but your sense of communication can tell you when things are not right. Ask for a retake when they are not. The cost is minimal while you are still on the set and have all the participants handy. If you insist on quality work, your production team will too.

Motion Picture Production

Although the technical quality of television improves daily, it still cannot match the motion picture in sharpness of image and clarity. Film can make time almost stand still (as in slow-motion photography) and leap ahead (as we watch a flower's month-long life cycle pass in a minute). It can make big things seem small enough to be visually understandable and small things big enough to see their every detail. Viewed in a darkened room on a large screen, the motion picture demands and captures viewers' attention as no other medium can. And, since the master film can be retained, each film lasts until it becomes obsolete.

There are several good reasons for making public relations films, from cost efficiency to corporate vanity. Make sure you know why film was selected to deliver your message before you begin a film. Good films can be long-term assets. But, mistakes are costly, since poorly conceived or produced films can damage the client substantially. As writer-manager, you want to be sure that the medium can meet your client's objectives.

Public relations films serve four purposes:

1. To directly appeal for support of the client. A hotel might sponsor a film on the beauty of Hawaii and Hotel "X" to be shown to prospective tourists.

2. To inform, motivate or convince client employees about the organizations for which they work.

3. To advocate a client's stand on a particular issue or tell an important story. The sponsor's identity is usually limited to screen credits before or after the film.

4. To document and promote an industry, but not the client or its specific products. A film on the health benefits of all Florida citrus (not a particular brand name) might be sponsored by Florida citrus growers.

Unless your client has an in-house motion picture production facility, equipment and team, it's best to contract with an outside film producer to shoot the film, edit it to your specifications and provide you with the finished print. Unlike videotape, which can be recorded over, once motion picture film is shot, it cannot be used again.

Most public relations films are produced in the 16-millimeter size, which is usable in most theaters. Additionally, most motion picture users, such as schools, churches, community groups and companies, have access to 16mm projectors. It also transfers well onto videotape, should the client later decide to exhibit it that way.

You should bring four tools to the producer of your film: (1) **the script;** (2) **the storyboard,** a sketch of each shot in the film; (3) **the treatment,** or scene-by-scene explanation of everything that will go on at a location; and (4) **the synopsis,** a one-page overview of the film. Using these tools and a technical expert who knows the background and objectives (such as you), producers and their teams put together the film.

Normally, you'll want to plan at least six weeks in advance for a film. Location or special-action films need even more time to plan and coordinate. Film making is expensive. It takes careful planning and much expertise to do it efficiently. As a writer-manager, you may be best qualified to represent the client's interests in a public relations film.

Delivering the Message

Long before a message is written and produced, the public relations team decides to whom it will be delivered and how. Occasionally you may be asked to oversee the delivery process. Perhaps the best advice is that you should treat each message for what it is: a valuable piece of property that cannot achieve its objective without timely and proper delivery.

For years, public relations releases were "shotgunned" out to every newspaper, magazine or broadcast station around. Small wonder that city editors felt dumped on by public relations releases and ignored many of them.

The key to successful delivery is to get messages only to those media or other channels capable of reaching the desired publics. Who they are should have been decided in the planning stage. Now your task is to get the messages to them.

The best way to get a release where it belongs is to deliver it yourself or personally phone it in. But that's expensive and could be counterproductive if you used it for other than most important messages. The next level might be same-day postal service or overnight delivery services. The next level of importance could be FAX or first class mail delivery. Multiple-destination releases can be handled by a number of computerized services. The key is to match the delivery process to the importance and urgency of the message.

Take the trouble to find out how your writing products are being distributed in their final form. If distribution is sloppy or slipshod, exert your influence as a coordinating manager. It would be unfortunate to lose the value of a great message after it had gone that far.

Chapter Summary

This chapter discussed ways the writer can help manage the writing process. The importance of managing the writing process well was considered, as was the case for the writer (who best knows the writing process) managing the writing process.

The knowledge and skills required to manage public relations writing well were noted as: understanding the process, its forms and purposes; budgeting time, talent and funds; and understanding senior managers' writing outlooks.

Writer-manager tasks were seen as self-management, management of in-house programs for which one is part-author and manager of projects contracted to outside groups. Time management, negotiating skills, proofreading and follow-through were said to be critical to self-management. Managing in-house projects calls for special skills in objectivity, tact and leadership. Managing outside writing requires getting well-qualified writers who are able to understand the client organization. It also requires the ability to negotiate good prices and see the work through.

Managing communicators requires that the writer-manager be aware of the special sensitivities and motivations of artistic people. The manager issues the challenge and controls the action in general, but gives the artists creative autonomy. For the very talented, formalities are few and quirks accepted.

The chapter told how to guide one's message through the coordination and approval process. The manager was advised to negotiate when possible, but to stand firm on honesty and integrity, insisting politely on the proper course. Points and guidelines were offered for improving coordinating efficiency.

Contracting for the production of final message forms was discussed for print, audiovisual and film messages. Considerable discussion focused on the production of printed publications because this is the area writers are expected to be most familiar with. Videotape and motion picture film productions were seen as those most requiring independent professional producers to achieve high quality messages.

The writer-manager's involvement in distribution was seen as a backup or follow-up requirement for activity presumably planned well beforehand, but one meriting overseeing to ensure that valuable messages were not lost en route to their destinations.

A Writing Exercise

Situation: You are a senior writer for Moremark Telecom. The company makes and markets a cordless cellular telephone, invented by Tom Moremark, the president and CEO. Moremark has worldwide sales of $100 million annually from distribution points in 20 countries. All manufacturing and assembly are done in Taiwan. The phone has good transmission and reception for up to 100 miles, and in-flight up to 40,000 feet. It is a high-priced communications tool, the sales of which seem to have flattened out in the past two years. The units have stabilized in cost at about $5,000 per unit. The company's 200 Taiwanese workers and 100 American managers and sales people are well paid and seem to enjoy their work.

Two months ago Moremark, as CEO, envisioned a 30-minute motion picture, "The Moremark Story," a history of his business career and the development of the company. Parts of it would be shot at the factory, the Chicago company headquarters and at all the sales locations. Response from all sections of the company has been close to ecstatic. All of the field office managers have written in with segments to be shot at their locations. All the inputs have now been turned over to you, as the only one in the company who seems to know anything about "that side of communication." The CEO is very enthusiastic and wants to know the best way to go about it.

Assignment: Your boss, the director of corporate affairs, thinks you have been tossed a box of rattlesnakes. She assigns you to study the situation and write a 300–500 word discussion paper on the film idea. In it, you are to first analyze the pros and cons of making such a film, taking care not to offend Moremark in his enthusiasm. Based on your analysis of the film's value and how it might best be produced, you are to recommend how the film should be produced. You are also to decide whether it should be produced and why, or why not. If not, what vehicle would you recommend that might tell the story more efficiently?

Food for Thought

1. Why do you believe that people who are gifted artists are seldom made managers of communication organizations?
2. What are the pros and cons of writers being used to manage writing programs? Do you think it is useful or counterproductive for them to do so?
3. Do you believe that video news release productions should be required to run a credit line that identifies the sponsor of the segment? Defend your position.
4. What percent of their time do you believe corporate CEOs should spend on communications? How should that time be spent? What percent should be spent on speeches, videotapes, articles, and other methods? Defend your position.
5. What are some of the collateral values of producing your message in print that cannot be duplicated through other media?

References for Further Study

Bivins, Thomas. *Handbook for Public Relations Writing.* Lincolnwood, Ill.: NTC Business Books, 1988, 265–275.

Brody, E. W. *The Business of Public Relations.* New York: Praeger, 1987.

Brody, E. W. *Public Relations Programming and Production.* New York: Praeger, 1988.

Click, J. William, and Russell N. Baird. *Magazine Editing and Production,* 5th ed. Dubuque, Iowa: Wm. C. Brown Publishers, 1990.

Granville, W. Hough. *Managing Business Operations and Organizations.* Fullerton, Calif.: Granville W. Hough, 1984.

Grunig, James E., and Todd Hunt. *Managing Public Relations.* New York: Holt, Rinehart and Winston, 1984, 443–496.

Lavine, John M., and Daniel B. Wackman. *Managing Media Organizations.* New York: Longman, 1988.

Matthews, Downs. *How to Manage Employee Publications.* Bartlesville, Okla.: Joe Williams, 1988, 89–129.

Nolte, Lawrence W., and Dennis L. Wilcox. *Effective Publicity: How to Reach the Public.* New York: John Wiley & Sons, 1984, 269–361.

Reuss, Carol, and Donn E. Silvis, (eds.). *Inside Organizational Communication,* 2d ed. New York: Longman, 1985.

Seitel, Fraser P. *The Practice of Public Relations.* Columbus, Ohio: Merrill, 1987.

Turner, Ruth. "24 Aids to Successful Proofreading." *tips & tactics.* August 20, 1978.

Wilcox, Dennis L., Phillip H. Ault and Warren F. Agee. *Public Relations: Strategies and Tactics.* New York: Harper & Row, 1989.

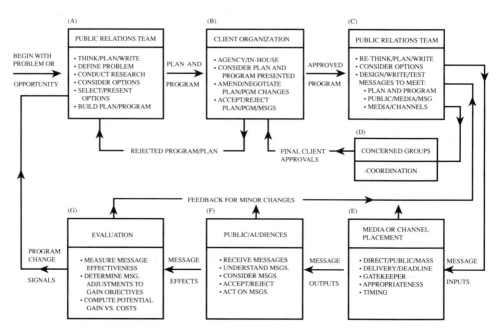

Through the testing process public relations writers determine the adequacy of their work. Thus, both the preparation and action are evaluated. Evaluation and correction occur at all stages in the process. But the crucial measure is to determine how well the message does what it was designed to do. The result of this measure helps determine how future messages should be changed to achieve objectives.

TESTING YOUR WRITING EFFECTIVENESS

Introduction

This chapter discusses evaluation of public relations writing, or **how well the message did what it was designed to do.** Though many public relations people don't evaluate their work well, it is one of the most important things they can do. If you can't measure your performance, how can you improve?

Public relations writers have historically resisted evaluating their work. Even the results-oriented Public Relations Society of America did not require contestants for its most prestigious awards to provide evaluation information with their entries until 1982 (Cutlip, Center and Broom 1985, 289). Some writers apparently believe that publication by itself is proof of the value of their work. Some admit a fear of failure or rejection and would rather not know.

The reality is, however, that evaluation of writing is critical. If we can measure its effectiveness while the campaign is in progress, changes can be made to improve the results. That is the message of block G in figure 2.1. Minor errors can be corrected and the corrections fed back into the message process immediately. The impact of major errors can be determined and compensated for. And major program changes can be considered by management and made before they become disasters. Finally, if we don't know what was wrong with past messages, we are liable to repeat those errors and hurt ourselves and our clients in the future.

Given the importance of evaluation research to public relations writing, you need to know how to conduct it. This chapter addresses the concepts, skills and techniques necessary for evaluation research.

A PROFESSIONAL TIP:
Measuring the Results

Increasingly, public relations programs are expected to make something happen, with a growing emphasis on measuring results. And increasingly, that is becoming the case.

Practitioners are making great strides in developing useful techniques and applying tools in the planning and evaluation stages of public relations campaigns. Clip analysis still remains widespread in terms of judging total numbers of people reached, especially in a media relations program. However, newer measurement tools like the Ketchum Publicity Planning and Tracking Model move the evaluation task to new heights by defining how well specific messages reached a finite target audience, thus ensuring that a public relations program delivered what it promised.

More qualitative measurement can be applied to changing attitudes through pre- and post-research, while improved employee communication can lead to increased productivity or resolution of labor unrest. In a marketing sense, public relations programs can also be measured in terms of increasing sales and moving product.

Paul H. Alvarez, APR, author of *What Happens in Public Relations* and former chairman of the Counselors Academy of Public Relations Society of America, is vice chairman of Ketchum Communications. He is also president of Public Relations Society of America's Foundation for Public Relations Research and Education.

Copyright © 1991 Paul Alvarez.
Used with permission.

The Concept of Evaluation

To conduct an effective evaluation, one must know what it is. "Evaluation research refers to the process of judging the effectiveness of program planning, implementation and impact" (Wimmer and Dominick 1987, 366–368). For our purposes, it is intended to determine what happened as a result of a writing program and why. When based on preconceived notions, its effectiveness is diminished. Cutlip, Center and Broom (1985 291–294) offer 10 basic steps to help assure objectivity in evaluation research. They are here modified and presented as seven steps for the public relations writer:

1. Fashion an agreement before the program begins on what evaluation research will be done, and its objectives, uses and criteria. For a recruitment PSA used in an American Red Cross membership drive, one measure of success would be the difference in membership before and after the campaign. Another might be to find out by survey why those nonmembers receiving the messages did not join. Yet another might be why some stations did not use the PSA.

2. Build the evaluation into the plan and get the client's support for it before you begin. Evaluation research, like everything else in the program, takes effort and money. Build your evaluation into the plan as specific research steps. In the Red Cross case above, you might want to plan for and get a commitment from management to pay for the survey of nonjoiners, for example.

3. Specify your program objectives beforehand in ways that can be appropriately measured. One program objective might be "to write, produce, distribute and assure publication of messages that will help increase American Red Cross membership in Alachua County by at least 10 percent during its 90-day membership drive." The objective is clear and measurable, even though it may be difficult to determine how much of its achievement can be specifically attributed to your messages. In the real world, many uncontrolled factors can contribute to change. Nevertheless, you would be able to provide an estimate of the value of your work.

4. Keep complete records on the evaluation methods used and their results. Things often happen fast during a public relations campaign. If you don't keep accurate and complete records, you will not be able to accurately reconstruct your actions later. Often the results can unearth factors you did not expect to influence the program. For example, in one membership drive, new memberships were found to correlate significantly with pleasant weather. People came by to sign up when the weather was nice. That was not an anticipated factor, but daily records of memberships allowed it to be determined.

5. Use evaluation results to improve the program. Clearly, you can best justify your research by using it to improve the results of the campaign while it is still in progress. If you determine early in the campaign that there are very few new memberships coming from a certain part of the county, you can find ways to get more messages to that area and perhaps improve the results there.

6. Report results and program adjustments to management in ways that contribute to management's primary objectives. A good way to show results in the Red Cross membership drive could be numbers of new members per dollar spent on the campaign. Red Cross leaders would want their funds to be mostly spent on charity, not membership campaigns.

7. Where applicable, share evaluation findings with colleagues so that they may be applied generally. Although not all research findings are generalizable, some might be useful in unforeseen ways. For example, the finding that messages from local celebrities attract more Red Cross recruits than messages from national celebrities might be useful information for leaders of the area's American Cancer Society.

Kinds of Evaluation Research

Although clearly necessary, evaluation research is, "about as elusive as finding the Holy Grail" (Pavlik 1987, 65). The fundamental problems are to decide what to measure and how to go about it. According to Reeves (1983 in Pavlik 1987, 65), full documentation of media effects requires evidence from four sources: (1) the content of the message; (2) audience exposure to the message; (3) how the audience was affected; and (4) situations when effects may or may not occur. Dozier (1984; Pavlik 1987, 66–67), surveying San Diego, Calif., public relations practitioners, found three major evaluation styles:

1. Scientific impact evaluation, which uses objective quantitative methods to determine program impact.

2. Seat-of-the pants evaluation, a personalized, subjective evaluation based on anecdotes, casual observation and the practitioner's judgment to determine effectiveness.

3. Scientific dissemination evaluation, which uses quantitative methods to examine **message distribution,** assuming that higher message dissemination correlates with greater message publication and impact.

Most evaluation research in public relations is of the "seat-of-the-pants" style, with considerable mixing of methods. It is important to press for more scientific evaluation research in writing and other facets of public relations. However, this does not mean that subjective evaluation cannot be of value to writers. Much intuitive evaluation by experts in many fields is based on sound, but undetermined underlying predictors.

Stages of the Evaluation Process

Evaluation research intrudes into many stages of the writing process. Some scholars separate it into "formative evaluation," which occurs in the planning and operational stages, and "summative evaluation," which occurs after a campaign is completed (Scriven 1967).

For our purposes here, however, it may be best to look at evaluation research in the four traditional public relations process areas: (1) definition and research, (2) planning and programming, (3) communication and other action and (4) evaluation and redirection.

Definition and Research

In this initial phase of the public relations writing process, most errors are due to inadequate research or unverified assumptions. Incomplete research can negate the finest writing program. For example, a United Nations' specialist, asked to review a comprehensive family planning campaign in Asia during the early 1980s, found that the health services and contraceptive devices promoted by the campaign were not available in many rural target areas (Woods 1982; Cutlip, Center and Broom 1985, 294). Program coordinators had not made sure that the services and devices were on hand. At best, the campaign messages created a demand that could not be met. At worst, they destroyed the credibility of the client. Either way, the messages were ineffective.

Inaccurate assumptions can cause writers to produce messages that fail too. During the 1988 U.S. vice presidential TV debate, Republican candidate Senator Dan Quayle drew parallels between himself and John F. Kennedy. His opponent, Democratic candidate Senator Lloyd Bentsen, saying that he had known and worked with Kennedy, responded, "Senator, you're no John Kennedy." The Democrats exploited this exchange considerably. Apparently, Quayle and his writers assumed that the candidate's youth and good looks could be exploited by comparing him to Kennedy. Kennedy's heroic war record (compared to Quayle's noncombat service in the National Guard), brilliance and martyrdom should have led Quayle and his advisors to examine and question this assumption.

How, then, can writers assure that their research has not overlooked any key facts? How can they keep from making incorrect assumptions? No answer is foolproof. Avoiding incorrect assumptions requires mastery of logic (see, for example, Merrill and Odell 1983). However, asking the right questions can help avoid most of the lapses in research that encourage such assumptions. All public relations situations have some things in common: (1) a client organization, (2) a problem or opportunity facing the client with possible public relations solutions, (3) a public relations team (one person or many, a division of the client organization or an outside firm), (4) one or more publics who affect or are affected by the situation, (5) messages or other actions that may be useful, (6) media or other channels through which messages may be sent to the publics, and (7) environmental factors (social, political, economic, religious, psychological and sociological) that may influence the outcome. If the writer examines each of these common areas, asking the traditional reporter's **who, what, where, when, why and how,** there will be few important facts overlooked.

Planning and Programming

Evaluation is a continual and integral part of planning and programming as well. Planning and programming problems usually occur because managers at some level do not think the project important enough to merit their review. As a public relations writer, it is to your advantage to force that review (see chapter 11).

For example, based on research, you may project a 20 percent increase in disposable income over the next five years for the average U.S. resident. Thus, you project new markets for your publishing company and plan for your writing team to produce 10 new books. Your corporate financial advisor may see the future differently, and have more expertise and information on which to base projections. But, if you can't get her to review and endorse your plan, you may have trouble selling it to the rest of the company. Also, involving her adds to and strengthens your information base and subsequent decisions.

The next major impact that evaluation has on planning is in the formation of objectives. If objectives can be properly quantified, evaluation becomes, in part, a measure of their achievement. Suppose you were part of a public relations planning team for the client group "Stop AIDS Now." A goal might be: "To maximize public knowledge of SAN and its fight to stop AIDS." Two supporting objectives might be: (1) To produce an information brochure on SAN, its goals, objectives and activities, and distribute it to each SAN staff member and volunteer in the two months before the start of the campaign; and (2) To record and produce 10 PSAs about SAN and its fight against AIDS, telling listeners how they can help, and distribute these PSAs to the five top radio stations in the top-20 radio markets in the nation (one PSA per week to each station for 10 weeks), with the first arriving one week before the campaign starts. There could be several more objectives to support this goal, but these two can let us see the evaluation process.

The success of objective one could be measured in several ways, including judging the quality of the brochure. But a direct approach would be to survey a random sample of SAN staff members and volunteers to see how many got the brochure before the campaign began. If 90 percent or more said "yes," we could call the results "excellent," 80–89 percent could be "good," 70–79 percent "acceptable," and anything less "unsatisfactory."

For objective two, the public affairs directors of the 100 stations could be randomly surveyed to see how many received all PSAs on time. A percentage score similar to that for objective one could be used for evaluation. Note that this rating does not determine whether the PSAs were broadcast, since the objective called for measures of production and delivery. That would be a somewhat better measure, but still not a measure of results.

A final critical planning and programming evaluation procedure is pretesting. It is important to test procedures before applying them, especially those that haven't been used before. The more scientific you can make such tests, the better. Focus groups and surveys are very useful evaluation tools (see chapters 5 and 13). But even if you cannot afford such evaluation research, find ways to pretest. One way is to call on experts.

A simple example shows how important this can be. A campaign for introducing a new product in Japan (a new type of umbrella) called for each person reading promotional material to receive a gift of a child's umbrella in the same style. An expert on Japan, asked to clear it, suggested that the gift would be counterproductive because of the "on," or obligation it places the recipient under. Although the Japanese know that promotional gifts are different from gifts of friendship, the expert suggested that there may still be a feeling of resentment about being placed under an "on" by someone who is not a friend. Because of the expert's advice, the gift idea was dropped.

TABLE 12.1. The Public Relations Writer's Self-Evaluation

1. Readability/listenability:
   A. Best reading grade level for the target public   _____
   B. Computed Flesch/Fang level for this message   _____
   C. Score: difference between A and B above   _____
2. Score 0–10 minus points on writing quality, with 0 being best and 10 the worst.   _____
3. Typographical and spelling errors. Use a computer spelling checker, if possible. Score two minus points for each error, except those for proper nouns.   _____
4. Score 10 minus points for each misspelled proper noun, except the client's name. Score 40 minus points for misspelling the client's name.   _____
5. Score two minus points for each error in grammar, punctuation, abbreviation, capitalization and style.   _____
6. Score two minus points for each improper use of a word (e.g., infer for imply, capital for capitol, stationary for stationery, etc.).   _____
7. Score 10 minus points for each factual error.   _____
8. Score 10 minus points for each stated or implied assumption or premise that is incorrect.   _____
9. Award 0–10 minus points for the weakness with which you made the central idea of the message (0 means you were perfect).   _____
10. Award 40 minus points for each legal flaw or error in the message.   _____
11. Total your minus points for items 1–10.   _____
                                                                                        100
12. Subtract your total minus points (line 11) from 100 to determine your score.   _____

Communication and Other Actions

At this point, you are ready to write, produce and distribute your messages. Each step from now on, merits evaluation in the following ways:

Self Evaluation

You could and should be your toughest critic. However, it's easy to lose objectivity when evaluating your own work. Table 12.1 provides a systematic checklist for self evaluation.

Item 10 of table 12.1, for example, refers to errors with legal consequences and penalties for your client (see chapter 14 for a discussion of such errors). You simply can't make this kind of error and survive.

As a professional, you should score 90 or above on this evaluation to have a successful message. A student writer should score at least 70 points.

TABLE 12.2. Sample Pretest Evaluation Form for Judges

INSTRUCTIONS: Please read the attached proposed public relations message and Part I of this form. Then evaluate the message as requested in Part II. Your evaluation will be averaged with that of four or more other experts.

Part I: To be completed by the writer:

1. Title or subject of work: _____
2. Public it is intended for: _____
3. Channel or medium intended for: _____
4. Planned release date: _____
5. Central idea or purpose: _____

Part II: To be completed by media expert: Please rate each of the following areas on a score of 1–10, with 10 being the highest. If you are unable to rate an area for any reason, write "N/A" in the scoring block.

A. Title (if given)   _____
B. Quality of visual or audio production materials provided with the message   _____

1. Writer's definition of the public   _____
2. How well the intended channel is suited to the desired public and the
   intended message   _____
3. How well the message frames the central idea   _____
4. Accuracy of the facts reported   _____
5. Adequacy of the assumptions made   _____
6. Quality of writing   _____
7. Readability/listenability for chosen public   _____
8. Logical organization of message   _____
9. Technical accuracy (grammar, typos, spelling, abbreviations, capitalization) _____
10. Your overall evaluation of the message   _____
Quality Score (add scores 1–10)   _____
Is the message usable as it is?   Yes ____   No ____
If not, is it usable, accepting your comments?   Yes ____   No ____

Thank you for your evaluation. Please add any comments you care to make in the space below:

Peer Evaluation

Each message should be previewed and evaluated by experts. Table 12.2 is a useful example of such evaluation. Try to get at least five evaluators who are fellow public relations writers, colleagues and cultural experts for each message. It is most convenient for students to use classmates, and for professional writers to ask co-workers for peer evaluations. Writers outside the organization will often cooperate on a *quid pro quo* basis. Expect to score 90 points or above as a professional writer, 70 points or above as a student.

Messages Produced

Too often practitioners use the number of messages produced as a measure of success. It is certainly a measure of effort. If you wrote and produced 100 messages, you did considerable work. Nevertheless, the proper measure in a management-by-objectives approach is not how many messages were produced, but what percentage of those were effective.

Messages Delivered

Messages delivered may not constitute absolute success either, but you are getting closer. What percentage of the messages you planned to deliver actually got delivered? If enough messages are delivered, some will surely be used. This used to be the basis of the "shotgun" approach in public relations. It works to some extent, but is not cost effective. However, it is another useful measure to help determine what went right or wrong. Score yourself on the number of messages delivered on time to planned destinations. You can determine if your messages got delivered by calling the appropriate media contact to check. If your release or tape came back undelivered, you know your media list needs immediate updating.

Messages Placed

Again, you are a step closer to measuring effectiveness if you can determine what percentage of messages delivered were printed or broadcast by the media. You can determine this by calling your media contacts and asking—at the risk of annoying them. Many public relations teams send self-addressed, postage-paid cards with their materials, asking to be told if their message was used, and, if so, when.

Some radio and television stations have a standard "bill" they send for all PSAs used. This notes the dates and times the spot was aired, cites the commercial cost equivalent and says "paid by station X as a public service." However, if you want to be sure, you have to either monitor the media or hire someone to do it for you.

A traditional placement measure compares "column inches." For example, each time a release is published in any way, the result is measured as if it were one standard newspaper column in width. The total column inches from all such publishings then becomes the measure of success.

There are a number of agencies that will clip articles or record mentions about your clients in designated publications or broadcasts. These services are expensive, but useful. The primary measure here, then, might be percentage of delivered messages that were published or broadcast at least once. Secondary measures might be for those aired or printed more than once in a specific media outlet.

Exposure per Message

This measure is more realistic since, all things being equal, the more people are exposed to a message, the greater the chance of it being effective. Potential exposure to all publics is easy to measure. For example, let's say that our message was published in all editions (we have to check to make sure) of a major newspaper with an Audit Bureau of Circulation guaranteed weekday (it's different on Sunday) circulation of one million. If the readership-per-paper is three for that newspaper, that means three million people might have seen our message. But since only about 10 percent of those who read the newspaper probably saw our message, a better estimate is 300,000 readers. That's still very good exposure. When we add that to the probable exposure figures for all other media that used our message, we have a quantifiable estimate of the size of our audience. Exposure computations for the broadcast media are similar, except that audience estimates come from ratings published by agencies such as A. C. Nielsen or Arbitron.

Column-inch Circulation

This is a variation of the exposure rating that combines the amount of coverage with the circulation of the print or market of the broadcast media. For newspapers, that could be measured as: $K \times$ Circ. $\times$ CI. "K" is the measure for readers-per-paper times the percentage of a newspaper a person normally reads (say, $3 \times .10 = .3$). "Circ." would be the confirmed circulation of that paper for the edition in which your release was published. And "CI" would indicate the size of the published story expressed in column inches. Given the above, four column inches published in a 50,000 circulation edition would measure $.3 \times 50,000 \times 4 = 60,000$ units. That measure hasn't much meaning until you can compare it with others made the same way. Then it can become useful.

For broadcasting, the procedure becomes a bit more complicated. In this case, "Circ." would be the market area of the station that is broadcasting the message (say, 500,000 people). "K" would be the "rating" or percentage (say, 12 percent of people watching or listening at the time of broadcast). "CI" can be roughly approximated. A standard column inch with 10-point type contains an average of 30 words. A normal broadcast announcement averages about 150 words per minute. So there are about five column inches in a one-minute broadcast. Each 12 seconds, then, equals a column inch. So CI equals the number of seconds the message was broadcast, divided by 12. Given all this, a 48-second spot could be computed as: $K \times$ Circ. $\times$ CI $= .12 \times 50,000 \times 48/12 = 24,000$ units.

To be more valuable, these figures would need more modification to better evaluate the target audience. Twelve percent of the station's 500,000 viewers, or 60,000 people, may be watching a message about your client. But how many of those are members

TABLE 12.3. Evaluation of Message Exposure

INSTRUCTIONS: Attached are two messages. The first is a copy of a release or other message product as it was delivered to a medium. The second is a copy of the message as it was used by the medium indicated. Please read the release, the published or broadcast message and Part I of this evaluation sheet. Then evaluate the potential of the message for being read, heard or seen and understood by the target audience. Instructions are given for each step. Your evaluations will be averaged with those of at least four other media experts.

Part I: To be completed by the writer:

1. Title or subject of work: _____
2. Public it was intended for: _____
3. Channel or medium using it: _____
4. Intended use date: _____ Actual use date: _____ Edition/Time of use _____
5. Central idea or purpose: _____

Part II: To be completed by media expert. Please rate each of the following areas on a score of 1–10, with 10 being the highest. Your rating should focus on how well the media results meet the writer's purpose and the potential of the media results for being read, heard or seen. If you cannot rate an area for any reason, write "N/A" in the scoring block.

1. Headline or title used by medium _____
2. Quality of visual or audio products used by medium _____
3. Essential elements of the writer's message retained in the published or broadcast message _____
4. Value of the placement (time/location) of the published or broadcast message in reaching the public targeted by the writer _____
5. Accuracy of the published or broadcast message in comparison to the writer's product _____
6. Readability/listenability of published or broadcast message for the desired public _____
7. Quality of writing of the published or broadcast message _____
8. Logical organization of the published or broadcast message _____
9. Technical accuracy of the published or broadcast message (grammar, typos, spelling, abbreviations, word usage) _____
10. Your overall evaluation of the published or broadcast message _____

Potential Score (add scores 1–10) _____

The percentage of the target public that you estimate will actually be exposed to the message _____

Thank you for your evaluation. Please add any comments you may care to make in the space below:

of your target public? If it is a television message asking business-women to act as Big Sisters and is aired at 5 p.m. on a weekday, you probably won't reach more than 10 percent of your audience.

The authors find that averaging media experts' judgments of several meaningful factors is the most valuable measure of potential exposure. It takes time and may not be relevant in all cases, but is good for random checks or special considerations. A format for potential exposure evaluation can be seen in table 12.3.

Message Attention

Those who actually attend to a message represent another step in the chain of writing evaluation. If we knew that people read, heard or saw our message, then it stands to good reason that some of those people will believe the message and act upon it.

We normally attempt to measure reception and understanding together. Sometimes, we also try to measure agreement, retention and action at the same time. But that is much more complex. Finding out who paid attention to the message and understood it is a simple, but often costly procedure.

Existing broadcast measurement systems may incorporate attention and sometimes comprehension questions. The A. C. Nielsen Company uses the "diary" system, where members of a household keep a written log of programs heard or seen. Although useful, this system is biased because those participating may differ from the average person in their listening or viewing habits. Nielsen and the Arbitron Company also measure television viewing through household meters that indicate when a set is on and what channel it is receiving. However, who watched at what time is again written in logs kept by family members.

AGB Television Research's "People Meter" requires each family member to punch a button on a personal console for viewing selections. That information is instantly relayed to central computers for processing. This latter method could be valuable for public relations PSAs, since they are often aired between programs or during public service programs. If you knew when your announcement was aired and could afford the rating data, you could find out precisely which members of your targeted public saw it. Of course, people could punch each other's buttons, but that doesn't appear to happen often (DeFleur and Dennis 1988, 354–355).

Telephone interviews can be used, either during or after a program, to determine what is being or was watched, what was learned from it, and to solicit opinions that might reveal an attitude change. Such interviews and polls are discussed in chapters 5 and 13.

Random surveys may also be used to effectively measure readership (see chapter 13). There are several levels of readership surveys. In the first, an article is shown to a respondent, who is then asked if she or he has seen, or "noted" it. A second level determines if the respondent has read more than half the article. The Daniel Starch method asks the respondent to name the advertiser on ads as a second level, and asks which was read most for a third level. Another level requires "unaided recall," where respondents are asked if they saw or read the latest issue of publication "X." If they did, they are asked which articles they could recall from it.

Understanding

Understanding can be reasonably determined by readability measures (for more about readability, see chapter 7). The traditional measure of determining under-standing is by testing, something students are familiar with. The most systematic test is to randomly select subjects from those who read or heard the message and provide them written questions on it. Generally, a 75 percent average correct response rate indicates a reasonable understanding. This measure is biased in some cases, since those who could not comprehend the message might not be able to understand the questions either. This is overcome by asking the questions verbally in person (most effective) or by phone (most economical) in conjunction with the readership test. It is the method most used to determine actual reader and listener comprehension of messages.

Yielding

How many of your readers yielded to what message? We won't really explore this deeper, more complex factor of attitude change. As noted in chapter 2, attitudes are very difficult to change. But people can comply with your message without changing their attitudes.

Also, not all people who yield to your message will act on it. Indeed, some of the yielding you may ask for can't be tested. Your message may have convinced students to be more accepting of the handicapped. But how could you know that? Short of measuring action, the best way may be by asking. Following political speeches, people are often interviewed to see if their opinions changed and to what extent. Following the U.S. presidential and vice presidential debates in 1988, national surveys were conducted to find out "who won?" These questions were asked in the context of who the respondent favored prior to the debate. Most people who had opinions before a debate did not change their minds. But some who had not yet made up their minds about whom to vote for, moved toward the person they believed to be most effective. You can take similar measures.

You can also get readers or listeners who are not totally convinced to take actions in support of your client. For example, a new product release might provide a telephone number for people who want more information to call. A person who calls may not be convinced, but will probably be leaning your way. Speakers often offer further information on their topics in brochures or other written handouts. Measuring the percentage of those attending who take away brochures with them gives a useful indication of interest. Some who oppose the speaker may take these, but the percentage is small. Information displays often have coupons attached to messages about products or services. Some groups measure the percentage of people who read the message and take a coupon as an indication of yielding. Others measure the number who respond with an "800" telephone call. That doesn't mean they'll buy the product or attend the event or order the service, but any physically supportive act has a generally positive effect.

Retaining

How do you get people to retain your message? Even after being persuaded to act in support of your message, many people simply forget. That may be a measure of the relative importance of the action to them.

a. Repetition. The easiest way to get people to retain messages is through repetition. If you can present the message in a variety of ways through a variety of media, you can maximize retention. As pointed out in chapter 2, however, this can be overdone. Aim for about four repetitions per public. That's hard to guarantee in public relations programs, because only a small portion of the messages ever reach the desired publics, even under ideal circumstances. Using clipping, listening and viewing services, calculate how many times each message reached each public. If the average is less than three, you cannot be confident that your message will be retained.

b. Originality. Assuring retention is also a function of the originality of your message. What unique tactic did you use to make the message memorable? If you came up with "Where's the Beef?" or Joe Isuzu and gave it the repetition and variation advertising did, many people would remember the message. A few public relations campaigns have been equally memorable. Helped by the Ad Council, Smokey the Bear's forest conservation message is not likely to be forgotten.

c. Surveys. Retention can be measured through surveys, in conjunction with readership and other surveys, or through measuring action. Say 100 people read your new product display and picked up postcards through which they could ask for additional information. If 75 of those people send the cards in within the next two weeks, you may assume that your message contributed to this high retention. Sometimes people act immediately after being exposed to your message and thus deny you the opportunity of testing their retention. If their actions support your client, however, you won't mind.

Action

What you ultimately seek, however, is some positive action by the target publics in response to your message. The behavioral change you desire is the acid test of public relations. It implies (but may not necessarily mean) that the other steps have been achieved.

The best measure of positive action is how close you came to achieving the desired objective. For a motorcycle safety campaign in California, an objective might be: "To conceive, create, write, produce and deliver print, video and audio messages sufficient to cause a 20 percent increase in helmet use by motorcyclists in California this year." You can test this systematically by randomly comparing the percentage of cyclists wearing helmets before and after the campaign. If your planning was complete, this procedure would have been projected as an evaluation measure from the beginning.

Your plan should also set what levels below 20 percent would be considered satisfactory. And since the client approved your plan, this measure will be accepted as authentic. Perhaps you agreed that a 15 percent level would be satisfactory. At any rate, if your count shows you achieved the minimum acceptable level, you could be properly proud. The increase would not prove that your campaign was the sole cause for change. Other factors such as weather, religion or war may have contributed to it. Nor could you be sure which message contributed most. But you could be confident that your program had contributed significantly, if helmet wearing had not changed by 20 percent or more during similar periods of time prior to your campaign.

Many desired public relations actions can be **overtly measured:** for example, the number of people attending a neighborhood meeting to discuss a voter initiative you publicized, or the number of people contributing to a charity campaign you organized.

Actions of interest can be **observed indirectly or unobtrusively.** One organization handed out copies of a brochure about itself to all visitors. The brochure had been carefully tested over two years and was believed to be an accurate representation of the organization. The number of brochures handed out each day was recorded and compared to the number found in the trash at the inn where the guests stayed. The premise was that people who were positively impressed by public relations presentations during their visits would not throw such brochures away.

Additionally, we can randomly survey our publics to get their **self-reports** on how successful our campaigns were. After a campaign to get people to eat less cholesterol-producing foods, we could ask respondents: "Do you eat more low cholesterol foods today than you did six months ago?" While people can lie, we generally find a high level of honesty in such responses.

The Bottom Line

Organizational units are continually looking for ways to measure their **contributions to organizational objectives.** These are extremely difficult to do in public relations with any assurance. There are ways, however, in which writers can show how their productivity correlates with success (Tirone 1977, 24–25). If you write for an association, this might be done via a **membership** measure. For example, yearly costs of the association's writing expenses (writers' salaries and benefits, writing equipment, supplies and facilities provided) might be compared to numbers of members in the association for the same period. **Charitable contributions** received by a major charity could be graphed against numbers of message products produced. **Profits** could be compared to average qualitative evaluations of messages by public relations firms. The value of corporate stock could be compared to the quality of annual reports produced. Any combination of these measures might work.

Most writers do not attempt to link writing effectiveness to the bottom line because the organizational bottom line is influenced strongly by many factors beyond writing. But CEOs appreciate quantitative measures. Search for meaningful comparison measures. A word of warning, however: "Don't ask the question if you can't stand the answer." Once you initiate the comparison, it may become standard and you will have to live with it. Be sure you can find two measures that have an influence on one another. Also, be sure it is understood that comparison or correlation does not necessarily mean causation. The quality of writing in your annual report may vary with overall prices in the stock market, but could hardly be expected to have completely caused them.

Evaluation and Redirection

All the best evaluation measures in the world won't work unless they are properly analyzed and acted upon quickly. So, how do you evaluate your evaluation and redirection efforts? The first measure is **how well and completely it was planned and executed.** Did you design, coordinate and write into the plan evaluation procedures for every step of the public relations problem-solving process? Several have been offered in this chapter. It is important that you, your bosses and managers select evaluation measures that you have confidence in and are prepared to measure adequately.

Two, **were your evaluation procedures appropriate for the size of your organization?** For example, if you have only one writer, it will be difficult to correlate writing tasks with profits.

Three, **are the procedures selected ones that you** or others in the organization **can do without hurting the program?**

Four, **are the tests and evaluations integrated smoothly into the organization's functions?** Will they be made objectively and fairly, preferably by members who are not doing the work they are evaluating?

You also must have **a procedure for analyzing evaluations and deciding** what needs to be done next. No matter how efficient your procedure, you will need informed managers to decide its significance and implement changes. There are three basic choices when a program is evaluated: (1) continue as is, (2) continue with specified changes, or (3) terminate the program.

Most organizations appraise ongoing programs at least weekly, usually during regular staff meetings. At such meetings, the project leader briefs management and staff on the status of the project, as well as on specific problems, with supporting evidence from measured evaluations. Then the public relations team makes recommendations. These are discussed by managers and staff. Additional information is requested from the public relations team, if necessary. Finally, the CEO or another manager decides what should be done with the project.

The public relations team bases future action on such decisions. Writers move in to rewrite messages or prepare new ones. Even if the project is to be terminated, there are many public relations actions that need to be taken. Repeated evaluations should be conducted so that the correct decisions can be made and implemented. Writers have a special responsibility to evaluate the impact of their work and be ready to make positive changes.

Chapter Summary

This chapter addressed public relations writing evaluation, why it is important and how one might go about it. It is important to improve current operations and to avoid repeating past mistakes. Evaluation, like other elements of a public relations program, requires advance planning. Well-planned objectives are described as the best vehicles for testing effectiveness.

Conceptually, evaluation was described as the effectiveness of three phases in public relations writing: planning, implementation and impact. Seven steps are proposed to bring writing evaluation from concept to reality: (1) prior agreement on measures, (2) including evaluation in planning, (3) using objectives achievement as measures, (4) keeping records, (5) using results to improve effectiveness, (6) reporting results to management in useful ways, and (7) sharing results with colleagues.

A review of past public relations evaluation showed that most efforts fall into three categories: scientific impact research, informal "seat-of-the-pants" research, and scientific dissemination research. Of these, informal evaluation research predominates.

Stages of the campaign during which writing may be usefully evaluated were viewed and several outcomes noted. This chapter examined writing evaluation in the four traditional public relations problem solving stages: definition and research, planning and programming, communication and other actions, and evaluation and redirection.

Key measurement points in definition and research noted were adequacy of research and accuracy of assumptions. Planning and programming concentrate on prior agreement of measures, involvement of management and staff in evaluation decisions, alignment of measures with objectives, and pretesting.

Evaluation during the implementation stage was categorized into: (1) self-evaluation, (2) peer evaluation, (3) comparison of numbers and types of messages planned with those actually produced and delivered on time, (4) percentage of delivered messages actually printed or aired, (5) exposures per message to all publics and to target publics; percentages of those who received messages who (6) attended, (7) understood, (8) were persuaded, (9) retained the messages, and (10) took the desired actions. Some ways were suggested by which writing effectiveness might be compared with the attainment of overall organizational success goals such as profit, membership and funds raised.

Key points made for the evaluation and redirection phase concerned what was done with the evaluations. Although objective evaluations were emphasized, interpretation was shown to be subjective, requiring experience and judgment. Finally, it was emphasized that findings and analysis must be acted upon and that procedures for analysis and action should be regular functions of organizations depending on public relations writing.

A Writing Exercise

Situation: You are a writer for the National Society for Integrating the Blind, an educational and charitable association dedicated to mainstreaming and normalizing the lives of America's blind citizens. Its president, Dr. Harry Mather, has devoted his life to the society. Both his parents were blind. He has now perfected his life's work, the Radar Analyzed Directed Sound System. RADSS promises to revolutionize life for the blind. Wearing what appear to be normal sun glasses, a hearing aid and a $6'' \times 6'' \times 1''$ RADSS pack, a blind person can walk anywhere at normal speed, using sound signals from the RADSS radar to avoid obstacles.

Mather wants to get the set to 10,000 blind Americans during its first year, and to continue at this pace until all who need it are so equipped. The RADSS packages cost $10,000 each, so the year's target is $100 million. He recognizes the sensitivity of asking for so much, but believes it necessary if his technological breakthrough is to be properly used. He has asked you to plan the writing program. You propose a three-part strategy: (1) direct appeals to those blind persons who can afford to pay the $10,000 for their own RADSS, (2) appeals to families of the blind who are able to fund a RADSS for their relatives, and (3) an appeal to donors to pay for the sets of others. Mather agrees with your strategy, but wants to know how many of what kinds of messages should go to whom. He is also concerned that such a large fund drive might get off track. He asks how you'll know if the program works.

Assignment: Prepare a memo for Mather. Explain what messages will be produced for whom, how they will be delivered and how you will keep a continual evaluation going to assure that messages to the three groups are effective and on target.

Food for Thought

1. Many successful public relations practitioners say that useful evaluation of public relations products is not possible. How would you convince such people that some useful objective evaluations are possible for public relations writing?
2. What are the potential benefits and liabilities of tying public relations writing variables to corporate profits?
3. Which public relations evaluation research do you consider more valuable, formative or summative? Why?
4. What are some steps that you can take to make your writing self-evaluation more objective and valid? Justify each.
5. What five evaluation procedures do you believe would be most effective for a corporate speech writer? Justify each.

References for Further Study

Barlow, Walter, and Carl Kaufman. "Public Relations and Economic Literacy." *Public Relations Review* 1:2 (Summer 1975):143–22.

Caro, Francis G. *Readings in Evaluation Research,* 2nd ed. New York: Russell Sage Foundation, 1977.

Cutlip, Scott M., Allen H. Center and Glen M. Broom. *Effective Public Relations,* 6th ed. Englewood Cliffs, N.J.: Prentice-Hall, 1985.

DeFleur, Melvin L., and Everett E. Dennis. *Understanding Mass Communication,* 3d ed. Boston: Houghton Mifflin, 1988.

Dozier, David M. "Program Evaluation and the Roles of Practitioners." *Public Relations Review* 10:2 (1982):12–32.

Fang, Irving E. "The 'Easy Listening Formula.' " *Journal of Broadcasting* 11 (Winter 1966–1967):63–68.

Foulger, Davis. "A Simplified Flesch Formula." *Journalism Quarterly,* 55 (Spring 1978): 167, 202.

"Measuring the Effectiveness of Public Relations." *Public Relations Review* (Special Issue) 4:4 (Winter 1977).

Merrill, John C., and S. Jack Odell. *Philosophy and Journalism.* New York: Longman, 1983.

Morrisey, George. *Management by Objectives and Results for Business and Industry,* 2nd ed. Reading, Mass.: Addison-Wesley, 1977.

Nager, Norman R., and T. Harrell Allen. *Public Relations Management by Objectives.* New York: Longman, 1984, 167–230.

Pavlik, John V. *Public Relations: What Research Tells Us.* Newbury Park, Calif.: Sage, 1987, 65–69.

Reeves, B. (1983). "Now You See Them, Now You Don't: Demonstrating Effects of Communication Programs." *Public Relations Quarterly* 28:3 (1987):40–55.

Rossi, Peter, and Howard E. Freeman. *Evaluation: A Systematic Approach.* Beverly Hills: Sage, 1982.

Rutman, Leonard. *Planning Useful Evaluations: Evaluability Assessment.* Beverly Hills: Sage, 1980.

Scriven, M. *The Methodology of Evaluation.* Chicago: Rand McNally, 1967.

Struening, Elmer L. and Marilyn B. Brewer, eds. *Handbook of Evaluation Research.* Beverly Hills: Sage, 1983.

Sutton, Sharyn. "Are We Measuring the Right Things?" *PR Week* March 29–April 3, 1988, 9.

Swinehart, James W. "Evaluating Public Relations." *Public Relations Journal* (July 1979): 13–16.

Taylor, Wilson. "Cloze Procedure: A New Tool for Measuring Readability." *Journalism Quarterly* 30: 4(1953):415–433.

Tirone, James F. "Measuring the Bell System's Public Relations." *Public Relations Review* 3: 4(1977):21–38.

Weiss, Carol H. *Evaluating Research: Methods for Assessing Program Effectiveness.* Englewood Cliffs, N.J.: Prentice-Hall, 1972.

Wimmer, Roger D., and Joseph P. Dominick. *Mass Media Research: An Introduction,* 2nd ed. Belmont, Calif.: Wadsworth, 1987, 363–368.

Woods, John L. *Making Rural Development Projects More Effective: A Systems Approach.* Bangkok: United Nations Development Programme, 1982.

P A R T

5

BEYOND THE BASIC MESSAGE:
ADVANCED WRITING STRATEGIES

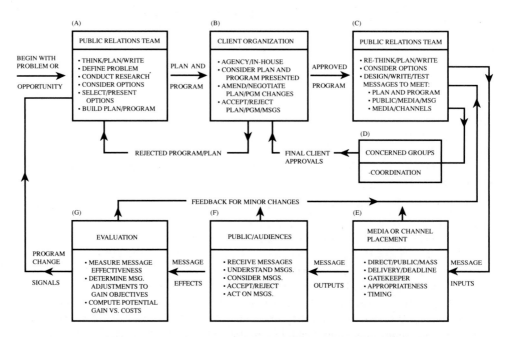

(A)		(B)		(C)
PUBLIC RELATIONS TEAM		**CLIENT ORGANIZATION**		**PUBLIC RELATIONS TEAM**

BEGIN WITH PROBLEM OR

OPPORTUNITY

(A) PUBLIC RELATIONS TEAM
- THINK/PLAN/WRITE
- DEFINE PROBLEM
- CONDUCT RESEARCH
- CONSIDER OPTIONS
- SELECT/PRESENT OPTIONS
- BUILD PLAN/PROGRAM

PLAN AND

PROGRAM

(B) CLIENT ORGANIZATION
- AGENCY/IN-HOUSE
- CONSIDER PLAN AND PROGRAM PRESENTED
- AMEND/NEGOTIATE PLAN/PGM CHANGES
- ACCEPT/REJECT PLAN/PGM/MSGS

APPROVED

PROGRAM

(C) PUBLIC RELATIONS TEAM
- RE-THINK/PLAN/WRITE
- CONSIDER OPTIONS
- DESIGN/WRITE/TEST MESSAGES TO MEET:
  - PLAN AND PROGRAM
  - PUBLIC/MEDIA/MSG
  - MEDIA/CHANNELS

REJECTED PROGRAM/PLAN

FINAL CLIENT APPROVALS

(D) CONCERNED GROUPS

-COORDINATION

FEEDBACK FOR MINOR CHANGES

(G) EVALUATION

PROGRAM CHANGE

SIGNALS

- MEASURE MESSAGE EFFECTIVENESS
- DETERMINE MSG. ADJUSTMENTS TO GAIN OBJECTIVES
- COMPUTE POTENTIAL GAIN VS. COSTS

MESSAGE

EFFECTS

(F) PUBLIC/AUDIENCES
- RECEIVE MESSAGES
- UNDERSTAND MSGS.
- CONSIDER MSGS.
- ACCEPT/REJECT
- ACT ON MSGS.

MESSAGE

OUTPUTS

(E) MEDIA OR CHANNEL PLACEMENT
- DIRECT/PUBLIC/MASS
- DELIVERY/DEADLINE
- GATEKEEPER
- APPROPRIATENESS
- TIMING

MESSAGE

INPUTS

Experiments and surveys are research techniques writers for public relations sometimes undertake. More often, however, writers are required to review such research, analyze it and interpret it objectively for concerned publics. This calls for a sophisticated knowledge of survey and experimental techniques, as well as the ability to explain complex issues simply and directly.

SURVEYS AND EXPERIMENTS
IN PUBLIC RELATIONS WRITING

Introduction

Let's start with a story. Scott Fagerstrom, a reporter for *The Orange County Register,* had this to write a couple of weeks before Pope John Paul II's 1987 visit to Los Angeles:

> Pope John Paul II's upcoming visit to Southern California will be: (A) a colossal waste of money, or (B) a pretty good deal.
>
> It depends on which Catholic is doing the calculating.
>
> Top church authorities say the pope's Sept. 15–16 Los Angeles stop will cost as much as $3 million. The pope will be here 47 hours, which means the visit should cost about $62,830 an hour—including the hours he's asleep.
>
> "That's crazy," said Rio Parfrey, founder of a new Catholic worker shelter and soup kitchen for the poor in downtown Santa Ana. "If the pope's visit could be cut by only one hour, that money could keep the center open for years," she said.
>
> "With all the hurting, hungry people around, spending $62,830 an hour for the pope and his entourage to visit California boggles my mind," she said.
>
> Considering the four million Catholics in Southern California, though, the cost of next month's papal visit—about 75 cents per Catholic—is a bargain, said the Most Rev. Norman McFarland, bishop of the Diocese of Orange. In any given two-day period, Californians may spend more just for beer, he said. (*The Orange County Register,* August 30, 1987, A3).

A PROFESSIONAL TIP:
Know Your Audience

The final test: Does what's written communicate or motivate effectively? The first questions: Who is your target audience? What do you want them to do, believe or know? What issues, interests and values do they bring to your subject? What's their education level? Where and how are they likely to encounter what's written? All that affects content, structure, vocabulary, style and your point of departure. You can use formal research to test the audience reaction and response—or just find a tough reader and don't debate the feedback. But before writing a word, research, understand and develop an empathy for the audience; then be your own relentless, lifetime critic.

Betsy Plank, APR, past president of the Public Relations Society of America, former agency executive and assistant vice president of corporate communications, Illinois Bell, is a public relations consultant.

Who's right? A coherent answer to this dilemma rests on a knowledge of statistics, of populations and samples and of research in general. Before the terms frighten you, try to think about statistics as information mostly in the shape of numbers and research as an intelligent way of discovering, interpreting and using this information.

We'll let you figure the answer to Fagerstrom's question after you have read this chapter.

As discussed in chapters 4, 5 and 12, and depicted in block A of figure 2.1, public relations writers are affected by research in three ways:

1. They may use it to find out about their *publics*, how it thinks and feels and how much it knows about a topic the writers are interested in communicating about. Public relations practitioner Betsy Plank sums up this aspect of research nicely in her Professional Tip above.

For example, you may be interested in writing a PSA to get mothers to have their children fingerprinted for safety reasons (case noted in chapter 8). But you don't know what appeal to use.

Rather than depend on intuition, you ask the mothers in your audience about their feelings regarding fingerprinting. During the investigation, you discover that many mothers like the idea but are worried that the fingerprinting ink may be toxic. You change the direction of your research, this time to find out from the police if the inks are toxic. You talk to police officers from several precincts. The answer everywhere is no. Now you not only know what your public's concern is, but you know what your message is going to be. You also have used a common research method, namely a survey, to solve your problem.

2. They may use research not only for audience understanding and message development, but also to evaluate the content and impact of the messages they write. The readability formulas discussed in chapter 7 are public relations writers' research devices that fall into this category.

3. In addition, topics they write about, media distribution, the source and the message may all involve research and statistics. An example of this is when writers have to report and explain the results of an employee survey to their audiences.

Understanding has to precede application. Our objective in this chapter is to help you understand the terms and concepts of research so that you may be able to understand and apply them to your writing projects.

Types of Research

Research is a systematic and reliable way of asking questions and getting answers. The question addressed by this section is: In what types of settings can research investigations take place?

Public relations writers can use one of four formal research settings to ask their questions. These are:

1. Experiment, in which people are questioned and observed, and answers sought in an artificial and tightly-controlled environment.

2. Field research, where the researcher observes people in their natural environment. For example, a public relations writer who has been asked to write a feature on how people communicate, may observe employees conversing in the lunch room, or around the water fountain.

3. Unobtrusive or nonreactive research (Babbie 1986, 266). All of the library research discussed in chapter 4, as well as some field research, falls into this category.

4. Survey, where the writer obtains information by administering some form of a questionnaire to or interviewing (also see chapter 5 for personal interviews) large numbers of people in real-world settings.

This chapter focuses on the usefulness of surveys and experiments as research tools for the public relations writer.

The Survey and Public Relations Writing

Public relations writers use surveys for public relations audit purposes, i.e., to find out about the opinions, attitudes and information needs and expectations of a variety of publics.

Survey research, like any other research approach, has its own strengths and weaknesses. Among its strengths are:

1. **Its ability to explain the characteristics (attitudes, behaviors, needs, expectations) of large populations fairly accurately.**
2. **Its ability to tap multiple rather than single issues via questionnaires.**

Its weakness is an inability to tell the public relations writer about the context or "total life situation in which respondents (the people the writer is interested in) are thinking and acting" (Babbie 1986, 232), as field research can.

Types of Surveys

There are three main types of surveys: mail surveys, telephone surveys and personal interview surveys.

Mail Surveys

Here, information is gathered by mailing questionnaires to large numbers of people called **respondents.** The respondents then complete these questionnaires in the privacy of their homes or other places. Researchers usually enclose a self-addressed, stamped envelope that the respondents can use to mail the questionnaires back.

Mail surveys are advantageous because:

1. **They allow the researcher to collect information from large numbers of people scattered over a wide geographic area.**
2. **They assure respondents of anonymity, thus encouraging them to complete and mail the questionnaire back, especially if the questions asked are about a sensitive subject.**
3. **They are relatively inexpensive.**

Mail surveys, however, are not without their disadvantages:

1. **Often they are only as good as the researchers' mailing lists.** If lists are incomplete, outdated or inaccurate, chances are you will never be able to reach many of the people you are interested in.
2. **They have to compete with other mail people get.** Thus, the chances of questionnaires getting tossed or placed aside are very good. Because of this, mail surveys suffer from a low response rate. Usually, between 20–40 percent of the people surveyed mail completed questionnaires back to the researcher.

3. They may be stopped by bureaucratic screens. In some cases, people other than the ones you are interested in may complete the questionnaire. This is often true of corporate executives, who may assign the task of completing questionnaires they receive to juniors, assistants and secretaries (Wimmer and Dominick 1987, 122).

You can improve response rates of mail surveys by:

1. **Including a self-addressed and stamped envelope.**
2. **Offering inducements.**
3. **Attractively packaging the questionnaire.**
4. **Keeping the questionnaires short, clear and understandable.** People get impatient with, and toss out, long and confusing questionnaires.
5. **Sending follow-up cards to those who do not return your questionnaires.** This gives you a chance to offer to send the respondent another questionnaire should it be lost or misplaced.

Telephone Surveys

In this type of survey, questions are asked over the telephone. Telephone surveys are able to cover as much ground as mail surveys. They are, however, often more expensive than mail surveys because of the costs in long distance telephone rates and training telephone interviewers. They also force respondents to make spot decisions about whether they want to participate in the survey or not. Depending upon the subject, this may or may not work to the advantage of the researcher.

Telephone surveys can be made to work by:

1. Keeping the telephone questions (and the interview itself) **simple, short and uncluttered.**
2. Training interviewers to be **polite, nonjudgmental, impartial and faithful** to the text of the questionnaire.
3. **Offering to call back** at another and more convenient time if the respondent is engaged in some other activity.
4. **Being considerate** to respondents and not disturbing them late at night, early in the morning or during dinner time.

Personal Interview Surveys

This involves sending trained interviewers from door to door, collecting information from people. Of the three survey types, this is the most expensive. Labor, transportation and interviewer training costs can be prohibitive if the information is being gathered from large numbers of people who are geographically dispersed.

Typically, two types of strategies are employed in personal interviews. The first is the **unstructured interview** (see chapter 5 for more on this), in which the interviewers ask broad questions and have the liberty to follow up on leads which may arise during the interview. The second is the **structured interview,** where the interviewer is required to stick to a questionnaire.

Despite the costs, surveys using personal interviews can be rewarding. They permit the researcher (or the interviewer) a chance to use visual and other aids, be flexible when necessary and observe and record the environment in which the interview is conducted. Thus, properly used, personal interviews can yield rich data for the researcher.

Samples and Sample Selection

The next two questions, and ones related to the issue of setting, are: to what public or publics must the researcher's questions be directed and how many people must respond in order to get reliable results? This concern directly leads the public relations writer-researcher to issues of sampling.

Population

The publics the writer-researchers are seeking to examine are determined by the questions they want answers to. For example, if the research issue of interest is, how many employees in Company X read the contents of the company's newsletter, then the public of interest is "all employees of Company X." In research jargon, this public—consisting of all of the people the researcher is interested in studying—is called a **study population.** The people who belong to a population are known as its **elements.**

When researchers measure, observe or talk to everyone in a population, they are said to be taking a census. Census-taking would occur if the writer-researcher asked all employees of Company X whether or not they read the company newsletter.

Taking a census is easy enough if the population is limited, as is the case with the employee populations of most companies. But what about conducting a census in a company such as General Motors that has several hundred thousand employees worldwide? Given the costs of survey research, census-taking in such situations becomes unreasonably costly and time consuming.

Fortunately, there is a way of studying populations without examining every member of that population—**sampling.**

Sampling

This is a procedure whereby the researcher is able to infer about the opinions, attitudes, needs and expectations of the study population by examining or sampling some of its members or elements.

To be able to infer the characteristics of a population from a sample, researchers have to be sure that the sample mirrors its parent in important respects. They achieve this by paying attention to two characteristics of the sample—sample size and sample representativeness.

Sample Size

How large should a sample be in order to accurately portray its parent population? In theory, the larger the sample size, the more closely it begins to resemble the parent population. In other words, the larger the sample, the closer the correspondence between what is observed in the sample and what could be observed in the population (if a census were taken). Thus, the larger the sample, the less error-prone your observations are likely to be. This notion is subsumed under the concept of sampling error, which is the range of error your actual findings could be prone to.

Sampling error can be calculated using the formula:

$$se = \sqrt{\frac{p(q)}{n}}$$

where *p* = an observation of interest
***q* = (100-p), and**
***n* is the sample size**

Let's assume you have a feeling that nobody reads the newsletter you so painstakingly put out week after week. So you decide to run a survey among company employees. The question is: "Do you (the employees) think that we should do away with the newsletter? Yes or no?" Your company has 10,000 employees, but you decide to question (or sample) only 500 of them. The surveys come back. Sixty percent of those surveyed say the newsletter should be done away with. This is your *p,* or observation of interest. No response can ever exceed 100 percent. So, if 60 percent of those employees surveyed wanted the newsletter done away with, (100–60) or 40 percent of the employees didn't. This is your *q.*

Plugging the figures into the formula:

$$se = \sqrt{\frac{60(40)}{500}} = \sqrt{\frac{2,400}{500}} = \sqrt{4.8} = 2.19\%$$

The sampling error of your finding that 60 percent of the employees want to do away with the newsletter is ± 2.19. That is to say, the percentage of employees who actually wanted the newsletter done away with could be anywhere between 57.81 percent $(60 - 2.19)$ and 62.19 percent $(60 + 2.19)$.

Sampling error is directly related to sample size. The larger the sample, the smaller the sampling error, and the greater your confidence in your findings. The following are sampling errors for the newsletter survey based on different sample sizes:

Sample Size	Sampling Error $\pm\%$
10	15.49
50	6.93
100	4.90
500	2.19
1,000	1.55
2,000	1.10
5,000	0.69
10,000	0.49

The gains in accuracy, as one goes beyond a sample size of 500, are rarely sufficient in communication research to justify the extra costs of surveying additional people. Most national polls reported by newspapers and television rarely have sample sizes of more than about 1,600 people to represent 249 million Americans. For this reason, you can be confident that your findings from a sample of 500 employees fairly accurately reflect the feelings of 10,000 employees in the above newsletter example.

When poll results are reported in newspapers or on television, one other piece of information related to sampling error is mentioned. This is the **confidence level,** which is usually reported as a percentage. Thus, if the "should-the-newsletter-be-dumped" study reported a confidence level of 95 percent, it would be claiming that if it repeated the same study on the same size sample 100 times, the sampling error 95 times out of the 100 would be 2.19. In other words, you would be 95 percent certain about the margin of error of your findings.

Table 13.1 demonstrates how the public relations writer can interpret and explain sampling error and confidence level. Note how the 95 percent confidence level is written as "in 19 cases out of 20 . . ."

Sample Representativeness

Sampling theory not only requires that you have sufficient numbers of people in your sample, but that these people be representative of the sampled population. The sample should contain all of the characteristics of the parent population in similar proportions.

Sampling representatives can be ensured by the manner in which decisions are made as to whom from a given population can or cannot be included in the sample.

Nonprobability Samples

Two broad types of sampling procedures are available to the writer-researcher. The first of these is the nonprobability procedure in which sample decisions are based on **convenience** (whoever is available), your own **judgment** or the judgment of experts, or

TABLE 13.1. Reporting Polls

How the Poll was Conducted
The New York Times

The New York Times survey of delegates to the Republican National Convention involved telephone interviews conducted July 22 through August 4 with 739 randomly selected delegates. The sample was drawn from the list of 2,277 total delegates to the Republican convention.

The New York Times survey of Democratic delegates, which was taken before their convention, involved telephone interviews conducted from June 20 through July 12 with 1,059 randomly selected delegates.

The sample was drawn from the list of 4,203 total delegates to the Democratic convention.

In some cases, public officials answered the survey through their spokesmen.

In theory, in 19 cases out of 20, results based on such samples will differ by no more than plus or minus 3 percentage points from what would have been obtained by interviewing all the delegates to each party's convention.

The potential sampling error for smaller subgroups can be larger.

---

the need to meet some **quota** based on prespecified characteristics or your prior knowledge of the population. Samples selected through such procedures are called convenience, judgment and quota samples respectively.

Nonprobability samples are not based on universally accepted selection principles. They may be haphazard, expedient and biased by the researcher's own haste or whims. Above all, as the term nonprobability suggests, such sampling procedures do not give every person in or every characteristic of a population an equal chance to be included in the sample. Also, sampling error cannot be calculated in nonprobability samples, thereby diminishing confidence in the sample's representativeness. Therefore, nonprobability samples should be approached with caution, since we cannot infer that sample results apply to the population.

Probability Samples

By contrast, probability samples are chosen in accordance with universally accepted principles of chance. They are designed to free the sample from the particular biases of the researcher and give every person in a population an equal and known chance of being included.

There are several probability sampling techniques that the writer-researcher should know about.

Simple Random Sample

Such samples may be chosen via a table of random numbers and involve several steps. The first step is to obtain a master list of all the subjects in the population you are interested in (usually, some group of people). Such a list is called a **sampling frame.** Class rosters and employee lists are examples of sampling frames.

The next step would be to assign a number to each person in the sampling frame. Let's assume that you have 44 employees who are listed in your company roster in alphabetical order. Also assume that you want to pull a sample of five people out of this sampling frame. Give each person a number, thus:

1. Apple, David
2. Biddle, Joe
3. Brookfield, Peter
  . .
  . .
  . .

44. Zinger, Zoe

Select a random numbers table. This is merely a table containing numbers randomly generated by a computer and whose occurrence cannot be predicted by any mathematical formula (Ray and Ravizza 1988, 136). The following is part of such a table:

29820	96783	29400	21840	15035	34537
02050	89728	17937	37621	47075	42080
83197	33732	05810	24813	86902	60397
99324	51281	**84463**	60563	79312	93454

Next, close your eyes and choose a random starting point. Assume that your finger falls on the number 84463. Since you don't have more than 44 employees, use only the last two digits in each number. From the random starting point, move in any predetermined direction across the page. Say you are going to read up the page. Sixty-three doesn't count because it is a number greater than 44. Ignore it and move to the next number. Ten falls within 44, so pick the 10th person on your list as the first member of your sample. Move up another number. Thirty-seven is also a valid number. Pick the 37th person on your list to be the second member of your sample. Keep moving in this fashion until you have selected your sample of five.

A version of this procedure called the random digit dialing method is commonly used for telephone surveys. The sampling frames are provided by the telephone directories. The usual practice is to have a computer randomly generate the last four digits of a telephone number. A computer can also be used to provide random numbers individually to simplify the above procedure.

Telephone directories are not complete sampling frames, since all phone numbers may not be listed and some people do not have telephones. Therefore, you should be cautious about using them.

Systematic Random Sample

If you do not want to bother using a random numbers table, you may want to consider a systematic random sampling procedure. Three steps are needed. The first is to obtain a sampling frame or list of the population you are interested in surveying. Let's keep the sampling frame of the 44 employees we used earlier to examine the simple random sample.

Next calculate the **sampling interval.** For this, you need two pieces of information—the sample size you desire and the size of the sampling frame. In this case, assume that you need a sample size of 11 out of a sampling frame of 44.

$$\text{Sampling Interval (SI)} \quad = \quad \frac{\textbf{Population Size}}{\textbf{Sample Size}}$$

$$\text{SI} \quad = \quad \frac{44}{11}$$

$$\text{SI} \quad = \quad 4$$

Now, closing your eyes again, randomly pick the first name from the sampling frame or list. Then, moving up or down the list, pick every **fourth** person until you have your sample of 11 employees.

Stratified Sample

Most real world populations contain subgroups that researchers may want represented proportionately in your sample. If this is your objective, then you may need a stratified sampling procedure.

Essentially, this involves breaking up your population into homogeneous subgroups, and sampling from these. The process of breaking down populations into subgroups is called **stratification.** Populations can be stratified on the basis of any number of conditions, including gender, position in a hierarchy, occupation or college class. While using this sampling procedure, the researcher must ensure that the sample contains the same proportion of elements from the subgroup as does the population.

For example, you wish to stratify your sample on the basis of corporate hierarchy and senior managers account for two percent of the employee population. Also assume that you wish to draw a sample of 1,000 employees. The same proportion of senior managers should be present in your sample, i.e., two percent, or 20, managers.

Types of Questions

Having decided on the sample, writer-researchers need to figure out what kinds of questions to ask of the people in the sample. They have a choice of four basic types of questions. These are: nominal questions, ordinal questions, interval questions and ratio questions.

Nominal Questions

These are questions that are designed to break the sample down into exclusive categories the researcher is interested in. All demographic questions, or questions aimed at finding out information such as a person's gender, race, political affiliation and religion, fall into this category.

When you set up the response categories for a nominal question, i.e., the boxes you want people to place themselves in, make sure these are both **exhaustive** and **mutually exclusive**. By exhaustive, we mean that you should be able to list all possible response categories within a characteristic you are interested in measuring. If there are too many categories, you are allowed to list the major ones and follow it up with an "other" box. For example, all ethnic origins in a group could be determined by this question:

Q. Please indicate your ethnic origin.
[ ] **Black**
[ ] **Hispanic**
[ ] **American Indian or Alaskan native**
[ ] **Caucasian**
[ ] **Asian**
[ ] **Other**

By mutual exclusivity, we mean that you should not give your respondents a chance to place themselves in more than one category. Take this **incorrect** example:

Q. Please indicate your income.
[ ] **$10,000 or less**
[ ] **$10,000 to $20,000**
[ ] **$20,000 to $30,000**
[ ] **$30,000 or more**

The categories that go with this question are exhaustive. Your respondents would be able to place themselves in some category. In fact, some people may be able to place themselves in two categories. For example, people earning $20,000 could place themselves either in the second or third boxes, thereby destroying the integrity of your classification. You could solve this problem by structuring the categories slightly differently, as in this **correct** example:

Q. Please indicate your income.
[ ] **$10,000 or less**
[ ] **$10,001 to $20,000**
[ ] **$20,001 to $30,000**
[ ] **$30,001 or more**

Now you have mutually exclusive categories that you can productively work from.

Ordinal Questions

These are questions offering answer choices that can be ordered or ranked in a logical way. They are commonly used to measure the strength of people's attitudes about a variety of issues. Ordinal questions with the answer categories of "strongly agree," "agree," "disagree," "strongly disagree" and "undecided" are called Likert-type scales or questions:

Beside each of the statements presented below, please indicate whether you Strongly Agree (SA), Agree (A), Disagree (D), Strongly Disagree (SD) or Have No Opinion (N).

	SA	A	D	SD	N
a. I'm happy with my job.	[ ]	[ ]	[ ]	[ ]	[ ]
b. I enjoy the respect of my fellow workers.	[ ]	[ ]	[ ]	[ ]	[ ]
c. People care about my opinions in this company.	[ ]	[ ]	[ ]	[ ]	[ ]

When several Likert-type questions are arranged in the form of statements, as in the above example, the arrangement is called a **matrix question.**

A second type of ordinal question is the **semantic differential.** It is used to evaluate meaning and is useful for testing communication messages or formats. You might test the content of a PSA script you wrote using the semantic differential thus:

Listed below are several pairs of opposite words or phrases with the numbers 1 to 7. For each pair, please indicate the number which best describes your reaction to the message.

Too short	1	2	3	4	5	6	7	**Too long**
Discouraging	1	2	3	4	5	6	7	**Encouraging**
Comforting	1	2	3	4	5	6	7	**Alarming**
Well done	1	2	3	4	5	6	7	**Poorly done**
Not informative	1	2	3	4	5	6	7	**Informative**

Interval Questions

These resemble ordinal questions, except that the scales the answers are made on are assumed to have known intervals, but not a true zero point. For example, if you were measuring room temperature, you would use a thermometer. The temperature points on the thermometer are set equally apart. However, a thermometer does not have a true zero point because temperature exists even at zero degrees.

IQ is another example of an interval scale. Its midpoint is 115 and an evolution to a higher or lesser IQ is presumed to take place every 15 points on either side of this midpoint. But there is no true zero, so one cannot argue that a person with an IQ of 80 is exactly half as intelligent as a person with an IQ of 160.

Ratio Questions

These are questions to which answers have known and equal intervals and true zero points, thereby allowing comparisons. Such questions may be used by the writer-researcher to find answers to questions such as how much time members of an audience spend reading newspapers, watching television or listening to radio. Example:

> **Q. On the average, how many hours a day do you spend watching television? (Specify the actual time spent to the closest hour.) The answers could range between zero (don't watch at all) and 24 hours.**
>
> **0   1   2   3   4   5   6   7   8   9 . . . 24**

Because there is a true zero point on this scale of "0" hours, we are able to say that a person watching four hours of television spends twice as much time with it as does a person watching two hours.

Guidelines for Developing Questions

The quality of answers you get from people generally depends on the quality of the questions you ask them. Here are some guidelines for developing and asking intelligent questions.

   1. Keep it simple, short and clear. Long, tedious and confusing questions try people's patience and keep them from completing your survey. You can achieve simplicity, brevity and clarity by keeping the language at the level of the respondent and by restricting each question to one idea. When you include more than one idea in a question, you run the risk of posing a **double-barreled question.** Such questions are fruitless and leave you to wonder which part of the question the person's answer was meant for. This is an example of a double-barreled question.

> **Do you read newspapers or watch television?**
> **Yes** _____
> **No** _____

   2. Avoid using biased or loaded words in your questions. These are words that have connotations beyond the scope of your line of questioning and "encourage respondents to answer in a particular way" (Babbie 1986, 132). Table 13.2 shows how changing the loaded word "welfare" to the more benign "assistance to the poor" affects the results. About the Clinton Reilly poll's use of the words "guaranteed benefits" and "state regulation":

> **Those are fighting words to Babbie, who said that a term like "guaranteed benefits" is guaranteed to get a positive response, while "government regulation" is a proven turnoff.**

The other survey, the California Poll, took its wording from the state's ballot pamphlet, Babbie said.

The difference in results was dramatic. The no-fault campaign found its initiative winning. The California Poll showed it losing (Kalfus 1988, A1).

3. People have fragile egos: Don't bully them by being unnecessarily blunt (Miller 1978, 75), offensive and insensitive.

4. Avoid using negative terms (Babbie 1986, 129). Unless you determine that it is absolutely necessary, purge negative terms from your questions. If you are after unpleasant orientations (What don't you like about the job?), "give your respondents a chance to express positive feelings" by asking them what they like about the job (Miller 1978, 75).

Survey research has become a frequently used source of information for public relations writers and journalists. Less common, yet, nevertheless important to understand, is experimental research.

The Experiment and Public Relations Writing

Experimental research is valuable to public relations writers. It allows them to explain and predict communication effects with a high degree of confidence. Experimentation is expensive, technically complex and time consuming, thus rarely done by the public relations writer. But you will undoubtedly be expected to contract and oversee experimental research when your client organization needs it to support writing assignments. And you will frequently be called upon to read, analyze and report on the results of experiments and other important research by others in your organization.

Defining the Experiment

An experiment is **a research process which allows us to compare two or more roughly equivalent groups of subjects after having exposed one of these groups to some unique condition.**

The groups are usually drawn from the same population. For example, you might give each person in a group a number and then use a random drawing of numbers to assign each person to one group or the other.

The two groups are called the "control" and "experimental" groups. The control group is used as the basis for comparison. It is measured without receiving the experimental treatment. The experimental group is submitted to some unique stimulus which the control group is not. Actually, there could be more than one experimental group but that would not change the basic procedure.

TABLE 13.2. Poll Wording

The way a question is worded can affect a poll's results.

Example:
  Subject: Welfare
  Q. "Are we spending too much, too little or about the right amount on welfare?"
  A. Too little: 23.6 percent
  Q. "Are we spending too much, too little or about the right amount on assistance to the poor?"
  A. Too little: 69.5 percent
  Source: 1988 Survey by the National Opinion Research Center of the University of Chicago.

Subject: Auto Insurance Proposition 103

Clinton Reilly's poll:
Q. "Still another initiative on the November ballot, Prop. 103, sponsored by a group called Voter Revolt and Ralph Nader, would establish state regulation of the insurance industry."
YES 37 percent
NO 32 percent
UNDECIDED 31 percent

Mervin Field's poll:

Q. "Would reduce auto and other property and casualty insurance rates. Requires an elected insurance commissioner's approval of rates and prohibits price fixing and discrimination. (Sponsored by consumer groups and Ralph Nader)"
YES 74 percent
NO 12 percent
UNDECIDED 14 percent

Subject: Auto Insurance Proposition 104

Clinton Reilly's poll:
Q. "Another initiative on the November ballot, Prop. 104, sponsored by California insurance companies, would establish no-fault auto insurance under which guaranteed benefits are paid to auto accident victims by their own insurance company, regardless of fault."
YES 37 percent
NO 33 percent
UNDECIDED 30 percent

Mervin Field's poll:

Q. "Would establish no-fault insurance for automobile accidents. Reduces rates for two years and restricts future regulation. (Sponsored by California insurance companies)"
Yes 28 percent
NO 50 percent
UNDECIDED 22 percent

Source: Clinton Reilly Campaigns, The California Poll.
(Reilly's results are from a 1,000-sample survey conducted from Sept. 11 to Sept. 15.
Field's poll was conducted among 773 registered voters between Sept. 6 and 13.)

After the experimental group has received its special treatment, both groups are measured on some outcome variable the researcher is interested in. Results of the measures are then compared. If the experiment has been properly controlled and is free of other influences, we may presume that the changed variable caused the difference in measures. If the groups measured were randomly selected, sufficiently large and representative of a larger population, we could then infer that similar results would occur using the same treatment on other segments of the same population.

Let's consider a simple example. Suppose you want to know whether the students of your 2,000-member department of communication are influenced by a writer's status or position when they evaluate a piece of writing. You get a list of all students in the department and have a computer program randomly select 500. Sample size is very important, as we have seen earlier. For now, let's accept that 500 is an adequate sample size. You get all 500 of them to gather in one place on a given date at a given time.

Your computer program has also randomly divided the 500 into two equal groups. Each group is given the same essay to read, with one exception. The control group's copies show the writer as "T. Hardy, an English student at King's College, London." The experimental group's essays are said to be written by "T. Hardy, dean of King's College School of English Studies and president of the Universal Society of English Scholars." After reading the essays, members of both groups are asked to rank the two authors in a questionnaire designed to evaluate source credibility. If there are statistically significant differences between the average rank given to T. Hardy, the dean, and T. Hardy, the student, by the two groups, you may infer that the status of the source influences evaluation of source credibility for students in your department.

The key value of the experiment is that it allows the researcher to look at cause-and-effect relationships. It is the only research approach which allows the researcher (and subsequently the writer) to say that one activity is the major cause of a certain outcome. Because of experimental research results, we can say with some certainty, for example, that corporate advertising can change people's beliefs about a company (Grass 1977, 39–50).

Guidelines for Writing about Experiments

Public relations writers report on experiments using the same basic rules they use for all writing. The message must be tailored for a specific public via the medium being used. Writing must be clear and comprehensible, attention-grabbing and interesting. It must assume that the reader has little knowledge in most cases. But, as before, assume equal intelligence. All you have learned about writing for public relations applies to writing about experimental research. But there are a few issues that deserve special consideration.

You must assist readers in evaluating the research presented, because they may not be familiar with its norms. For example, if an experiment used a significance level of 0.10, you would want to point out that the lowest level normally used in research is 0.05. That is, you would accept the results of an experiment if it was rigorous enough to produce the same outcome 95 times out of 100 (significance = 0.05), rather than the less rigorous 90 times out of 100 (significance = 0.10). Sometimes interpretations of results are not made clearly. An experiment might show that public relations is three percent more effective in getting across a message than is advertising. But if the experiment's margin of error is $+/-5$ percent, you may need to inform the reader that statistically there is no difference in the effectiveness of public relations and advertising, based on the results.

It is important to either remove or explain terms with which your readers may not be familiar. As noted in this chapter and others, words such as sample, population and respondent have precise meanings in research. It is not necessary to go into technical explanations that will be of little use to the reader. Instead, use lay terms. For example, you might categorize the *chi-square* test as a mathematical measure used to determine whether differences between groups are accidental or mean the groups are truly different.

Try to work as much as possible using the body of knowledge which you and the reader have in common. A reader who may be confused by the "null hypothesis" (the hypothesis that suggests there is no relationship between the variables or groups being studied) should have no trouble in understanding that if two groups are alike, then any averages of their characteristics should be similar. Some who might need an explanation of "the mean" probably understand the concept of "average" very well.

Experiments, like other scientific research, attempt to find answers to problems for which no answers exist, to solve problems that have not previously been solved or to confirm answers we know intuitively to be true. Make sure the experiment's purpose is clear, whether its hypothesis is supported or not. The research hypothesis may be a bit too formal for the writing style you are using. But you should state very clearly its essence so the reader can understand exactly what the experimenter was trying to prove. Using the study's general research questions, rather than the specific working hypothesis, is often effective.

Hypothesis: With all other factors controlled for, students listening to a research lecture delivered at 180 words per minute will give it a higher credibility rating than they will for the same lecture delivered at 120 words per minute.

Research Question: Does the speed of delivery of a speech affect the credibility of the speaker?

An experiment is a special kind of research. Make certain the reader understands what constitute the experimental and control groups, what treatment is being applied to each and what independent variable is being manipulated for its effect on what dependent variable.

Obviously, you will want to announce the results, but it's not necessary to use research terminology. Instead of saying, "We may reject the null hypothesis," you might say, "Results showed a greater information gain among those receiving the video message than among those receiving the print message."

What does it all mean? One of the great strengths of experimental research is that it allows one to be reasonably certain that a change in one variable caused a change in another. How that knowledge can be applied depends on the experimenter's discussion and conclusions and the writer's research. If video message transmission enhances understanding for 11th graders, might it not do so for all high school students? How can this knowledge be applied in other situations? If it works for AIDS, might it not also work for drugs? Discussing possible implications is very useful but the writer must be careful. A common error in general news reporting on scientific studies is the writer's penchant for making inferences not justified by research findings. If you are in doubt, get experts to help you make the proper interpretation.

Interpreting and Reporting Research

Readers of reports on survey and experimental research generally use the information either to gain knowledge and understanding about a field in which they have interest or to apply the findings to some interests of their own. Since one of the aims of research is to increase knowledge, public relations writers attempt to achieve it by presenting all the useful information in understandable and interesting reports. Although the basics of public relations writing remain the same in each type of writing approach, there are some special considerations required in writing about experimental and survey research.

Guidelines for Analyzing Research Reports

The National Council on Public Polls has produced a set of questions readers should want to know about polling research reports (Angione 1977, "Polls and Surveys"). These can be productively used as guidelines on what should be in a report of an experiment as well.

1. Highlight the Sponsor. The sponsor of the research should be named, and information given about how the reader may obtain a copy of the report. We do not expect experimental research to be skewed by those paying for it and a clear indication of the sponsor will show that the researcher has no doubts on that score. Credentials and affiliation of the researcher should also be indicated.

2. Date and Locale. Indicate when and where the research was conducted. It sometimes takes a year or more for research reports to be published and some writers hesitate to show this information for fear the report will seem out of date. But conditions, especially the conditions of people, change over time. Knowing when and where the research took place allows readers to judge for themselves.

3. Methodology. Describe how the information was gathered. There is a great deal of difference in the minds of some people in the reliability of person-to-person, telephone survey, letter, laboratory and field data.

4. Language. Describe the wording of any letters or questionnaires used. As chapters 4 and 5 and earlier segments of this chapter reveal, wording, word order, tone of voice and even order of presentation of questions can sometimes bias results.

5. Sample Selection. Indicate how the sample was selected and whether or not the selection was random. If it was not, inferences cannot be made about the population to which the sample belonged.

6. Sample Size. Indicate the sizes of the sample and the total population, as well as sampling error. Even a random sample will not produce accurate results if it is too small. Also show the level of significance set by the researcher and its correlated confidence interval.

7. Internal Samples. If smaller groups within the sample are cited, indicate how large they are and the usefulness of the information learned. For example, in a video versus print experiment, you might find that 11th graders of Asian background do 90 percent better in the print group than in the video group. But if only five Asian students took part in the experiment, that sample could give no indication at all about Asian students in general.

8. Comparisons. Indicate how these results compare with other contemporary work. Although this experiment may be different than any done before, there will have been research reported which is at least, in part, similar to it. How do the findings compare?

Chapter Summary

This chapter began with a broad listing of the public relations writer's use of research. Essentially, the writer uses it for understanding information needs of the audience, and to test, develop and evaluate messages. In addition to all these, the public relations writer may be forced to write about research topics. For these reasons, this chapter is emphatic about the need for public relations writers to understand research and its concepts.

Next, the chapter addressed the notion of survey research and how it is distinct from experimental, field and non-reactive research. From this section of the chapter arose a discussion of the three types of surveys—mail, telephone and personal interviews.

From there, it moved to concerns about samples and sampling techniques, focusing largely on probability sampling procedures, such as simple random sampling, systematic random sampling and stratified sampling. This logically led into issues of question writing and questionnaire construction and types of questions relevant for public relations research.

This chapter also examined the experiment as it is used in public relations writing. It defined the experiment as research which allows comparison of similar groups after one or more groups has been exposed to some changed condition.

It explained experimental groups as those to which change is applied and control groups as those which are compared to the experimental groups after this change. Independent variables are seen as those which are altered in order to provide change in dependent variables. The key value of the experiment was described as proving cause and effect.

The laboratory experiment was described as research at its purest, due to the experimenter's ability to control all its aspects. Experimentation was seen to have liabilities, due to its high costs in time, expertise, efforts and funds.

Finally, pointers were given about what to look for and what to write about when reading and writing about experiments conducted by others. Basically, this writing is like other public relations writing, considering the message, medium and public being addressed. Several key differences were noted, however, and the reader was provided with guidelines for writing informal reports on experiments.

Research Exercises

1. At the beginning of the chapter, you read about the dilemma of the pope's visit. Who has the better argument? To answer this question, you will not only have to address issues of sampling but also test the logic of the assumptions made by Parfrey and McFarland. Prepare a one-page analysis of the situation.
2. You are a public relations writer-researcher in a company that employs 2,000 employees. You wish to determine what percentage of your company's employees read the newsletter you publish every month. Ideally, you would like to get each employee's response. However, due to budget constraints, you decide on a sample size of 200. If you conducted the survey and found that 55 percent of the employees don't read your company's newsletter, what would the sampling error of your finding be?
3. Using table 13.1 as a model, write a brief report on how your survey was conducted. You may assume that the confidence level is 90 percent.

Writing Exercises

Two writing exercises are presented here. The first asks you to evaluate an experimental research report written by someone else. The second presents you with the results of an experiment and asks you to write a report on it. Both these exercises will verify your ability to analyze experiments and determine how they should be written for specific publics.

Exercise One: Reviewing an Experimental Report

Instructions: Read and analyze the following article on "Food and Cancer." Consider it in light of what you learned in this chapter. Then write a 200-word review of the article for *Public Relations Journal.* The article was written for the food section of the *Washington Post.* You may rewrite the article for your own purposes. But the purpose here is to analyze the article in light of its medium, message and intended publics, and review it for your medium and publics.

Food and Cancer

Can the food you eat affect your chances of getting cancer? Members of Washington, D.C.-based Jackson-Andrew Public Relations didn't use to think so but they believe it now. Ten of its members developed cancer in the past decade, which could have been prevented by proper diet.

One hundred members of the firm took part in a 10-year experiment on food and cancer which ended this year. The Jackson-Andrew participants were part of a larger experiment conducted by the National Council on Health and Nutrition involving 1,000 professionals in the city. Jackson-Andrew specializes in health public relations.

In each firm, participants were randomly separated into two equal groups. One half ate whatever they wanted, while the other half ate only foods specified by a group of doctors from the council. These foods consisted primarily of deep green and leafy vegetables, fish and cheese and whole grain cereals. Fried foods and red meat were not allowed. Those taking part were on their honor not to deviate from the designated food list.

At the experiment's conclusion, the council reported that 10 percent fewer cases of cancer developed among the careful eaters than among the free eaters. The council's privately published report concluded that "the results seem to indicate that the types of food eaten can have a significant effect on one's chances of developing cancer in this professional group."

Exercise Two: Writing About an Experiment

Instructions: Presented below is a research brief on an experiment. Review the brief carefully. Then, using information from this chapter and your knowledge of writing, write a report on the research for the business section of the *Dallas Morning News.*

Research Brief: Racial Bias and Public Relations Credibility

1. Researcher: John Haymount, Ph.D., professor of communications, Texas Northern University.

2. Research Hypothesis: Students presented with a new product promotional message by a white source will evaluate the message more positively than the same message from a black source.

3. Subjects: 224 freshman students in the School of Communications, Texas Northern University. Students were randomly assigned to two equal groups, titled White Source Group and Black Source Group.

4. Procedure: Both groups were convened simultaneously in adjacent university classrooms. Each group was presented with a new product release on "Sleep-Study," an audiotape program designed to enhance learning while a person sleeps. Both releases were exactly the same except for one factor. Both cited Al A. Pattah, president of the Improved Study Group of Dallas, quoting his major points on Sleep-Study as a useful product. The single difference in the releases provided to subjects in the White Source Group and the Black Source Group was that for the former, Pattah was said to be "white" and for the latter he was said to be "black." After reading the release, each subject was asked to complete a Hill Standard Message Evaluation Questionnaire. Mean scores of the evaluations of the two groups were compared.

5. Independent Variable: Sleep-Study new product release.

6. Dependent Variable: Hill Standard Message Evaluation Questionnaire.

7. Significance Level Selected: 0.05.

8. Confidence Interval: $+/-5\%$.

9. Statistical Test: Comparison of Means (z score).

10. Finding: $z = 2.58$, $p < .01$.

11. Results: Null hypothesis rejected.

12. Conclusion: Perceived race can affect evaluation of public relations messages by students in this area.

Food for Thought

1. It is often said that research and creativity don't mix. In fact, some people believe that including research in a creative program is a sure way of destroying it (the creative program). Do you believe this to be true? If so, why? If not, why not?

2. Because the experiment allows us to say with some authority that a manipulation in one variable can cause a predictable change in another variable, it is a most powerful research tool. Knowing this, why do you suppose that the experiment is so little used for public relations research?

3. Reporters writing about experiments often project the meaning of the results far beyond that logically allowed. What are some reasons why this tendency might occur?

4. If you wanted to do an experiment testing whether donation requests by print, video or audio messages were most effective with college students, how would you set it up?

References for Further Study

Angione, Howard. *The Associated Press Stylebook and Libel Manual.* New York: The Associated Press, 1977.

Babbie, Earl. *The Practice of Social Research,* 4th ed. Belmont, Calif.: Wadsworth, 1986.

Fagerstrom, Scott. "Cost of Papal Visit: Question of Priorities." *The Orange County Register.* August 30, 1987. A3.

French, Christopher, ed. *The Associated Press Stylebook and Libel Manual.* New York: The Associated Press, 1987.

Grass, R. C. "Measuring the Effects of Corporate Advertising." *Public Relations Review* 3:4(1977):39–50.

Kalfus, Marilyn. "Political Polls can be Misleading if Questions are Loaded." *The Orange County Register.* October 31, 1988, A1.

Kish, Leslie. *Survey Sampling.* New York: Wiley, 1965.

Miller, Delbert C. *Handbook of Research Design and Social Measurement,* 3rd ed. New York: Longman, 1978.

Ray, William J. and Richard Ravizza. *Method Toward a Science of Behavior and Experience.* Belmont, Calif.: Wadsworth, 1988.

Wimmer, Roger D. and Joseph R. Dominick. *Mass Media Research: An Introduction.* Belmont, Calif.: Wadsworth, 1987.

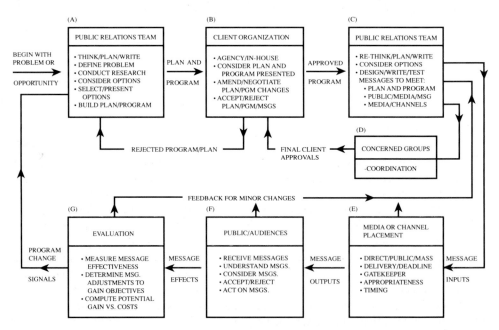

BEGIN WITH
PROBLEM OR

OPPORTUNITY

(A)

PUBLIC RELATIONS TEAM

• THINK/PLAN/WRITE
• DEFINE PROBLEM
• CONDUCT RESEARCH
• CONSIDER OPTIONS
• SELECT/PRESENT
  OPTIONS
• BUILD PLAN/PROGRAM

PLAN AND

PROGRAM

(B)

CLIENT ORGANIZATION

• AGENCY/IN-HOUSE
• CONSIDER PLAN AND
  PROGRAM PRESENTED
• AMEND/NEGOTIATE
  PLAN/PGM CHANGES
• ACCEPT/REJECT
  PLAN/PGM/MSGS

APPROVED

PROGRAM

(C)

PUBLIC RELATIONS TEAM

• RE-THINK/PLAN/WRITE
• CONSIDER OPTIONS
• DESIGN/WRITE/TEST
  MESSAGES TO MEET:
  • PLAN AND PROGRAM
  • PUBLIC/MEDIA/MSG
  • MEDIA/CHANNELS

REJECTED PROGRAM/PLAN

FINAL CLIENT
APPROVALS

(D)

CONCERNED GROUPS

-COORDINATION

FEEDBACK FOR MINOR CHANGES

(G)

EVALUATION

• MEASURE MESSAGE
  EFFECTIVENESS
• DETERMINE MSG.
  ADJUSTMENTS TO
  GAIN OBJECTIVES
• COMPUTE POTENTIAL
  GAIN VS. COSTS

PROGRAM
CHANGE

SIGNALS

MESSAGE

EFFECTS

(F)

PUBLIC/AUDIENCES

• RECEIVE MESSAGES
• UNDERSTAND MSGS.
• CONSIDER MSGS.
• ACCEPT/REJECT
• ACT ON MSGS.

MESSAGE

OUTPUTS

(E)

MEDIA OR CHANNEL
PLACEMENT

• DIRECT/PUBLIC/MASS
• DELIVERY/DEADLINE
• GATEKEEPER
• APPROPRIATENESS
• TIMING

MESSAGE

INPUTS

Law and ethics are of concern in every step of the writing process. But they are most critical in the planning, designing, writing, and coordination of messages. Writers may know how to check the legality of their words, but they must first be aware that those words are suspect. Key considerations in public relations writing are information disclosure laws, diminished worth laws (especially libel, privacy, copyright, and trademark law), corporate publication laws, and ethical conventions.

LEGAL AND ETHICAL IMPLICATIONS OF PUBLIC RELATIONS WRITING

Introduction

Much of the information we have about American institutions—be they commercial or nonprofit—comes to us from public relations sources via mass media and other information channels. Public relations messages tell us how such institutions operate, whether they are financially sound or not and what their economic, social, technological and other contributions to society are. Thus, public relations writers play a valuable role in moving social, economic and business information around society.

However, public relations activities are not completely free and unrestrained. They are subject to many restrictions. Some of these come from the organizations the writers work for. Others come from federal and state laws governing the use and dissemination of information. Yet others come from personal values and the ethical codes of the professional associations the writers belong to.

Our objective here is to provide you with an understanding of legal and ethical constraints on public relations writing. While interpreting and applying this information to your writing assignments, keep the following points in mind:

First, our discussion is limited only to some legal and ethical issues that directly apply to public relations writing. Master these. They will serve you and your clients well. Also, take the time to explore legal and ethical issues not addressed here.

A PROFESSIONAL TIP:
Law and Ethics

As an attorney who is also in public relations, I occasionally shudder when I observe the unnecessary jeopardy to which some public relations practitioners expose their companies or clients. Basic knowledge of the law is essential for anyone who hopes to have a successful and lengthy career as a public relations writer. It behooves the practitioner to stay abreast of the constantly changing laws involving libel, slander, copyrights, trademarks and disclosure. Public relations firms have been held liable for issuing false or misleading information on behalf of their clients.

The codes of ethics of the Public Relations Society of America, the International Public Relations Association, the International Association of Business Communicators and other professional groups will also have a bearing on the ethical consequences of your writings.

William J. Corbett, APR, is vice president of communications for the American Institute of Certified Public Accountants. An attorney, part-time judge and public relations veteran of more than 25 years, he served as director of public relations (worldwide) for Avon Products Inc. for 16 years before joining the AICPA in 1984. He is currently president of the International Public Relations Association.

Likewise, take the time to study the ethics codes of professional bodies such as the Public Relations Society of America and the International Association of Business Communicators. These codes provide valuable guidelines for ethically appropriate behaviors for the public relations writer and practitioner.

Second, recognize that we are not trying to make lawyers of you. When you have even the slightest doubt about the legality of something you may write for a client, consult a lawyer. Likewise, when your doubts are of an ethical nature—and this chapter does not provide you with a satisfactory answer—consult officers of the PRSA or IABC. If they cannot help you resolve your dilemma, at least they will be able to refer you to an ethics expert who can.

In general, the legal constraints on public relations writers can be organized around four topic areas. These are:

1. Information disclosure laws
2. Diminished worth laws
3. Corporate publications laws
4. Ethical conventions

We will examine each area and its implications for public relations writing in the remainder of the chapter.

Information Disclosure Laws

Disclosure of Financial Information

Securities Acts

Many people use the information companies issue about themselves to make investment decisions, i.e., decisions to buy, hold or sell stock. The more information people have, and the more reliable this information is, the more intelligent their investment decisions are likely to be.

Individual needs for such information are protected by the **Securities Act of 1933,** the **Securities Exchange Act of 1934,** and the **Investment Company Act of 1940.** These laws were enacted in good part to prevent the misinformation and speculation that led to the stock market crash in 1929. Collectively, they force publicly-held organizations—companies that trade stocks on the nation's stock exchanges over the counter—to promptly, accurately and widely disseminate a variety of **material information,** both favorable and unfavorable, about themselves, so people can use it to buy, hold or sell stock wisely.

The securities acts are policed and enforced by the **Securities and Exchange Commission.**

Public relations writers play a critical role in the dissemination of material information. By channeling news releases through a variety of print and electronic media, they are able to get such information quickly and accurately to the investing public. This centrality of public relations to the accurate and prompt disclosure of material information has been recognized by the SEC (1963).

Corporate Material Information

This generally is information that has the potential to affect the value of a company's stock. According to the **American Stock Exchange Guide** (1987, 3), the following are some categories of material information. For each category, we have provided examples of the lead paragraph of an appropriate news release. As will become clear, the burden of composing and distributing such information generally falls upon the public relations department of the organization.

1. Development of a significant new product, or a significant new discovery. This usually is a healthy sign. The value of company stock generally tends to increase following the announcement of the introduction of a new product or the discovery of a new process. Following is an example of a release to signal such an event:

> **June 14, 1990**
> **Scientists working for Futuristic Biomedical Co. have produced a drug that shrinks and destroys cancer cells in laboratory rats. John P. Doe, chief scientist of the company's cancer research group, said that the development of the drug "signified the first major step toward a cancer cure for humans." The drug, code named ZZZZ, . . .**

2. Major changes in the management structure of a company. This includes announcements about the hiring, firing, promotion or demotion of key company executives such as the president and chief executive officer and vice presidents of marketing, finance and other major divisions. Sometimes, news of this nature has a positive impact on investors, as when a company hires a dynamic person to head it:

> **June 14, 1990**
> **The Futuristic Biomedical Co. today named Dallas financier John P. Doe as its president and chief executive officer. Doe rose to national prominence by turning around the troubled Speedy Motor Co. . . .**

At other times, management changes can spell bad news and scare investors away:

> **June 14, 1990**
> **John P. Doe stepped down as the president and chief executive officer of Futuristic Biomedical Co. after a company spokesman acknowledged that claims about a cure for cancer may have been based on fraudulent data . . .**

However, if management changes are due to a legitimate or harmless reason and there is a smooth transfer of power, then such news may not adversely affect the stock of a company:

> **June 14, 1990**
> **A spokeswoman for Futuristic Biomedical Co. said that John P. Doe has resigned as president and chief executive officer. Jim Z. Smith, the company's vice president for finance, will step in as acting president until the board decides on a permanent replacement. Doe said he plans to explore other, as yet undisclosed, business options . . .**

3. News about a company buying or selling a significant asset. Acquisitions are normally a sign of a company's good health and welcome news for the investor. Selling a company can also be good news if there is a positive reason for the sale:

June 14, 1990
The XYZ Co. is putting up its Health Care Unit for sale so it can concentrate on its consumer product line . . .

The sale of an asset can be bad news if it is accompanied by stories of mismanagement, operating losses and the like:

June 14, 1990
The XYZ Co. put up its Health Care Unit for sale after the unit reported a $13 million loss in earnings in the first six months of this year . . .

4. News about a joint venture or merger with, or acquisition of, another company. Such announcements are often viewed by the investing public as positive developments. They stimulate investment and are often accompanied by increases in stock value. The following are some examples of news releases that follow such developments:

Joint Venture

June 14, 1990
The Futuristic Biomedical Co. will team up with the USP Pharmaceutical Group of Great Britain to produce an AIDS vaccine. This collaboration is expected to produce the first commercially viable AIDS vaccine by the end of 1993. The USP Pharmaceutical Group has already completed animal tests of the vaccine and is ready to begin clinical trials by the start of 1992 . . .

Merger

June 14, 1990
The Futuristic Biomedical Co. today announced that talks have been completed to pave the way for merging its operations with the Bedrock Pharmaceutical Group of Los Angeles. The unified companies will be known as the Cureall Biomedical and Pharmaceutical Group . . .

Acquisition

June 14, 1990
The Futuristic Biomedical Co. today announced that it will buy the Los Angeles-based Bedrock Pharmaceutical Group for $1.6 billion. The purchase will make Futuristic the largest pharmaceutical company in the United States . . .

5. News about a company acquiring or losing a significant contract. The former is a healthy sign and good news for the investor. The latter is troublesome news and potentially unsettling for both the company and the investor.

New Contracts

June 14, 1990
The Futuristic Aerospace Co. today received an order for 20 FAC-311 civilian jet aircraft from the Los Angeles-based Commuter Airlines. The FAC-311 is a mid-range jetliner costing $33 million . . .

Lost Contracts

June 14, 1990
The Futuristic Aerospace Co. will lay off 4,000 employees, following the cancellation by the Department of Defense of the $1 billion hypersonic jetliner contract. The company had only a year earlier been awarded the prestigious contract . . .

6. Major litigation. Lawsuits are always bad news, especially since companies can lose huge sums of money in damages, sometimes close to or in excess of what they are actually worth. Such announcements are unsettling for both companies and investors.

June 14, 1990
The Futuristic Biomedical Co. announced today that it will pay $21 million to settle a class-action suit brought Feb. 10 against it by 10 former shareholders . . .

7. Information about stock offerings and dividends. Such information is of special interest to investors, since it provides them with opportunities to buy new stock or see how current investments are faring.

Stock Offerings

June 14, 1990
The Futuristic Biomedical Co. today registered intent with the Securities and Exchange Commission office in New York to seek $530 million in new stock. It is the biggest company filing since the October 1987 stock market collapse . . .

Dividends

June 14, 1990
The Futuristic Biomedical Co. announced today that it is planning to raise its dividend 12 percent and buy back 5 million shares. Chief Executive Officer John P. Doe said, "We are doing this to assure shareholders that there is no danger of one investor owning a major stake in the company . . ."

Other material events calling for disclosure under the securities laws are: plans to borrow funds; annual earnings; major disputes with workers and their unions; bankruptcy filings; worker layoffs and plant closings. In short, any major event that is likely to signal the good or ill health of a company requires disclosure (Newsom and Scott 1985, 414–415).

Disclosure Guidelines

Most rules for when and how material information about publicly-held companies must be released are provided by three agencies. These are the SEC, the New York Stock Exchange and the American Stock Exchange. These three institutions generally agree that material information must be distributed on a **mass scale, promptly, simultaneously** and **speedily.**

In particular, the NYSE and AMEX recommend or require that material information be disseminated immediately via press releases to newspapers such as *The New York Times* and *The Wall Street Journal,* general news services such as The Associated Press and United Press International, financial wire services such as Dow Jones and Reuters, and specialized financial information channels such as the Standard and Poor's Corporation and Moody's Investor Service (Simon 1984, 335–336). Material information released via mail to individual newspapers and other media organizations is considered to be too slow to meet the promptness requirement. Similarly, all releases must show that they are intended **"FOR IMMEDIATE RELEASE."** Releases that have an "embargo" or "hold for release" date are not acceptable.

These extensive disclosure guidelines are intended to ensure that everyone who may need or want to use the information has it at the same time. They are also designed to prevent organizational "insiders," including public relations people, from exploiting and financially benefiting from the material information before such information reaches the general public.

Insider Trading

Since public relations writers are closely involved in the dissemination of information, they must be especially careful not to violate disclosure rules. Violations commonly occur in two ways—insider trading and misinformation.

The act of companies or individuals selectively distributing or using information not yet disclosed to the public for personal gain is known as "insider trading." The AMEX considers as insiders all persons who come into contact with material information before it is made public (Walsh 1986, 10). Since public relations writers compose financial press releases, they generally have prior access to such information. Thus, they are considered as "insiders," especially since the landmark *Texas Gulf Sulphur* (1968; 1969) case (Newsom and Scott 1985, 413; Walsh 1986, 10). In this case, according to the federal court of appeals, the company's public relations manager used material undisclosed information to his own advantage. The company was also found guilty of issuing a press release that falsely and misleadingly downplayed a significant mineral ore discovery.

Insider trading is a serious infraction of the securities acts, punishable with fines and imprisonment.

There were at least two major insider trading cases involving public relations professionals in the mid-'80s. In the first, the SEC accused R. F. Hengen Inc., a financial public relations firm, of passing confidential information to a stockholder that Puritan Fashions Corp., a client, would not be able to meet previously and publicly announced earnings and sales projections. This stockholder, in turn, passed the information to another stockholder. Between them, the two "sold or advised sales of more than $2 million [in Puritan stock] before the public announcement [of Puritan's inability to meet the earlier earnings and sales projections] was made" (Walsh 1986, 10).

Another case of insider trading involved Anthony M. Franco while he was national president of PRSA. According to the SEC (complaint no. 11206, August 26, 1986), Franco, a consultant to Crowley, Milner and Co., had prior knowledge that the company would soon be acquired by the Oakland Holding Co. Such information usually makes stock prices rise when announced. The SEC further charged that Franco used this information to direct his stockbroker to buy 3,000 shares of Crowley stock one day before the acquisition was publicly announced. Franco avoided prosecution by signing an SEC consent decree. People who sign such decrees essentially neither admit nor deny an SEC charge. However, the incident damaged Franco's professional credibility, forcing him, among other things, to resign his presidency of and membership in the PRSA.

The lesson here is that the handling of financial information is a serious responsibility. Do not play favorites with the information or use it for personal gain. Such practices are against the law and could endanger your career and freedom.

Misinformation

Section 10(b) of the Securities Exchange Act of 1934 and rule 10b–5 of the SEC both make it unlawful for any person, including public relations writers (and their companies), to mislead investing publics by making false or incomplete statements about material facts or engaging in fraudulent or deceitful acts or practices.

Misinformation can occur in one of two ways. The first is when a company denies or lies about a material development for fear that such news, especially if it is negative, could discourage investment and hurt the value of its stock. This happened in the *Basic v. Levinson* (1988) case involving the December 1978 agreement to merge Basic Inc. and Combustion Engineering Inc.

Before the official announcement was made, the value of Basic stock had begun rising amid rumors of the impending merger. Basic officials responded by publicly denying the rumors even as merger talks were taking place. As late as November 6, 1978, company directors said they were unaware of the possibility of the merger (Savage 1988, 17).

After the merger was announced, several stockholders sued Basic Inc., stating that they had been misled into selling their stock at prices "artificially depressed" by the company's denials (Shillinglaw 1988, 1). Ruling for the stockholders, the Supreme Court said, "Misleading statements denying rumors of an impending merger may provide investors with sufficient basis to win damages from the company" (Savage 1988, 1). Lawyer Wayne Cross estimated that damage awards to the stockholders could be as high as $20 million (Ibid, 1).

The other manner in which misinformation takes place is through misrepresentation, distortion and omission of pertinent facts.

In 1972, the SEC accused Pig'n' Whistle, a Chicago-based restaurant and motel chain, of distributing false and misleading media releases about two properties it had purchased—the Mary Ann Baking Co., and the Holiday Lodge near Lake Tahoe. The releases themselves were written for Pig'n' Whistle by Financial Relations Board Inc., a public relations firm. The SEC rebuked Financial Relations for not verifying the accuracy of the information, adding that the company "should have done independent research before allowing any release to leave its offices" (Newsom and Scott 1985, 413).

Likewise, in 1984, the SEC found fault with the Howard Bronson public relations firm for making false and misleading statements about a client (Cutlip 1985, 26–27).

These cases are important to you for two reasons. They not only emphasize the illegality, potential for civil damages and, or, criminal penalties of misinforming investing publics about material facts but also place partial responsibility for researching and verifying such facts upon the public relations writer.

Disclosure of Product Information

Other federal agencies besides the SEC may investigate a company accused of making false and misleading statements, especially if these pertain to material developments about products. (See accompanying story on the FDA.)

FDA Tells Company to Revise Drug Description
By
Irvin Molotsky

WASHINGTON—The Food and Drug Administration has taken the unusual step of telling a drug manufacturer to recall a press release it had issued on the safety and effectiveness of one of its medicines.

The federal agency accused ICN Pharmaceuticals of Costa Mesa, Calif., of issuing a press kit that included false or misleading statements about its drug, Virazole. The drug had been approved by the agency for the treatment of respiratory syncytial virus infection, but the FDA said that the press release exaggerated both the severity of the illness it was designed to treat and the effectiveness of the drug in treating other illnesses.

A spokesman for the agency said that the action, initiated in a letter on March 24, [1986] appeared to be only the second time it had moved in such a way against a drug maker. The previous incident, he said, involved a press release promoting the drug Oraflex that was distributed by Eli Lilly & Co.

The federal agency cited the following statement in the press release as false or misleading: "Virazole holds a great potential because of its broad-spectrum antiviral action. The drug's usefulness in combating respiratory syncytial virus, influenza, measles, chicken pox, herpes simplex and herpes zoster, hepatitis A, Lassa fever and sandfly fever has been demonstrated in worldwide clinical research."

In a letter to the chairman of ICN, Milan Panic, the agency said: "The press kit grossly exaggerates the efficacy of Virazole beyond the single, limited indication provided in the approved labeling in that there are numerous representations and suggestions of efficacy in a wide variety of viral infections."

The FDA spokesman, William Grigg, said that the agency could take the action because press releases were regarded as extensions of drug labeling, over which it has authority.

Other government agencies, like the Securities and Exchange Commission, have acted against press releases issued by corporations.

An official of the American Civil Liberties Union said he did not know enough about the case for comment on whether the action constituted a First Amendment free-speech issue.

Officers of ICN would not comment on the case. Owen Daley, a senior vice president of Hill & Knowlton, the public relations company that distributed the press material said: "They are prepared to demonstrate to the FDA that they did not misrepresent deliberately approval of this product for the purposes for which it was not intended."

As to his own concern's role, Daley said: "Hill & Knowlton did not prepare the press release. We were assured by ICN that the substance was correct."

In its letter to Panic, the Food and Drug Administration said: "Generally we believe that the press kit and related materials have resulted in the communication of false and (or) misleading concepts concerning the safety and efficacy of Virazole."

In addition, the FDA charged that the press kit "misrepresents the safety profile of Virazole, as currently known."

The FDA told ICN that it must provide a list of all recipients of its press release and send them a new corrected description. Failing that, the agency said ICN faced seizure of the drug on the ground of mislabeling.

Copyright © 1986 The New York Times Company. Reprinted with permission.

Public relations materials containing false and misleading information about products could also be investigated by the Federal Trade Commission or state attorneys general as deceptive advertising (Overbeck 1989, 206). This agency polices, among other things, public relations activities as they relate to product promotion.

If public relations messages are obscene or fraudulent and are distributed through postal channels, then the writer could risk a criminal investigation by the U.S. Postal Service.

Writing Problems and Solutions

While writing product announcements or any material news release, watch out for six types of word problems. These are:
1. Nonfact
2. The puff word
3. Sweeping generalizations
4. Legitimization
5. Misleading and out-of-context words
6. Improper connotation

Nonfact

This includes practices such as:

a. Half-truth: This is usually achieved by communicating the advantages of a material development but not its problems. For example, a company might announce the development of a potentially important vaccine but neglect to inform audiences that the testing process was flawed.

b. Untruth: Here the writer may communicate an outright lie, such as, "Arcane [brand] aspirin **will cure** the common cold" (Pember 1987, 517). The Pig'n' Whistle and Basic Inc. cases referred to earlier fall into this category.

c. Speculation: Here, the writer might make product or other claims beyond those grounded in fact. The ICN Pharmaceutical case cited earlier demonstrates the problems speculation can create for a company.

There is no room in public relations writing for speculation, half-truths or falsehoods. Make sure that all your work is frank, honest and scrupulously accurate.

The Puff Word

Companies are often proud of their products and other achievements, and are not averse to praising them. A common practice is for public relations writers to use "puff" words, or adjectives and verbs which exaggerate the qualities of people and things. For example, they might use the word "amazing" to describe a client's product, "unprecedented" to describe a stock offering, "spectacular" or "breathtaking" to describe a client's corporate headquarters and "genius" or "wizard" to describe a newly-appointed CEO.

If for no other reason than their low credibility, public relations writers must avoid using puff words. You can deal with puffery in two ways. One is by eliminating it from your messages. Chapter 7 offers some guidelines on how this can be done. Alternately, you can replace them with specific, fact-based descriptions. For example, instead of saying "a product of revolutionary fabric-coating biotechnology," say, "The fabric coating breathes and behaves like human skin."

Likewise,

Instead of	Say
This computer can remain operational under AMAZINGLY-HIGH temperature conditions.	This computer can function in temperatures as high as 150° F.
The company president, John P. Doe, has a DISTINGUISHED educational background.	The company president, John P. Doe has a Ph.D. in business administration from Harvard University.
This company made a HUGE profit.	This company made a profit of $35 million.

The revised descriptions are not only accurate, but have a better chance of creating the impact that you may have expected by using puff words.

Sweeping Generalizations

This is a variation of puffery in which writers make vague means-something-for-everyone statements about the product or material development in question. For example, they might say, "The drug has the potential to cure most common illnesses," without stating what these illnesses are.

In such cases, the remedy is again specificity. Be specific about what your product will do. Base your statements on systematically researched facts. Having done this, you might rewrite your drug release thus:

> **The drug has the potential to cure common illnesses such as stomach flu and diarrhea.**

Legitimization

Here, the writers may use words and phrases which suggest that the information they are conveying has been validated by independent and authoritative sources. In such instances, the writers may also fall short of identifying the corroborating authority. Common legitimization phrases to watch out for are:

> **Independent tests show that . . . It has been demonstrated in worldwide clinical research . . .**

If you feel compelled to use legitimizing language, go a step further and identify the validating authority. For example:

> **Clinical tests conducted by the Futuristic Biomedical Co. of Santa Ana, Calif., show that the drug has the potential to cure common illnesses such as stomach flu and diarrhea.**

Misleading and Out-of-Context Words

These are words of profound and serious meaning that can appropriately be used in some situations. Public relations writers can get their clients into trouble by using such words as "breakthrough" and "new" indiscriminately and out of context.

According to Van Deusen (1967, 27), the word "breakthrough" is a "fair and accurate description," if it represents a product development of "major importance representing a capability that has been sought for many years." Thus, it could be used to describe recent developments in cold fusion, stealth technology and superconductivity.

Unfortunately, the word is used indiscriminately in product releases, causing "government agencies to show their teeth but not as a by-product of laughter" (Simon 1969, 532).

When you are tempted to use "breakthrough" to describe a client's product or technology, apply Van Deusen's definition to it. If it fits, use it. If not, avoid it.

TABLE 14.1.   AMEX Writing Guidelines

Exchange Requirements—The content of a press release or other public announcement is as important as its timing. Each announcement should:

(i) be factual, clear and succinct;

(ii) contain sufficient quantitative information to allow investors to evaluate its relative importance to the activities of the company;

(iii) be balanced and fair, i.e., the announcement should avoid the following:

— The omission of important unfavorable facts or the slighting of such facts (e.g., by "burying" them at the end of a press release).

— The presentation of favorable possibilities as certain or as more probable than is actually the case.

— The presentation of projections without sufficient qualification or without sufficient factual basis.

— Negative statements phrased so as to create positive implications, e.g., "The company cannot now predict whether the development will have a materially favorable effect on its earnings," (creating the implication that the effect will be favorable even if not materially favorable), or, "The company expects that the development will not have a materially favorable effect on earnings in the immediate future," (creating the implication that the development will eventually have a materially favorable effect).

— The use of promotional jargon calculated to excite rather than to inform.

(iv) avoid over-technical language and should be expressed to the extent possible in language comprehensible to the layman;

(v) explain, if the consequences or effects of the information on the company's future prospects cannot be assessed, why this is so; and

(vi) clarify and point out any reasonable alternatives where the public announcement undertakes to interpret information disclosed.

Copyright © 1987. American Stock Exchange. Reprinted with permission.

Improper Connotation

Here, the writer communicates false ideas by a subtle and improper arrangement of words and phrases. As an example of this, Pember (1987, 517) cites the two messages Listerine carried on its label, "Kills Germs by Millions on Contact," followed by, "For General Oral Hygiene, Bad Breath, Colds and Resultant Sores." The FTC concluded that the messages were deceptive since they conveyed the impression that Listerine, the germ killer, could cure, even prevent, colds.

A similar situation might arise when a writer uses a news report format to disguise an ad. Under the provisions of the Bourne Newspaper Publicity Law of 1912, such messages must be clearly identified as advertising material. The writer may achieve this by boxing the material and placing the word "Advertisement" prominently above it.

The lesson for the public relations writer is that the regulating bodies not only look for individual words that deceive, but also the overall effect created by the arrangement of words in a message. The law is not intended "for the protection of experts only, but also for the public which includes the ignorant, the unthinking and the credulous who do not stop to analyze but are governed by appearance and general impression" (Simon 1969, 389).

Some more writing guidelines are provided in Table 14.1.

To summarize, avoid puff words, speculative statements, vague generalizations, difficult words, deceptive arrangements of words and phrases, half-truths and falsehoods in your material releases. Make sure your information is thoroughly researched and substantiated.

Finally, remember these are not only sound guidelines for disclosing material information, but good general writing principles as well.

Diminished Worth Laws

This section examines the following laws and their implications for the public relations writer:

1. Libel law
2. Privacy law
3. Copyright law
4. Trademark law

These laws are collectively called "diminished worth" laws because they are designed to protect the personal, social and economic value of people and artifacts (products, services and artistic creations) from decreasing. The libel and privacy laws protect people, while the copyright and trademark laws protect artifacts.

In the case of *Dorr v. United States* (1904), the U.S. Supreme Court defined defamation as:

> An utterance tending to impugn (i.e., damage and destroy) the honesty, virtue or reputation, or publish the alleged or natural defects of a person and thereby expose him [or her] to public hatred, contempt and ridicule.

Both libel and slander are forms of defamation. The difference generally is that slander is spoken defamation whereas libel is written or printed defamation. Since public relations messages, even those that are spoken, are usually scripted, libel is a more distinct possibility for the public relations writer than slander.

Libel

On the Sept. 25, 1980, telecast of NBC television's "Tomorrow" program, actor Chevy Chase said of fellow actor Cary Grant, "I understand he's a homo." Grant sued Chase for $10 million. After three years of negotiations, Grant reportedly settled for $1 million in damages (Scott 1988, 2).

This case illustrates two points. One, that libel is a serious, damaging and expensive matter. Two, when we think of libel, we usually think about celebrities, but rarely about public relations writers.

Simon (1969) was among the first to point out the implications of the defamation laws to the practice of public relations. He wrote:

> As prime company communicator, the PR man is constantly concerned with possible exposure—either of his company or himself—to claims of libel and slander. Even a news release or newspaper interview may open this door. As company communications and statements become more competitive and aggressive, the possibilities increase (212).

Simon's prediction came true in the *Hutchinson v. Proxmire* (1979) case, "in which Senator William Proxmire was [successfully] sued for libel after awarding his 'Golden Fleece of the Month Award' (for wasteful expenditure of public funds) to Michigan scientist Dr. Ronald Hutchinson" (Walsh 1982, 8).

Hutchinson, the research director of a public mental hospital, was also principal investigator of federally-funded research on animal aggression. Believing Hutchinson's research to be wasteful, the Wisconsin Democrat said that the scientist was putting the "bite" on the American taxpayer and making a "monkey" of the American people.

In this case, the libelous material was published in a news release and newsletter put out by the Senator's office.

Elements of Libel

Thus, libel is the publication of information which tends to damage people's social or business reputations, defames their character and negatively affects their abilities to conduct business (Walsh 1982, 8).

Four conditions need to be met for a situation to become libelous: (1) The use of defamatory words; (2) Identification; (3) Publication of libelous information; and (4) Fault.

1. Use of Defamatory Words

Plainly, inherent in every definition of libel is the notion that the reputation of a person must be adversely affected by the published material. This happens when public relations writers use negative and derogatory words in their messages. The examples used earlier qualify because they state or imply that a person is a sexual deviant misuser of public funds.

Some defamatory words, such as "thief," "swindler," "drug addict," "arsonist" or "alcoholic" are easy enough to recognize. Others are not as easy to identify, and include words such as "bankruptcy" and "creative accountant" or "creative financier" (Walsh 1982, 8).

In general, according to Pember (1987, 129–135), the following categories of words have the potential to libel people:

a. Words that either explicitly or implicitly portray people as law breakers or criminals.

b. Words that depict the sexual practices and lifestyles of individuals. These include words such as "queer" and "gay."

c. Words that attack a person's religious and political affiliations. It is, for example, defamatory to say that "a Catholic was denied the right of Holy Communion . . . , for to most people, it suggests some ghastly kind of behavior by the excommunicant" (Pember 1987, 131). Likewise, it may be defamatory to say that someone has been "stripped of citizenship. Charging someone with being a traitor or spy or with urging sedition or anarchy or revolution are all defamatory statements" (Ibid).

d. Words that attack a person's integrity through an examination of his or her personal life and qualities. These include words and phrases that question a person's honesty, imply drug use, suggest a poor credit rating or indicate the presence of venereal or other contagious diseases.

e. Words and phrases that portray people as incompetent or dishonest businesspersons or professionals.

f. Words that question the abilities of organizations to do honest business.

g. Words that undermine confidence in a product. This is generally referred to as "trade libel."

How do you decide what is defamatory and what is not? A simple test would be to ask yourself if you would: (a) think any less of a person, organization or product after reading the words you just used to describe them; and (b) feel uncomfortable if other people used similar words to describe you in public. If the answer to either question is yes, chances are you could have a potentially libelous message. It might be a good idea to run such messages, or any you are uncomfortable with, by your client's lawyers.

Libel law also looks at photographs (*Peck v. Tribune,* 1909), and cartoons and caricatures (*Brown v. Harrington,* 1911) as extensions of words. If they are derogatory, then there is the risk of a libel suit. Thus, public relations writers must not only be careful about the words they choose, but also about any illustrations accompanying their messages.

2. Identification

Defamatory words by themselves do not constitute libel. For a libel suit to proceed, the person defamed by the words must be identified by the public relations writer. Identification takes place when the defamatory words are directed to a named person. In the examples used at the beginning of this section, the defamed persons were clearly named. Actor Chevy Chase called actor Cary Grant a homosexual on television. Likewise, Dr. Hutchinson was plainly identified as the person allegedly misusing public funds.

Sometimes, the defamed person is not identified by name. There may be clues in the message that point a finger at him or her. In such cases, the courts may acknowledge that identification has taken place. Frederick Hope (in *Hope v. Hearst Corp.,* 1961) successfully argued that there was sufficient information in a gossip column about an affair between an unnamed ex-FBI agent and a wealthy socialite to identify him as that agent. Hope collected $58,000 (Pember 1987, 122).

Thus, the public relations writer must pay attention to the libelous consequences of contextual information as well. (See The Sugarcoat Case Study for more about this.)

The Sugarcoat Case Study

Background Information: You are a staff writer in the public relations department of the Sugarcoat Corp. The company manufactures an assortment of candy and sugar coating for medicines. It has assets of $3.2 billion, 75,000 stockholders, and is located in Washington, D.C.

Situation: One morning, you arrive at work and are told to immediately see your boss, the vice president for public relations. You step into his office and find him extremely distraught and agitated (he can't take pressure too well). The gist of the message he gives you is this:

Thomas A. Kitkat, president, absconded late last evening with more than $1 million in company cash. Also missing is Debbie M. Dietrich, recently promoted to the position of company executive secretary. It is no secret that the two have a fondness for each other. Dietrich's appointment book shows that she was to have joined Kitkat for dinner at the popular Georgetown restaurant, Gourmay Corner. The money was discovered missing about 10 p.m. after company guards found financial manager Sam P. Bear unconscious in his office. Security officials believe that Bear's keys were used to get at the money. Bear himself escaped serious injury and is resting at home. The police were called in. Their own investigations show that Kitkat and Dietrich were booked on a flight to Paradise City in the country of Timbuktoo. The United States does not have an extradition treaty with Timbuktoo.

The Question: Normally, you would research the situation thoroughly before doing anything about it. This time, you discover there is not much else to go by. Determining that you have a material development here, you decide to write a media release (with some of the above information) for use by newspapers and the wire services.

How would you compose this release? We posed this question to several of our students. Here are four versions of the story and an analysis of each of them:

Version 1

Public Relations Department
Sugarcoat Corporation
514 Gooey Lane
Washington, D.C. 20005

Contact: John P. Doe
Day: (000) 000 0000
Night: (000) 000 0000

June 14, 1990

FOR IMMEDIATE RELEASE

WASHINGTON—The Sugarcoat Corp. today reported missing more than $1 million from its headquarters.

Company officials learned of the loss last night after security personnel found finance manager Sam P. Bear unconscious in his office. Bear escaped serious injury.

Police are investigating the incident.

Analysis of Version 1

This writer excludes information about the missing president from the story. This may not be a good idea for the following reasons:

1. By calling in the police, company officials have already released the information into the public domain. Reporters may learn of it either by accident or because they were tipped off by anonymous police sources. If this happened, the company might be forced to defend itself against rumors, speculation and colorful media stories about the Kitkat-Dietrich connection and the role of the pair in the case of the missing money.

2. Because the president is missing, it is a serious material development that the investment community needs to know about. If just the couple was missing, the company could have waited the statutory 24 hours before worrying about them. But here, not only is the couple missing, but so is the money. Hence, the urgency about notifying the police. The Timbuktoo factor further complicates the issue. Being the first to release information about Kitkat in an orderly fashion ensures that the company retains control over the information; minimizes the possibility of rumor and speculation; and provides a reasonable and truthful explanation to the investment community and other relevant publics about the incident.

3. If the media got the information from police sources and printed the story or if rumors got started, because this is a material development, the company would have to immediately clarify the situation anyway.

Version 2

Recognizing that the Kitkat part of the story needed to be told, writer #2 wrote the following story:

WASHINGTON—The Sugarcoat Corp. today reported that it is missing more than $1 million from its local headquarters.

Company officials learned of the loss last night after security personnel found finance manager Sam P. Bear unconscious in his office.

Police are investigating the incident.

The company president, Thomas A. Kitkat, is also missing and is believed to have taken the money. According to police reports, he was booked on a flight to Paradise City, Timbuktoo, along with his secretary, Debbie M. Dietrich.

The United States does not have an extradition treaty with Timbuktoo.

Analysis of Version 2

Though we don't know for sure who took the money; whether the deed was done by one, two or many thieves; or, indeed if the money was stolen at all; the writer places the "theft" of the money squarely upon the missing couple. The writer is on dangerously libelous ground for the following reasons:

1. Only the police may officially label a person a suspect. Only the courts may proclaim a person guilty of a crime. In this instance, even the police have not officially named a suspect.

2. The disclosure of the plane ticket information lends legitimacy to the idea that Kitkat and Dietrich stole the money. The writer has no real evidence that the pair did indeed fly to Paradise City. Anyone can book a flight in anyone else's name. That mere fact does not automatically mean that the person(s) so booked were aboard that plane.

Thus, the writer has quite possibly unleashed a barrage of scandalous media stories. She has also possibly exposed the company (and herself) to a libel suit. Remember, all the writer has is her boss' word that Kitkat ran away with the money. It may later turn out, for example, that the theft (if indeed it was a theft) was the work of a third person who held Kitkat and Dietrich hostage because they happened to catch him or her in the act.

If Kitkat and Dietrich are later found innocent, the writer (and Sugarcoat Corp.) may be sued for invasion of privacy. Kitkat and Dietrich's personal relationship is nobody's business but theirs.

The moral of the story: Be careful. Never speculate, no matter how strong the temptation.

Version 3

WASHINGTON—The Sugarcoat Corp. today announced that it is missing more than $1 million from its local headquarters.

Company officials learned of the loss last night after security personnel found finance manager Sam P. Bear unconscious in his office. Bear escaped serious injury.

The company president, Thomas A. Kitkat, is also feared missing.

The police are investigating both incidents.

Analysis of Version 3

Here, the writer avoids some of the privacy issues confounding version 2 by not mentioning Dietrich. The writer does not call Kitkat a thief. However, because the writer positions the missing president part of the story next to the missing money part without an adequate explanation of the connection between the two, readers may be left with the impression (or jump to the conclusion) that Kitkat took the money. If Kitkat is later proven innocent, the writer (and the company) may be staring at a libel suit.

Version 4

WASHINGTON—The Sugarcoat Corp. today announced that it is missing more than $1 million from its local headquarters.

The loss was discovered last night after security personnel found finance manager Sam P. Bear unconscious in his office. Bear escaped serious injury. No explanation has yet been found to account for the missing money.

In an apparently unrelated incident, the company president Thomas A. Kitkat is also feared missing. There is no evidence, however, linking Kitkat's possible disappearance with the missing money.

Both incidents are being investigated by the police.

The $3.2 billion company manufactures candy and sugar coatings for medicines.

Analysis of Version 4

Now, the writer has it all together. The missing money is reported; so is the missing president, and the relationship between the two incidents is made clear. The writer does not speculate about Kitkat taking the money or even that there was a theft. By not mentioning Dietrich, the writer minimizes the possibility of a privacy suit.

Should it later be proven that Kitkat (and Dietrich) took the money, the writer can update the media on new developments (again without speculating and leaving the actual accusations and the indictments to the police and courts).

3. Publication of Libelous Information

The third condition necessary for libel is publication or other dissemination. For this to happen, only one person other than the person being defamed and the writer needs to see the message. Thus, it would be to the public relations writer's advantage to edit, proof and recheck memos, letters, newsletter articles, press releases and other messages before they are printed, broadcast or otherwise distributed to publics.

4. Fault

The fourth condition of libel is fault. Here, it must be shown that the public relations writer was negligent or careless with the facts or showed a reckless disregard for the truth.

According to Simon (1984, 324), public relations writers can be negligent by: (a) publishing a libelous story by mistake; (b) mistakenly identifying an innocent person because of a typographical or spelling error; and (c) not carefully proofing their copy, thus failing to spot and remove libelous content.

In the landmark *Gertz v. Welch* (1974) case, the U.S. Supreme Court held that a publisher of defamatory material about individuals who are neither public officials nor public figures may not claim any constitutional privilege against liability. Individual states have been left to set standards of liability as long as it is not liability without fault. Because of this, public relations writers should be familiar with state laws and rulings about negligence which may differ significantly. More importantly, they should recognize that the law is not forgiving of typographical and other copy errors that some writers may consider trivial.

In certain circumstances, the negligence standard is not applicable. Then, a disregard for the truth, also referred to as malice, must be established before a libel suit can succeed, thus placing a much heavier burden of proof on the plaintiff (*New York Times v. Sullivan,* 1964). For example, on April 4, 1988, the Supreme Court found that Walter Jacobson, anchor and commentator for WBBM-TV, had uttered deliberate falsehoods about tobacco advertising in a 1981 commentary. A key portion of the commentary read: "An attempt should be made, say Viceroy slicksters, to relate the cigarette to pot, wine, beer and sex. Do not communicate health or health-related points" (Taylor 1988, 11). The U.S. Supreme Court affirmed the findings of lower courts that there was sufficient evidence to establish that Jacobson made the statements despite not finding any pot, sex, wine or beer ads by Viceroy. Also, the fact that Jacobson's assistant destroyed key documents that may have helped the tobacco company prove its case, reinforced the court's opinion that the commentary was malicious. The Brown and Williamson Tobacco Company was awarded a little more than $3 million in damages (Ibid.)

Defenses Against Libel

When faced with a libel suit, the public relations writer can fall back on the following defenses:

1. **That the published words are the truth and can be supported by legally acceptable and verifiable proof.**
2. **That the published words were made in the public interest or in an appropriate context.**

Assume that PRSA informs its members via a newsletter report that John P. Doe has been expelled from the society following his conviction in court for mail fraud.

The message is truthful. The statement cannot damage Doe's reputation any more than the court decision has. It is also a recorded judgment of the only institution in the country with the authority to convict people for proven crimes. Thus, the information is verifiable. PRSA's comment is also fair because not to do otherwise might damage its professional integrity. Besides, the members ought to know.

Thus, the newsletter story meets both the truth and fair comment requirements and thus is not actionable.

Public versus Private Figures

Libel law offers greater protection to private individuals than it does to public figures. There are two reasons for this. One, public figures are presumed to have access to mass media and other public information channels to defend themselves from libelous material. By contrast, the only recourse private individuals have is the law courts.

A second reason is that controversy and personal attacks are often recognized as the price people have to pay for achieving public recognition. In the course of public debate, some public figures may be maligned. But in order to preserve the environment of free debate which is so valued under the First Amendment of the U.S. Constitution, the "threat of libel actions is minimized" (Pember 1987, 147).

There are three types of public figures:

1. Public Officials. This includes people such as mayors, city managers, senators and members of Congress who hold public office and whose official actions affect a wide variety of people. In *New York Times v. Sullivan* (1964), the U.S. Supreme Court held that where public officials are concerned, malice must be proved to establish libel.

2. Public Figures. These are opinion leaders and influential persons such as actors and actresses. In some instances, business executives like Donald Trump achieve the status of a public figure because they are regularly in the public limelight.

3. Limited Public Figures. This category consists of people who are temporarily thrust into the public limelight because of their involvement in events. When the events end, limited public figures generally become private individuals again.

However, public relations writers must not allow themselves to be affected by these distinctions. They should ensure that their messages do not libel anyone, private or public.

Privacy

Generally, privacy law, which also varies from state to state, is designed to protect the private lives of people from being invaded by the glare of publicity. Specifically, privacy law is not one but four distinct entities (Prosser 1971, 739). These are:

1. Disclosure of private facts, i.e., personal and confidential information
This aspect of privacy law ties it very closely to libel law (see The Sugarcoat case study earlier in this chapter). Often, libel suits arise because private and embarrassing information about people is used to undermine their public reputations.

Some types of information protected by this part of the privacy law are:

A. Information about a person's financial history and status which, if revealed publicly, can be embarrassing or demeaning. Thus, it is potentially dangerous for public relations writers to imply, for example, that a person is bankrupt, owes money or lives beyond his or her means.

B. Information about a person's medical history or health status. It is inappropriate for public relations writers to, for example, publicly comment that a person is an alcoholic, or has AIDS or cancer.

Model Consent Release

In consideration of the sum of (amount) dollar(s) and other valuable consideration, the receipt of which is hereby acknowledged, I certify to being over 21 years of age and hereby give (organization's name), its successors and assigns and those acting under its permission or upon its authority, the unqualified right and permission to reproduce, copyright, publish, circulate or otherwise use photographic reproductions or likenesses of me and/or my name. This authorization and release covers the use of said material in any published form and any medium of advertising, publicity or trade in any part of the world for 10 years from the date of this release or as long as I am an employee of said organization.

Furthermore, for the consideration above mentioned, I, for myself, my heirs, executors, administrators or assigns, sell, assign and transfer to the organization, its successors and assigns, all my rights, title and interests in and to all reproductions taken of me by representatives of the organization. This agreement fully represents all terms and considerations and no other inducements, statements or promises have been made to me.

Signature: (employee)
Date:
Signature: (organization representative)
Date:

(While this model consent release provides most of the requirements of a valid release form, each organization should consider its special circumstances before designing a consent form. As written, this model may or may not provide adequate protection.)

Reprinted with permission from the Sept. 1983 issue of the *Public Relations Journal.*
Copyright © 1983 Public Relations Society of America.

C. Comments about a person's sexual preference. The public relations writer is cautioned against reporting, for example, that a named employee is gay or bisexual.

It must be noted that the privacy law is similarly affected by the distinction between public and private persons, as is libel law.

2. Publication of information that portrays a person in false light

This is important to the public relations writer because it involves publicity that creates wrong impressions about people in the minds of an organization's publics. "This kind of privacy case might be described as a libel case but without defamation" (Overbeck 1989, 81).

Simplified Model Consent Release

I, _____ , give _____
  (Consenter's full name)   **(organization's name)**
**permission to use photographs of me for any lawful purpose related to the
organization's business activities, including advertising and publicity, for the
next 10 years. I am 21 or more years old. I (have received adequate
compensation/do not desire compensation) for this permission.**

Signature: _____   **Date:** _____
          (Consenter)

Signature: _____   **Date:** _____
          (Organization representative)

---

3. Intrusion

This happens when a person uses equipment such as tape recorders or video cameras
to record another person's activities or words without that person's permission. Public
relations writers normally interview many people for their stories. None of these interviews should be recorded or videotaped without the written permission of the person
being so documented. There are no exceptions to this rule.

4. Misappropriation (invasion of the right of publicity)

This occurs when a public relations writer uses a person's photograph or likeness in
organizational or promotional literature without permission. Most organizations have
a standard consent form that public relations writers are well advised to use.

While the Model Consent Release on the previous page fills legal requirements for
most organizations, some prefer to use a more simplified version like that above.

Copyright Law

Public relations writers generate vast numbers of messages for their clients. Some of
these are original, unique, artistic and thus valuable. Others may be based on the creative works of other writers. How can public relations writers protect their original
works from being misused by others? Also, how can they avoid the legal tangles that
may arise when they use creative materials produced by others? Answering these and
other questions about the protection, use and misuse of literary products requires an
understanding of copyright law.

Definition and Scope

Generally, obtaining copyright is an important means of: "protecting one's creative efforts. (It gives) authors and other creative persons (the ownership of, and) monopoly on the use of their creations for a certain period of time" (Dunn 1986, 181). Copyright protection is provided by the Copyright Act, enacted in 1909 and last revised in 1988, to:

1. Literary works as such, fiction and nonfiction books; poems; and articles, feature stories, opinion pieces and columns appearing in newspapers, magazines, newsletters and house journals.

2. Musical works, including lyrics.

3. Motion picture and other audiovisual productions such as commercial and corporate newscasts, video news releases, features, training films and PSAs.

4. Other works of art such as sculptures, graphic arrangements, photographs, murals and paintings.

Copyright protection is given to the style, presentation and expression of ideas, not to the ideas themselves. Similarly, the facts and particular expression of historical and scientific facts can be protected, but not the facts themselves (Overbeck 1989, 89).

Obtaining Copyright

Any type of work listed above can be officially copyrighted by sending two copies of the work, a completed application form and a $10 fee to the U.S. Copyright Office at the Library of Congress, Washington, D.C. 20559. Copyrighted works are authorized to carry the legend, "Copyright (year) (name of the person or institution owning the copyright)." Sometimes, the universal copyright symbol is used in the legend instead of the word. However, legal experts recommend the use of both to prevent international copyright violations:

Copyright © 1991 P. Doe
Copyright © 1991 Mobil Corp.

Duration of Copyright

The Copyright Act distinguishes between two types of creative properties. The first is "original," which is protected for the duration of the life of an author (or the last surviving author in the case of multiple authorships) plus 50 years.

The second type of creative property is called "work for hire." As the name suggests, such property is usually commissioned by and created for other people. An example might be a speech an organization pays a public relations professional to write. In such cases, the commissioning organization usually files for and owns the copyright. Such works are protected for 75 years from the date of publication (the day the speech is delivered), or 100 years from the date of creation (the day the completed speech was delivered to the client by the writer), whichever causes the copyright to expire sooner.

Public Domain

After the specified periods of time, copyrighted works pass into public domain; that is, they cease to be protected by the Copyright Act and can be used by anyone without permission or payment of royalty.

Conventions for Use

We have said that public relations writers may build their messages upon the creative expression of others. When these messages are copyrighted, the following protocol needs to be followed:

Obtaining Permission

The copyright law gives owners the right to monopolize and profit from their creations. Anyone else reproducing, printing, dramatizing, translating or otherwise using copyrighted materials must obtain the owner's written permission. Figure 14.1 shows the form we used to obtain permission for use of copyrighted materials in this book. Sometimes, the user may have to pay the owner a fee or royalty. In such cases, the amount varies with the nature of the request, the use the material is being put to and the perceived profit or gain for the user.

Exceptions

The copyright law falls short of giving owners absolute monopoly. That is, in some instances, small portions of copyrighted materials can be used without the owner's permission. These instances, listed in the "fair use" doctrine of the Copyright Act, are:

1. Use for nonprofit or noncommercial purposes. Usually this aspect of the fair use doctrine is pertinent to teachers, scholars and reporters who may use copyrighted materials for advancement of knowledge or in public interest. Public relations writers should be cautious about invoking this argument since much of what they write can be used for commercial gain.

2. Use of material that is not readily available. This includes use of copyrighted materials that are out of print. However, Pember (1987, 473) cautions against using this excuse to reproduce works that have never been formally published or "consumable materials like workbooks, standardized tests and so forth."

3. Use of limited or small portions of copyrighted materials. As textbook authors, we are told that we may not directly quote a passage of more than 250 words from a copyrighted work without the author's permission. However, the courts judge this case by case by looking at the overall damage the quoted material is likely to do to the commercial value of the copyrighted work. For example, in *Harper & Row v. The Nation* (1986), the U.S. Supreme Court decided that *The Nation* violated copyright law when it published a 300-word passage from former U.S. President Gerald Ford's memoirs before Harper & Row had a chance to publish it.

July 14, 1988

Ms. Barbara Wruck
Manager, Corporate Communications
Coleco Corporate Center
999 Quaker Lane South
West Hartford, CT 06110

I am preparing a book and accompanying ancillaries on <u>PR Writing</u> to be published by Wm. C. Brown Company Publishers. May I please have your permission to quote from

Your publication <u>Press release</u>

by <u>Coleco Corporate Center</u>

the following material: <u>"Oh my gosh! The Cabbage Patch Talking Kids have</u>

<u>arrived in New York City" I would like to make some kind of a composite</u>

<u>of the first and last page (enc.) to demonstrate how you use and care for</u>

trade-

in my book and its ancillaries and in future revisions and editions thereof, including nonexclusive marks world rights in all languages. These rights will in no way restrict republication of your material in any other form by you or others authorized by you. Should you not control these rights in their entirety, would you kindly let me know whom else I must write.

Unless you indicate otherwise, I will use the following credit line:

<u>Reprinted with the permission of Coleco Industries</u>

I would greatly appreciate your consent to this request. For your convenience a release form is provided below and a copy of this letter is enclosed for your files.

Sincerely yours,

Lalit Acharya, Assistant Professor
Department of Communications
California State University, Fullerton
Fullerton, California 92634

I (We) grant permission for the use requested above.

Barbara Wruck

Date _7/21/88_

▶ **Figure 14.1.** Permission request for copyrighted materials.

Keep in mind that the fair use provisions of the Copyright Act are complex. There are no easy answers to what constitutes substantial use and what is fair and marginal use. If you have doubts, consult a lawyer before acting.

Acknowledging Permission

When copyrighted material is used with the owner's permission, it must be acknowledged by reproducing the copyright notice (Copyright © 1991 Wm. C. Brown Company Publishers) and a permission notice (Reprinted with permission). The tabled materials in this book provide several examples of copyright acknowledgement.

Penalties for Copyright Violation

If you violate the copyright law, you and your client could be sued for actual damages (your net profits from the work based on the unauthorized use of copyrighted material), statutory damages, attorney fees and other litigation costs.

It is interesting to note that even owners of unregistered copyrights are protected from infringement by the law, even if to a lesser extent. Such persons usually register the work and then file a lawsuit and are entitled to actual damages, but not statutory damages and legal costs.

Trademark Law

Fabrica D'Armi P. Beretta, an Italian arms manufacturer since the late 15th century, sued General Motors (maker of the Beretta automobile) July 19, 1988, for $250 million for trademark infringement. The Italian company claimed that its "centuries-old reputation for fine workmanship would be ruined if the carmaker continues producing the four-wheeled Beretta" ("Arms Maker Sues," 1988, C3). The company also claimed that it "had registered trademarks in this country for the Beretta name as far back as 1954," and that "it had warned GM about using the Beretta name before the automaker unveiled the Chevrolet model in 1987" (Ibid.)

According to a 1989 report, GM—in order to keep the Beretta name for its automobile—acknowledged Beretta's predominant right to use the name and donated $500,000 to the Beretta Foundation for Cancer Research in Switzerland ("Beretta Cites GM Accord" 1989, B4).

This lawsuit demonstrates the fierceness with which companies protect and preserve their trademarks. These are unique symbols, names, logos or expressions companies use to identify their products. **Coke®, Kleenex®** and **Xerox®** are examples of familiar trademarks. Other, less familiar trademarks are included in Table 14.2. When such unique symbols are used to identify services, they are called "servicemarks."

Trademarks are protected by the 1946 Lanham Act, extensively revised by Congress in the Trademark Law Revision Act of 1988. This act gives a trademark infinite life, provided its owner works hard to retain its uniqueness. When trademarks are allowed

TABLE 14.2.   Some Common and Uncommon Trademarks

Ajax   household cleaners, detergent
American Express   financial services and charge cards
Apple   computers
Ben Gay   muscle pain relieving ointment
Big Mac   hamburger
Budweiser   beer
Chap Stick   lip balm
Chuck Wagon   dog food
Coke   soft cola drink
Cover Girl   make-up and facial care products
Duracell   batteries
Ex-Lax   laxatives
Glad   plastic and trash bags
IBM   computers
Kleenex   tissues
Kodacolor   photographic film
Listerine   mouthwash
Nutrasweet   artificial sweeteners and sugar substitutes
Realtors   or real estate agents who are members of the National Association of Realtors
Rolodex   card files
Snickers   candy bars
Stetson   hats
Xerox   photocopy machines

to be misused, they lapse into unprotected generic words that anyone may use in whatever fashion they choose. For example, the Du Pont Company allowed its trademark "cellophane" to be appropriated and abused by a variety of people. When the company finally tried to rescue its trademark in a court battle, it was too late. The trademark had lost its exclusivity and had become a generic term for transparent wrapping.

Trademark Protection

Trademarks can be protected in three ways: (a) by placing ads reminding others of the uniqueness of the trademark; (b) by policing the marketplace to make sure that other people are not abusing a trademark; and (c) by making sure that a trademark symbol stands out every time it is used in organizational or other literature.

Public relations writers are involved in the care and protection of trademarks in two ways: by writing copy for the trademark reminder ads; and by ensuring that trademarks are properly highlighted in organizational literature.

Figures 14.2, 14.3, and 14.4 illustrate how public relations writers may properly use, identify, highlight and protect trademark symbols in their writing.

You—each and every employee—play a most valuable role in preserving and enhancing our trademarks. For this reason it is important that you thoroughly understand how our trademarks are to be used.

A *trademark* is a word (or several words), a name, a symbol (such as one or more letters, or numbers, or a design), or any combination of these, used to identify the goods of our company. Some well-known trademarks are KODAK, LYSOL, and TEFLON. The mere use of a trademark to identify and distinguish the goods of our company from those of another creates trademark rights. However, in order to obtain additional advantages most companies register their trademarks in the United States Patent and Trademark Office.

The *generic* name is the common descriptive name of the product it identifies. For example, "instant lather shaving cream" is the generic name that goes with RISE and "depilatory cream" is the generic name that goes with NAIR.

A trademark must not be confused with a *trade name*, which identifies a company. COKE is a trademark of The Coca-Cola Company. "The Coca-Cola Company" is the trade name.

Trademarks must be protected and cared for or they will be lost. Many trademarks which were once the proud possessions of corporate families have been lost because they were misused. Some famous *former* trademarks are: escalator, kerosene, shredded wheat, cellophane and mimeograph. A trademark is lost when it becomes *generic*, i.e. when it has come to mean the product as distinguished from a certain brand of the product.

If our trademarks became generic, they could be used by anyone and would no longer indicate to the public that the products on which they were used, were made, supplied or sold by our company.

Our company's trademarks are well-known and signify to the purchaser that he is buying quality products from a company with a reputation for dependability and integrity.

Trademarks are one of our most important assets and should be treated with the care due something so valuable.

It is relatively easy to protect and care for trademarks. You need only follow the simple rules listed here. These rules should be followed on all business documents, advertising literature, displays, packaging, labels and correspondence.

If you have any questions relating to the rules of trademark use, call the Trademark Department.

How to care for trademarks.

1. Trademarks are loners. They must be distinguished in print from other words and must appear in a distinctive manner.

A trademark should always be used in a manner which will distinguish it from the surrounding text. Capitalize trademarks completely, or use initial caps with quotes, or as a minimum use initial caps. The generic product name should not be capitalized. If the material is being prepared by a printer, other suitable alternatives for distinguishing the trademarks are to place it in italics, bolder-faced type or a different color.

Example
ARRID cream deodorant
"Arrid" cream deodorant
Arrid cream deodorant

▶ **Figure 14.2.** A guide to the care of trademarks. Reprinted with the permission of the United States Trademark Association.

2. Trademarks are status seekers and ask that they be followed by a notice of their status.

Whenever possible a trademark notice should follow the mark. As a minimum requirement, it should be used at least once in each piece of printed matter and preferably the first time the trademark appears. If a trademark has been registered in the U.S. Patent and Trademark Office, the registration notice ® or "*Reg. U.S. Pat. & Tm. Off." should be used. The ® or Reg. U.S. Pat. & Tm. Off. should never be used if the trademark has not been registered for the product concerned. In such a case, the letters TM should follow the mark or an asterisk can be used to refer to a footnote stating, "*A trademark of — — — —".

Example
ANSCOMATIC® camera
SHEETROCK* gypsum wallboard
XYZ™
XYZ†

*Reg. U.S. Pat. & Tm. Off.
™(if the mark is not yet registered)
†A trademark of X Company

3. Trademarks like good company and should be accompanied by the generic name for the product they identify.

A trademark is a proper adjective and should, whenever possible, be followed by the common descriptive name (noun) of the product. This should be done at least the first time the trademark appears in a piece of printed material.

Example

Trademark	Generic Name
KODAK®	cameras
JEEP®	vehicles
VASELINE®	petroleum jelly
LEVI'S®	jeans and sportswear

The word *brand* may also be used to reduce the possibility that the trademark will be thought of as the generic name for the product, or a line of products. When used, it should always appear in small print.

Example
BAND-AID® brand adhesive bandages
SCOTCH® brand transparent tape
PYREX® brand heat-resistant glassware

4. Trademarks are not clinging vines. They are never possessive.

Never use a trademark in the possessive form.

Example
Correct—
The good taste of FRENCHETTE® low calorie salad dressings. The fine quality of PAMPERS® disposable diapers.

Wrong—
FRENCHETTE'S good taste
PAMPERS' fine quality

▶ **Figure 14.2** *(continued)*

5. Trademarks are singular.

Since a trademark is not a noun, it should never be used in the plural form.

Please note, however, that some trademarks actually end with "s" such as KEDS®, COETS®, Q-Tips®.

Example
Correct—
Take some pictures with KODACOLOR® film.
The doctor prescribed MILTOWN® tranquilizer tablets.

Wrong—
Take some KODACOLORS.
The doctor prescribed MILTOWNS.

6. Trademarks are never common. They are always proper.

Trademarks are proper adjectives and should never be used as common descriptive adjectives.

Thus, never use a trademark for a raw material to describe finished products made from it.

Example
Correct—
This flotation equipment made of STYROFOAM® plastic foam can be readily installed.

Wrong—
This STYROFOAM® flotation equipment can be readily installed.

Since a trademark is a proper adjective and not a verb, it should never be used as a verb.

Example
Correct—
Make six copies on the XEROX® copier.
            or
Make a photocopy.
Polish your car with SIMONIZ® paste wax.

Wrong—
XEROX® the report
SIMONIZ® your car

7. Trademarks are proud of the companies that own them.

If it is not readily apparent who owns the trademark, for example, where the company letterhead is not being used, a notice of ownership should be given. This can be accomplished by placing an asterisk after the trademark, which refers to a footnote stating that the trademark is the brand name for a product which is made by our company.

Example
JELL-O*
*JELL-O is a registered trademark for dessert products made by General Foods.

★   ★   ★   ★   ★

And, if you still have questions about trademarks, call the Trademark Department.

THE UNITED STATES TRADEMARK ASSOCIATION
6 East 45th Street, New York, New York 10017

▶ **Figure 14.2**   *(continued)*

INDUSTRIES, INC.

COLECO CORPORATE CENTER

FOR IMMEDIATE RELEASE
September 17, 1987

CONTACT:

Cynthia Plaisted/Bob Bagar
Bozell, Jacobs, Kenyon & Eckhardt
(212) 484-7400
         or
Donna Wolf, Manager
Corporate Communications
Coleco Industries, Inc.
(203) 725-6617

①

OH MY GOSH! THE CABBAGE PATCH TALKING KIDS ®
HAVE ARRIVED IN NEW YORK CITY

         New York, NY -- An eager public of grown-ups and kids alike
② were enthralled today as Xavier Roberts, creator of the CABBAGE
    PATCH KIDS®, arrived at "BABYLAND On Fifth" in a 35-foot
    s-t-r-e-t-c-h Kidmobile, filled to the roof with the first of
    the CABBAGE PATCH TALKING KIDS®.

         Speaking with obvious pride, both Xavier Roberts and Brian
    Clarke agreed that while there are other talking toys available, the
    TALKING KIDS represent the unbeatable combination of advanced   ③
③ technology with the tremendous appeal that has made all CABBAGE
    PATCH KIDS so popular.

         The enthusiastic reaction of today's crowd prompted both
    gentlemen to advise potential parents to "adopt early!"

                              # # # #

④   © 1987 CABBAGE PATCH KIDS® and all related trademarks are owned
     by and licensed from Original Appalachian Artworks, Inc.,
     Cleveland, Georgia, U.S.A. All Rights Reserved.

▶ **Figure 14.3.   Acknowledging and protecting trademarks.** Public relations writers can do this through capitalization plus the ™ symbol ①; capitalization plus the ® symbol ②; capitalization only ③; and trademark acknowledgment statements ④. © 1987 Coleco Industries, Inc. Reprinted with permission.

THE WORD FRIGIDAIRE ALWAYS ENDS WITH A CAPITAL "R."

The capital "R" has a circle around it, too. Because Frigidaire® is more than an ordinary word, it's our registered trademark.

To many, it means the finest quality refrigerator available. It's a name that's so popular some people call every refrigerator a Frigidaire® Unfortunately, that's wrong.

Only Frigidaire® refrigerators have the quality, engineering and heritage to bear the name.

So if a refrigerator really is a Frigidaire® say so.

If it's not, use the other word that ends with an "R". Refrigerator. We would **Frigidaire®** appreciate it. **HERE TODAY. HERE TOMORROW.**

One of the White Consolidated Industries

WASHINGTON JOURNALISM REVIEW

▶ **Figure 14.4.**   Protection of the registered trademark. Copyright © White Consolidated Industries, Inc. Reprinted with permission.

Corporate Publications Laws

Public relations writers spend a considerable portion of their time writing corporate publications such as newsletters and brochures. Thus, they must be aware of some special legal concerns that touch upon the planning, editing, publication and distribution of such material.

Publication

Since corporate publications, even those intended primarily for internal publics, end up reaching external audiences, the writer is vulnerable to libel and privacy lawsuits.

We have already provided writing guidelines for minimizing the danger of a libel suit. The corporate writer can similarly minimize the danger of a privacy lawsuit by:

1. Making sure that employees who are mentioned in corporate literature are currently employed by the organization. Writers (and their companies) using names and photographs of persons no longer working for them may be sued for invasion of privacy.

2. Ensuring that written permission is obtained from all employees whose names and photographs appear in corporate literature. Some companies have employees sign a generalized consent form covering all prospective uses of their names and photographs in promotional literature (Simon 1969, 583). Permission may not be necessary when an employee's name and photograph are used in connection with company events that are newsworthy, as, for example, a newsletter story about a workplace safety campaign. Likewise, employees' names and photographs may be used without permission for company events the employees are associated with, such as development of a new product (Ibid.)

3. Ensuring that trademarks (and their owners) are properly cared for and highlighted in company literature. This has already been discussed. However, a point to note is that the title of a corporate publication is registerable as a trademark. If it has been, the writer must take care to highlight this fact.

4. Ensuring that all literary properties belonging to the company are copyrighted and thus protected. Such properties include: original stories and articles, freelance articles commissioned by the writer, artwork, cartoons and photographs, technical literature, films, video and audiotapes.

Republication

Public relations writers often reprint media news stories or features in their company publications. If they do, they must:

1. Ensure that they have obtained copyright permission to reprint the article. Note that media stories are copyrighted and not republishable without permission.

2. Ensure that written permission is obtained from individuals repeatedly mentioned in media stories, especially if such stories are going to be reprinted and distributed by companies for promotional purposes. In 1959, the Mosler Safe Co. reprinted and distributed a news story about a fire along with a circular recommending purchase of its fireproof safes. The original news story contained several references to a "Mr. Flores" as having been at the site of the fire. Flores objected to his name being used by Mosler for advertising purposes. He sued and won (Simon 1969, 584).

Distribution

Just as the securities laws govern the distribution of information, the Robinson-Patman Act of 1962 regulates the distribution of corporate publications.

Corporate publications contain large amounts of valuable information about a company's performance, philosophy, products and services. Often, a company's dealers, suppliers and customers will use such information in their own plans for doing business with the company. Recognizing this, companies may send multiple copies to some clients for their own use.

According to the provisions of the Robinson-Patman Act, companies are bound to treat all customers equally. This means that all people doing business with a company must get roughly the same quantities of corporate publications as their competitors do. If a company plays favorites in the distribution of such publications, it can be investigated by the FTC.

The Robinson-Patman Act also requires company publications accepting paid advertising to offer this opportunity to all of its clients. This is to ensure that some clients are not unfairly strong-armed into advertising in a company's publications.

Ethical Conventions

Between January 1986 and February 1987, the SEC charged 13 people and at least one company with insider trading. Among those accused were Ivan Boesky, a Wall Street investor, who was fined a record $100 million, and Anthony Franco, whose case we have already discussed.

In April 1988, former White House spokesman Larry Speakes said that he invented a quotation and attributed it without permission to President Ronald Reagan during a 1985 summit meeting with Soviet leader Mikhail Gorbachev. The fictitious quotation: "The world breathes easier because we [Mr. Reagan and Mr. Gorbachev] are talking together."

Less than a week after his admission, Speakes resigned his position as vice president of communications at Merrill Lynch.

These incidents focused national attention on the need for more rigorous ethical standards in business, and more importantly, in public relations.

Definition

Ethics is a complex concept, difficult to define and practice. According to Wilcox, Ault and Agee (1986, 108):

> **Ethics refers to a value system by which a person determines what is right or wrong, fair or unfair, just or unjust. It is expressed through moral behavior in specific situations.**

Thus, ethics, for the most part, are people's judgments about whether particular actions are right or wrong. Unfortunately, such judgments are complicated by society's standards about what is or isn't ethical at a given point in time; by the person's upbringing and cultural background; and by the constraints of the specific situation meriting the ethical decision.

Recognizing this difficulty, we offer some guidelines to help the public relations writer figure out what is ethical behavior and what is not. Our discussion is centered around four themes: public interest, good taste, fair play and performance.

Public Interest

Much of what the public relations writer generates impacts society. Because of their public values, public relations messages are regulated by the laws discussed so far.

Many of the actions that are illegal—insider trading, misrepresentation—are also unethical. The PRSA code, perhaps the most authoritative source of public relations ethics, recognizes this parallel between good law and good ethics. Its interpretation of ethical financial relations (see table 14.4) merits reading as an ethical reaffirmation of good law. It threads together, as the general code does (see table 14.3), the ethical view that public relations best serves the public interest through truth, honesty and integrity.

To achieve this, the public relations writer must avoid:

1. Composing messages that hurt the credibility and undermine the effectiveness of governmental institutions. The Speakes case is an example of this. Marlin Fitzwater, Speakes' successor at the White House, reacted angrily and said that the comments had cast aspersions on the Presidency of the United States as well as his (Fitzwater's) position.

2. Composing messages encouraging anarchy and subversion of the Constitution and government of the United States.

3. Selling, even inadvertently giving away, sensitive information (defense secrets and other information vital to national security) to representatives of foreign governments. This is especially important if the writer is retained by foreign-based clients.

4. Composing messages that are insensitive and incite racial and other types of hatred, contempt, ridicule and violence.

5. Composing misleading and inaccurate messages. This has already been discussed in the law segment.

Good Taste

This generally means avoiding words, phrases and messages that are obscene, racist, derogatory, demeaning or offensive. In a burst of offensive publicity, the Sigma Chi fraternity plastered the University of Colorado-Boulder campus with rush posters that included the photograph of an obese, nude black woman. Its caption: "Black Mama Jama says rush Sigma Chi." In the lower right corner of the poster was the message, "Come play with me" (Phemister 1978, 1). Some of the posters appeared on Jan. 18, the day honoring the slain civil rights leader, Martin Luther King Jr. The fraternity acknowledged that the poster was in bad taste after it drew cries of outrage from campus minority and other groups (Ibid.)

TABLE 14.3. Code of Professional Standards for the Practice of Public Relations

---

Public Relations Society of America

---

1. A member shall conduct his or her professional life in accord with **public interest.**

2. A member shall exemplify high standards of **honesty and integrity** while carrying out dual obligations to a client or employer and to the democratic process.

3. A member shall **deal fairly** with the public, with past or present clients or employers, and with fellow practitioners, giving due respect to the ideal of free inquiry and to the opinions of others.

4. A member shall adhere to the highest standards of **accuracy and truth,** avoiding extravagant claims or unfair comparisons and giving credit for ideas and words borrowed from others.

5. A member shall not knowingly disseminate **false or misleading information** and shall act promptly to correct erroneous communications for which he or she is responsible.

6. A member shall not engage in any practice which has the purpose of **corrupting** the integrity of channels of communications or the processes of government.

7. A member shall be prepared to **identify publicly** the name of the client or employer on whose behalf any public communication is made.

8. A member shall not use any individual or organization professing to serve or represent an announced cause, or professing to be independent or unbiased, but actually serving another or **undisclosed interest.**

9. A member shall not **guarantee the achievement** of specified results beyond the member's direct control.

10. A member shall **not represent conflicting** or competing interests without the express consent of those concerned, given after a full disclosure of the facts.

11. A member shall not place himself or herself in a position where the member's **personal interest is or may be in conflict** with an obligation to an employer or client, or others, without full disclosure of such interests to all involved.

12. A member shall **not accept fees, commissions, gifts or any other consideration** from anyone except clients or employers for whom services are performed without their express consent, given after full disclosure of the facts.

13. A member shall scrupulously safeguard the **confidences and privacy rights of** present, former and prospective clients or employers.

14. A member shall not intentionally **damage the professional reputation** or practice of another practitioner.

15. If a member has evidence that another member has been guilty of unethical, illegal, or unfair practices, including those in violation of this Code, the member is obligated to present the information promptly to the proper authorities of the Society for action in accordance with the procedure set forth in Article XII of the Bylaws.

16. A member called as a witness in a proceeding for the enforcement of the Code is obligated to appear, unless excused for sufficient reason by the judicial panel.

17. A member shall, as soon as possible, sever relations with any organization or individual if such relationship requires conduct contrary to the articles of this Code.

This Code was adopted by the PRSA Assembly in 1988. It replaces a Code of Ethics in force since 1950 and revised in 1954, 1959, 1963, 1977 and 1983.

TABLE 14.4. An Interpretation of the PRSA Code as It Applies to Financial Public Relations

1. It is the responsibility of PRSA members who practice financial public relations to be thoroughly familiar with and understand the rules and regulations of the SEC and the laws it administers, as well as other laws, rules and regulations affecting financial public relations, and to act in accordance with their letter and spirit. In carrying out this responsibility, members shall also seek legal counsel, when appropriate, on matters concerning financial public relations.

2. Members shall adhere to the general policy of making full and timely disclosure of corporate information on behalf of clients or employers. The information disclosed shall be accurate, clear and understandable. The purpose of such disclosure is to provide the investing public with all material information affecting security values or influencing investment decisions. In complying with the duty of full and timely disclosure, members shall present all material facts, including those adverse to the company. They shall exercise care to ascertain the facts and to disseminate only information they believe to be accurate. They shall not knowingly omit information, the omission of which might make a release false or misleading. Under no circumstances shall members participate in any activity designed to mislead or manipulate the price of a company's securities.

3. Members shall publicly disclose or release information promptly so as to avoid the possibility of any use of the information by an insider or third party. To that end, members shall make every effort to comply with the spirit and intent of the timely-disclosure policies of the stock exchanges, NASD, and the SEC. Material information shall be made available on an equal basis.

4. Members shall not disclose confidential information the disclosure of which might be adverse to a valid corporate purpose or interest and whose disclosure is not required by the timely-disclosure provisions of the law. During any such period of non-disclosure, members shall not directly or indirectly: (a) communicate the confidential information to any other person, or (b) buy or sell or in any other way deal in the company's securities where the confidential information may materially affect the market for the security when disclosed. Material information shall be disclosed publicly as soon as its confidential status has terminated or the requirement of timely disclosure takes effect.

5. During the registration period, members shall not engage in practices designed to precondition the market for such securities. During registration, the issuance of forecasts, projections, predictions about sales and earnings or opinions concerning security values or other aspects of the future performance of the company, shall be in accordance with current SEC regulations and statements of policy. In the case of companies whose securities are publicly held, the normal flow of factual information to shareholders and the investing public shall continue during the registration period.

6. Where members have any reason to doubt that projections have an adequate basis in fact, they shall satisfy themselves as to the adequacy of the projections prior to disseminating them.

7. Acting in concert with clients or employers, members shall act promptly to correct false or misleading information or rumors concerning clients' or employers' securities or business whenever they have reason to believe such information or rumors are materially affecting investor attitudes.

8. Members shall not issue descriptive materials designed or written in such a fashion as to appear to be, contrary to fact, an independent third-party endorsement or recommendation of a company or a security. Whenever members issue material for clients or employers, either in their own names or in the name of someone other than the clients or employers, they shall disclose in large type and in prominent position on the face of the material the source of such material and the existence of the issuer's client or employer relationship.

9. Members shall not use inside information for personal gain. However, this is not intended to prohibit members from making bona fide investments in their company's or client's securities insofar as they can make such investment without the benefit of material inside information.

TABLE 14.4 (*continued*)

10. Members shall not accept compensation that would place them in a position of conflict with their duty to a client, employer, or the investing public. Members shall not accept stock options from clients or employers nor accept securities as compensation at a price below market price except as part of an overall plan for corporate employees.

11. Members shall act so as to maintain the integrity of channels of public communication. They shall not pay or permit to be paid to any publication or other communications medium any consideration in exchange for publicizing a company, except through clearly recognizable paid advertising.

12. Members shall in general be guided by the PRSA Declaration of Principles and the Code of Professional Standards for the Practice of Public Relations of which this is an official interpretation.

Fair Play

This includes avoiding:

1. Composing messages that undermine the professional reputation of fellow public relations practitioners. Exceptions are when the writer has proof that a practitioner has engaged in "unethical, illegal or unfair practices" (see Articles 14 and 15 of the PRSA Code in Table 14.3).

2. Using or conveying confidential information provided by past or present clients to others for personal profit.

3. Accepting writing assignments from competing clients without their knowledge and permission.

Performance

This involves guaranteeing results beyond the capabilities of the public relations writer. For example, writers cannot promise clients that their press releases will be used. This is because the writers do not control the editorial processes and personnel that determine what will appear in a newspaper.

Another aspect of performance is failing to do the best job the public relations writer can, and is being paid to do.

Consequences

Public relations writers who violate the canons of ethical behavior:

1. Also violate the law in many instances, thus jeopardizing their freedom and careers.

2. Destroy their personal and professional credibility and sense of worth. Such writers are of no use to clients.

3. Damage the credibility and reputations of their clients. Executives at Merrill Lynch were reportedly upset and concerned that the credibility of their organization had been seriously damaged by Speakes' revelations.

4. Demean and undermine the profession of public relations by their behavior. The Speakes incident, which focused a lot of negative public attention on the public relations profession, was denounced by public relations practitioners as a breach of professional ethics.

Chapter Summary

In this chapter, we walked you through some of the legal and ethical implications of public relations writing.

We started off with a discussion of the laws regulating the disclosure of financial and other material information. We examined the securities laws and their implications for public relations writers. In particular, we examined insider trading and misrepresentation, and their penalties. We also alerted the public relations writer to policing agencies such as the SEC, the FTC, the FDA and the U.S. Postal Service.

Next examined were laws of diminished worth such as libel, privacy, copyright and trademark and their relationship to the public relations writer.

The chapter also explained some special legal considerations for writers and managers who plan, edit, publish and distribute corporate publications.

The last section of the chapter dealt with ethical considerations facing the public relations writer and the consequences of violating them.

A final word. A sound understanding of the law and ethics of public relations writing will probably be one of your most prized possessions. Learn and guard this information well. Your survival as a writer may well depend upon it. Above all, never hesitate to consult a lawyer.

Writing Exercises

1. *Situation:* You are a staff writer in the public relations department of the Sugarcoat Corp. This Washington, D.C., company is the largest manufacturer of candy (get creative with the brand names) and sugar coatings for medicines. It has assets of $3.2 billion and 75,000 stockholders. One afternoon, you are given the following information (scribbled on the back of an old memo, of course) by your colorful and eccentric boss, the vice president for public relations.

The facts according to your boss:

At an emergency meeting this morning, Thomas Kitkat, chairman and founder of the company, announced that he is resigning due to a terminal case of cancer. He said that he has less than six months to live. The shocked board quickly moved to appoint Harry Softsell, senior vice president of marketing, as interim chairman, promising to find a permanent replacement within six months.

Some background information:

Kitkat, 62, has a wife, Martha, and two sons, Peter and Paul. He is an alumnus of Harvard University, where he obtained an M.B.A. degree in 1952. He has since served on the board of directors of the Futuristic Biomedical Corp., the Advanced Aerospace Corp. and the Laserbeam Telephone Co. Kitkat was responsible for turning the small candy company he founded in 1973 into the giant Sugarcoat Corp.

His tenure as chairman of Sugarcoat, however, has not been without its share of controversy. Only last year, he was said to have been involved in a scandalous relationship with an executive secretary (Debbie Dietrich, now no longer with the company).

Harry Softsell is no Harvard mogul. He comes from a relatively obscure background, having graduated with an M.B.A. from the small Wakamasha University in the state of Washington. Known as a slick operator, Softsell mesmerized corporate executives into accelerating him into his present position in marketing. It took him six years to become vice president—no one else in the company has done it in less than 17 years—a position he has held for two years. Softsell is an ambitious man. His burning desire to become chairman is no secret.

2. Though your boss gives you the information, the board members would like him (and you) to hold off giving the information to the media for a few days, until "we get over the shock of what we have just heard."

What do you think? Should this information be released immediately? If so, give two reasons why in a memo to your boss.

3. Evaluate the Sugarcoat information for legally sensitive material. For each legal trap that you find:
—Specify what law or laws are in possible violation.
—Zero in on the specific nature of the violation. For example, if you think privacy law is in possible violation, state whether this is because of appropriation, intrusion or publication of false facts.

4. Using the Sugarcoat information, prepare two lists: one of information you would use in a media release; the other of information you would exclude from a media release.

5. Using guidelines provided in chapters 7 and 8, write a legally acceptable one-page media release for use by newspapers and wire services. Use a media release format.

6. If you were using the Sugarcoat information for a story in the next edition of the company publication, *Gooey Times,* would you include Debbie Dietrich's name in the story? If the answer is no, provide two reasons why you could not use that information in a corporate publication.

7. You wish to reprint an Associated Press feature about Thomas Kitkat in a special forthcoming issue of *Gooey Times,* bidding Kitkat farewell. The AP feature appeared in the *Wall Street Journal.* Who owns copyright on this story? How would you go about making sure so you can obtain permission? Outline the steps you would take to find this information, and obtain permission.

8. If you felt the information needed to be released immediately and your boss (and board) pressured you against it, what actions would you take to safeguard your own professional credibility?

Food for Thought

1. McCammond (1987, 8) posed the following ethical dilemma: A well-known athlete is charged with selling drugs and planning and carrying out, with others, the death of a young married couple. His attorney calls you, a close friend, to advise and assist him in handling the intense media interest in the case. During the period before the trial, you learn that the athlete was, in fact, a drug dealer and did participate in the murder. The lawyer tells you that the information is privileged. You decide to await the outcome of the trial. The lawyer is able to get his client acquitted. What should you do?

   How would you handle this situation according to the guidelines provided by the PRSA Code? Also, if you were already working for Sugarcoat Corp. as a staff writer, what additional steps might you need to take before agreeing to handle the athlete's media relations?

2. You are working for the Advanced Armaments Corp. as a senior public relations writer. Often, because of your seniority, your advice is sought regarding disclosure of material information. Your company completes production of a field gun. Unfortunately, because someone goofed, the information surrounding the development of the gun was not properly classified. You recommend that the company, being a public company, must comply with the securities laws and immediately issue a media release. However, your superiors have been told by representatives of the Pentagon that any such release would jeopardize national security. They, in turn, tell you not to release the information.

   What would you do? Why? Be specific.

3. Assume that you are in the same situation outlined in 2, above; only this time, the U.S. is in a state of war with the Russian-backed regime in the state of Karanjistan.

What would you do now? Why? Be specific.

References for Further Study

American Stock Exchange Disclosure Policies. New York: AMEX, Securities and Exchange Commission, 1987.

"Arms Maker Sues GM over Beretta Name." *The Orange County Register.* July 20, 1988, C3.

Baskin, Otis W. and Craig E. Aronoff. *Public Relations: The Profession and The Practice.* Dubuque, Iowa: Wm. C. Brown, 1988.

"Beretta Cites GM Accord." *The New York Times.* February 24, 1989, B4.

Cutlip, Scott M. "Attendant Responsibility: Public Relations and the SEC." *Public Relations Journal.* January 1985.

Dunn, S. Watson. *Public Relations: A Contemporary Approach.* New York: Harper & Row, 1986.

McCammond, Donald B. "The Right Choice." *Public Relations Journal.* February 1987.

Newsom, Doug and Alan Scott. *This Is PR: The Realities of Public Relations.* Belmont, Calif.: Wadsworth, 1985.

Overbeck, Wayne. *Communications Law, 1989–1990.* California State University, Fullerton (Unpublished manuscript).

Pember, Don R. *Mass Media Law,* 4th ed. Dubuque, Iowa: Wm. C. Brown, 1987.

Phemister, Heidi. "Sigma Chi Flier Sparks Protest." Colorado University *Campus Press.* January 22, 1978, 1.

Prosser, William L. *Law of Torts,* 4th ed. St. Paul, Minn.: West Publishing, 1971.

Register News Services. "Editor Indicted." *The Orange County Register.* June 28, 1988, A8.

Savage, David G. "Justices Say Firm Can't Lie about Merger Talks." *The Los Angeles Times.* March 8, 1988, 1, 17.

Scott, Walter. "Personality Parade." *Parade.* June 26, 1988, 2.

Securities and Exchange Commission. *Special Study of the Securities Market.* Washington, D.C.: U.S. Government Printing Office, 1963.

Shillinglaw, James. "Court Disclosure Decision Sparks IR Sector Criticism." *PR Week.* March 14–20, 1988, 1, 5.

Simon, Morton J. *Public Relations Law.* New York: AppleCentury Crofts, 1969.

Simon, Raymond. *Public Relations: Concepts and Practices.* New York: John Wiley & Sons, 1984.

Taylor, Stuart, Jr. "Justices Uphold $3 Million Libel Award on CBS." *The New York Times.* April 5, 1988, 11.

VanDusen, Donald T. "Technical Publicity Means Special Handling." *Public Relations Journal.* June 1964, 26–28.

Walsh, Frank. "Libel: The Principles Also Apply to Public Relations Tools." *Public Relations Journal.* May 1982, 8.

Walsh, Frank. "Public Relations Firm Charged with Inside Trading." *Public Relations Journal,* May 1986, 10.

Wilcox, Dennis L., Phillip H. Ault and Warren K. Agee. *Public Relations: Strategies and Tactics.* New York: Harper & Row, 1986.

Case References

Brown v. Harrington, 268 Mass. 600, 95 N.E. 655 (1911).

Dorr v. United States, 195 U.S. 138 (1904).

Gertz v. Welch, 418 U.S. 323, 94 S.Ct. 2977 (1974).

Harper & Row Publishers v. The Nation Enterprises, 105 S.Ct. 2218 (1985).

Hope v. Hearst Corp., 294 F 2d 681 (1961).

New York Times v. Sullivan, 376 U.S. 254, 84 S.Ct. 710 (1964).

Peck v. Tribune, 214 U.S. 185 (1909).

Texas Gulf Sulphur Co., 401F.2d 833 (2d Cir. 1968), 394 U.S. 976 (1969).

INDEX